Foundations for Tracing Intuition

The study of intuition and its relation to thoughtful reasoning is a burgeoning research topic in psychology and beyond. While the area has the potential to radically transform our conception of the mind and decision making, the procedures used for establishing empirical conclusions have often been vaguely formulated and obscure. This book fills a gap in the field by providing a range of methods for exploring intuition experimentally and thereby enhancing the collection of new data.

The book begins by summarizing current challenges in the study of intuition and gives a new foundation for intuition research. Going beyond classical dual-process models, a new scheme is introduced to classify the different types of processes usually collected under the label of intuition. These new classifications range from learning approaches to complex cue integration models.

The book then goes on to describe the wide variety of behavioural methods available to investigate these processes, including information search tracing, think aloud protocols, maximum likelihood methods, eye-tracking, and physiological and non-physiological measures of affective responses. It also discusses paradigms to investigate implicit associations and causal intuitions, video-based approaches to expert research, methods to induce specific decision modes as well as questionnaires to assess individual preferences for intuition or deliberation.

By uniquely providing the basis for exploring intuition by introducing the different methods and their applications in a step-by-step manner, this text is an invaluable reference for individual research projects. It is also very useful as a course book for advanced decision-making courses, and could inspire experimental explorations of intuition in psychology, behavioural economics, empirical legal studies and clinical decision making.

Andreas Glöckner is head of the research group Intuitive Experts at the Max Planck Institute for Research on Collective Goods, Bonn. In addition, since 2004 he has worked as an independent consultant for human resources.

Cilia Witteman is professor of Diagnostic Decision Making at the Behavioural Science Institute of the Radboud University Nijmegen. She has been secretary/treasurer of the European Association for Decision Making since 2005.

Foundations for Tracing Intuition

Challenges and Methods

Andreas Glöckner and Cilia Witteman

ΨPsychology Press
Taylor & Francis Group

HOVE AND NEW YORK

First published in 2010
by Psychology Press
27 Church Road, Hove, East Sussex, BN3 2FA

Simultaneously published in the USA and Canada
by Psychology Press
711 Third Avenue, New York, NY 10017

*Psychology Press is an imprint of the Taylor & Francis Group,
an Informa business*

First issued in paperback 2012

Typeset in Times by RefineCatch Limited, Bungay, Suffolk

Cover design by Andy Ward

British Library Cataloguing in Publication Data
A catalogue record for this book is available from the British Library

Library of Congress Cataloging in Publication Data
Foundations for tracing intuition : challenges and methods / [edited by]
Andreas Glöckner and Cilia Witteman.
    p. cm.
  Includes bibliographical references and index.
  ISBN 978–1–84872–019–0 (hbk.)
  1. Intuition. I. Glöckner, Andreas, 1975– II. Witteman, Cilia, 1954–
  BF315.5.F68 2010
  153.4′4–dc22   2009026724

ISBN: 978–1–84872–019–0 (hbk)
ISBN: 978–0–415–64787–8 (pbk)

Contents

Contributors

Cornelia Betsch, University of Erfurt, Center for Empirical Research in Economics and Behavioural Sciences, CEREB, Postfach 900221, D-99105 Erfurt, Germany.

Ralf Brand, University of Potsdam, Department of Sport and Exercise Psychology, Am Neuen Palais 10, Haus 2, D-14469 Potsdam, Germany.

Arndt Bröder, Universität Bonn, Institut für Psychologie, Allgemeine Psychologie 1, Kaiser-Karl-Ring 9, D-53111 Bonn, Germany.

Marieke de Vries, Leiden University Medical Center, Department of Medical Decision Making, J10-S, PO Box 9600, 2300 RC Leiden, The Netherlands.

Stephan Dickert, Max Planck Institute for Research on Collective Goods, Kurt-Schumacher-Str. 10, D-53113 Bonn, Germany.

Guus Dietvorst, Department of Psychology, University of Amsterdam, Roetersstraat 15, 1018 WB Amsterdam, The Netherlands.

Andreas Glöckner, Max Planck Institute for Research on Collective Goods, Kurt-Schumacher-Str. 10, D-53113 Bonn, Germany.

York Hagmayer, Universität Göttingen, Georg Elias Müller Institut für Psychologie, Gosslerstr. 14, D-37073 Göttingen, Germany.

Daniel Hausmann, University of Zurich, Social and Health Psychology, Binzmühlestrasse 14/Box 14, 8050 Zurich, Switzerland.

Guy Hochman, Faculty of Industrial Engineering and Management, Technion – Israel Institute of Technology, Office: Cooper 401, Technion City, Haifa 32000, Israel.

Rob Holland, Department of Social Psychology, University of Nijmegen, P.O. Box 9104, 6500 HE Nijmegen, The Netherlands.

Nina Horstmann, Max Planck Institute for Research on Collective Goods, Kurt-Schumacher-Str. 10, D-53113 Bonn, Germany.

Paola Iannello, Catholic University of Sacred Heart, Department of Psychology, Largo Gemelli 1, 20123 Milano, Italy.

Georg Jahn, University of Greifswald, Department of Psychology, Franz-Mehring-Str. 47, D-1748 Greifswald, Germany.

Pieter Koele, University of Amsterdam, Roetersstraat 15, 1018 WB Amsterdam, The Netherlands.

Elisabeth Norman, Faculty of Psychology, University of Bergen, Christiesgt. 12, 5015 Bergen, Norway and Haukeland University Hospital, Bergen, Norway.

Henning Plessner, University of Leipzig, Department of Psychology, Seeburgstraße 14–20, D-04103 Leipzig, Germany.

Frank Renkewitz, University of Erfurt, Department of Psychology, Postfach 900221, D-99105 Erfurt, Germany.

Stefan Ryf, University of Zurich, General Psychology (Cognition), Binzmühlestrasse 14/22, CH-8050 Zurich, Switzerland.

Michael Schulte-Mecklenbeck, Faculty of Psychology, University of Bergen, Christiesgt. 12, 5015 Bergen, Norway.

Geoffrey Schweizer, University of Potsdam, Department of Sport and Exercise Psychology, Am Neuen Palais 10, Haus 2, D-14469 Potsdam, Germany.

Erwin van Geenen, Utrecht Medical Center, P.O. Box 855 00, 3508 GA, Utrecht, The Netherlands.

Cilia Witteman, Radboud University Nijmegen, P.O. Box 9104 (6th floor), 6500 HE Nijmegen, The Netherlands.

Eldad Yechiam, Behavioral Science Area, Faculty of Industrial Engineering and Management, Technion – Israel Institute of Technology, Haifa 32000, Israel.

1 Foundations for tracing intuition

Models, findings, categorizations

Andreas Glöckner and Cilia Witteman

Introduction

Every day people make a multitude of judgments and decisions which differ in complexity and importance. The question how people make these decisions has attracted research interest over many years. Why did some decisions which were based on long deliberation turn out to be bluntly wrong – leading to the break-down of mighty companies and organizations, to financial or political crisis and even wars? How can, on the other hand, complex decision tasks sometimes be solved in the blink of an eye? Obviously, processes that are not only based on deliberate, conscious information processing play a crucial role. We automatically record parts of the information we are confronted with, and are able to use this knowledge in later decisions. Parts of these processes concern conscious information selection, retrieval and processing, other parts operate completely automatically and unconsciously. Both kinds of processes interact. This could lead to a conscious over-writing of initial intuitive choice tendencies. The reverse could also happen: unconscious processes may modify the outcomes of seemingly completely deliberate decisions. They may lead us to act against our deliberate intentions, or they may generate feelings that one should select an option without knowing where this feeling comes from. They may produce vague feelings warning us that although all the facts speak for option A something feels wrong and another option should be selected, and they may even produce insights in complex tasks just in the moment when we stop deliberatively reflecting about them. These phenomena are as fascinating as they are complex and decision research has only just started to unravel them.

In November 2007 we conducted a workshop on *Measuring Intuition and Expertise* at the Max Planck Institute for Research on Collective Goods, Bonn. The aim of this workshop was to bring together decision researchers who have investigated expertise, intuition and the interplay of automatic and deliberate processes in decision making to present and discuss recent methodological approaches and to develop ideas for further methodological improvements. This volume is based on the talks presented there, and on the discussions held at and after the workshop. We aim to present different perspectives on intuition and different methodological approaches, which should enable graduate students and scientists from different fields (i.e., psychology, decision sciences, cognitive sciences, behavioural economics, and behavioural law and economics) to use them in their research. In this chapter we provide a theoretical basis for the different methodological approaches described in the rest of this volume.

What is intuition?

There are quite a few controversies surrounding the study of intuition. Controversy starts with the definition of intuition, and further concerns its properties, the scope and the homogeneity of the phenomenon, its working mechanism, its distinction from deliberation, its relatedness to affect, and its dependence on experience. To illustrate that there is partial agreement but also controversy about the definition of intuition, we cite four examples:

> "The outcomes [of intuition] are typically approximate (not precise) and often experienced in the form of feelings (not words)" (p. 9). "The correlates are speed, and confidence" (p. 10). "Intuition or intuitive responses are reached with little apparent effort, and typically without conscious awareness; they involve little or no conscious deliberation" (p. 14) "[but are reached] in a largely tacit, unintentional, automatic, passive process" (p. 21). "We know, but we do not know why" (p. 29) (all in Hogarth, 2001).

> Intuition is an involuntary, difficult-to-articulate, affect-laden recognition or judgment, based upon prior learning and experiences, which is arrived at rapidly, through holistic associations and without deliberative or conscious rational thought. (Sadler-Smith, 2008, p. 31)

> Intuition is the way we translate our experiences into judgments and decisions. It's the ability to make decisions using patterns to recognize what's going on in a situation and to recognize the typical action scripts with which to react. Once experienced intuitive decision makers see a pattern, any decision they have to make is usually obvious. (Klein, 2003, p. 13)

> Intuition is a process of thinking. The input to this process is mostly provided by knowledge stored in long-term memory that has been primarily acquired via associative learning. The input is processed automatically and without conscious awareness. The output of the process is a feeling that can serve as a basis for judgments and decisions. (Betsch, 2008, p. 4)

From the above definitions we derive the common ground which we will rely on in this volume: Most definitions agree that intuition is based on automatic processes which rely on knowledge structures that are acquired by different kinds of learning. They operate at least partially without people's awareness and result in feelings, signals, or interpretations. Assumptions concerning the underlying processes and consequently also concerning further properties of these processes diverge. In this volume we refrain from trying to unify these perspectives. On the contrary, we suggest that intuition is used as a label for different kinds of automatic processes and we will aim to categorize them into four general types.

In this chapter, we will first discuss why tracing intuition is challenging, and we summarize some historical background to the investigation of intuition. Next the distinction between intuition and deliberation as well as assumptions concerning the interplay of both will be described. Then we turn to a discussion of the processes underlying intuition. We suggest a classification of types of intuition according to four rather different underlying learning and retrieval or information integration processes, and we sort existing models accordingly (see also Glöckner and Witteman, in press). Neuroscientific results are outlined that support the hypothesis that the processes exist and seem to operate at least partially independently. Turning back to the distinction between intuition and deliberation, different factors are described that are supposed to influence the activation of one or the other process. Also, the relation between intuition and expertise, as based on extensive learning, is briefly discussed. We show that the suggested types of intuition allow for rather similar predictions concerning when it will lead to good or bad decisions. Finally, the structure of the book is outlined.

The challenge of tracing intuition

The importance of improving our scientific understanding of intuitive processes in judgment and decision making has been prominently highlighted in several influential publications (e.g., Kahneman & Frederick, 2002; Plessner, Betsch, & Betsch, 2008). Automatic, intuitive processes seem to be particularly important for professional decision makers such as clinicians, managers, and judges (Agor, 1986; Beach, 1996; Glöckner, 2008b; Glöckner & Engel, 2008; Guthrie, Rachlinski, & Wistrich, 2007; Klein, 2003; Klein, Orasanu, Calderwood, & Zsambok, 1993), but these processes also enable lay persons to come to good decisions quickly (Glöckner & Betsch, 2008a, 2008b, 2008c; Glöckner & Dickert, under review; Glöckner & Herbold, in press). The theoretical and the practical importance of intuition have attracted many decision researchers to start investigating the topic empirically. However, there are at least four major challenges that "intuition" researchers face: ambiguity of the concept intuition and a multitude of models, underspecification of models, methodological challenges to trace unconscious processes, and interactions of the research method with cognitive processes.

Concerning the first point: intuition is used as a common label for a set of phenomena that are likely to be based on completely different cognitive mechanisms (cf. definitions above). Hence, it is probably a waste of time to ask the question what "intuition really is". It is more fruitful to concentrate on one class of mechanisms and to investigate them first separately and later on in their interaction with other ones. We provide a simple classification of mechanisms below that reduces the multitude of models to a few basic processes that could be specifically explored.

Second, some models of intuition are still in the process of being elaborated and hence they are sometimes underspecified in that they do not allow the derivation of clear behavioural predictions. We advise researchers to focus on models that are well specified or to use (and explicate) additional specifying assumptions that make them testable (if not done so by the authors themselves) (see Glöckner, chapter 5, this volume; Glöckner & Herbold, in press). Note, however, that intuition is a phenomenon for complex information integration processes. That means that better specified models for intuition are usually mathematically somewhat complex (but see Gigerenzer, 2007). Researchers should take the time to understand the underlying concepts as well as the math and not focus on the simplest models only. Increasingly, computer tools are available to derive predictions from mathematically complex intuition models (see Glöckner, chapter 5, this volume; for materials and links see www.intuitive-experts.de – Resources).

Third, one of the major challenges for exploring automatic-intuitive processes is that some of the traditional methods used in behavioural decision research are simply not suitable for capturing implicit, unconscious processes or have to be modified to do so. In this volume we describe methods ranging from "technical" approaches such as information-search tracing via eye-tracking (Norman & Schulte-Mecklenbeck, chapter 2, this volume) or physiological measures (Hochman, Glöckner, & Yechiam, chapter 8, this volume) to applying classical behavioural approaches such as the analysis of choices (Bröder, chapter 4, this volume), decision times and confidence (Glöckner, chapter 5, this volume), the usage of verbal protocols (Witteman & van Geenen, chapter 3, this volume), and many more.

The final issue is closely related to the previous one. It has been shown that research methods such as computer-based information search paradigms (see Norman & Schulte-Mecklenbeck, chapter 2, this volume) influence whether persons rely on automatic-intuitive processes or whether they apply simple deliberate short-cut strategies (Glöckner & Betsch, 2008c). Hence, researchers should be very sensitive concerning the influence of context factors which are induced by the research method. Otherwise the results might not generalize to real world settings. This is particularly true for the investigation of experts' intuitions, which should be based on content rich, externally valid materials that are representative for the environment in which experts act (cf. Schweizer, Plessner, & Brand, chapter 6, this volume). Of course, content rich materials often decrease internal validity of the study. In some cases it might be appropriate to take a stepwise approach, starting investigation with well controlled material and applying content rich material afterwards (cf. Glöckner, chapter 5, this volume).

Some historical context

In early work on decision making, researchers proposed very general theories which did not aim to describe processes (i.e., process models) but merely outcomes (i.e., input-output models). One important example is classic expected utility models, which assume that individuals choose the option with the highest expected utility, which is the sum of the utilities of all outcomes multiplied by the probability that these outcomes occur (Savage, 1954; von Neumann & Morgenstern, 1944). The later Nobel-prize winner Herbert A. Simon (1955) drew attention to the decision process. He challenged the assumption that people maximize utility. He argued that people might not rely on deliberate calculations of weighted sums in their decisions, because the limitations of cognitive capacity and the multitude of decision options do not allow them to do so. Essentially two alternative process model approaches have been suggested. The first is based on the idea of adaptive strategy selection. People might use effortful weighted sum calculations in a few important situations only (Beach & Mitchell, 1978; Payne, Bettman, & Johnson, 1988). In other situations, for instance under time pressure, they might rely on short-cut strategies, so called heuristics. Heuristics were conceptualized as simple strategies which consist of stepwise cognitive operations and are carried out deliberately. An example would be the lexicographic strategies (Fishburn, 1974), which assume that people compare options by considering attributes in a stepwise manner and selecting the option that is best on the first differentiating attribute without considering the remaining attributes. The second approach suggests that people might utilize partially automatic processes, which means that they use the huge computational and storage power of the brain to overcome the obvious limitations of their conscious cognitive capacity.[1] Reliance on automatic-intuitive processes often leads to surprisingly good judgments and choices, but under certain circumstances also causes systematic biases. In their intriguing work on heuristics and biases a group of researchers around Daniel Kahneman and Amos Tversky (e.g., Kahneman, Slovic, & Tversky, 1982) showed, among other things,[2] that in probability judgments people often rely on feelings of representativeness and availability, and anchor their judgments on (sometimes irrelevant) information. A group of researchers elaborating on Brunswik's (1955) lens model showed in many studies that people's (intuitive) judgments follow a weighted linear integration of cues (e.g., Brehmer, 1994; Doherty & Brehmer, 1997; Doherty & Kurz, 1996; Hammond, Hamm, Grassia, & Pearson, 1987).[3]

The distinction between a set of deliberate rule-based processes and reliance on intuitive automatic processes is reflected in many dual-process models, which are described next.

Dual-process models

Dual-process models come in different flavours. Most models postulate that people rely either on deliberate (conscious, controlled) or intuitive (automatic, unconscious) reasoning, or on certain combinations of both. Classic models have been proposed early in cognitive psychology (Schneider & Shiffrin, 1977; Shiffrin & Schneider, 1977). Later they have been introduced to social psychology as the elaboration likelihood model (Petty & Cacioppo, 1986) or the heuristic systematic model (Chen & Chaiken, 1999) which describe phenomena such as persuasion and attitude change. Since then, the influence of automatic processes on social cognition has repeatedly been highlighted (Bargh, 1996; Bargh & Chartrand, 1999; Kruglanski et al., 2003; Strack & Deutsch, 2004). In judgment and decision-making research dual-processing theories were sometimes referred to, but for a long time they received surprisingly little attention. This changed with several influential publications by Kahneman and colleagues (Gilovich, Griffin, & Kahneman, 2002; Kahneman, 2003; Kahneman & Frederick, 2002) who, among other things, summarized properties of the two processes based on a set of other dual-processing theories (e.g., Epstein, 1990; Sloman, 2002).

In a recent review Evans (2008) suggested a classification of dual-processing models into a) models that assume a clear distinction between the two kinds of processes and an initial selection between them based on certain variables (e.g. Petty & Cacioppo, 1986), b) models that assume a parallel activation of both kinds of processes (Sloman, 2002), and c) default-interventionist models which assume that automatic processes are always activated first and that additional deliberate processes are activated only if it is necessary to intervene, correct or support reasoning of automatic-intuitive processes (Evans, 2007; Glöckner & Betsch, 2008b; Guthrie et al., 2007; Haidt, 2001; Hogarth, 2001; Kahneman & Frederick, 2002).[4]

Despite these differences, most models agree on very general properties of the two kinds of processes. Deliberate processes are supposed to consist of conscious, controlled application of rules and computations. The core property of the intuitive processes is that they operate (at least partially) automatically and without conscious control.[5] Apart from this basic agreement, there is major divergence concerning the nature and functioning of intuitive processes. Predictions concerning the underlying information integration processes are often vague. Evans (2008) concluded:

> it emerges that (a) there are multiple kinds of implicit processes described by different theorists and (b) not all of the proposed attributes of the two kinds of processing can be sensibly mapped on to two systems as currently conceived. It is suggested that while some dual-process theories are concerned with parallel competing processes involving explicit and implicit knowledge systems, others are concerned with the influence

of preconscious processes that contextualize and shape deliberative reasoning and decision-making. (p. 255)

We agree with the general point that there are multiple kinds of intuition, but we will suggest a more specific classification of the underlying processes in the next section.

The processes underlying intuition

Although the different theoretical approaches diverge about the question where intuition comes from, most agree that intuition does not just "fall from heaven" but that it is acquired through learning processes, and that there are some systematic processes of retrieval or integration of information that generate intuitions and unconscious influences on choice behaviour (see definitions above). Models can be categorized according to the format in which information is thought to be stored in memory and the specification of the retrieval or information integration processes. Without aiming to be exhaustive we discuss four partially complementary types of processes, suggested in Glöckner and Witteman (in press), which are summarized in Table 1.1. As mentioned above, we argue that "intuition" is an umbrella term for these and other kinds of processes. From this perspective it is not useful to discuss which types of processes cover "real intuition". Researchers investigating intuition should clearly define which kind of processes they are investigating and refrain from using the term intuition without further qualification.

Associative intuition: simple learning-retrieval

In interaction with their environment people record a surprising amount of information both consciously and unconsciously. Even if they do not intend to do so, people automatically record frequencies of events (Hasher & Zacks, 1979; Zacks, Hasher, & Sanft, 1982), values of options (Betsch, Plessner, Schwieren, & Gütig, 2001), and they acquire even complex artificial rules through implicit learning (Reber, 1993). Presenting neutral (i.e., a new brand name) with unconditioned stimuli (i.e., a beautiful face) leads to acquiring evaluative reactions (e.g., feelings of liking or disliking) (cf. evaluative conditioning, e.g., Walther, 2002; Walther & Grigoriadis, 2004). A similar effect of increased liking of an object can be reached by merely presenting the object repeatedly (Zajonc, 1968, 1980). Similarly, according to classic findings in conditioning the application of punishment (reward) after a certain choice behaviour reduces (increases) its prevalence rate (Skinner, 1938) while people are not necessarily aware of it. It has, for instance, been shown that people acquire affective reactions towards options before they become consciously aware that they should not choose them (Bechara, Damasio, Tranel, & Damasio, 1997). Of course more complex learning mechanisms such as (implicit) social learning (Bandura, 1977) or learning from feedback

Table 1.1 Types of intuition

Types	Description
Associative intuition: simple learning-retrieval	*Learning:* Reinforcement and association learning (classical conditioning/evaluative conditioning/signal learning, operant/instrumental conditioning); social learning; implicit recording of frequencies and values *Retrieval:* Intuition as mere feelings of liking and disliking; intuition as affective arousal; intuition as the activation of the previously successful behavioural option
Matching intuition: exemplar/prototype learning-retrieval	*Learning:* Acquisition of exemplars, prototypes, images, schemas *Retrieval:* Comparison with exemplars (prompting and echo); comparison with prototypes; comparison of images
Accumulative intuition: evidence accumulation	*Source of information:* Memory traces (from both above perspectives) and/or currently perceived information *Integration:* Accumulation of evidence based on quick automatic process; random sampling proportional to the importance of the information; overall (cognitive or affective) evaluation is compared with threshold
Constructive intuition: construction of mental representations	*Source of information:* Memory traces (from both above perspectives) and/or currently perceived information *Integration:* Activation of related information; automatic construction of consistent mental representations; accentuation of evidence (coherence shifts); the result (e.g., chose option A) or the whole automatically constructed interpretation of the problem enters awareness

Note: Modified after Glöckner, A. & Witteman, C.L.M. (in press). Beyond dual-process models: A categorization of processes underlying intuitive judgment and decision making. *Thinking & Reasoning.*

(Reber, 1993; Klein, 2003) might also change knowledge structures that later on automatically influence choices.

Obviously, the learning mechanisms mentioned above provide a multitude of sources for different kinds of "intuition": a) intuition as mere feelings of liking and disliking which we take into account in our choices, b) intuition as affective arousal which might influence our reaction to an option, or c) intuition as the activation of the previously successful behavioural option when we are confronted with a similar task. The first possibility is elaborated in the affect heuristic (Finucane, Alhakami, Slovic, & Johnson, 2000; Slovic, Finucane, Peters, & MacGregor, 2002) which assumes that from experience people acquire so called "affective tags" which are related to options. These tags are activated as soon as people are confronted with options, and the option with the more positive affective tag is selected. The idea that general affective arousal states are activated when confronted with specific options or situations is reflected in the second view: the somatic marker hypothesis (Damasio, 1994). Somatic markers or gut feelings are supposed to warn people away from bad outcomes and alert them to good outcomes. The third view is reflected in routine models of decision making according to which people's choices are heavily influenced by previous experience (Betsch, Brinkmann, Fiedler, & Breining, 1999; Betsch & Haberstroh, 2005; Betsch, Haberstroh, & Höhle, 2002). In many cases the routine option is instantly selected without consideration of other information and without conscious awareness. Repeatedly reinforced options (i.e., routines) are maintained even when there is clear information that it would be better to deviate from them (Betsch, Haberstroh, Glöckner, Haar, & Fiedler, 2001). It has been shown that particularly under time pressure people fall back on their routines and decide against explicitly formed intentions (Betsch, Haberstroh, Molter, & Glöckner, 2004).

Matching intuition: exemplar/prototype learning-retrieval

A different class of theories suggests that parts of intuition might rely on more complex learning and retrieval processes that include the storage of multiple exemplars, matching of situations or objects to prototypes or retrieval from multiple-trace memory. The MINERVA-DM model (Dougherty, Gettys, & Ogden, 1999; cf. Hintzman, 1988) explains likelihood judgments as a result of complex memory retrieval processes in multiple-trace memory systems. According to the model, each experience with an object is separately stored in memory as a single trace. Intuition, in the sense of a feeling towards an option, is an "echo" that results from automatically comparing the current object or situation to all similar experiences stored in memory. Along similar lines of thought, intuition might be understood as generating estimates based on the sampling of instances from memory (Fiedler, 2000, 2008; Unkelbach, Fiedler, & Freytag, 2007). In a similar vein, the Recognition-Primed decision model (Klein, 1993) postulates that complex pattern-recognition processes underlie intuition: A situation generates cues that are compared to memory traces and that enable people to recognize patterns (which make sense of a situation) that activate action scripts (routines for responding). This takes place in an instant, without conscious thought. Somewhat similar, image theory (Beach & Mitchell, 1987; Mitchell & Beach, 1990) postulates an automatic pattern matching process of different images (e.g., trajectory image: What do I want to achieve? and projected image: Do I get there on the current track?) that direct decisions.

Both perspectives discussed so far highlight the importance of learning and retrieval processes for intuition. The models discussed in the follo-wing paragraphs focus more on automatic information *integration* processes which could take into account information from memory but also currently perceived information.

Accumulative intuition: evidence accumulation

Evidence accumulation and diffusion models (Busemeyer & Townsend, 1993; Ratcliff, 1978; Ratcliff & McKoon, 2008) assume that people select options based on automatic information sampling processes. Information is repeatedly inspected and added up, partially relying on automatic processes. According to decision field theory (Busemeyer & Johnson, 2004; Busemeyer & Townsend, 1993), for instance, the inspection rate of each single piece of information is proportional to its importance, which leads to an approximation of a weighted linear information integration without deliberately calculating weighted sums. As soon as the evidence for one option reaches a certain threshold this option is selected. In recent formulations of the theory (Busemeyer & Johnson, 2004) it is argued that evidence is not accumulated in a deliberate manner but that it is integrated automatically into an overall affective valence measure. Decision field theory is a very general model. It is mathematically well specified and allows for very precise predictions. Information underlying a decision can both be currently available and sampled from memory. Hence, evidence accumulation models can account for decision processes that are akin to perception. They assume that the intuition to select one or the other option relies on automatic processes of accumulating evidence.

Constructive intuition: construction of mental representations

Taking an even more complex perspective, it has been argued that information is not only accumulated, retrieved from memory and matched to exemplars, but that people construct mental representations of the task based on information provided and further relevant information that is activated in memory. In contrast to evidence accumulation models, evidence is not only added up but constellations are preserved. Information is also not only matched to existing exemplars but mental representations go beyond existing information in forming new consistent interpretations and possibly also by combining elements creatively in new ways. Good shapes ("Gestalts") are formed by maximizing consistency given the constellation of information (McClelland & Rumelhart, 1981; Read, Vanman, & Miller, 1997; Rumelhart & McClelland, 1982; Wertheimer, 1938). The underlying processes can be mathematically captured using parallel constraint satisfaction (PCS) network models which have also been applied to judgments and decisions (Glöckner & Betsch, 2008b; Glöckner & Herbold, in press; Holyoak & Simon, 1999; Thagard, 1989; Thagard & Millgram, 1995).

According to PCS models, as soon as people are confronted with decision tasks, mental representations (for a broad overview see Holyoak & Spellman, 1993; cf. mental models, Johnson-Laird, 1983) are constructed. These can be conceptualized as networks which contain information directly provided as well as related information activated in memory. Spreading activation in the network is used to find the best possible interpretation. This interpretation is constructed by an automatic process in which contrary facts are devalued and supporting facts are highlighted (cf. Montgomery, 1989; Svenson, 1992). Often the mental representation and the processes to construct the interpretation are completely unconscious and only the result enters awareness. We feel that we should choose this option without knowing why. In other cases, only a part of the mental representation will be unconscious. However, unconscious nodes that are connected with the conscious ones might produce a feeling that although all facts speak for selecting option A something is wrong with it – which might induce increased deliberation.[6]

Findings from neuroscience with relation to the suggested types of processes

Results from neuroscience have started to contribute to our understanding of intuitive and deliberate processes. In this volume we focus on behavioural measures which, from our point of view, still have lots of potentials to increase our knowledge of these processes without using expensive technology. Many of the methods we discuss could be usefully applied without neuro-scientific methods or they could be used to supplement them with crucial additional data. Yet we will report some of the recent findings in neuroscience on the localization of intuition and will particularly focus on findings that relate to the types of processes suggested above and taken together support the hypothesis that these different types of processes operate at least partially independently because they are related to different brain areas.

Early attempts to locate intuitive and deliberate processes led to unclear results about which brain areas would be involved. Recently, Lieberman (2007), a social cognitive neuroscientist, has investigated which neural systems support among other things deliberate and automatic processes (see also Lieberman, Gaunt, Gilbert, & Trope, 2002; Satpute & Lieberman, 2006). He warns that his results are preliminary, but he has found consistent associations between deliberate processing and activations in the lateral and medial prefrontal cortex, the lateral and medial parietal cortex, and the medial temporal lobe, which together he calls the neural correlates of the C (reflective) system; and between automatic processes and activations in the amygdala, the ventromedial prefrontal cortex, and the lateral temporal cortex, which he calls the neural correlates of the X (reflexive) system.

In a different line of research based on patients with very specific brain damages (Damasio, 1994), it has been argued that the anterior prefrontal cortex is related to the ability to generate affective reactions necessary for efficient decision making in experience based tasks (Bechara, Damasio, Damasio, & Anderson, 1994; Bechara, Damasio, Tranel, & Damasio, 2005; Damasio, 1994; but see also Yechiam, Busemeyer, Stout, & Bechara, 2005). This indicates that the learning and/or retrieval of affective tags as suggested by the affect heuristic might be related with the anterior prefrontal cortex.

A taxonomy has been suggested that distinguishes between vigilance and access to conscious report, as well as between subliminal, preconscious and conscious processing. According to this taxonomy "conscious perception is systematically associated with surges of parieto-frontal activity causing top-down amplification" (Dehaene, Changeux, Naccache, Sackur, & Sergent, 2006, p. 204).

In support of evidence accumulation models it has been shown that there are single cells in monkey brains for which activation correlates substantially with the amount of evidence accumulated in favour of an option (Dehaene, 2008; Shadlen, Kiani, Hanks, & Churchland, 2008; Yang & Shadlen, 2007). In support of the parallel constraint satisfaction model, it has been shown that the anterior cingulate cortex (ACC) is connected with monitoring conflict (i.e., inconsistency) between pieces of information (Botvinick et al., 2004; cf. also Lieberman, 2007; van Veen & Carter, 2002a, 2002b, 2006; van Veen, Holroyd, Cohen, Stenger, & Carter, 2004). If high conflict is detected, lateral areas are activated that could be related to more deliberate reasoning processes (see also De Neys & Glumicic, 2008; De Neys, Vartanian, & Goel, 2008). This supports the view that intuition comes first, and that the possible later activation of deliberate processes is based on the detection of inconsistency.

In sum, there seems to be initial support for the hypothesis that different types of intuitive processes exist and that they might be related with somewhat different areas in the brain. We argue that the categorization introduced above is also essential for a useful application of neuroscientific methods to investigate intuitive processes and might explain results which appear at first glance to be conflicting.

Factors influencing the activation of intuitive and deliberate processes

Some dual-processing models that assume a clear distinction between the two kinds of processing and an early selection of one of them, postulate that people's motivation and capacity are the major factors that determine which kind of processing is selected (Petty & Cacioppo, 1986). Low motivation and low capacity for computations induce more intuitive processing. Hammond and colleagues (1987) suggested a more differentiated view and argued that a multitude of task characteristics moves processing on a cognitive continuum from more intuitive to more deliberate (i.e., complexity of the task / number of cues high vs. low; measurement of cues is perceptual vs. objective; cue values are continuous vs. dichotomous; redundancy among cues is high vs. low; task is holistic vs. can be easily split into simpler sub-tasks; degree of certainty in the task is low vs. high; information is displayed simultaneously vs. serially; available time period is brief vs. long). Parallel constraint satisfaction models (Glöckner & Betsch, 2008b) assume that deliberation is activated based on an endogenous variable which is the result of automatic processes. Deliberation is activated if the automatic consistency maximizing processes cannot construct a sufficiently consistent interpretation of the task. The level of consistency that is reached is determined by the structure of the mental representation (cf. criteria suggested by Hammond et al.). The aspired consistency level could be influenced by different factors such as importance of the task, capacity, person specific factors, mood, and expertise (see also Horstmann, Hausmann, & Ryf, chapter 12, this volume).

Expert intuition

Expert intuition is often discussed as a special kind of intuition, yet it is not fundamentally different from other types except in its being based on significant, often dedicated, explicit learning (Klein, 2003; Sadler-Smith, 2008; see also Schweizer, Plessner, & Brand, chapter 6, this volume; Witteman & van Geenen, chapter 3, this volume). As a result, expert intuition is domain-specific. It allows experts to assess situations quickly and correctly, spotting anomalies and recognizing the viable options. It is sometimes mistrusted, since intuitive experts are not easily able to explain their decisions. However, and again similar to other types of intuition, if learning has taken place in representative situations and with adequate feedback, the decisions from expert intuition will be correct as well as efficiently fast. It has recently been suggested that the parallel constraint satisfaction approach to decision making allows integrating decision making on different levels of expertise and can account for a multitude of classical findings concerning expertise development and experts' performance (Herbig & Glöckner, 2009) by assuming differences in mental representations that are caused by the different amount of experience.

The quality of decisions based on intuition and deliberation

One of the assumptions of most economists and a prediction of some adaptive strategy selection models is that more thorough decision strategies will usually lead to better choices (e.g., Beach & Mitchell, 1978). Hence, following the instruction to deliberate instead of using spontaneous intuitive estimations should usually increase decision quality. Interestingly, in certain situations it has been shown that more deliberation leads to worse judgments and decisions (Wilson & Schooler, 1991) and that people sometimes produce better choices if they are distracted from reflecting on a task before making a choice compared to when they are not (Bos, Dijksterhuis, & van Baaren, 2008; Dijksterhuis, Bos, Nordgren, & van Baaren, 2006; but see Acker, 2008). Plessner and Czenna (2008) present a review of studies that show mixed findings concerning the quality of intuitive and deliberate decision making. In light of the different processes underlying intuition as discussed so far this is not very surprising and additionally supports the different type of processes hypothesis.

We argue that researchers should concentrate on investigating the processes underlying intuition first before making strong claims about its performance.

The further development and testing of elaborated process models is necessary to allow stable predictions. The models and findings we described above are a starting point. The methodological tools to proceed are provided in this volume.

Interestingly, from all four approaches discussed above, namely learning models, evidence accumulation models, exemplar sampling models and parallel constraint satisfaction models, rather similar predictions can be derived concerning the answer to the question when intuition will lead to good choices:

1   Automatic mechanisms provide good choices as long as the information with which they are fed is unbiased, representative and sufficient. The learning experiences should be representative and if this is the case, the better option will be chosen; the evidence accumulation process should be proportional to the importance and if so, choices will follow rational norms; the sampling of exemplars should be representative for the problem and if so, then the estimation will be correct; and the constructed mental representation should correctly represent the underlying problem structure and if so, then the highlighted interpretation will be the correct one.
2   Unconscious and conscious processes can both bias the information input to the computational mechanisms. Both kinds of biases can be due to motivational or emotional factors or they could simply be induced by properties of the task (e.g., salience, availability).
3   Conscious mechanisms can in principle be used to correct for biased information, although it might be questioned whether people can detect biased information and whether they are able to compensate properly (instead of possible over- or under-shooting). Recent evidence indicates that people are often well able to handle the former issue. When solving classic judgment and decision making tasks, people typically detect that they are biased when giving intuitive responses (De Neys & Glumicic, 2008).

The fact that these predictions of the models may be similar does not mean that the discussed models or mechanisms cannot be differentiated empirically. Methods described in this volume should allow the identification of mechanisms that drive choices in certain situations. As argued above, however, we assume that although most of the models describe different affective/ automatic processes or describe them on a different level of abstraction, yet all these processes influence choice behaviour. The commonly used label "intuition" consequently refers to a collection of different processes and it is a fascinating challenge for researchers to explore them separately and in their interaction (cf. Glöckner, 2008a, 2008b).

Overview of the book

The current chapter gave a theoretical basis for the book by providing a short review of current models and by differentiating the processes that are collected under the label intuition. This should help researchers to specify the kind of intuition (or processes) he or she really wants to investigate. Chapters 2 to 5 describe traditional methods that are often used in behavioural decision research and explain how these methods might be used to capture not only deliberate but also intuitive processes. In chapter 2, Norman and Schulte-Mecklenbeck describe methods for tracing information search such as Mouselab and eye-tracking and discuss how they can be used to reveal intuitive information processing as well. In chapter 3, Witteman and van Geenen describe how self-report methods may be used to determine whether people deliberate or use some kind of intuition. In chapter 4, Bröder describes how individuals' information integration processes in deliberate but also in intuitive decisions may be inferred from the statistical analysis of choices. Elaborating on this method, in chapter 5, Glöckner goes one step further and exemplarily shows how specific predictions concerning choices, confidence and decision time can be derived from intuitive and deliberate strategies and how data could be compared with these predictions in a statistically sound way. In both chapters easy to use tools are provided to do the mathematically complex analyses. Chapters 6 to 12 explain further methods that go beyond the basic and traditional ones. Chapter 6 by Schweizer, Plessner, and Brand shows how video may be used as a tool for analyzing and understanding the cognitive processes that underlie experts' intuitive decision making (i.e., professional soccer referees). In chapter 7, Holland and de Vries detail some measures often used in social cognition research, such as the Implicit Association Task, which can be used to capture intuition based reactions as well. In chapter 8, Hochman, Glöckner and Yechiam describe how physiological measures such as skin conductance response and pupil diameter can be used to investigate the components of intuition that are related to affective reactions and arousal. Hagmayer, in chapter 9, outlines how causal intuitions can be investigated. In chapter 10, Dickert discusses the role of emotion, mood and affect in decision making and presents behavioural methods to measure affective responses in deliberate but especially in intuitive decision making. In chapter 11, Renkewitz and Jahn discuss methods from cognitive psychology based on eye-tracking to investigate implicit memory-search processes. Finally, in chapter 12, Horstmann, Hausmann, and Ryf discuss methods for efficiently inducing individuals to use deliberate or intuitive processes and methods for checking the success of these manipulations.

Chapters 13 and 14 discuss whether a predilection for more intuitive or more deliberate reasoning can be understood as a general relatively time-stable behavioural tendency (i.e., a personality trait) that may be measured with self-reports, and whether these measures have predictive value for decision making. In chapter 13, Koele and Dietvorst take a critical view on these measures and discuss their internal validity and their construct validity. C. Betsch and Iannello describe and analyze in chapter 14 several existing scales and discuss their interrelations as well as their external validity. In line with our core argument in the current chapter, they also suggest for the trait perspective a differentiation of different kinds of intuition and deliberation and suggest scales that can be used to measure them.

The chapters mainly stand on their own and it is not necessary to read them all in order. Exceptions are chapters 4 (Bröder) and 5 (Glöckner) and chapters 13 (Koele & Dietvorst) and 14 (Betsch & Ianello) which partially complement each other.

We conclude the book with a summing-up chapter (Witteman & Glöckner, chapter 15) in which we illustrate how each of the methods can be applied to elicit different apects of intuition, using legal decisions as an example.

Authors' note

We thank Tilmann Betsch, Christoph Engel, Janet Kleber and Nina Horstmann for helpful comments on earlier drafts of this chapter which helped to improve it considerably.

Notes

1 Note that this could of course also be considered a kind of strategy that is adaptively selected.
2 Of course, Kahneman and Tversky also developed Prospect Theory as a descriptive model for risky choices that postulates weighted integration of subjective "values" and probabilities (Kahneman & Tversky, 1979; Tversky & Kahneman, 1992). Predictions concerning the process of information integration can however only be derived based on additional process asumptions which are not part of the theory (Glöckner & Betsch, 2008a; Glöckner & Herbold, in press).
3 Note that for a long time intuition was mainly investigated for judgments and less considered in research on preferential decisions (Goldstein & Hogarth, 1997).
4 The later view is theoretical also more in line with uni-model approaches (Kruglanski & Orehek, 2007; Kruglanski & Thompson, 1999) and cognitive continuum theory (Hammond et al., 1987).
5 Note that there is some confusion concerning the usage of the term *heuristics*. According to the adaptive decision maker perspective (Gigerenzer & Todd, 1999; Payne et al., 1988), heuristics are shortcut strategies that rely on simple deliberate calculations. Consequently, they rely on deliberate processes. According to the heuristics and biases perspective (Gilovich et al., 2002; Kahneman et al., 1982), heuristics are based on automatic-intuitive processes. Some dual-process models equate both and put them together in one category (Chen & Chaiken, 1999; Gigerenzer, 2007; Petty & Cacioppo, 1986). This simplification seems to be inappropriate from a processing perspective. We strongly suggest to differentiate between both interpretations and to specify if one refers to *Payne-heuristics* (i.e., simple deliberate processes) or *Kahneman-heuristics* (i.e., automatic-intuitive processes).
6 Note that the model can also account for the related phenomenon of insights: Although all evidence has been seen the solution is only found if these elements are

brought in a new relation. This might sometimes happen if persons start thinking about other completely unrelated things (e.g., Kekulé's benzene rings).

References

Acker, F. (2008). New findings on unconscious versus conscious thought in decision making: Additional empirical data and meta-analysis. *Judgment and Decision Making*, *3*(4), 292–303.

Agor, W. (1986). *The logic of intuitive decision making: A research-based approach for top management*. Westport: Greenwood Press.

Bandura, A. (1977). *Social learning theory*. Oxford, England: Prentice-Hall.

Bargh, J. A. (1996). Automaticity in social psychology. In E. T. Higgins & A. W. Kruglanski (Eds.), *Social psychology: Handbook of basic principles* (pp. 169–183). New York, NY: Guilford Press.

Bargh, J. A., & Chartrand, T. L. (1999). The unbearable automaticity of being. *American Psychologist*, *54*(7), 462–479.

Beach, L. R. (1996). *Decision making in the workplace: A unified perspective*. Hillsdale, NJ, England: Lawrence Erlbaum Associates, Inc.

Beach, L. R., & Mitchell, T. R. (1978). A contingency model for the selection of decision strategies. *Academy of Management Review*, *3*, 439–449.

Beach, L. R., & Mitchell, T. R. (1987). Image Theory: Principles, goals, and plans in decision making. *Acta Psychologica*, *66*(3), 201–220.

Bechara, A., Damasio, A. R., Damasio, H., & Anderson, S. W. (1994). Insensitivity to future consequences following damage to human prefrontal cortex. *Cognition*, *50*(1–3), 7–15.

Bechara, A., Damasio, H., Tranel, D., & Damasio, A. R. (1997). Deciding advantageously before knowing the advantageous strategy. *Science*, *275*(5304), 1293–1294.

Bechara, A., Damasio, H., Tranel, D., & Damasio, A. R. (2005). The Iowa Gambling Task and the somatic marker hypothesis: Some questions and answers. *Trends in Cognitive Sciences*, *9*(4), 159–162.

Betsch, T. (2008). The nature of intuition and its neglect in research on judgment and decision making. In H. Plessner, C. Betsch & T. Betsch (Eds.), *Intuition in judgment and decision making* (pp. 3–22). Mahwah, NJ: Lawrence Erlbaum Associates Publishers.

Betsch, T., Brinkmann, B. J., Fiedler, K., & Breining, K. (1999). When prior knowledge overrules new evidence: Adaptive use of decision strategies and the role of behavioral routines. *Swiss Journal of Psychology – Zeitschrift fur Psychologie – Revue Suisse de Psychologie*, *58*(3), 151–160.

Betsch, T., & Haberstroh, S. (2005). Current research on routine decision making: Advances and prospects. In T. Betsch & S. Haberstroh (Eds.), *The routines of decision making* (pp. 359–376). Mahwah, NJ: Lawrence Erlbaum Associates Publishers.

Betsch, T., Haberstroh, S., Glöckner, A., Haar, T., & Fiedler, K. (2001). The effects of routine strength on adaptation and information search in recurrent decision making. *Organizational Behavior and Human Decision Processes*, *84*(1), 23–53.

Betsch, T., Haberstroh, S., & Höhle, C. (2002). Explaining routinized decision making: A review of theories and models. *Theory & Psychology*, *12*(4), 453–488.

Betsch, T., Haberstroh, S., Molter, B., & Glöckner, A. (2004). Oops, I did it again – relapse errors in routinized decision making. *Organizational Behavior and Human Decision Processes*, *93*(1), 62–74.

Betsch, T., Plessner, H., Schwieren, C., & Gütig, R. (2001). I like it but I don't know why: A value-account approach to implicit attitude formation. *Personality and Social Psychology Bulletin, 27*(2), 242–253.

Bos, M. W., Dijksterhuis, A., & van Baaren, R. B. (2008). On the goal-dependency of unconscious thought. *Journal of Experimental Social Psychology, 44*(4), 1114–1120.

Botvinick, M., Braver, T. S., Yeung, N., Ullsperger, M., Carter, C. S., & Cohen, J. D. (2004). Conflict monitoring: Computational and empirical studies. In M. I. Posner (Ed.), *Cognitive neuroscience of attention* (pp. 91–102). New York, NY: Guilford Press.

Brehmer, B. (1994). The psychology of linear judgement models. *Acta Psychologica, 87*, 137–154.

Brunswik, E. (1955). Representative design and the probability theory in a functional psychology. *Psychological Review, 62*, 193–217.

Busemeyer, J. R., & Johnson, J. G. (2004). Computational models of decision making. In D. J. Koehler & N. Harvey (Eds.), *Blackwell handbook of judgment and decision making* (pp. 133–154). Malden, MA: Blackwell Publishing.

Busemeyer, J. R., & Townsend, J. T. (1993). Decision field theory: A dynamic-cognitive approach to decision making in an uncertain environment. *Psychological Review, 100*(3), 432–459.

Chen, S., & Chaiken, S. (1999). The heuristic-systematic model in its broader context. In S. Chaiken & Y. Trope (Eds.), *Dual-process theories in social psychology* (pp. 73–96). New York, NY: Guilford Press.

Damasio, A. R. (1994). *Descartes' error: Emotion, reason, and the human brain.* New York: Putnam Publishing.

De Neys, W., & Glumicic, T. (2008). Conflict monitoring in dual process theories of thinking. *Cognition, 106*, 1248–1299.

De Neys, W., Vartanian, O., & Goel, V. (2008). Smarter than we think: When our brains detect that we are biased. *Psychological Science, 19*(5), 483–489.

Dehaene, S. (2008). Conscious and non-conscious processes: Distinct forms of evidence accumulation? In C. Engel & W. Singer (Eds.), *Better than conscious? Decision making, the human mind, and implications for institutions* (pp. 21–50). Cambridge, MA: MIT Press.

Dehaene, S., Changeux, J.-P., Naccache, L., Sackur, J., & Sergent, C. (2006). Conscious, preconscious, and subliminal processing: A testable taxonomy. *Trends in Cognitive Sciences, 10*(5), 204–211.

Dijksterhuis, A., Bos, M. W., Nordgren, L. F., & van Baaren, R. B. (2006). On making the right choice: The deliberation-without-attention effect. *Science, 311*(5763), 1005–1007.

Doherty, M. E., & Brehmer, B. (1997). The paramorphic representation of clinical judgment: A thirty-year retrospective. In W. M. Goldstein & R. M. Hogarth (Eds.), *Research on judgment and decision making: Currents, connections, and controversies* (pp. 537–551). New York: Cambridge University Press.

Doherty, M. E., & Kurz, E. M. (1996). Social judgment theory. *Thinking & Reasoning, 2*(2–3), 109–140.

Dougherty, M. R. P., Gettys, C. F., & Ogden, E. E. (1999). MINERVA-DM: A memory processes model for judgments of likelihood. *Psychological Review, 106*(1), 180–209.

Epstein, S. (1990). Cognitive-experiential self-theory. In L. A. Pervin (Ed.), *Handbook of personality: Theory and research* (pp. 165–192). New York, NY: Guilford Press.

Evans, J. S. B. T. (2007). On the resolution of conflict in dual process theories of reasoning. *Thinking & Reasoning, 13*(4), 321–339.

Evans, J. S. B. T. (2008). Dual-processing accounts of reasoning, judgment, and social cognition. *Annual Review of Psychology, 59,* 255–278.

Fiedler, K. (2000). Beware of samples! A cognitive-ecological sampling approach to judgment biases. *Psychological Review, 107*(4), 659–676.

Fiedler, K. (2008). The ultimate sampling dilemma in experience-based decision making. *Journal of Experimental Psychology: Learning, Memory, and Cognition, 34*(1), 186–203.

Finucane, M. L., Alhakami, A., Slovic, P., & Johnson, S. M. (2000). The affect heuristic in judgments of risks and benefits. *Journal of Behavioral Decision Making, 13*(1), 1–17.

Fishburn, P. C. (1974). Lexicographic orders, utilities, and decision rules: A survey. *Management Science, 20,* 1442–1472.

Gigerenzer, G. (2007). *Gut feelings: The intelligence of the unconscious.* New York: Viking Press.

Gigerenzer, G., & Todd, P. M. (1999). Fast and frugal heuristics: The adaptive toolbox. In *Simple heuristics that make us smart* (pp. 3–34). New York, NY: Oxford University Press.

Gilovich, T., Griffin, D., & Kahneman, D. (2002). *Heuristics and biases: The psychology of intuitive judgment.* New York, NY: Cambridge University Press.

Glöckner, A. (2008a). Does intuition beat fast and frugal heuristics? A systematic empirical analysis. In H. Plessner, C. Betsch & T. Betsch (Eds.), *Intuition in judgment and decision making* (pp. 309–325). Mahwah, NJ: Lawrence Erlbaum.

Glöckner, A. (2008b). How evolution outwits bounded rationality: The efficient interaction of automatic and deliberate processes in decision making and implications for institutions. In C. Engel & W. Singer (Eds.), *Better than conscious? Decision making, the human mind, and implications for institutions* (pp. 259–284). Cambridge, MA: MIT Press.

Glöckner, A., & Betsch, T. (2008a). Do people make decisions under risk based on ignorance? An empirical test of the Priority Heuristic against Cumulative Prospect Theory. *Organizational Behavior and Human Decision Processes, 107*(1), 75–95.

Glöckner, A., & Betsch, T. (2008b). Modeling option and strategy choices with connectionist networks: Towards an integrative model of automatic and deliberate decision making. *Judgment and Decision Making, 3*(3), 215–228.

Glöckner, A., & Betsch, T. (2008c). Multiple-reason decision making based on automatic processing. *Journal of Experimental Psychology: Learning, Memory, and Cognition, 34*(5), 1055–1075.

Glöckner, A., & Dickert, S. (under review). Base-rate respect by intuition: Approximating rational choices in base-rate tasks with multiple cues.

Glöckner, A., & Engel, C. (2008). Can we trust intuitive jurors? An experimental analysis. *MPI Collective Goods Preprint, No. 38. Available at SSRN:* http://ssrn.com/abstract=1307580.

Glöckner, A., & Herbold, A.-K. (in press). An eye-tracking study on information processing in risky decisions: Evidence for compensatory strategies based on automatic processes. *Journal of Behavioral Decision Making.*

Glöckner, A., & Witteman, C. L. M. (in press). Beyond dual-process models: A categorization of processes underlying intuitive judgment and decision making. *Thinking & Reasoning.*

Goldstein, W. M., & Hogarth, R. M. (1997). Judgment and decision research: Some historical context. In W. M. Goldstein & R. M. Hogarth (Eds.), *Research on judgment and decision making: Currents, connections, and controversies* (pp. 3–65). New York, NY: Cambridge University Press.

Guthrie, C., Rachlinski, J. J., & Wistrich, A. J. (2007). Blinking on the bench: How judges decide cases. *Cornell Law Review*, *93*(1), 1–44.

Haidt, J. (2001). The emotional dog and its rational tail: A social intuitionist approach to moral judgment. *Psychological Review*, *108*(4), 814–834.

Hammond, K. R., Hamm, R. M., Grassia, J., & Pearson, T. (1987). Direct comparison of the efficacy of intuitive and analytical cognition in expert judgment. *IEEE Transactions on Systems, Man, & Cybernetics*, *17*(5), 753–770.

Hasher, L., & Zacks, R. T. (1979). Automatic and effortful processes in memory. *Journal of Experimental Psychology: General*, *108*(3), 356–388.

Herbig, B., & Glöckner, A. (2009). Experts and decision making: First steps towards a unifying theory of decision making in novices, intermediates and experts. *MPI Collective Goods Preprint, No. 2009/2. Available at SSRN: http://ssrn.com/abstract=1337449.*

Hintzman, D. L. (1988). Judgments of frequency and recognition memory in a multiple-trace memory model. *Psychological Review*, *95*(4), 528–551.

Hogarth, R. M. (2001). *Educating intuition.* Chicago, IL: University of Chicago Press.

Holyoak, K. J., & Simon, D. (1999). Bidirectional reasoning in decision making by constraint satisfaction. *Journal of Experimental Psychology: General*, *128*(1), 3–31.

Holyoak, K. J., & Spellman, B. A. (1993). Thinking. *Annual Review of Psychology*, *44*, 265–315.

Johnson-Laird, P. N. (1983). *Mental models: Towards a cognitive science of language, inference, and consciousness.* Cambridge, MA: Harvard University Press.

Kahneman, D. (2003). A perspective on judgment and choice: Mapping bounded rationality. *American Psychologist*, *58*(9), 697–720.

Kahneman, D., & Frederick, S. (2002). Representativeness revisited: Attribute substitution in intuitive judgment. In T. Gilovich, D. Griffin & D. Kahneman (Eds.), *Heuristics and biases: The psychology of intuitive judgment* (pp. 49–81). New York, NY: Cambridge University Press.

Kahneman, D., Slovic, P., & Tversky, A. (Eds.). (1982). *Judgment under uncertainty: Heuristics and biases.* Cambridge, MA: Cambridge University Press.

Kahneman, D., & Tversky, A. (1979). Prospect theory: An analysis of decision under risk. *Econometrica*, *47*, 263–292.

Klein, G. A. (1993). A recognition-primed decision (RPD) model of rapid decision making. In G. A. Klein, J. Orasanu, R. Calderwood & C. E. Zsambok (Eds.), *Decision making in action: Models and methods* (pp. 138–147). Westport, CT: Ablex Publishing.

Klein, G. A. (2003). *Intuition at work.* New York: Doubleday.

Klein, G. A., Orasanu, J., Calderwood, R., & Zsambok, C. E. (1993). *Decision making in action: Models and methods.* Westport, CT: Ablex Publishing.

Kruglanski, A. W., Chun, W. Y., Erb, H. P., Pierro, A., Mannetti, L., & Spiegel, S. (2003). A parametric unimodel of human judgment: Integrating dual-process frameworks in social cognition from a single-mode perspective. In J. P. Forgas, K. D. Williams & W. von Hippel (Eds.), *Social judgments: Implicit and explicit processes* (pp. 137–161). New York, NY: Cambridge University Press.

Kruglanski, A. W., & Orehek, E. (2007). Partitioning the domain of social inference:

Dual mode and systems models and their alternatives. *Annual Review of Psychology*, *58*, 291–316.

Kruglanski, A. W., & Thompson, E. P. (1999). Persuasion by a single route: A view from the unimodel. *Psychological Inquiry*, *10*(2), 83–109.

Lieberman, M. D. (2007). Social cognitive neuroscience: A review of core processes. *Annual Review of Psychology*, *58*, 259–289.

Lieberman, M. D., Gaunt, R., Gilbert, D. T., & Trope, Y. (2002). Reflexion and reflection: A social cognitive neuroscience approach to attributional inference. In M. P. Zanna (Ed.), *Advances in experimental social psychology, Vol. 34* (pp. 199–249). San Diego, CA: Academic Press.

McClelland, J. L., & Rumelhart, D. E. (1981). An interactive activation model of context effects in letter perception: I. An account of basic findings. *Psychological Review*, *88*(5), 375–407.

Mitchell, T. R., & Beach, L. R. (1990). ". . . Do I love thee? Let me count . . .": Toward an understanding of intuitive and automatic decision making. *Organizational Behavior and Human Decision Processes*, *47*(1), 1–20.

Montgomery, H. (1989). From cognition to action: The search for dominance in decision making. In H. Montgomery & O. Svenson (Eds.), *Process and structure in human decision making* (pp. 23–49). Oxford, England: John Wiley & Sons.

Payne, J. W., Bettman, J. R., & Johnson, E. J. (1988). Adaptive strategy selection in decision making. *Journal of Experimental Psychology: Learning, Memory, and Cognition*, *14*(3), 534–552.

Petty, R., & Cacioppo, J. (1986). *Communication and persuasion: Central and peripheral routes to attitude change*. New York: Springer.

Plessner, H., Betsch, C., & Betsch, T. (2008). *Intuition in judgment and decision making*. Mahwah, NJ: Lawrence Erlbaum Associates Publishers.

Plessner, H., & Czenna, S. (2008). The benefits of intuition. In H. Plessner, C. Betsch & T. Betsch (Eds.), *Intuition in judgment and decision making* (pp. 251–265). Mahwah, NJ: Lawrence Erlbaum Associates Publishers.

Ratcliff, R. (1978). A theory of memory retrieval. *Psychological Review*, *85*(2), 59–108.

Ratcliff, R., & McKoon, G. (2008). The diffusion decision model: Theory and data for two-choice decision tasks. *Neural Computation*, *20*(4), 873–922.

Read, S. J., Vanman, E. J., & Miller, L. C. (1997). Connectionism, parallel constraint satisfaction processes, and Gestalt principles: (Re)introducing cognitive dynamics to social psychology. *Personality and Social Psychology Review*, *1*(1), 26–53.

Reber, A. S. (1993). *Implicit learning and tacit knowledge: An essay on the cognitive unconscious. Oxford psychology series, No. 19*. New York: Oxford University Press.

Rumelhart, D. E., & McClelland, J. L. (1982). An interactive activation model of context effects in letter perception: II. The contextual enhancement effect and some tests and extensions of the model. *Psychological Review*, *89*(1), 60–94.

Sadler-Smith, E. (2008). *Inside intuition*. New York: Routledge/Taylor & Francis Group.

Satpute, A. B., & Lieberman, M. D. (2006). Integrating automatic and controlled processes into neurocognitive models of social cognition. *Brain Research*, *1079*(1), 86–97.

Savage, L. J. (1954). *The foundations of statistics* (2nd ed.). New York: Dover.

Schneider, W., & Shiffrin, R. M. (1977). Controlled and automatic human information processing: I. Detection, search, and attention. *Psychological Review*, *84*(1), 1–66.

Shadlen, M. N., Kiani, R., Hanks, T. D., & Churchland, A. K. (2008). Neurobiology of decision making: An intentional framework. In C. Engel & W. Singer (Eds.), *Better than conscious? Decision making, the human mind, and implications for institutions.* Cambridge, MA: MIT Press.

Shiffrin, R. M., & Schneider, W. (1977). Controlled and automatic human information processing: II. Perceptual learning, automatic attending and a general theory. *Psychological Review, 84*(2), 127–190.

Simon, H. A. (1955). A behavioural model of rational choice. *The Quarterly Journal of Economics, 69,* 99–118.

Skinner, B. F. (1938). *The behavior of organisms.* New York: Appleton-Century-Crofts.

Sloman, S. A. (2002). Two systems of reasoning. In T. Gilovich, D. Griffin & D. Kahneman (Eds.), *Heuristics and biases: The psychology of intuitive judgment* (pp. 379–396). New York: Cambridge University Press.

Slovic, P., Finucane, M., Peters, E., & MacGregor, D. G. (2002). The affect heuristic. In T. Gilovich, D. Griffin & D. Kahneman (Eds.), *Heuristics and biases: The psychology of intuitive judgment* (pp. 397–420). New York, NY: Cambridge University Press.

Strack, F., & Deutsch, R. (2004). Reflective and impulsive determinants of social behavior. *Personality and Social Psychology Review, 8*(3), 220–247.

Svenson, O. (1992). Differentiation and Consolidation Theory of human decision making: A frame of reference for the study of pre- and post-decision processes. *Acta Psychologica, 80*(1–3), 143–168.

Thagard, P. (1989). Explanatory coherence. *Behavioral and Brain Sciences, 12*(3), 435–502.

Thagard, P., & Millgram, E. (1995). Inference to the best plan: A coherence theory of decision. In A. Ram & D. B. Leake (Eds.), *Goal-driven learning* (pp. 439–454). Cambridge, MA: MIT Press.

Tversky, A., & Kahneman, D. (1992). Advances in prospect theory: Cumulative representation of uncertainty. *Journal of Risk and Uncertainty, 5,* 297–323.

Unkelbach, C., Fiedler, K., & Freytag, P. (2007). Information repetition in evaluative judgments: Easy to monitor, hard to control. *Organizational Behavior and Human Decision Processes, 103*(1), 37–52.

van Veen, V., & Carter, C. S. (2002a). The anterior cingulate as a conflict monitor: fMRI and ERP studies. *Physiology & Behavior, 77*(4–5), 477–482.

van Veen, V., & Carter, C. S. (2002b). The timing of action-monitoring processes in the anterior cingulate cortex. *Journal of Cognitive Neuroscience, 14*(4), 593–602.

van Veen, V., & Carter, C. S. (2006). Conflict and cognitive control in the brain. *Current Directions in Psychological Science, 15*(5), 237–240.

van Veen, V., Holroyd, C. B., Cohen, J. D., Stenger, V. A., & Carter, C. S. (2004). Errors without conflict: Implications for performance monitoring theories of anterior cingulate cortex. *Brain and Cognition, 56*(2), 267–276.

von Neumann, J., & Morgenstern, O. (1944). *Theory of games and economic behavior* (1st ed.). Princeton, NJ: Princeton University Press.

Walther, E. (2002). Guilty by mere association: Evaluative conditioning and the spreading attitude effect. *Journal of Personality and Social Psychology, 82*(6), 919–934.

Walther, E., & Grigoriadis, S. (2004). Why sad people like shoes better: The influence of mood on the evaluative conditioning of consumer attitudes. *Psychology & Marketing, 21*(10), 755–773.

Wertheimer, M. (1938). Gestalt theory. In W. D. Ellis (Ed.), *A source book of Gestalt psychology* (pp. 1–11). London, England: Kegan Paul, Trench, Trubner & Company.

Wilson, T. D., & Schooler, J. W. (1991). Thinking too much: Introspection can reduce the quality of preferences and decisions. *Journal of Personality and Social Psychology, 60*(2), 181–192.

Yang, T., & Shadlen, M. N. (2007). Probabilistic reasoning by neurons. *Nature, 447*(7148), 1075–1080.

Yechiam, E., Busemeyer, J. R., Stout, J. C., & Bechara, A. (2005). Using cognitive models to map relations between neuropsychological disorders and human decision-making deficits. *Psychological Science, 16*(12), 973–978.

Zacks, R. T., Hasher, L., & Sanft, H. (1982). Automatic encoding of event frequency: Further findings. *Journal of Experimental Psychology: Learning, Memory, and Cognition, 8*(2), 106–116.

Zajonc, R. B. (1968). Attitudinal effects of mere exposure. *Journal of Personality and Social Psychology, 9*(2, Pt.2), 1–27.

Zajonc, R. B. (1980). Feeling and thinking: Preferences need no inferences. *American Psychologist, 35*(2), 151–175.

2 Take a quick click at that!

Mouselab and eye-tracking as tools to measure intuition

Elisabeth Norman and
Michael Schulte-Mecklenbeck

Introduction

When investigating literature in intuitive decision making one will often find references or applications of a dual-systems approach (Stanovich & West, 2000). Within this framework intuition is viewed as the counterpart of rationality, and the two information-processing systems are thought to be largely independent. As pointed out by Glöckner and Witteman (chapter 1, this volume), a wide variety of cognitive mechanisms might be involved in intuitive decision making, ranging from simple learning mechanisms to the construction of complex mental representations. What they all seem to have in common is that their influence on decision making is largely *automatic*.

Automaticity in the context of decision making

A common view of automaticity is that it refers to mental processes that are effortless, unconscious and involuntary – they operate without cognitive effort, conscious control or monitoring (Bargh & Chartrand, 1999). In a classic study Bargh, Chen, and Burrows (1996) found that priming participants with words associated with either politeness or rudeness influenced their tendency to act politely or rudely in a staged social situation, even when participants showed no conscious awareness of this influence. How can we then measure the influence of automatic processes in decision making?

Automaticity is often associated with implicit or unconscious aspects of our mental processing. These labels are used interchangeably in the decision-making literature and will be treated likewise here, although our readers should be aware that there are some debates about the degree of overlap between these concepts in the consciousness literature (see e.g., Tzelgov, 1997). Implied in the model of Glöckner and Witteman (chapter 1, this volume) is that automaticity involves the unintentional application of complex knowledge structures that are in themselves not consciously represented.

One approach to studying intuition in decision making is to focus on the automaticity of the information integration process itself (Glöckner & Betsch, 2008a, 2008b; Glöckner & Herbold, 2008). The central question is whether the decision maker integrates available information in a more controlled and serial manner, or in a more automatic and parallel manner. We later give examples of how this has been done.

Given the close association between automaticity and implicit or unconscious cognition, an alternative approach is to investigate whether decision makers showed conscious awareness of the basis of their decision. To decide whether a certain decision should be regarded as intuitive and characterized by automatic processing, one then needs to apply testable operational criteria of conscious awareness. Depending on the focus of the researcher, one might want to address whether the applied knowledge was unconscious, whether the intention to apply the knowledge was unconscious, or both. Because the measurement of consciousness is rarely addressed in the decision-making literature, we will now exemplify how this can be done.

Measuring consciousness

Let us briefly turn to the implicit cognition domain. Implicit cognition refers to cognitive activity that influences a person's behaviour and judgment, while the person is not consciously aware of this activity and/or its influence on performance. Examples include implicit memory (Schachter, 1987), implicit learning (Reber, 1989; see also Glöckner & Witteman, chapter 1, this volume) and implicit attitudes (Greenwald, McGhee, & Schwartz, 1998; see also Holland & de Vries, chapter 7, this volume).

In research on implicit cognition several operational criteria for consciousness have been put forward. These mainly apply to whether knowledge is consciously represented or not. For the time being we will restrict ourselves to a classic principle: Knowledge or processing is regarded as unconscious when it is above an objective but below a subjective threshold (Cheesman & Merikle, 2003; Dienes & Berry, 1997). An objective threshold refers to whether the knowledge or process is expressed on overt behaviour, e.g., the ability to make discriminatory responses in line with this knowledge in a forced-choice situation. A subjective threshold refers to whether the person shows metacognitive awareness as reflected in a verbal report measure. For example, in a classic study of intuition by Bowers, Regehr, Balthazard, and Parker (1990), participants were shown two word triads on each trial, e.g., the words *playing, credit, report*, and *still, pages, music*. Only one triad in each pair was semantically coherent in the sense that all three words in the triad were semantically related to a fourth word that was not presented. (In our example, all three words on the first triad were semantically related to the word *card.*) While participants showed no ability to verbally report the common associate, they showed an intuitive preference for the internally coherent triads on a forced-choice measure. Participants showed an intuitive preference for a certain decision alternative, even when the knowledge was not consciously represented – the preference was above an objective but below a subjective threshold. Recently, it has been found that trials where the coherence was perceived intuitively are associated with a different pattern of brain activity than correctly solved trials, as measured by fMRI (Ilg et al., 2007). It has also been found that undetected coherence gives rise to specific patterns of facial muscle reactions (Topolinski, Likowski, Weyers, & Strack, in press), which could be seen as yet another objective measure.

This criterion can be applied to decision-making situations, where dissociations between objective and subjective assessment of participants' preferences are indicative of intuitive decision making.

From outcomes to process measures

So far, research on intuitive decision making has largely focused on explicit choices rather than on the processes leading up to these choices. This focus on outcomes per se is not necessarily a problem as long as models make different predictions for decisions under different conditions (see Glöckner & Witteman, chapter 1, this volume; Bröder, chapter 4, this volume; Glöckner, chapter 5, this volume). However, the way in which outcome measures have been applied to intuitive decision making seems problematic especially concerning two points: Limited choice sets and deliberate choices. Participants are given a choice between a limited set of options, where choosing anything but the pre-defined "rational" alternative is regarded as "intuitive" (Hammond, Hamm, Grassia, & Pearson, 1987). They state their choice most often by saying or writing down which response alternative they prefer. This mainly reflects conscious preferences. However, if intuition is viewed as the outcome of largely automatic and unconscious processes, this type of measurement does not, on its own, allow for differentiation between intuition and deliberation.

Candidate methodological tools

It is clear that additional methodological tools are needed which are more likely to reflect the intuitive, automatic decision-making process. Several candidates are presented in this book, including confidence and decision time (Glöckner, chapter 5, this volume), specific self-report (Witteman & van Geenen, chapter 3, this volume), physiological measures (Hochman, Glöckner, & Yechiam, chapter 8, this volume) and implicit associations (Holland & de Vries, chapter 7, this volume).

In this chapter we explore whether Mouselab and eye-tracking (see also Renkewitz & Jahn, chapter 11, this volume), which are commonly used in the study of deliberate decision making, can also be used to explore intuitive decision making. Our main focus will be on whether these methods allow us to identify situations where a dissociation between objective and subjective measures indicates that the person is not consciously aware of the basis of his or her decision. We now discuss each of these tools in turn.

Mouselab

Mouselab is a computer program that records the acquisition of information that is presented in a matrix. The roots of Mouselab go back to studies with information boards (literal boards with envelopes attached to them, e.g., Payne, 1976). With the commercial introduction of computers, new ways to record information acquisition were created. Computer monitors replaced information boards as presentation devices, and keyboards were used to indicate which cell should be opened (Payne & Braunstein, 1978). In the next developmental step the computer mouse was introduced as a pointing device and Mouselab found its name.

Theoretical concepts close to Mouselab

Mouselab is closely related to the adaptive decision maker (ADM) framework (Payne, Bettman, & Johnson, 1988, 1993). In this framework the decision maker is understood as an information processor, with limited capabilities, who adapts to the environment at hand. This adaption is based on considering a trade-off between the accuracy of a certain strategy and the effort that this strategy requires. Putting a strategy on a continuum, optimal or normative versus random choice, determines its accuracy (see Payne et al., 1988 for several visualizations of such continua). To estimate the effort a strategy requires the authors went back to the ideas in production systems (Newell & Simon, 1972) and elementary information processes (EIP; Huber, 1980). First a strategy is broken down into simple operations or EIPs such as READ, COMPARE, ADD . . ., then the number of EIPs necessary determines the effort for the given strategy. An interesting application of this approach is presented in Lohse and Johnson (1996), where the time needed to execute an EIP was used to build predictions for how long it would take the participant to finish different conditions of a task.

In the ADM framework, the decision maker can learn from prior experience, which eases strategy selection and availability. While the ADM framework does not directly refer to intuitive processes the authors acknowledge that the choice of a strategy is bound to a conscious process plus a "learned contingency between elements of the task and the relative effort and accuracy of a decision strategy" (Payne et al., 1993, p. 14).

Citation record of Mouselab studies

To evaluate the impact Mouselab has had in decision-making research an ISI Web of Science search with the keyword combination: "decision making" and "mouselab" was conducted (see Table 2.1). The citation count is reported and a subjective categorization into different research areas performed. Citation numbers were cut-off at a minimum of 15 citations because of a long tail of studies with only few citations.

Table 2.1 Influential Mouselab studies based on their citation count

Publication	Citation count	Area
Payne, Bettman & Johnson (1988)	372	Gambles, multi-variate
Costa-Gomes, Crawford, and Broseta (2001)	67	Gambles
Bröder (2003)	44	Heuristics
Levin, Huneke, and Jasper (2000)	37	Consumer decision making
Lohse and Johnson (1996)	32	Method comparison
Dhar, Nowlis, and Sherman (1999)	26	Consumer decision making
Dhar, Nowlis, and Sherman (2000)	24	Consumer decision making
Lurie (2004)	17	Consumer decision making

In the literature, a broad area of applications for Mouselab can be found ranging from research on gambles (Costa-Gomes, Crawford, & Broseta, 2001; Payne et al., 1988) and heuristics (Bröder, 2003) to method comparisons (Lohse & Johnson, 1996). Half of the published studies are situated in the area of consumer decision making (Dhar, Nowlis, & Sherman, 1999, 2000; Levin, Huneke, & Jasper, 2000; Lurie, 2004). More important for our topic, all of the studies are concerned with the question of deliberate decision making. Only a small number of papers can be found that use Mouselab in the area of intuition, namely a series of studies by Glöckner and Betsch (2008a, 2008b), which we will discuss in more detail below.

Setting up a Mouselab study

There are different flavours of Mouselab available which can be used online or offline in a laboratory (e.g., MouselabWeb, Willemsen and Johnson, 2008, or Web Mouselab, Payne, 2005). In what follows we will use MouselabWeb as an example because it is freely available and frequently updated. The basic design of a MouselabWeb page is a matrix-like setup (e.g., Figure 2.1, but see Glöckner and Betsch, 2008a, Experiment 3, for a different setup) of an arbitrary number of information cells. Each information unit is presented in a box which is covered by an overlay. Simply moving the mouse pointer over one of the boxes shows the participant the content. Upon leaving the box area the information is covered again. The closing of a box, after leaving the box area, can be suppressed in a design where re-acquisitions are of less interest.

For setting up a MouselabWeb experiment a program within the MouselabWeb package called "Designer" is very useful. The Designer helps creating the basic matrix layout with the information boxes. There are sophisticated counterbalancing options available to avoid unwanted effects of, e.g., reading order. In a process tracing study the reading order (left to right in

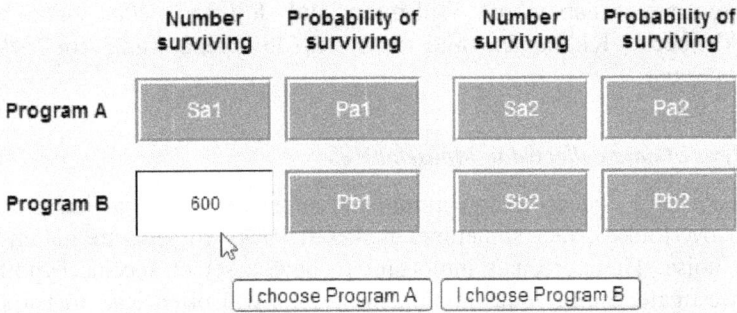

Figure 2.1 Example of a MouselabWeb setup in a framing study. There are eight cells, with different labels, of which seven are closed and one open, displaying a value of 600. At the bottom of the figure the participant can select the option he prefers.

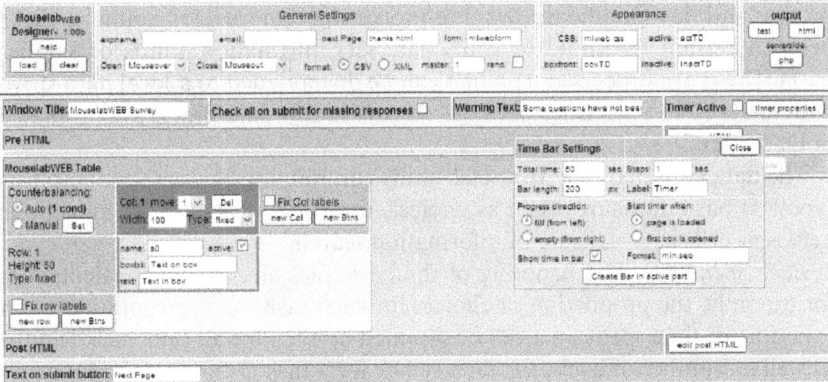

Figure 2.2 MouselabWeb Designer.

Western cultures) can have an effect on the acquisition order of information. The heart of the Designer (see Figure 2.2) is the MouselabWeb Table which helps to create the actual information matrix. Each cell is automatically named after pressing "new Col" or "new Row", but it is highly recommended to change cell naming to something sensible in reference to the desired content because the cell labels are reflected in the data-sets. For each cell the status can be set to *active*, to have actual search capabilities, or *passive*, e.g., for adding column or row names. Two additional fields ask for the text on the box (boxtxt) and the actual information (text).

If the research question asks for time restrictions the latest version of MouselabWeb (1.0 beta, as of December 2008) provides the option of adding a timer bar that either counts down from or up to a pre-defined value in seconds. This feature can be useful to run studies with time constraints, e.g., Glöckner and Betsch (2008b). Again several options to fine tune this feature are available (see Willemsen and Johnson, 2008 or Schulte-Mecklenbeck, Kühberger, and Ranyard, in preparation, for detailed instructions).

Analysis of data collected in MouselabWeb

MouselabWeb collects a large amount of information per participant. This, often overlooked, fact sometimes makes it tricky to separate actual data from noise. Therefore it is important to have a set of specific hypotheses to investigate. Simply data mining the results will often lead to tears and frustration. MouselabWeb is event driven, i.e., each event (click, cell opening) generates a data row with a time-stamp. It is therefore hard to specify the amount of data generated for a certain experiment length.[1] However, it is clear that several kilobytes of data per person are to be expected when running a MouselabWeb study. Access to the results of a study can be gained with the "Datalyzer" application which offers a convenient way to pre-process and download data-sets. Pre-processing removes, for example, clicks below a certain threshold or splits data-sets into halves, thirds or smaller parts. These pre-processed data files can be downloaded to a local hard-drive and analyzed in a statistics package. Access to raw data files is also available in Datalyzer.

The data collected in a Mouselab study can roughly be organized into two types: 1) basic measures such as choices, time and clicks and 2) transitions betweens cells as a measure of information search.

Basic measures. The handling of the basic measures involves calculating, for example, the proportion of choices for each task type or condition in an experiment; time spent on a cell or summed up time for all cells (task length) as well as number of clicks for each cell or for a task. Note that the time and click measures are often correlated and result in highly similar patterns. The following statistics are sufficient with the "basic measures" in most cases: proportions and ratio analysis, means, ANOVAs, MANOVAs, time series and Random Effect Models. For each of these it is common practice to log-transform click and time measures in order to get more normal distributed variables.

Transitions between cells. There are four possible types of transitions in an information search task using a matrix layout: A Type II transition (see Figure 2.3) corresponds to an alternative-wise search pattern, where the transition moves within the same alternative but changes the attribute. A Type III transition is attribute based, where the transition stays within the same attribute but changes the alternative. These are the transitions most often analyzed in decision-making studies. However, Type I transitions (no transition, the same information item is inspected again) and Type IV transitions (a diagonal transition, which switches alternative as well as attribute) hold valuable information, too.

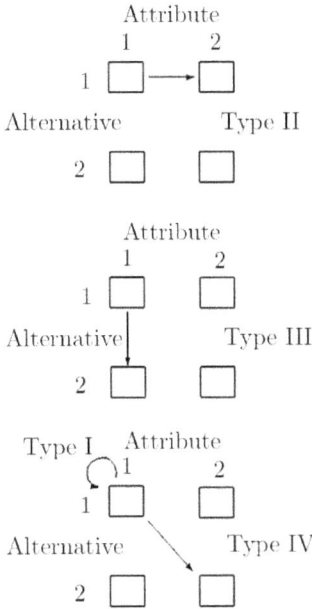

Figure 2.3 Types of information selection.

Transitions are tricky in the sense that the above mentioned "simple" approaches are not sufficient for this type of analysis. Therefore several indices have been suggested to condense data based on transitions into measures that can be handled more easily.

The Search Index (SI), based on work of Payne (1976), is also often referred to as the Payne Index in the literature. Assuming that the total number of within-alternative transitions is $N_{alternative}$ (Type II) and the total number of across-attribute moves is $N_{attribute}$ (Type III), the Search Index is the ratio:

$$SI = \frac{N_{alternative} - N_{attribute}}{N_{alternative} + N_{attribute}} \tag{1}$$

This index ranges from −1.00 to 1.00 indicating a completely attribute based vs. a completely alternative based information search respectively. If there are equal numbers of both types of transitions, the index equals 0. A positive index value is often assumed to indicate the usage of compensatory strategies (e.g., equal weight strategies), whereas a negative index value is interpreted as indicator for more non-compensatory strategies (e.g., lexico-graphic strategies).

Böckenholt and Hynan (1994) showed in a simulation study that the SI is unreliable when the number of alternatives and attributes is not identical.

When the number of attributes is larger than the number of alternatives a positive SI index is more likely and when the number of attributes is smaller than the number of alternatives a negative SI index is more likely. In order to overcome the problems identified with SI, the authors introduced a strategy measure (SM) that compared the observed frequency of transitions against those expected by chance (see Formula 2 in the original notation).

$$SM = \frac{\sqrt{N\left(\frac{AD}{N}\right)(r_a - r_d) - (D - A)}}{\sqrt{A^2(D - 1) + D^2(A - 1)}} \tag{2}$$

Here N denotes the total number of cell openings; A and D define the information matrix with A defined as the number of alternatives and D as the number of dimensions; r_a is the frequency of alternative-wise transitions (Type II), r_d is the frequency of dimension-wise transitions (Type III).

Several other approaches to represent transitions and search behaviour were introduced by different authors: Van Raaij (1977) approached the problem with an index that compared the first and second half of the search process to the total number of cell openings. Koele and Westenberg (1995) suggested to combine the variability of searches with the depth of searches in a compensation index denoted C and showed the psychometric properties of this index to be superior to SI.

The above described simple measures represent overt, voluntary responses (i.e., moving the mouse cursor and clicking). It becomes clear that most of them are useful as dependent variables in questions regarding deliberate search behaviour and indeed they have mostly been used in that domain. We now turn to whether information search patterns measured in Mouselab can also be used to identify more intuitive processes. One way to identify intuitive processes would be to show that large amounts of information are integrated in a largely automatic manner. Another would be to show that a preference for a certain option is revealed on objective but not subjective indices. Objective measures would here include fixation times, opening length, information search patterns and response times. The subjective measure would be explicit choice.

Mouselab: a tool for studying intuitive decision making?

So far only a handful of studies have applied Mouselab for investigating intuitive decision making (Glöckner & Betsch, 2008a, 2008b). The basic setup of these studies involved presenting participants with a series of decisions between two or three alternatives, e.g., to decide which city has more inhabitants. Participants were for instance presented with a number of cues for each decision alternative, together with information about the relative validity of each cue.

Two variants of Mouselab were used in these studies. One was the traditional setup where information is hidden behind boxes and information search behaviour can be measured through standard Mouselab data (see e.g., Glöckner & Betsch, 2008b, Experiment 2). Another variant was to present information in an open matrix, and to infer decision strategy from the explicit choice (see e.g., Glöckner & Betsch, 2008b, Experiment 1).

These studies show that people are able to integrate information in a weighted compensatory manner very quickly. The observed decision times were interpreted as being far below the time necessary to integrate information deliberately. Inspired by Hammond et al. (1987) this was taken to indicate the usage of computationally powerful automatic-intuitive processes. However, a comparison between an Open-Mouselab setup in which all information was instantly presented on the screen and a classic Mouselab setup in which information had to be deliberately looked up using the mouse-pointer indicated that the classic Mouselab might hinder information search and that it might induce the application of deliberate strategies. Glöckner and Betsch (2008b) therefore recommend that Mouselab might not be the optimal tool to study intuition.

Based on the few studies available, a tentative conclusion is that Mouselab, at least in its traditional closed cell format, is relatively limited as a tool for studying intuitive processes or even promotes more deliberate processes (Glöckner & Betsch, 2008b, Experiment 2). While the open matrix display seems to encourage more intuitive processing (Glöckner & Betsch, 2008b, Experiment 1) it comes with the downside of not recording mouse movements. It hence takes us back to insight on the pure choices level, which is fine for some research questions but makes us incapable of investigating information search behaviour. Mouselab therefore seems to have limited usefulness for researchers interested in testing specific hypotheses about the automaticity of information search and knowledge integration derived from different theoretical models of decision making (see Glöckner & Betsch, 2008b). It is also of limited value for researchers who want to look for dissociations between objective and subjective measures of consciousness, e.g., observing whether information search behaviour starts favouring one decision alternative before an explicit choice is made.

Eye-tracking

An eye-tracker measures eye positions and eye movements. Interest in vision in general and eye-movements in particular has a long history dating back to Kepler and his work on the optics of the eyes in the seventeenth century. In the nineteenth century Javal (1878) realized that reading involved short stops and not a smooth transition from one word to the next, an observation that led to one of the central measures in eye-tracking research: fixations (stabilized position of the retina). With the turn of the century and the introduction of more sophisticated eye-tracking devices this research grew rapidly. Yarbus (1967) made an important contribution that emphasized the serial processing of pictures which was well in contrast to the dominating view of Gestalt psychology's parallel, one-step process. The author demonstrated that the task given to a participant greatly influenced the scan path of the eyes (the pattern generated by a series of fixations) while the actual stimulus stayed the same. While these first attempts seem somewhat crude from today's perspective they laid the groundwork for modern eye-tracking research and technology.

Theoretical concepts close to eye-tracking

Several theoretical concepts are relevant for understanding eye-tracking data. We will briefly review two that closely connect to decision-making research and intuition. From a process perspective the levels-of-processing framework (Craik & Lockhart, 1972) had a huge influence on cognitive psychology in general and eye-tracking specifically. A two-level model is assumed for visual stimuli in which objects are first localized in the environment (pre-attentive or ambient), then a selection of information is further analyzed on the second level (attentive or focal). Several additional levels of processing have been suggested, with the semantic and metacognitive levels being the more prominent ones (Velichkovsky, Rother, Kopf, Donhofer, & Joos, 2002).

The strong "eye-mind hypothesis" (Just & Carpenter, 1980) postulates a direct mapping of fixation length to the actual length of a cognitive process, since a good deal of the visual information during fixation seems to be accessed and processed instantaneously. There has been a broad discussion of this hypothesis and less strong versions were formulated. Today it is more generally agreed that in addition to an overt orientation system that guides the eyes, a secondary covert system provides attentional guidance. The combination of fixation patterns and fixation time can be used to determine whether a strategy was influenced more by automatic or controlled processes (Glöckner & Herbold, 2008).

Citation record of eye-tracking studies

To evaluate the impact of eye-tracking in decision-making research an ISI Web of Science search with the keyword combination: "decision making" and "eye-tracking" was performed (the same procedure was used as above in the Mouselab section, see Table 2.2).

Consumer research again shows up often in terms of published papers. In the method comparison class we find Lohse and Johnson (1996) again, which is to our knowledge the only work that compares Mouselab with eye-tracking as tools for measuring deliberate decision making. One strong contestant in a

Table 2.2 Influential eye-tracking studies based on their citation count

Publication	Citation count	Area
Russo and Dosher (1983)	200	Gambles
Lohse and Johnson (1996)	32	Method comparison
Russo and Leclerc (1994)	22	Consumer research
Pieters, Rosbergen, and Wedel (1999)	22	Consumer research
Pieters and Warlop (1999)	18	Consumer research

literature search is Russo and Dosher (1983) in a study using simple gamble stimuli. Since 1983 this paper has been cited 200 times and surely it has had a large impact on different research areas. Only one study uses eye-tracking in the area of intuition in decision making, namely Glöckner and Herbold (2008), and this study will be described in more detail later.

Setting up an eye-tracking study

The market for eye-tracking systems is large. Walthew (2008) lists 23 websites for commercial and open source (free) eye-tracking systems which provide hardware as well as software solutions, often in a convenient package. As a different approach, without an actual eye-tracker, "Flashlight" (Schulte-Mecklenbeck, Murphy, & Hutzler, in preparation) could be used. All of these require instructions specific to each system so it is not sufficient or feasible (as in the Mouselab example above) to provide a general guide. Therefore we will try to highlight important issues independent of one specific technology and refer the reader to the eye-tracking manual of the system at hand as well as to Russo's chapter on eye-tracking in decision-making research in Schulte-Mecklenbeck, Kühberger, and Ranyard (in preparation).

Multiple methods are available to record eye movements. The most commonly used method today (Video-Based Combined Pupil/Corneal Reflection) involves projecting an infrared light on the eye and measuring the corneal reflection ("Purkinje reflections") of this light relative to the pupil centre location with a camera.

There are two types of video-based systems which differ in the location of the camera. In remote mounted systems the camera is often installed underneath or above the presentation monitor (see Figure 2.4, top part), or built within a box including a chin rest (most often in high resolution eye-trackers). A computer monitor is used to present stimuli in the visual field of the participant. Head movement is not desired and either compensated through head tracking (i.e., the camera following small head movements) of the camera or a chin rest. More mobility for the participant is provided with a head-mounted system which has a fixed connection between the participant's head and the camera, most often through a helmet (see Figure 2.4, bottom part) or

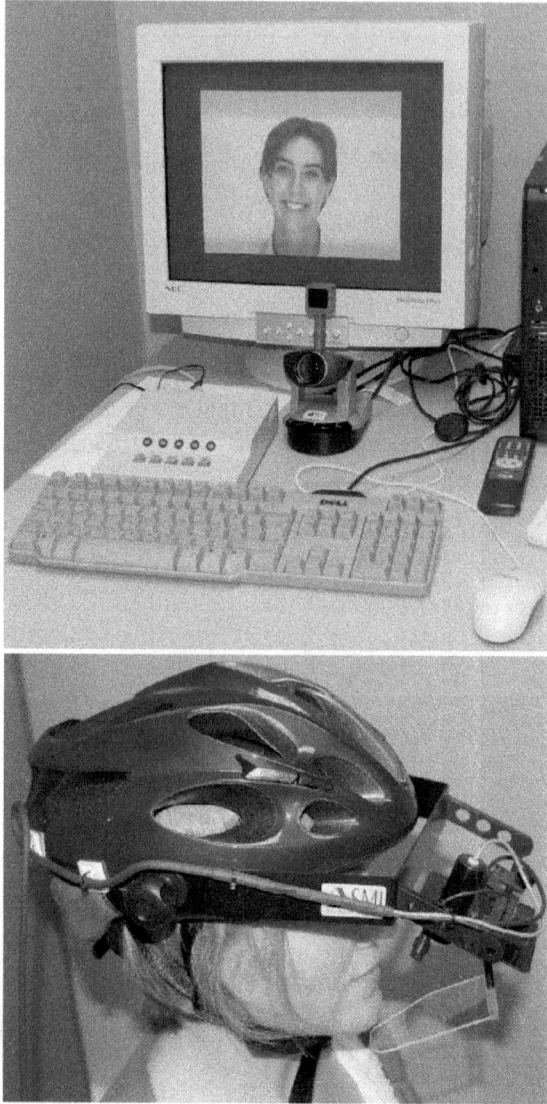

Figure 2.4 Remote mounted system with the camera underneath the presentation monitor (top part), head mounted system with the camera built into the helmet (bottom part).

through glasses. With such a system the participant can move freely and investigate the environment, e.g., in a supermarket or museum.

A calibration process precedes eye-tracking studies using the corneal reflection method. Most often this includes displaying several fixation crosses in the extreme positions of the viewing area (outer left, outer right, top, bottom). The eye-tracker then calculates the Point of Regard (POR) in these positions to be able to estimate all the PORs in-between for the actual measurements. While the calibration process is very smooth in many systems today, especially Tobii systems (http://www.tobii.com) excel here, there are still participants for which the calibration is very hard or impossible, e.g., due to very dark eyes and resulting problems for the system to identify the pupil.

Analysis of data collected with an eye-tracker

Depending on the sampling rate of the eye-tracking system, raw data files can grow to several Megabytes for a short recording session for one person. A 60 Hz eye tracker records the position of the eyes 60 times per second which results in 36,000 measurements for a ten minute experiment. It is important to keep this in mind when preparing an experiment! Eye-tracking systems are delivered with software that helps to get a grip on this data volume by running basic analyses for the user.

Two measures are central to the analysis of eye movements: fixations and saccades. (A third important measure is *smooth pursuit* which refers to the tracking of moving objects. We will not describe this measure in more detail, because it is less relevant to decision making and intuition as it is researched at the moment.) Saccades refer to rapid eye movements used in repositioning the fovea to a new location in the visual environment (usually lasting 10–100 ms). A saccade can be voluntarily invoked or reflexive in order to correct the position of the eyes. Fixations refer to the phase in an eye movement sequence where the retina is stabilized over a stationary object (usually lasting 250–300 ms). The interesting paradox with fixations is that while it seems that the eyes rest on one position there is actual movement which can be categorized in three classes: tremor, drifts and micro-saccades. (Tremor is a very small, high frequency (90 Hz) movement, drift refers to low frequency movements parallel to tremor and between micro-saccades which are fast movements around 25 ms. See Martinez-Conde, Macknik, and Hubel, 2004 for more details.) Without this movement a sharp picture of the environment would not be possible.

In Mouselab there is a clear connection between an information cell in the matrix and the actual relevant information for the participant. Only the opening of a cell is recorded as actual data – moving the mouse around the information matrix is not reflected in the final data-set. For eye-tracking studies the whole stimulus (most often a picture) is used to record the positions of the eyes, i.e., fixations on the whole stimulus area are reflected in the final data-set. To make an analysis more focused on the parts of a stimulus that are relevant for the research question, areas of interest (AOI) can be defined. If a fixation falls inside an AOI it is recognized as data, if it falls outside an AOI it is left out of the analysis. The above mentioned indices can easily be used with AOIs, too. More commonly used in eye-tracking research are the percentage of fixations within an AOI and re-acquisitions of an AOI.

Eye-tracking: a tool for studying intuitive decision making?

In decision-making research, there is so far only one study that specifically addresses whether eye movements can reflect intuitive decision making. Glöckner and Herbold (2008) presented their participants with a series of two-alternative gambles where information about the two gambles was presented in matrix layout in separate halves of the screen. Eye movements were recorded and choice behaviour was measured. Different strategies derived from Cumulative Prospect Theory (Tversky & Kahneman, 1992), Priority Heuristic (Brandstätter, Gigerenzer, & Hertwig, 2006) and Decision Field Theory (Busemeyer & Townsend, 1993) were tested. More compensatory (within alternative) than non-compensatory (between alternative) search behaviour was observed (a result well in line with, e.g., Johnson, Schulte-Mecklenbeck, and Willemsen, 2008). Interesting for our purpose was that results were best explained by models that, at least partially, are claimed to rely on intuitive components in the decision-making process (Decision Field Theory and Parallel Constraint Satisfaction (PCS) Models, e.g., Glöckner & Betsch, 2008c; Thagard & Millgram, 1995). For example, analysis of fixation patterns (the number of fixations and the duration of fixations in each AOI) indicated that most of the observed fixations were rather fast (< 250 ms) indicating short inspections. Long fixations (> 500 ms) were found only seldom indicating only few deliberate processing steps. Additionally there was a tendency for participants to make within-gamble comparisons and to show an unequal distribution of fixations over gambles, which were also taken to reflect automatic processing.

How does this study address the possible dissociation between objective and subjective measures that would indicate that the basis of the decision was unconscious? One objective measure might be visual attention shifts. There are several examples showing that visual attention shifts, measured by eye-tracking, can indicate a preference for a certain decision alternative before a conscious preference has evolved (see e.g., Bridgeman, 1992; Holm, Eriksson, & Andersson, 2008; Ryan & Cohen, 2004). Eye movements can be seen as a type of objective measurement that also reflects non-intentional characteristics of behaviour (see Seth, Dienes, Cleeremans, Overgaard, & Pessoa, 2008, for further discussion about objective and subjective measures). Because these studies also applied subjective report measures of participants' conscious preferences, these examples illustrate the type of dissociation between objective and subjective measures that would be needed to indicate that participants were not consciously aware of the basis of their decision.

Glöckner and Herbold (2008) actually explored this question. They found that participants attended relatively more to the option they later chose than to the other option, before the actual choice was made. This was taken as additional evidence that the decision relied on intuitive processes.

Eye-tracking also allows for measurement of pupil dilation, which is an indicator of autonomic activation. In principle, differences in autonomic activation toward different options before a conscious preference has developed could be seen as another indicator of intuitive processing. In implicit cognition research, it has been found that implicit learning of a complex stimulus pattern can be predicted by pupil dilation preceding each of a series of classification judgements (Bierman, 2004). However, we are not aware of examples applying pupil dilation measures in this way in more traditional decision research.

In conclusion, Glöckner and Herbold's (2008) study suggests that attention shifts as measured by eye-tracking can be sensitive (objective) measures of intuitive decision processes, because they sometimes precede conscious preferences measured by explicit choice behaviour (i.e., a subjective measure). Whether pupil dilation can be an equally valid dependent (objective) measure remains to be shown.

Discussion and critical remarks

We now address some general concerns related to the measurement of intuitive processes in decision making, and their relevance for the empirical studies we have described.

As pointed out in the introduction, intuitive decision making is most often equated with the involvement of automatic processes. Automaticity in this context implies the unintentional application of complex knowledge structures, and/or lack of conscious awareness of the details of these knowledge structures. We suggested that a starting point for exploring this would be to apply a fundamental criterion of consciousness, namely dissociation between objective and subjective measures that supposedly reflect the same underlying knowledge.

In this chapter we wanted to explore whether two well-established process-tracing tools, namely Mouselab and eye-tracking, could be used to study intuitive decision making. To illustrate their applicability we summarized some central findings from a series of studies by Glöckner and Betsch (2008a, 2008b) and Glöckner and Herbold (2008). A wide variety of objective behavioural measures were used in these studies, including fixation times, opening length, information search patterns and response times. Our focus was mainly on those objective measures that would indicate an unconscious preference for the to-be-chosen option before a conscious preference for this option had evolved.

Especially the study using eye-tracking (Glöckner & Herbold, 2008) illustrates how attention shifts sometimes indicate a preference toward one option before this option is explicitly chosen. However, how do we know that this reflects *intuitive* decision making rather than more deliberate processing? More precisely, how do we know that the intuitive preference developed independently of, faster than, or in the absence of, a more conscious preference that could be reflected on subjective measures? The answer is that we do not know as long as explicit choice, the only subjective measure included, was always measured after the various objective measures. In principle, a conscious preference for a certain option could have developed in parallel with, or before participants started to show a selective attentional preference for this option. Therefore, a better procedure would be to collect subjective measures of preferences (e.g., explicit choice) at regular intervals while the person is considering the different options. This would more closely parallel procedures used in implicit cognition research. For example, in the classic study by Bowers et al. (1990), subjective awareness measures always preceded objective forced-choice measures, and intuitive preferences indicated by forced-choice were only measured for the subset of trials for which the participant had reported no explicit solution.

For the sake of simplicity, we so far only discussed one criterion for unconscious cognition, namely dissociation between objective and subjective measurements. In the decision-making experiments we have discussed, a subjective measure of preference is the actual choice behaviour, i.e., indicating one's choice by saying or writing down which response alternative one prefers. However, no single forced-choice measure is process-pure in the sense that it reflects only conscious (or unconscious) knowledge or processes, but is likely to be influenced by a mixture of these (Destrebecqz & Cleeremans, 2001). One solution is to combine the measurement of choice behaviour with measurement of subjective confidence ratings. The use of confidence ratings in the area of implicit cognition derives from higher-order thought theories, according to which a mental state is conscious if the person is meta-cognitively aware of being in that state (see Dienes & Perner, 1999, for a more detailed discussion). Let us take an example of how confidence ratings are used in implicit cognition research. In the training phase of an implicit learning experiment, participants acquire knowledge about a complex rule (e.g., an artificial grammar structure) by passive exposure to a series of stimuli that follow this rule. In a test phase, participants are presented with a series of novel stimuli, and have to decide whether each of these follow the rule or not. It is common to ask people to indicate their subjective confidence in each of these decisions. Learning is regarded as implicit if confidence is unrelated to accuracy (i.e., the zero-correlation criterion, Dienes, Altmann, Kwan, & Goode, 1995), or if classification accuracy is above chance when the participant claims to be guessing (i.e., the guessing criterion, Dienes et al., 1995). Although confidence judgements are sometimes included in studies of intuitive decision making they are used for a different purpose than in the implicit learning literature.

The central aim of this chapter was to show how the presented methods can be used to decide whether a certain decision is predominantly influenced by controlled/conscious processes or automatic/unconscious processes. However, we are aware that this approach might represent an over-simplification. In line with Hammond et al. (1987) we think that the distinction between deliberate and intuitive forms of processing might not be clear-cut. An assumption that is receiving increased popularity is that implicit cognition often gives rise to consciously experienced, "intuitive" feelings that reflect these implicit processes, sometimes referred to as cognitive feelings (Price & Norman, 2009) or fringe consciousness (Norman, Price, Duff, & Mentzoni, 2007). The study of cognitive feelings in decision making is associated with yet another set of methodological challenges (see Price & Norman, 2008).

Authors' note

Thanks to Daniel Hanss for comments. The preparation of this chapter was supported by a Helse Vest grant (# 911274) to the first author, and a Faculty of Psychology, University of Bergen grant (# 1751/1352) to the second author.

Note

1 Thanks to Martjin Willemsen for pointing this out to us.

References

Bargh, J. A., & Chartrand, T. L. (1999). The unbearable automaticity of being. *American Psychologist, 54*, 462–479.

Bargh, J. A., Chen, M., & Burrows, L. (1996). Automaticity of social behavior: Direct effects of trait construct and stereotype activation on action. *Journal of Personality and Social Psychology, 71*, 230–244.

Bierman, D. J. (2004). Non conscious processes preceding intuitive decisions. In *Proceedings of Bial Foundation 5th symposium: Behind and beyond the brain* (pp. 100–115). Portugal: Bial Foundation.

Böckenholt, U., & Hynan, L. S. (1994). Caveats on a process-tracing measure and a remedy. *Journal of Behavioral Decision Making, 7*, 103–117.

Bowers, K. S., Regehr, G., Balthazard, C., & Parker, K. (1990). Intuition in the context of discovery. *Cognitive Psychology, 22*, 72–110.

Brandstätter, E., Gigerenzer, G., & Hertwig, R. (2006). The Priority Heuristic: Making choices without trade-offs. *Psychological Review, 113*, 409–432.

Bridgeman, B. (1992). Conscious vs. unconscious processes: The case of vision. *Theory & Psychology, 2*, 73–88.

Bröder, A. (2003). Decision making with the "adaptive toolbox": Influence of environmental structure, intelligence, and working memory load. *Journal of Experimental Psychology: Learning, Memory and Cognition, 29*, 611–625.

Busemeyer, J. R. & Townsend, J. T. (1993). Decision field-theory: A dynamic-cognitive approach to decision-making in an uncertain environment. *Psychological Review, 100*, 432–459.

Cheesman, J., & Merikle, P. M. (2003): Distinguishing conscious from unconscious perceptual processes. In B. J. Baars, W. P. Banks, & J. B. Newman (Eds.). *Essential sources in the scientific study of consciousness* (pp. 519–540). Cambridge, MA: MIT Press.

Costa-Gomes, M., Crawford, V. P., & Broseta, B. (2001). Cognition and behavior in normal-form games: An experimental study. *Econometrica, 69*, 1193–1235.

Craik, F. I. M., & Lockhart, R. S. (1972). Levels of processing: A framework for memory research. *Journal of Verbal Learning and Verbal Behavior, 11*, 671–684.

Destrebecqz, A., & Cleeremans, A. (2001). Can sequence learning be implicit? New evidence with the process dissociation procedure. *Psychonomic Bulletin & Review, 8*, 343–350.

Dhar, R., Nowlis, S., & Sherman, S. (1999). Comparison effects on preference construction. *Journal of Consumer Research, 26*, 293–306.

Dhar, R., Nowlis, S., & Sherman, S. (2000). Trying hard or hardly trying: An analysis of context effects in choice. *Journal of Consumer Psychology, 9*, 189–200.

Dienes, Z., Altmann, G. T. M., Kwan, L., & Goode, A. (1995). Unconscious knowledge of artificial grammars is applied strategically. *Journal of Experimental Psychology: Learning, Memory, and Cognition, 21*, 1322–1338.

Dienes, Z., & Berry, D. (1997). Implicit learning: Below the subjective threshold. *Psychonomic Bulletin & Review, 4*, 3–23.

Dienes, Z., & Perner, J. (1999). A theory of implicit and explicit knowledge. *Behavioral and Brain Sciences, 22*, 735–808.

Glöckner, A., & Betsch, T. (2008a). Do people make decisions under risk based on ignorance? An empirical test of the priority heuristic against cumulative prospect theory. *Organizational Behavior and Human Decision Processes, 107*, 75–95.

Glöckner, A., & Betsch, T. (2008b). Multiple-reason decision making based on automatic processing. *Journal of Experimental Psychology: Learning, Memory and Cognition, 34*, 1055–1075.

Glöckner, A. & Betsch, T. (2008c). Modelling option and strategy choices with connectionist networks: Towards an integrative model of automatic and deliberate decision making. *Judgement and Decision Making, 3*, 215–228.

Glöckner, A., & Herbold, A. K. (2008). Information processing in decision under risk: Evidence for compensatory strategies based on automatic processes. *MPI Collective Goods Preprints.*

Greenwald, A., McGhee, D., & Schwartz, J. (1998). Measuring individual differences in implicit cognition: The implicit association test. *Journal of Personality and Social Psychology, 74*, 1464–1480.

Hammond, K. R., Hamm, R. M., Grassia, J., & Pearson, T. (1987). Direct comparison of the efficacy of intuitive and analytical cognition in expert judgment. *IEEE Transactions on Systems, Man, & Cybernetics, 17*, 753–770.

Holm, L., Eriksson, J., & Andersson, L. (2008). Looking as if you know: Systematic object inspection precedes object recognition. *Journal of Vision, 8*, 1–7.

Huber, O. (1980). The influence of some task variables on cognitive operations in an information processing decision model. *Acta Psychologica, 45*, 187–196.

Ilg, R., Vogeley, K., Goschke, T., Bolte, A., Shah, J. N., Pöppel, E., & Fink, G. R. (2007). Neural processes underlying intuitive coherence judgments as revealed by fMRI on a semantic judgment task. *NeuroImage, 38*, 228–238.

Javal, E. (1878). Essai sur la physiologie de la lecture [Essay on the physiology of reading]. *Annales d'Oculustique, 79*, 97–117.

Johnson, E. J., Schulte-Mecklenbeck, M., & Willemsen, M. (2008). Process models deserve process data. *Psychological Review, 115*, 263–272.

Just, M., & Carpenter, P. (1980). A theory of reading: From eye fixations to comprehension. *Psychological Review, 87*, 329–354.

Koele, P. & Westenberg, M. R. (1995). A compensation index for multiattribute decision strategies. *Psychonomic Bulletin & Review, 2*, 398–402.

Levin, I. P., Huneke, M., & Jasper, J. (2000). Information processing at successive stages of decision making: Need for cognition and inclusion-exclusion effects. *Organizational Behavior and Human Decision Processes*, *82*, 171–193.

Lohse, G., & Johnson, E. J. (1996). A comparison of two process tracing methods for choice tasks. *Organizational Behavior and Human Decision Processes*, *68*, 28–43.

Lurie, N. H. (2004). Decision making in information-rich environments: The role of information structure. *Journal of Consumer Research*, *30*, 473–486.

Martinez-Conde, S., Macknik, S. L., & Hubel, D. H. (2004). The role of fixational eye movements in visual perception. *Nature Neuroscience*, *5*, 229–240.

Newell, A., & Simon, H. A. (1972). *Human problem solving*. Engelwood: Prentice Hall.

Norman, E., Price, M. C., Duff, S. C., & Mentzoni, R. A. (2007). Gradations of awareness in a modified sequence learning task. *Consciousness and Cognition*, *16*, 809–837.

Payne, J. W. (1976). Task complexity and contingent processing in decision making: An information search and protocol analysis. *Organizational Behavior and Human Decicion Processes*, *16*, 366–387.

Payne, J. W. (2005). *Mouselab experimenter*. https://www.fuquaworld.duke.edu/blab/MouseLabExperimenter.jsp

Payne, J. W., Bettman, J. R., & Johnson, E. J. (1988). Adaptive strategy selection in decision making. *Journal of Experimental Psychology: Learning, Memory, and Cognition*, *14*, 534–552.

Payne, J. W., Bettman, J. R., & Johnson, E. J. (1993). *The adaptive decision maker*. New York: Cambridge University Press.

Payne, J. W., & Braunstein, M. L. (1978). Risky choice: An examination of information acquisition behavior. *Memory & Cognition*, *6*, 554–561.

Pieters, R., Rosbergen, E., & Wedel, M. (1999). Visual attention to repeated print advertising: A test of scanpath theory. *Journal of Marketing Research*, *36*, 424–438.

Pieters, R., & Warlop, L. (1999). Visual attention during brand choice: The impact of time pressure and task motivation. *International Journal of Research in Marketing*, *16*, 1–16.

Price, M. C., & Norman, E. (2008). Intuitive decisions on the fringes of consciousness: Are they conscious and does it matter? *Judgment and Decision Making*, *3*, 28–41.

Price, M. C., & Norman, E. (2009). Cognitive feelings. In P. Wilken, T. Bayne, & A. Cleeremans (Eds.), *Oxford companion to consciousness* (pp. 141–144). Oxford: Oxford University Press.

Reber, A. S. (1989). Implicit learning and tacit knowledge. *Journal of Experimental Psychology: General*, *118*, 219–235.

Russo, J. E., & Dosher, B. A. (1983). Strategies for multiattribute binary choice. *Journal of Experimental Psychology: Learning, Memory and Cognition*, *9*, 676–696.

Russo, J. E., & Leclerc, F. (1994). An eye-fixation analysis of choice processes for consumer nondurables. *The Journal of Consumer Research*, *21*, 274–290.

Ryan, J., & Cohen, N. (2004). The nature of change detection and online representations of scenes. *Journal of Experimental Psychology: Human Perception and Performance*, *30*, 988–1015.

Schacter, D. (1987). Implicit memory: History and current status. *Journal of Experimental Psychology: Learning, Memory, and Cognition*, *13*, 501–518.

Schulte-Mecklenbeck, M., Kühberger, A., & Ranyard, R. (Eds.) (in preparation). *A handbook of process tracing methods for decision research.* New York: Taylor & Francis.

Schulte-Mecklenbeck, M., Murphy, R. O., & Hutzler, F. (in preparation). *Flashlight – an online eye-tracking replacement.*

Seth, A. K., Dienes, Z., Cleeremans, A., Overgaard, M., & Pessoa, L. (2008). Measuring consciousness: Relating behavioural and neuropsychological approaches. *Trends in Cognitive Sciences, 12*, 314–321.

Stanovich, K. E., & West, R. F. (2000). Individual differences in reasoning: Implications for the rationality debate? *Behavioral and Brain Sciences, 23*, 645–665.

Thagard, P. & Millgram, E. (1995). Inference to the best plan: A coherence theory of decision goal-driven learning. In A. Ram & D.B. Leake (Eds.), *Goal-driven learning* (pp. 439–454). Cambridge, MA: MIT Press.

Topolinski, S., Likowski, K. U., Weyers, P., & Strack, F. (in press). The face of fluency: Semantic coherence automatically elicits a specific pattern of facial muscle reactions. *Cognition and Emotion.*

Tversky, A. & Kahneman, D. (1992). Advances in prospect theory: Cumulative representation of uncertainty. *Journal of Risk and Uncertainty, 5*, 297–323

Tzelgov, J. (1997). Specifying the relations between automaticity and consciousness: A theoretical note. *Consciousness and Cognition, 6*, 441–451.

Van Raaij, W.F. (1977). Consumer information processing for different information structures and formats. In W.D. Perreault (Ed.), *Advances in consumer research.* Vol. 4. (pp. 176–184). Provo, UT: Association for Consumer Research.

Velichkovsky, B., Rother, A., Kopf, M., Donhofer, S., & Joos, M. (2002). Towards an express-diagnostic for level of processing and hazard prerception. *Transportation Research Part F: Traffic Psychology and Behavior, 5*, 145–156.

Walthew, C. (2008). *Eye movement research website.* http://www.eyemovementresearch.com

Willemsen, M. C., & Johnson, E. J. (2008). *The MouselabWeb Page.* http://www.mouselabweb.org

Yarbus, A. L. (1967). *Eye movements and vision.* New York: Plenum.

3 Cognitive process analysis

Cilia Witteman and Erwin van Geenen

Introduction

Professionals in domains such as health care are accountable for their decisions to their clients. That means that they may be expected to make their decisions after conscious deliberation, although with increasing experience they might increasingly use short-cuts in their decision processes, or intuition (e.g. Klein, 2003). In this chapter we describe two closely related and partly overlapping methods to measure consciously accessible components of decision making. Both methods directly ask decision makers what and how they think. The first method, think-aloud, is also used as part of the second method, Cognitive Structure Analysis (CSA; Leddo & Cohen, 1989). With the think-aloud method, participants are asked to verbalize all the thoughts they attend to. With CSA, you acquire knowledge about decision processes in two steps: First the knowledge structures or mental representations that are involved in performing a task in the domain of interest are uncovered through interviews, and then the contents of these structures are elicited with think-aloud problem solving. Hence, CSA might be used to uncover formerly hidden information structures that underlie intuition (Glöckner & Witteman, chapter 1, this volume).

We will illustrate think-aloud with a study of psychotherapists who were asked to propose a treatment plan for a depressed patient (Witteman & Kunst, 1997). To decide upon the most suitable treatment, therapists have to weigh information from heterogeneous sources into an overall proposal. We will illustrate CSA with a decision situation in underwriting (Van Geenen, 2004; Van Geenen & Witteman, 2006). Underwriters are people employed by a health insurance company to assess risks and fix premiums. They have to make two consecutive decisions. First, they decide whether an applicant meets the statutory eligibility criteria (also called "technical" underwriting); second, they assess whether the medical costs and risks that are associated with the applicant are acceptable (called "medical" underwriting).

Application of think-aloud and CSA is quite time- and labour-intensive, as will be illustrated below; first conceptually and then the application. Both methods however yield very rich data, and are eminently suitable to find out about the contents of professionals' knowledge models. To date, they have not been used to trace intuition. In the final section we discuss how they might be used for that purpose, by revealing mental representations that are the basis for intuitive processes and showing when professionals deliberate and when they use their intuition.

Conceptual introduction of the methods

Think-aloud

One way to find out about professionals' thoughts and to uncover their knowledge models (cf. Schreiber et al., 2000) is to just ask them, and to trace their reasoning processes (Juslin & Montgomery, 1999). A well-known process-tracing technique is think-aloud: People are presented with problems and are asked to verbalize everything they are thinking while solving them (Ericsson & Simon, 1993; Van Someren, Barnard & Sandberg, 1994). This knowledge elicitation technique is often used to capture expert knowledge, to be used in the construction of expert systems or training material for novices (Witteman & Krol, 2005). The researcher studies word-by-word transcriptions (called "protocols") of the think-aloud sessions, to identify what reasoning strategies their subjects use. That explains why think-aloud is often referred to as a member of a group of methods that together are called "protocol analysis" (Ericsson & Simon, 1993), and that further includes talk-aloud and retrospective verbal reports. For more details about this technique of gathering and analysing verbal protocols and its validity see for instance Breuker and Wielinga, 1989; Ericsson and Simon, 1980, 1984, 1993; Svenson, 1979.

Think-aloud is perhaps the most widely used method to gain insight into people's cognitive processes (Ericsson, 2006; Schreiber et al., 2000). Think-aloud as a method derives from information-processing theories of human cognition. Its basic assumption is that cognitive processes can be seen as a sequence of mental states, which are transformed by a series of information processes (Ericsson & Simon, 1993). Information that is heeded in concurrent sequences of mental states is assumed to be held in short-term memory, a limited-capacity storage, and may subsequently be stored in long-term memory, with large capacity. Information-processing theories distinguish between the information sequences in short-term memory, and the processes that activate the information, such as recognition and retrieval. The idea is that the information sequence is directly accessible and can thus be reported verbally, while the processes whereby this information is activated cannot be verbalized.

Think-aloud is thus especially useful to learn about concurrently heeded information sequences. The focus of interest is how information is combined, whether decision makers use specific cognitive operations such as falsification of hypotheses, and the order in which decision steps are taken. It is less concerned with the contents of the thought processes, and does not reveal the domain knowledge used for the decision, nor does it reveal sequences of thought that have become automatic. The researcher has to make sure that the problem that the participants are asked to solve, requires them to engage in all reasoning behaviours that they normally use. If the problem is not representative of normal decision tasks, the results of the think-aloud are not necessarily comprehensive. Then again, this is true for all experimental and process-tracing studies of decision making: The tasks need to be ecologically valid and to require the full range of decision behaviours for their solution. Think-aloud has been criticized as a method: For example it would not mirror the thought processes that would occur when people do not think aloud, but Ericsson and Simon (1993) have shown in a number of studies that thinking aloud does not change the thought process, except that it moderately slows it down.

CSA

If a researcher wants to investigate both the thought processes and the contents of these processes, another method is more suitable. A technique that captures both, in separate steps, is Cognitive Structure Analysis (CSA; Leddo & Cohen, 1989). This technique first identifies how decision makers mentally structure their knowledge, and then what knowledge they use in these stuctures; in other words: first the syntax and then the semantics of knowledge (Stillings, Weisler, Chase, Feinstein, Garfield, & Rissland, 1995). Five possible knowledge structures are distinguished: Memory Organization Packets (MOPs), production rules, semantic networks, frames and mental models.

MOPs (Schank, 1982) are an extension of scripts (Schank & Abelson, 1977) which represent procedural knowledge. They describe for one specific event, with the most often used example being a visit to a restaurant, a chain of temporally and causally ordered events reaching a goal. For example: enter the restaurant, be shown to a table, read and choose from the menu, etc., ending with pay the bill and leave the restaurant, having attained the goal of eating a meal. *Production rules* take the form of if-then or condition-action propositions. An example would be If you are interested in the study of intuition, Then you read this book. You draw a conclusion either by reasoning forward from data that fit the condition, or backward from an action to infer a condition. *Semantic networks* are graphical representations of concepts related by arrows that are labelled with the type of relation (Quillian, 1968). A typical example is a taxonomy of concepts, with a superclass and subclasses related by is-an-instance-of links. You may have medication as a superclass, with as the subclasses medications for different types of diseases, such as headache-pills, pills for high blood pressure, cholesterol-lowering medicine, etc. . Subclasses inherit information from the superclass, in this example being curative. *Frames* are collections of slots and slot fillers that describe typical concepts (Minsky, 1975). A typical concept could be a disease, with the slots severity, duration, chronicity, etc. . For a prototypical disease these slots will have default fillers. Diabetes mellitus for example will be of medium severity, long duration, and chronic. Slots of frames can again be frames, for example in the frame for the concept "applicant" with slots for age, gender, etc., and for the framed concept disease. Frames "chunk" knowledge about a concept; they are used to complete knowledge about a concept. *Mental models* are mini-theories about concepts or events (Johnson-Laird, 1983). They represent how changes in a concept or event cause changes in other concepts or produce events in the theory. A mental model can be used to predict what will happen or explain what has happened. Clinicians will for example have a mental model of a disease, with symptoms and mechanisms, allowing them to conclude which medication may be expected to be helpful.

These five structures represent knowledge differently, and have been supported by psychological studies (Markman, 1999; Sowa, 2000). Each structure is identified by three discriminators: its basic unit (declarative or procedural knowledge: a concept or an event), its organizing principle (why is it used; for example to reach a goal, to determine causal relations or to identify co-occurrence) and its inferential use (how is it used; for example by forward chaining from a concept to a conclusion, by deciding that a concept inherits a value from a more general concept, or by completing a concept with attributes). In Table 3.1 we give an overview of the five stuctures and their discriminators. For the general description of the structures see above; for more detailed descriptions of the discriminators' organizing principle and inferential use, see below.

The organizing principles refer to the different goals of the structure: Chunking aims to group and link concepts together in a frame; a taxonomy aims to capture hierarchical and categorical relations between concepts in a semantic network; data-conclusion mapping aims to map data onto a condition part (if) of a production rule until a conclusion (then) is reached; goals are reached by connecting events in a MOP; and establishing causality is the aim of reasoning and explanations in mental models. The inferential use refers to the mechanism of inference in a knowledge structure. In a frame, information is used to expand and complete knowledge about a concept; in a

Table 3.1 Discriminators of the five knowledge structures in CSA

Knowledge structure	Basic unit	Organizing principle	Inferential use
Frame	Concept	Chunking	Concept completion
Semantic network		Taxonomy	Inheritance
Production rule	Event	Data-conclusion mapping	Forward and backward chaining
MOP		Goal	
Mental model	Event and concept	Causality	Prediction, explanation, conclusion

semantic network, attributes of a concept are inherited from other concepts in the network; in a production rule, conclusions are inferred from information through forward chaining or information from conclusions through backward chaining; in a MOP, a goal can similarly be reached through forward or backward chaining; and in a mental model, causal knowledge is used to generate predictions, explanations and conclusions.

When the researchers have identified a knowledge structure, they also, by implication, know which type of reasoning process takes place: the inferential use of the structure. For example, when participants use a mental model, they will be engaged in causal reasoning. Interviews with open and closed questions are used to elicit the knowledge structures. Subsequently, the professionals are asked to think aloud while solving some small domain problems, to acquire the contents of these knowledge structures.

Applications

Think-aloud

In our think-aloud study, we aimed to gain insight into decision processes of psychotherapists when they are asked to propose an intervention method for a depressed patient (Witteman & Kunst, 1997). Our question was whether psychotherapists make their treatment decisions according to the steps of a formal, optimal model for making treatment decisions, derived from general decision theory. This optimal model stipulates that, on the basis of information about the client and her or his complaint, different hypothetical treatment options should be proposed. Each of these should be weighed by making an inventory of its pros and cons. Eventually, the option that has the best foundation in justifying arguments should be chosen (cf. "The Diagnostic Cycle": De Bruyn, Ruijssenaars, Pameijer, & Van Aarle, 2003; and cf. the (Bayesian) weighted additive strategy: Glöckner, chapter 5, this volume). We expected that therapists would not follow this model, since making a therapy decision deliberately and in the optimal model's thorough manner (that is: generate pros and cons and calculate weighted sums) is just not feasible given therapists' (as people's in general) limitations of cognitive capacity as well as time pressure, due to the increasing focus on efficiency in mental health care. People have been found to overcome their cognitive limitations by "satisficing": by considering only one option at a time and deciding for the first option, provided they can satisfactorily substantiate it. Alternatives are only considered if the first option is unsatisfactory (Simon, 1955). This means that we expected that therapists would consider just one treatment option, which they would substantiate to their satisfaction through a focus on confirming information. In this think-aloud study we thus compared therapists' actual performance to the optimal model.

The therapists participated in the experiment individually. They all followed the same procedure (cf. Van Someren et al., 1994). After a brief training in thinking aloud, they were presented with the task. They were first asked to study, but not learn by heart, the case of Mr Johnson, who had been diagnosed as suffering from a major depression. Consultation with very experienced therapists had revealed that for this Mr Johnson there was no one treatment that could be said to be the best, but that different treatments were suitable, depending on the focus on different aspects of his complaints. Indeed, our participants came up with different treatment plans. That, however, was not the focus of our study; we were interested in the decision process, not the outcome. To disclose the process, participants were asked to read the following instruction aloud, from paper: "Imagine that Mr Johnson comes to you for treatment. Now please think aloud about how you would plan his therapy and why that would be your plan. You may, but need not, give all possible details, such as number of sessions a week. Please be more specific than, for example, proposing 'psychoanalysis'. Thus, we ask you to decide which intervention method or methods you would use to start therapy and to think aloud about everything you consider while you come to your treatment decision." The participants were asked to think aloud all the time until they reached their decision, taking as long as they needed. The participants' verbalizations were tape-recorded and then typed out verbatim, resulting in a hard copy protocol for each participant. Then each protocol was segmented into independent thoughts (sentences or groups of closely associated sentences). Each thought was subsequently coded into one of the categories presented in Table 3.2.

Coding the participants' thoughts into these categories enabled us to test our expectation that the psychotherapists' treatment decision processes would show that they do not adhere to the optimal model. That is: we did not expect them to propose different treatment options and weigh the pros and cons of each. We expected them to make their decisions by quickly

Table 3.2 Coding categories for protocol analysis with examples

Code	Category	Example
0	Orientation	"... behaviour therapy, since that is my approach ..."
1	Diagnosis	"... I see a depressed person ...", "... OK clearly a depression ..."
2	Interpretation	"... I see an inhibited person ...", "... he reminds me of ..."
3	Treatment option	"... I would propose a cognitive treatment ..."
4	Considerations:	
	1 Supporting	"... he has sufficient insight" (for a cognitive treatment)
	2 Disconfirming	"... he seems addicted" (with a client-centred treatment)
	3 Alternative	"... (client-centred) or possibly an assertiveness training"
5	Treatment plan	"... in a cognitive treatment I would try to give him self-insight, with indirect interventions, by giving homework assignments"

associating a treatment option with the case, and deciding after a subsequent confirmatory information search and hardly any consideration of altern- atives. We included a code for "Interpretation" (code 2) to capture this association, be it a thought about the most striking feature or general impression of the case or the resemblance to earlier, similar cases.

Our expectations were borne out. The participants generally did not gener- ate more than one treatment option, nor did they weigh their option by considering its pros and cons. Indeed, they all focussed on one treatment option only, for which they found support in the case description. Generally, the more global remarks (e.g. giving an interpretation or a therapy option) were found before the more specific remarks (i.e. considerations or specifica- tions of the treatment plan), indicating that the participants first assessed the situation (cf. Klein, 1998; Pliske & Klein, 2003) and that their decision followed after this assessment. More than half of the participants mentioned their orientation (code 0). The clearest example was "behaviour therapy – but then of course that is my orientation and I cannot do something I don't know anything about". All but one participant talked about the diagnosis in one way or another (code 1). Most participants agreed with the diagnosis, explicitly or implicitly, e.g. "the first thing to do is to clarify the source of his depression to him". All participants offered an interpretation (code 2) of the patient and/or his complaints before mentioning a therapy option (code 3). Usually only one option was mentioned. Most of the participants' subsequent considerations were found in sentences that confirmed the suit- ability of the therapy option (code 4.1). An instance taken from the report of a participant who decided upon assertiveness training is "aspects of his assertiveness have been tried". Only very few considerations were disconfirm- ing (code 4.2) and only with a quarter of the participants. In all instances disconfirmation took the form of mentioning risks associated with the chosen treatment plan. For example, a participant who opted for "a behaviour analy- sis followed by cognitive restructuring and assertiveness training", mentioned the risk that "he wants to have a helping hand, but I don't think we should let it get to the point that the therapist is the saving angel, I think we need to make clear, from the very beginning, that he has to do it himself". None of the participants who mentioned risks rejected their earlier option. All but one participant mentioned an alternative (code 4.3), but, as with disconfirming considerations, this alternative was never a serious option; it was rejected in the same sentence, as in for instance: "by concentrating on sexuality too soon it could become threatening and provoke fears I'd rather avoid". All partici- pants specified their treatment plan (code 5), both in the course of their decision process and in concluding sentences. An example is: "so to sum up, I think a cognitive therapy, with medication to provide a basis for treatment, a counselling therapy concentrating on main points, indirect interventions and homework assignments aimed at self insight".

The think-aloud study revealed that the optimal model was not the model actually used by the participants. Our practising psychotherapists did not propose different hypothetical treatment options, nor did they consciously weigh the option they proposed by making an inventory of its pros and cons. The option that was chosen was generally the only option they seriously considered, with alternatives always rejected in the same thought in which it was mentioned. The chosen option was generated after an interpretation of the client's complaints, and justified with confirmatory considerations. This has been one of the few studies that look at what happens, cognitively, between the input of client information and the output of the treatment decision (see also Caspar, 1997; Witteman, Harries, Bekker & Van Aarle, 2007).

CSA

In the study for which we used Cognitive Structure Analysis (CSA; Leddo & Cohen, 1989), we aimed to find out how underwriters cognitively structured, or mentally represented, the knowledge they used in their work, as well as what the content of these structures was (Van Geenen, 2004; Van Geenen & Witteman, 2006). We had no hypotheses about which structures they would use. We only knew that underwriters were unable to use a decision support system that used Bayesian statistics (for details of such systems see e.g. Pearl, 1988). This system asked underwriters to estimate for each factor that was identified as relevant to a decision, numerical probabilities of its absence or presence with an applicant. The system then combined these estimates into an assignment of the applicant into a risk group: low, medium or high. The underwriters had major difficulties giving their knowledge as numerical probabilities (cf. Witteman, Renooij, & Koele, 2007), and thought the system that required numerical probabilities was very uncomfortable to use and difficult to understand. This decision support system was consequently shelved.

The underwriters were interviewed individually. A structured interview was held with each participant, involving the following steps: 1) asking open questions about the underwriting process; 2) applying the discriminators (see Table 3.1) to form a hypothesis about which knowledge structure is used; 3) asking closed questions to test the hypothesis of step 2 and fill in the content of the knowledge structure; 4) summarizing the structure and contents and ask for verification; 5) repeating steps 2–4 until all knowledge structures and participants' uses are identified; 6) introducing small-scale problem solving to get an illustration of the use of the knowledge structures, asking participants to think aloud while solving them.

An example will elucidate the procedure. The first discriminator, the basic unit (concept or event) was assessed first. In answer to an open question: "Can you describe how you generally proceed in your underwriting, and what information you use?" (step 1), an underwriter would for example start talking about applicants and their disease. Both "applicant" and "disease" would be identified as concepts. With concepts, the hypothesized knowledge structures (step 2) would be frames or semantic networks (see Table 3.1).

To test whether a frame was used for applicant (step 3), the interviewer would try to assess the organizing principle: chunking, that is: grouping and linking elements to a concept. The appropriate closed question would be: "Can you ascribe attributes to the applicant?" The inferential use of frames: concept completion, that is: inferring additional attributes, was tested using the closed question: "If you consider an applicant, can you think of other attributes?" If a frame was indeed used for an applicant, then a participant might respectively answer "the applicant is 55 years old, his height is 1.80 metres and his weight is 120 kg", and "given his height and weight, the applicant's body mass index will be quite high".

To test whether a semantic network was used for disease, the interviewer would ask a closed question about the organizing principle taxonomy: "Could you place this disease in a taxonomy of other diseases?" With an affirmative answer, the probe for its inferential use, inheritance of information, would be: "Can you infer attributes of the disease from other diseases in the taxonomy?" If indeed the disease was mentally structured as a semantic network, the underwriter would for example for Crohn disease answer: "An important group of internal diseases concerns enteritis. The group can be subdivided into chronic and non-chronic enteritis. Crohn disease and colitis ulcerosa are two types of chronic enteritis". This shows that indeed the organizing principle was a taxonomy. An answer to the question about inferring attributes would then be: "A symptom of enteritis is recurrent abdominal cramp. Therefore, cramp is also found for Crohn disease". The inferential use was indeed inheritance of information.

Note that the questions about frames would also be used with the concept disease and the questions about semantic networks with applicant; the above only illustrates positive identifications of a knowledge structure. The closed questions to identify organizing principle and inferential use for each knowledge structure were prepared in advance. For example, for a production rule the question for its organizing principle would always be: "Can you describe <the event> in terms of if-then statements?", and the questions about inferential use: "Do you use data to infer conclusions? Do you use conclusions to deduce data?" The interviewer would only need to fill in the name of the identified concept or event.

The content of the knowledge structure was elicited by asking, for frames and semantic networks respectively: "Can you give some examples of the attributes of this applicant?", and "What other diseases are involved in the taxonomy, and how are they related to each other?". The answers were then summarized (step 4), and the participant was asked to endorse or adapt the structure and its contents. For example, "Is it true that with the concept 'applicant', you want to know their age, gender, height, weight, partner, child(ren), current insurance?" (a frame with its attributes), and a participant might endorse this, but add the attribute "current disease". Subsequently (step 5), from the answers to the open questions (step 1) other hypothesized knowledge structures (step 2) were treated similarly (testing and filling in (step 3) and summarizing for endorsement (step 4)).

Then small-scale problems were introduced, asking participants to think aloud while coming to a decision about real applications, to get a more comprehensive overview of the contents of the structures (step 6). Their verbalizations were tape-recorded, typed out, segmented and coded by two independent judges (cf. think-aloud above) into the discriminators of the five knowledge structures. If for example a participant said "the man got contaminated with HIV", this would be coded as the basic unit "event"; a subsequent "the man is HIV positive, that means he is rejected for private insurance", this would be coded as an "inferential use" of data-conclusion mapping.

All participants were found to use frames to represent many concepts, for example applicant and requested insurance. One of the attributes of applicant was medication, which itself was represented as a frame, with attributes such as name, strength, dose, and costs. Insurance products and diseases were represented as semantic network taxonomies by most applicants. Cervical cancer would be a "child" of cancer, and inherit all its attributes. Most participants applied production rules, for example: "if the medical costs exceed the underwriting norm, then reject the application". Memory Organization Packages (MOPs) were used by many participants to represent a fixed order of events, for example: first calculating the underwriting norm, then calculating the costs, and finally relating the costs to the norm. Most participants also used mental models, although quite simple ones, to represent for example everything they knew about a specific disease. As an example, a simple mental model that was used for diabetes mellitus contained: "Seriousness is dependent on treatment. The use of a diet constitutes a mild seriousness. The use of insulin constitutes a severe seriousness. Prognosis is dependent on the seriousness. A mild seriousness constitutes a good prognosis. A severe seriousness constitutes a poor prognosis".

In sum, all participants used the full range of knowledge structures in their description of the execution of the medical underwriting task, with different structures for different parts of the task. In our research, these results were used to propose the design of the user-interface of a knowledge-based system to support underwriting decisions (Van Geenen, 2004; Van Geenen & Witteman, 2009). Users of such a system do not have to distort their way of deciding to fit the requirements of the system, that is: they are not forced to come up with numerical probabilities, but they are presented with, for example, a visualized frame in which they can fill in the attribute values of an applicant, and with taxonomies of diseases.

Discussion of the methods

Think-aloud

We have successfully employed the think-aloud method in different studies (e.g. De Kwaadsteniet, Krol & Witteman, 2009; Denig, Witteman, & Schouten, 2002). It has also been used extensively in other domains, such as reading and comprehension (e.g. Magliano & Mills, 2003), medical decision making (e.g. Backlund, Skånér, Montgomery, Bring, & Strender, 2004), and human–computer interaction (e.g. Jaspers, Steen, Bos, & Geenen, 2004).

A think-aloud study requires thorough preparation by the researchers (Van Someren et al., 1994). They need to first get globally acquainted with the domain, then they need to select an appropriate task that is representative of the participants' normal work, and then they have to develop a coding scheme for the protocols. It also requires a typist, and at least two independent coders to score the protocols. Compared to an experimental manipulation of a variable of interest and tabulation of the resulting output, the work involved is much more time-consuming, but, contrary to such an experiment, it does give detailed information about the cognitive processes (but see also Norman & Schulte-Mecklenbeck, chapter 2, this volume; Bröder, chapter 4, this volume; Glöckner, chapter 5, this volume). In the context of this book it is important to note that think-aloud is most informative with advanced participants. Novices will not know enough, and experts will know too much: they will have automated (parts of) their thought processes, which will, consequently, sometimes not be available to short-term memory and thus also unavailable for verbal reports (Ericsson & Simon, 1993).

CSA

From reading the design of our CSA study, it will be clear that applying the method requires at least as much preparation from the researcher as the think-aloud method. For CSA the researchers must be highly trained and must have the discriminators at their fingertips to be able to apply them to what participants say during the interview. If that is too demanding, two sessions may be used instead of one single session: the first to get the participants' answers to the open questions and analyse the answers for possible knowledge structures (steps 1 and 2) and the second session to test and fill in the knowledge structures (steps 3 to 6). The researchers should be aware that there is a potential risk of eliciting the type of structures they have in mind rather than those actually representing the expert's knowledge.

While there are many published studies that have used the think-aloud method, there are considerably fewer that include Cognitive Structure Analysis. A technique that similarly captures the content of knowledge and reasoning in separate steps is Cognitive Task Analysis (CTA; Crandall, Klein, & Hoffman, 2006; Hoffman & Militello, 2008). This is a much better known technique, for which there are almost two million hits with Google Scholar. CTA is used to study cognition of professionals at work in real-world contexts. It models the contents of professionals' knowledge as well as their reasoning: What they know and how they think. Different methods are available for both. One interesting method to elicit and represent what professionals know is to ask them to draw concept maps (see www.ihmc.us for a free software download). To elicit their reasoning, CTA uses the think-aloud method. Specifically, CTA-developers advocate thinking-aloud problem solving. Using this method, mental strategies can be distinguished, for example breadth-first or depth-first search, and the sequence of reasoning steps can be charted. We used the less well-known CSA though, because CSA has an interesting unique point: It looks for the way knowledge is actually mentally represented, and allows the identification of different knowledge structures.

For researchers who study actual thinking by professionals, it is intrinsically interesting to know how people represent their knowledge and how they decide. Such knowledge is also very relevant for designers of knowledge systems, since it allows them to design really usable systems. The interface of a decision support system could mimic the users' representations, allowing for user centred interaction rather than a programmer centred interface. The probabilistic decision support system that had been built for the underwriters obviously was not user centred, and was subsequently never used.

Think-aloud and CSA to measure intuition and deliberation

The think-aloud method and CSA measure cognitive structures and processes that are accessible to conscious awareness. As noted above, automatic cognitive processes by definition operate without conscious awareness (see Glöckner & Witteman, chapter 1, this volume) and do not pass short-term memory and thus can not be verbalized. However, we may speculate about how thinking-aloud could provide information concerning the use of intuition. First, some extra coding categories could be added in the analysis of protocols, identifying the "inferential use" of the verbalized knowledge. One obvious category is the moment at which a decision is first mentioned. One of the major characteristics of intuition is that it is fast. Thus, if participants immediately mention their decision and only then continue to give reasons pro (and con), they may be assumed to have reached their (initial) decision intuitively, and their reasons could be called post-hoc justifications. In relation to the intuition models described in the theoretical chapter (Glöckner & Witteman, chapter 1, this volume), decision makers could use these more deliberate steps to reach the evidence threshold for deciding (cf. evidence accumulation models; Busemeyer & Johnson, 2004) or these justifications could be arrived at in deliberative construction processes to support maximizing consistency (cf. parallel constraint satisfaction models, Glöckner & Betsch, 2008a). If participants mention their decision only after their reasoning, they are more likely to have reached it by deliberate strategies in the narrower sense, namely by deliberately comparing information in a rule based manner. Another characteristic of intuition is that it is associative. Therefore an extra coding category could be associations. The more associations participants mention, for example: "this client reminds me of Mr X", the more they may be assumed to decide intuitively. Also, reasons that participants give for their decision could be counted. The more reasons, the more deliberation is used in the process. Note that this does not preclude the operation of automatic-intuitive processes at the same time (see Glöckner & Betsch, 2008a). And intuitive, forward reasoning could be distinguished from deliberative, backward reasoning. Intuitive responses are also characterized by high confidence. Thus an extra question, post-hoc, about participants' certainty about their decisions might be helpful, with the higher the confidence the more intuitive (but see Glöckner & Betsch, 2008b; see also Glöckner, chapter 9, this volume). Finally, it could be interesting to combine think-aloud with physiological measures (see Hochman, Glöckner, & Yechiam, chapter 8, this volume; cf. also Bechara, 2004; Damasio, 1994; Lieberman, 2000) to identify specific more affect-laden or cognitively effortful steps in the course of decision making.

According to lay-persons' interpretations of intuition (but see Glöckner & Witteman, chapter 1, this volume), one might think that years of experience would be a predictor of intuitive decision making. More experienced decision makers may be expected to be more intuitive, since considerations they have first made explicitly, may become implicit and may be skipped (cf. in the clinical domain Boshuizen, Bromme, & Gruber, 2004; Witteman & Van den Bercken, 2007). That would mean that their think-aloud protocols would be shorter. However, in line with more comprehensive models of the interplay between intuition and deliberation (i.e., interventionist models, parallel constraint satisfaction models, Glöckner & Betsch, 2008a), in the study we discussed above, we found no correlation between number of years of work experience and length of the protocols. Also, very experienced decision makers may sometimes reach their decisions more intuitively (for instance if there is a sufficient match to an exemplar or sufficiently clear evidence for one option; for more extensive model descriptions see Glöckner & Witteman, chapter 1, this volume) and thus faster than less experienced colleagues, but they also have more domain knowledge and thus continue their decision processes longer. Thus the difference is not in the length of the decision process, but in the manner in which it is reached.

References

Backlund, L., Skånér, Y., Montgomery, H., Bring, J., & Strender, L.-E. (2004). GPs' decisions on drug treatment for patients with high cholesterol values: A think-aloud study. *BMC Medical Informatics and Decision Making, 4,* 23

Bechara, A. (2004). The role of emotion in decision-making: Evidence from neurological patients with orbitofrontal damage. *Brain and Cognition, 55,* 20–40.

Boshuizen, H. P. A., Bromme, R., & Gruber, H. (Eds.). *Professional learning: Gaps and transitions on the way from novice to expert.* Dordrecht: Kluwer.

Breuker, J. A., & Wielinga, B. J. (1989). Model-driven knowledge acquisition. In: P. Guida and G. Tasso (Eds.), *Topics in the design of expert systems* (pp. 265–296). Amsterdam: North-Holland.

Busemeyer, J. R., & Johnson, J. G. (2004). Computational models of decision making. In D. J. Koehler & N. Harvey (Eds.), *Blackwell handbook of judgment and decision making* (pp. 133–154). Malden, MA: Blackwell Publishing.

Caspar, F. (1997). What goes on in a psychotherapist's mind? *Psychotherapy Research, 7*, 105–125.

Crandall, B., Klein, G., & Hoffman, R. R. (2006). *Working Minds: A practitioner's guide to cognitive task analysis.* Cambridge, MA: MIT Press.

Damasio, A. R. (1994). *Descartes' error: Emotion, reason, and the human brain.* London: Macmillan.

De Bruyn, E. E. J., Ruijssenaars, A. J. J. M., Pameijer, N. K., & Van Aarle, E. J. M. (2003). *De diagnostische cyclus: Een praktijkleer* [The diagnostic cycle: Learning in practice]. Leuven: Acco.

De Kwaadsteniet, L., Krol, N. P. C. M., & Witteman, C. L. M. (2009). Causality in psychodiagnosticians' mental representations of client information: A think aloud study. *Manuscript submitted for publication.*

Denig, P., Witteman, C. L. M. & Schouten, H. W. (2002). Scope and nature of prescribing decisions made by general practitioners. *Quality and Safety in Health Care, 11*, 137–143.

Ericsson, K. A. (2006). Protocol analysis and expert thought: Concurrent verbalizations of thinking during experts' performance on representative tasks. In K. A. Ericsson, N. Charness, P. J. Feltovich, & R. R. Hoffman (Eds.), *The Cambridge handbook of expertise and expert performance* (pp. 223–241). Cambridge: Cambridge University Press.

Ericsson, K.A., & Simon, H. A. (1980). Verbal reports as data. *Psychological Review, 87*, 215–251.

Ericsson, K.A., & Simon, H. A. (1984). *Protocol analysis: Verbal reports as data.* Boston: MIT Press.

Ericsson, K.A., & Simon, H. A. (1993). *Protocol analysis: Verbal reports as data* (2nd ed.). Boston: MIT Press.

Glöckner, A., & Betsch, T. (2008a). Modelling option and strategy choices with connectionist networks: Towards an integrative model of automatic and deliberate decision making. *Judgment and Decision Making, 3*, 215–228.

Glöckner, A., & Betsch, T. (2008b). Multiple-reason decision making based on automatic processing. *Journal of Experimental Psychology: Learning, Memory, and Cognition, 34*, 1055–1075.

Hoffman, R. R. & Militello, L. (2008). *Perspectives on Cognitive Task Analysis: Historical origins and modern communities of practice.* Hove, UK: Psychology Press.

Jaspers, M., Steen, T., Bos, C., & Geenen, M. (2004). The think aloud method: a guide to user interface design. *International Journal of Medical Informatics, 73*, 781–795.

Johnson-Laird, P. N. (1983). *Mental models.* Cambridge, MA: Harvard University Press.

Juslin, P., & Montgomery, H. (1999). *Judgment and decision-making: Neo-Brunswikian and process tracing approaches.* Mahwah, NJ: Lawrence Erlbaum Associates.

Klein, G. A. (1998). *Sources of Power: How people make decisions.* Cambridge, MA: MIT Press.

Klein, G. (2003). *Intuition at work: Why developing your gut instincts will make you better at what you do.* New York: Doubleday.

Leddo, J., & Cohen, M. S. (1989). Cognitive structure analysis: A technique for eliciting content and structure of expert knowledge. *Proceedings of the 1989 Conference on AI Systems in Government.* McLean, VA.

Lieberman, M. D. (2000). Intuition: A social cognitive neuroscience approach. *Psychological Bulletin, 126,* 109–137.

Magliano, J. P., & Mills, K. K. (2003). Assessing reading skill with a think-aloud procedure and latent semantic analysis. *Cognition and Instruction, 21,* 251–283.

Markman, A. B. (1999). *Knowledge representation.* London, UK: Lawrence Erlbaum.

Minsky, M. (1975). A framework for representing knowledge. In P. H. Winston (Ed.), *The psychology of computer vision* (pp. 211–280). New York: McGraw-Hill.

Pearl, J. (1988). *Probabilistic reasoning in intelligent systems.* San Mateo: Morgan-Kaufmann.

Pliske, R., Klein, G. A. (2003). The naturalistic decision-making perspective. In S. L. Schneider & J. Shanteau (Eds.), *Emerging perspectives on judgment and decision research* (pp. 559–585). Cambridge: Cambridge University Press.

Quillian, M. (1968). Semantic memory. In M. Minsky (Ed.), *Semantic information processing* (pp. 227–270). Cambridge, MA: MIT Press.

Schank, R. C. (1982). *Dynamic Memory.* Cambridge, UK: Cambridge University Press.

Schank. R. C., & Abelson, R. P. (1977). *Scripts, plans, goals and understanding.* Hillsdale, NJ: Lawrence Erlbaum.

Schreiber, G., Akkermans, H., Anjewierden, A., De Hoog, R., Shadbolt, N., Van de Velde, W., & Wielinga, B. (2000). *Knowledge engineering and management: The CommonKADS methodology.* Cambridge, MA: MIT Press.

Simon, H. A. (1955) A behavioral model of rational choice, *Quarterly Journal of Economics, 69,* 99–118.

Sowa, J. F. (2000). *Knowledge representation: Logical, philosophical, and computational foundations.* Pacific Grove, CA: Brooks/Cole Publishing Co.

Stillings, N. A., Weisler, S. E., Chase, C. H., Feinstein, M. H., Garfield, J. L., & Rissland, E. L. (1995). *Cognitive science: An introduction.* New York: Wiley.

Svenson, O. (1979). Process descriptions of decision making. *Organizational Behavior and Human Performance, 23,* 86–112.

Van Geenen, E. W. (2004). *Knowledge structures and the usability of knowledge systems: A study in health insurance underwriting.* Doctoral dissertation, Nijenrode University, The Netherlands.

Van Geenen, E. W., & Witteman, C. L. M. (2006). How experts reason: The acquisition of experts' knowledge structures. *The Knowledge Engineering Review, 21,* 335–344.

Van Geenen, E. W., & Witteman, C. L. M. (2009). Using knowledge structures to make useful systems usable. *Manuscript in preparation.*

Van Someren, M. W., Barnard, Y. F., & Sandberg, W. A. C. (1994). *The think aloud method.* London: Academic Press.

Witteman, C. L. M., Harries, C., Bekker, H. L., & Van Aarle, E. J. M (2007). Evaluating psychodiagnostic decisions. *Journal of Evaluation in Clinical Practice, 13,* 10–15.

Witteman, C. L. M., & Krol, N. P. C. M. (2005). Knowledge-based systems: Acquiring, modeling and representing human expertise for information systems. In H. van Oostendorp, L. Breure & A. Dillon (Eds.), *Creation, use and deployment of digital information* (pp.177–197). Mahwah, NJ: Lawrence Erlbaum Associates.

Witteman, C. L. M., & Kunst, H. (1997). Planning the treatment of a depressed patient. *Clinical Psychology and Psychotherapy*, *4*, 157–171.

Witteman, C. L. M., & Van den Bercken, J. H. L. (2007). Intermediate effects in psychodiagnostic classification. *European Journal of Psychological Assessment*, *23*, 56–61.

Witteman, C.L.M., Renooij, S., & Koele, P (2007). Medicine in words and numbers: A cross-sectional survey comparing probability assessment scales. *BMC Medical Informatics and Decision Making*, *7*, 1–8.

4 Outcome-based strategy classification

Arndt Bröder

Introduction

Many decision strategies or heuristics can be conceptualized as consisting of search rules, stopping rules, and decision rules (e.g. Gigerenzer, 2004; Payne, Bettman & Johnson, 1993). Search and stopping rules determine which information is looked for in what order, and when to stop information search. For example, if one plans to buy a DVD player, he or she will probably limit information search to certain brands and compare the available options with respect to several attributes that are considered to be important (e.g. price, longevity, disc formats supported etc.). If theories or models make different predictions about the parameters of information search like search order or depth of search, information search tracing methods (see Norman & Schulte-Mecklenbeck, chapter 2, this volume) can be used to differentiate between models. The *decision rule* on the other hand describes the manner of information integration after the search has stopped. You may, for instance, deliberate and weigh pros and cons of the DVD players, or you may decide according to the most important aspect, or you may just follow an overall intuition or feeling about the most preferred option. Note that a clear distinction between information search and later information integration is only assumed by some models. Many models that also account for intuition (see Glöckner & Witteman, chapter 1, this volume) assume an instant integration (e.g., accumulation) of information.

For researchers interested in investigating the decision rules people follow, process tracing techniques (see Norman & Schulte-Mecklenbeck, chapter 2, this volume) show at least three problems: First, looking at information does not imply that it is used in the later decision process. Hence, people may collect lots of information, but in the end, they might only use a small subset of it for deciding. Second, sometimes the information gathering process may not be observable, or the researcher does not want to interfere with it. For example, if decision making is memory-based, information search in memory cannot be observed, and often, researchers want to avoid using think-aloud techniques (see Witteman & van Geenen, chapter 3, this volume) not to disturb the process itself (Bröder & Schiffer, 2003b, 2006b). Third, participants may have only limited insight into their own cognitive processes and hence may not be able to report the decision rules they used (e.g. Nisbett & Wilson, 1977). The latter could be especially the case with intuitive decisions this book is dealing with. Nevertheless, researchers may be interested in the tacit information integration rules the decision makers follow (see also Glöckner, chapter 5, this volume). For example, do intuitions integrate lots of information unconsciously (e.g., Hammond, Hamm, Grassia, & Pearson, 1987; Glöckner & Betsch, 2008), or do they follow a single argument as Gigerenzer (2007) suggests?

To deal with these questions, it is therefore inevitable to analyze the structure of decision *outcomes*.[1] The trick is to design the decision situations in experiments in a way that each strategy of interest predicts a different pattern of choices across the decision items. The observed choices of real participants are compared to these predictions, and the best-fitting strategy is chosen as the one probably used by the participant. So far, so simple!

However, although the principle itself is quite easy, it is a nontrivial problem to find a good fit index that informs us about the best-fitting strategy. The first intuition of course is to count the number of correct predictions and choose the model that correctly predicted more of the participant's choices. Unfortunately, this method is restricted to situations in which each strategy under consideration makes a clear prediction in every single decision situation. Sometimes, however, strategies predict guessing for several items. How do we deal with those items? For an illustration, assume that a Model A makes definitive predictions for a whole item set. Model B, on the other hand, predicts guessing for 20% of the items, whereas it makes definitive predictions for the other 80% of items (some of the predictions are different from Model As). How do we count the 20% guessing cases? Imagine that after counting all responses, they show a 90% match with Model A. However, if we count only the 80% of items with clear predictions from both models, we might find 80% in line with Model A and 95% in line with Model B. What about the 20% guessing cases – should we ignore them? They probably contain information. Which model is better in this case?

This chapter introduces a generalized version of a maximum-likelihood strategy classification method described by Bröder and Schiffer (2003a) in the decision domain. For this method, simple response error models are formulated (assuming that participants sometimes make errors when using decision strategies), and the likelihood of the data is assessed for each of the considered strategies (via estimating the error probabilities). The model for which the data are most likely is selected as the strategy that presumably produced the data. In addition to the simple classification, the method provides the likelihood ratios as measures of confidence in the correctness of the classification.

First, I will give a conceptual introduction involving an illustrative example. Afterwards, general formulas will be derived for three different cases of applications involving binary choice and three-alternative choice. Each will be illustrated by a calculation example. Then, the spreadsheet tool coming with this chapter that allows for easily applying the strategy classification method (suitable for OpenOffice Calc, Macintosh iWork Numbers, or Microsoft Excel) will be explained briefly. Last, benefits and disadvantages of the method will be discussed.

Conceptual introduction of the method

Researchers often want to know more about the information integration processes during decision making, and when process tracing data are not available or the focus lies on the decision rule rather than the search rule, outcome-based inferences must be done.

An experiment will be designed in a way that different strategies predict different patterns of choices when they are applied without error. However, absolutely error-free responding will be quite rare, and it may turn out that none of the empirical choice patterns you observe perfectly fits one of the strategies you consider. What can be assessed in this case are the *conditional probabilities* of the observed data, given each of the strategies and response error. These probabilities are also called the *likelihoods* of the data.

The goal of the method proposed here is to identify an individual's decision strategy by finding the strategy for which the data are most likely. To do this, you need a) a plausible set of strategies, b) items that allow discrimination between different strategies, and c) a formal (yet simple) definition of response errors.

Set of considered strategies

Ideally, the researcher comes equipped with an a priori set of plausible strategies that can be applied in a specific type of problem, and the art of experimentation includes choosing different decision situations in which the predictions of the strategies differ. Consider, for example, a decision task used by my colleague Ben Newell and me in an unpublished study: In a first learning phase, participants predicted the colour of a plant's flower (yellow or blue) from several binary attributes like leaf size (large or small), bud shape (round or narrow), stem texture (smooth or segmented), and roots (radial or deep). They did so several hundred times and received feedback in every trial. This allowed them (in principle) to find out the validities of the four cues used to predict flower colour. In this environment, leaf size was the best (i.e., most valid) predictor, followed by roots, stem, and bud shape.[2] In a later task, we were interested how participants might integrate cue information for their predictions. We presented two plants in each trial (differing with respect to their cue patterns), and participants had to choose the plant with the higher likelihood of having a blue (rather than yellow) flower.

Following prior research and consultation of the literature, we thought of four plausible strategies to consider: "Take The Best", "Single Cue", "Equal

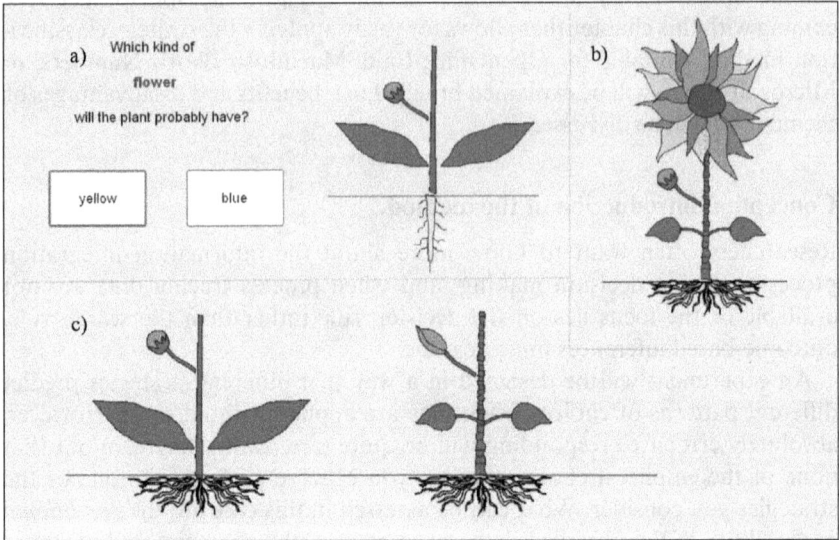

Figure 4.1 Example of the flower prediction task. In the learning phase (a), participants predicted the flower colour. They received feedback like in (b) (here
for a different cue combination). In the final decision phase, participants
had to choose the plant with a higher likelihood of having a blue flower
(original presentation coloured).

Weighting" and the "Weighted Additive Rule". The former two are simple
noncompensatory strategies, whereas the latter ones are compensatory. The
term "compensatory" means that bad cue values on important cues can be
compensated by good values on less important attributes. Take The Best
(TTB) is noncompensatory: It looks up the best cue. If this cue discriminates
between objects (e.g. large leaves vs. small leaves), TTB chooses the object
with the positive cue value (here: large leaves). If the leaves do not differ
between the plants, the next most valid cue is compared (roots), and so on.
Hence, TTB searches the cues in order of validity until one discriminating cue
is found, and the decision is based on this single cue. The single cue heuristic
(SC) is even thriftier because it only looks for the most valid cue and decides
according to this information. If this cue does not discriminate (the plants
both have large leaves), the strategy does not bother about including further
information but simply guesses! The equal weighting rule (EQW) is compensatory and counts the "pros" and "cons" for each option, disregarding their
variations in importance. If, however, both options have the same number of
positive attributes, EQW also guesses. The weighted additive strategy
(WADD) is conceptually the most complex rule because it entails weighting
the cues and adding them up in a weighted fashion. Hence, WADD uses all
information in the most sophisticated manner. There is evidence that this
weighted adding can be accomplished in an intuitive way (e.g., Glöckner,

2008), and claims about WADD's large cognitive costs in terms of effort have probably been overstated (Bröder & Newell, 2008).

Of course, any inferences about presumable heuristics used by participants are restricted to those considered in the strategy set, although many more potential strategies may be thought of. This may appear like a major drawback of the maximum likelihood method presented here. However, this is just a prima facie argument because *any* inference on unknown strategies must be restricted to the cases the researcher considers. The a priori definition of strategy sets does not prevent hypothesis generation about new strategies by carefully examining the data and potential bad fits of the strategies considered, but any experiment can only be designed to examine a limited set of potential cognitive processes. Hence, choosing the most representative and theoretically interesting strategies is a major task in planning research.

Discriminating items

With four strategies under consideration and binary choices, we can construct $2^4 = 16$ different patterns which yield a hypothetical maximum of 120 different item types if each pattern is combined with each other ($16^2/2 - 16/2$). However, note that depending on the set of strategies, the number of differentiating items for which the strategies make different predictions is usually drastically lower because strategy predictions overlap considerably. For some of the items, some distinctions between strategies are even logically impossible. For example, SC can never predict choosing another option than TTB if we exclude guessing cases: If the first cue discriminates, both predict choice of the option this cue predicts (and if it doesn't SC predicts a guess). Hence, there cannot be any items in which TTB firmly predicts the choice of option "A" while SC predicts "B". The only way to distinguish between these strategies then is to include the guessing cases, and we already mentioned the problems of simple fit indices such as the number of matches between data and predictions in this case. Also, with four binary cues like in the example (and cue weights in which the weighted sum of less valid cues exceeds the weight of one better cue) it is impossible to construct stimuli in which EQW and WADD make different predictions (since there must always be *more* positive cue values than less valid cues to compensate for negative values on a valid cue), and one is again confined to those items with ties in the number of positive cue values in order to disentangle both strategies – here, EQW predicts guessing.[3] Table 4.1 shows examples of six item types used in our flower prediction task that were used to differentiate between the four strategies.

The goal of experimentation should be to achieve a reliable classification. Therefore, the more differentiating items, the better. However, as we have seen, there are sometimes formal limits to the numbers of items that can be generated. Furthermore, researchers sometimes desire to use "representative" stimuli, and overrepresenting differentiating items may interfere with the

Table 4.1 Six examples of items to discriminate between the strategies SC, TTB, EQW, and WADD. "+" denotes a positive cue value, "–" denotes a negative cue value. Cues are ordered according to decreasing validity from top to bottom, predictions of the strategies are given in the second to last row ("0" is the prediction of a guess)

	Item type 1		Item type 2		Item type 3		Item type 4		Item type 5		Item type 6	
Option	A	B	A	B	A	B	A	B	A	B	A	B
Cue 1	+	–	+	+	+	–	+	+	+	–	–	–
Cue 2	–	–	+	–	–	+	+	–	+	+	+	–
Cue 3	–	+	–	–	+	+	–	–	–	+	–	+
Cue 4	+	–	+	+	–	–	–	+	–	+	–	+
Prediction	SC=A		SC=0		SC=A		SC=0		SC=A		SC=0	
	TTB=A		TTB=A		TTB=A		TTB=A		TTB=A		TTB=A	
	EQW=A		EQW=A		EQW=0		EQW=0		EQW=B		EQW=B	
	WADD=A		WADD=A		WADD=A		WADD=A		WADD=B		WADD=B	
	N=14		N=10		N=7		N=3		N=12		N=4	
Hypothetical data (No. of "A" choices)	13		9		3		1		3		2	

Note: For the WADD predictions it is assumed that the weighted sum of two less valid cues always exceeds the weight of the more valid cue.

research question. Third, if subjective cue orderings are used (e.g. Glöckner & Hodges, 2008) or if additional strategies are considered after running the experiment, you must often live with what you have. But evidently, strategies that do not make different choice predictions for at least a few items cannot be distinguished empirically using choice-based strategy classification alone (but see Glöckner, this volume).

Error model

Having chosen strategies and stimuli to differentiate them, the third ingredient for a likelihood-based classification is the error model incorporated in the strategies. If you assume that strategies are administered deterministically without any error, no probability estimation would be necessary. In fact, *any* choice of a person violating a strategy's prediction would rule out that the person used it. However, this error-free responding is quite implausible, and the variation in participants' response patterns would imply hundreds of different (and opaque) strategies. Under the assumption of randomly distributed errors in responding, formulas about the data likelihood (i.e., observation of a certain choice distribution) for each model can be derived. In principle, various error distributions are conceivable, but for the method used here, the simplest possible assumption about error-prone responding is used: We assume that participants use a consistent strategy throughout the experiment, but make an error with probability ε in each trial and hence erroneously choose the option not predicted by their strategy. With this simple error theory, the mathematics of the method boils down to simple binomial or trinomial probability distributions in the two- and three-alternative cases, respectively.[4] The probability ε is an unknown parameter which has to be estimated separately for each participant (see below). In addition to the strategy classification, this ε estimate provides additional information about the consistency with which the strategy is applied by the participant.

Running an experiment and collecting data

Once you have chosen your set of strategies and have generated items that potentially help to distinguish between the strategies, you can conduct your study and collect the respective data. You present the items to your participants and record their choices. Note, that the formal way of representing the cue patterns like in Table 4.1 does not necessarily match the actual presentation in an experiment. The positive and negative cue values are only formal placeholders for actual cue values. For instance, the flower prediction task involved presenting all cue values in a pictorial format, and all cues were visible simultaneously as depicted in Figure 4.1c. However, cue values can also be presented in a Mouselab-like matrix on the screen where participants have to uncover them actively (e.g., Bröder, 2003, Newell & Shanks, 2003, see also Norman & Schulte-Mecklenbeck, chapter 2, this volume). Still another variant are memory-based decisions in which participants had learned the cue patterns before and have to retrieve them from memory to make their decisions (e.g. Bröder & Schiffer, 2003b, 2006b; Glöckner & Hodges, 2008).

Although the display format might influence strategy selection, the only thing that matters for choice-based strategy classification is the formal structure of cue patterns that allow to discriminate strategies. Also, it is of course possible to add filler trials to your experiment that do not enter in your strategy classification later.[5]

Data and analysis

The result of your experiment will be a frequency distribution of choices for each of the item types employed. Hence, you assess how often each single participant chooses option A or B (or C in the three-alternative case). These frequencies form the basis of the likelihood estimation and the strategy classification. Of course, other data such as decision times can also be recorded, and they may provide valuable additional information about the decision process (e.g., Bröder & Gaissmaier, 2007), but the maximum likelihood classification is purely outcome-based and only uses the frequency distributions as a basis of inference. Classification techniques that use additional information are described by Glöckner (this volume).

In the next section, formulas are derived and explained how to estimate likelihood values for each considered strategy on the basis of observed frequency distributions of choices.

Application and formal basis of the method

I will present three cases of application that differ with respect to the number of alternatives and the error models behind the method.

First, some terminology will be introduced. Second, I will deal with the simplest case of binary choice, and I will explain how to apply it to the flower task in Table 4.1. Third, I will discuss two different variants of three-alternative choice problems that differ with respect to the setup of experimental items and the error models assumed.

Terminology

Let us denote the overall number of decision items in the experiment with N. If one has defined J different item types to differentiate strategies (e.g., $J = 6$ for the six item types in Table 4.1), each item type is indexed with j. In analogy, there are K strategies (1, 2, . . . k . . . K) considered ($K = 4$ in the example). There are different numbers of items of each type j in the experiment which are consequently denoted as n_j. It is also useful to define for each strategy k the number of items in which this strategy predicts a guess. We denote this number as n_{0k}. With these symbols, we have defined all quantities that are solely determined by the setup and design of our experiment without a reference to participants' behaviour.

Of course, we also need variables that are derived from our empirical observations. The number n_{jk} is the number of choices compatible with strategy k in all item types j where k makes a clear prediction (i.e., excluding the guessing cases of strategy k).

In addition to the variables defined by the design and by observation, there is also the unknown parameter ε_k which denotes the probability of making an error with strategy k to choose the non-predicted option, respectively. These probabilities are estimated from the data to maximize the likelihood of the data under the assumption of each strategy k.

These values are all we need to compute the likelihoods of the data, and an overview of the terminology can be found in Table 4.2.

Case 1: Binary choice

The probability of a given frequency of matches between strategy k and the observed choices for each item type j is given by the well-known *binomial distribution*. Remember that the binomial formula defines the probability $p(n_s|p, N)$ for the number n_s of observed successes in a series of N independent observations when the probability of a success in each trial is p. The binomial equation reads:

Table 4.2 Overview of terminology

Variables defined by experimental design

$1 \ldots j \ldots J$	Index of item types (J item types are in the experiment)
$1 \ldots k \ldots K$	Index of strategies (K strategies are compared)
N	Overall number of items in the experiment
n_j	Number of items of type j in the experiment
n_{0k}	Number of items in which strategy k predicts a "guess"

Observed variables

n_{jk}	Number of strategy-consistent choices for those item types with a clear prediction of strategy k
$n_{j\phi}$	Number of choices of dominated options in item type j (only in case 2)

Estimated parameters

ε_k	Error probability for choosing nonpredicted option of strategy k
ϕ	Error probability of choosing dominated option (only in case 2)

$$p(n_s | p, N) = \binom{N}{n_s} \times p^{n_s} \times (1-p)^{(N-n_s)} = \left(\frac{N!}{N! \times (N-n_s)!} \right)$$

$$\times p^{n_s} \times (1-p)^{(N-n_s)} \qquad (1)$$

For example, if you throw a fair die $N = 10$ times, the probability of getting exactly five times a "six" would be:

$$p(n_s = 5 | p = \frac{1}{6}, N = 10) = \left(\frac{10!}{10! \times 4!} \right) \times \left(\frac{1}{6} \right)^5 \times \left(\frac{5}{6} \right)^5 = 0.010853.$$

Hence, for our experiment, the probability of the data (i.e., n_{jk} matches between choices and strategy k in item type j) is given by equation (2) in which the terms of equation 1 have been replaced with our terminology.

$$p(n_{jk} | \varepsilon_k, n_j) = \binom{n_j}{n_{jk}} \times (1-\varepsilon)^{n_{jk}} \times \varepsilon^{(n_j - n_{jk})} = \left(\frac{n_j!}{n_{jk}! \times (n_j - n_{jk})!} \right)$$

$$\times (1-\varepsilon)^{n_{jk}} \times \varepsilon^{(n_j - n_{jk})} \qquad (2)$$

However, for all item types in which strategy predicts a guess one counts the number of choices of option "A", resulting in n_A, and the probability boils down to equation (3).[6]

$$p(n_A | \varepsilon = 0.5, n_{0k}) = \binom{n_{0k}}{n_A} \times 0.5^{n_A} \times 0.5^{(n_{0k} - n_A)} = \left(\frac{n_{0k}!}{n_A! \times (n_{0k} - n_A)!} \right) \times 0.5^{n_{0k}}$$

$$(3)$$

However, equations 2 and 3 only define the probabilities of the choices separately for each item type *j*, whereas our goal is to compute the overall probability of the observed choices. The joint probability of independent events is given by the product of all single event probabilities, and therefore the overall probability is given in equation (4) which is simply the product of the probabilities computed for each item types according to equations (2) and (3):

$$p(\vec{n}_{jk} | \varepsilon_k, \vec{n}_j) = \prod_{j=1}^{J} p(n_{jk} | \varepsilon_k, n_j) \tag{4}$$

In equation (4), $\varepsilon_k = 0.5$ in all item types in which strategy *k* predicts a guess. The formula simply states that the probability of a certain *vector* of frequencies (indicated by the arrow above the *n*'s) is simply given by the product of the probabilities of the constituent frequencies.

Up to this point, we have defined the theoretical probability of the choices, given a certain strategy which we denoted as the likelihood of the data, given this strategy. For the equations to be useful, however, an important ingredient is of course still missing: The unknown parameter ε, this is the error probability. For each strategy *k*, we want to choose ε_k in such a way that the likelihood of the data given that strategy is maximized. The maximum likelihood estimator of the success probability in a binomial distribution is simply the proportion of successes in a sequence of trials, and hence, the estimate of $(1 - \varepsilon_k)$ and ε_k is given in equation (5).

$$(1 = \hat{\varepsilon}_k) = \frac{\displaystyle\sum_{j=1}^{J} n_{jk}}{\displaystyle\sum_{j=1}^{J} n_j} \quad and \ \hat{\varepsilon}_k = \frac{\displaystyle\sum_{j=1}^{J} (n_j - n_{jk})}{\displaystyle\sum_{j=1}^{J} n_j} \tag{5}$$

Hence, you just count the number of strategy-compatible choices in items in which *k* makes a clear prediction and divide it by the total number of items in which this strategy makes a clear prediction. This maximum likelihood estimator of $(1 - \varepsilon_k)$ is plugged into equations (2) to (4) to compute the maximum likelihood of strategy *k*.[7]

A recipe and calculation example

Hence, in the binary case, the processing steps for obtaining likelihood values for all strategies are like this:

1) *Determine strategy-compatible choices per type and total number of errors*
   For each item type *j* count the number of choices that are in line with the prediction of the strategy *k*. This gives variable n_{jk}. Additionally,

determine the total number of strategy-errors by adding up all deviating choices. Do this for the items with clear predictions (i.e., no guessing) only.

2) *Determine error probability ε_k for each strategy*
Determine the error probability ε_k by dividing the total number of strategy-errors by the total number of tasks with clear predictions.

3) *Determine distribution in guessing tasks*
Count the number of "A" choices in item types in which strategy k predicts a guess.

4) *Single probability calculation for each task type*
Plug the error rate and the number of compatible choices into equations (2) and (3) to obtain the probabilities of data given the strategy k for each item type.

5) *Overall probability*
Multiply all single probabilities to obtain the joint probability.

For an illustration consider again the four strategies TTB, SC, EQW, and WADD in the flower prediction task. Imagine that a hypothetical participant had produced the choice frequencies in the last row of Table 4.1, i.e., he chose "A" 13, 9, 3, 1, 3, and 2 times in the item types 1 to 6, respectively. Since the "A" choices and "B" choices must add up to the total number of items of each type, the corresponding numbers of "B" choices are 1, 1, 4, 2, 9, and 2. For which strategy are these results most likely?

We will illustrate the computation only for one strategy, namely EQW. For step 1, we first compute the number of items in which EQW makes a clear prediction which excludes item types 3 and 4 in Table 4.1 and according to the second last row results in: $14 + 10 + 12 + 4 = 40$. From these items, $13 + 9 + 9 + 2 = 33$ match EQW's prediction, hence $(1 - \varepsilon) = (33/40) = 0.825$ and $\varepsilon = 0.175$. We plug the values into equation (3) for each of the six item types and multiply these equations (equation 4) which yields:

$$p(\vec{n}_{jk}|\varepsilon_k, N) = \binom{14}{13} \times 0.825^{13} \times 0.175^1 \times \binom{10}{9} \times 0.825^9 \times 0.175^1 \times \binom{7}{3}$$

$$\times 0.5^7 \times \binom{3}{1} \times 0.5^3 \times \binom{12}{9} \times 0.875^9 \times 0.175^3 \times \binom{4}{2} \times 0.825^2 \times 0.175^2$$

This can be simplified by rearranging the product terms and by adding the exponents of power function terms with the same base, yielding

$$p(\vec{n}_{jk}|\varepsilon_k, N) = \binom{14}{13} \times \binom{10}{9} \times \binom{7}{3} \times \binom{3}{1} \times \binom{12}{9} \times \binom{4}{2} \times 0.825^{33} \times 0.175^7$$

$$\times 0.5^{10} = 14 \times 10 \times 35 \times 3 \times 220 \times 6 \times 0.00174977$$

$$\times 0.00000503 \times 0.00097656 = 0.0001667$$

This likelihood of the data may seem small, but note that it denotes the probability of *exactly* the distribution you have observed which is only one of a huge class of possible distributions. Still, you will find that data are much more likely under the assumption of EQW than for any other of the strategies considered (TTB = 7.4 * 10^{-8}, WADD = 6.98 * 10^{-6}, SC = 2.5 * 10^{-8}). It is useful to divide these likelihoods to yield an *odds ratio* which tells you how much more likely the data are for EQW than for the other strategies. This provides a measure of how confident you can be in your classification. According to these results, the data are 2,253 times more likely for EQW than TTB, 24 times more likely than for WADD, and 6,668 times more likely than for SC. Odds ratios hovering around 1 tell you that your classification is not much more reliable than chance.[8]

But caution: The likelihood itself is not informative, but it must *always* be regarded together with the estimated error probability ε_k! This is because the binomial function is symmetric with respect to the event probability, and for example, $\varepsilon_k = 0.15$ will yield the same likelihood value as $\varepsilon_k = 0.85$. Obviously, however, the latter value would not make much sense because in this case, 85% of the choices would *not* be predicted by strategy k. Hence, merely computing the likelihood may favour a particular strategy as well as its exact opposite. Therefore, any likelihood accompanied by $\varepsilon_k > 0.50$ can never be interpreted in favour of strategy k. The rule is: First look at the ε_k, then look at the likelihoods!

If you want to use the maximum likelihood method, computing the example by hand once will be useful for a full comprehension. However, the computations are implemented also in the calculation spreadsheet that comes with this chapter and can be used to cross-check your own calculations.

Table 4.3 Probabilities of choosing certain options in (a) the two-alternative choice, (b) three-alternative choice with one dominated option, and (c) three-alternative choice without dominated option

	Observable response			
	Strategy-compatible choice	Strategy-incompatible choice	Choice of dominated option	Predicted guess
Two-alternative choice	$(1-\varepsilon)$	ε	–	0.5
Three-alternative choice with dominated option	$(1-\varepsilon-\phi)$	ε	ϕ	0.333
Three-alternative choice without dominated option	$(1-\varepsilon)$	$\varepsilon*0.5$	–	0.333

Case 2: Three-alternative choices with one (quasi-)dominated option

If you enter the realm of three-alternative choices, the basic logic of the maximum likelihood procedure remains the same, but the probability distribution for three exclusive and exhaustive events is now given by the *trinomial distribution* in equation (6):

$$p(n_1, n_2, n_3 | p_1, p_2, N) = \left(\frac{N!}{n_1! n_2! n_3!} \right) \times p_1^{n_1} \times p_2^{n_2} \times (1 - p_1 - p_2)^{n_3} \tag{6}$$

Here, the n_j are the three event frequencies (that add up to N), and p_1 and p_2 are the probabilities of events 1 and 2, respectively. The probability of event 3 is $1 - p_1 - p_2$ since the three events are exclusive and exhaustive. Hence, the formula is a simple extension of the binomial case.

However, the mapping of correct and wrong predictions of a strategy on the event probabilities in equation (6) is not as easy as in the binary choice task. If strategy k does not predict a guess in a trial, then there is of course one correct option a participant using this strategy can choose. However, when making a strategy application error, *two* different other options can be chosen, and the strategy itself does not predict which kind of error occurs. In principle, three-alternative choice problems for differentiating various strategies can be generated by just adding another option to each of the item types in Table 4.1. However, depending on the nature of this option, it would be worthwhile to consider very different error models. We will first deal with the situation in which a clearly inferior option is added which we will call the dominated or the quasi-dominated option. The more general case with a viable third option will be described in the next section.

As stated before, a dominated option is at least as weak as all other options on all attributes and weaker on at least one. No sensible decision rule would ever choose a dominated option. Another form of a basically inferior option is one which may be better than others on an unimportant cue, but all others are better on several more important cues. Although not strictly dominated, this option would be "quasi-dominated" relative to a set of sensible decision strategies. If we include such inferior options denoted as "C" in the set of alternatives, the choice of this alternative can be termed an error for each strategy. We can therefore denote the probability of choosing this option with a second error probability ϕ_k and this can simply be estimated by the relative frequency of "C" choices in all item types in which k does not predict a guess.

For each item type j, the likelihood of the data, given strategy k is then given by equation (7):

$$p(n_{jk}, n_\phi | \varepsilon_k, \phi_k, n_j) = \left(\frac{n_j!}{n_{jk}! n_\phi! (n_j - n_{jk} - n_\phi)!} \right) \times (1 - \varepsilon_k - \phi_k)^{n_{jk}}$$
$$\times \varepsilon_k^{(n_j - n_\phi - n_{jk})} \times \phi_k^{n_\phi} \tag{7}$$

Here, n_ϕ is the number of choices of the inferior option in all item types, in which strategy k does not predict a guess, ϕ_k is the probability of choosing the inferior option, and all other symbols have the same meaning as in equation (3). Note, that in all item types in which strategy k predicts a guess, $\varepsilon_k = \phi_k = 1/3$ is inserted into equation (7), yielding:

$$p(n_A, n_B | n_j) = \left(\frac{n_j!}{n_A! n_B! n_C!} \right) \times \left(\frac{1}{3} \right)^{n_j} \tag{8}$$

Here, n_A, n_B, and n_C are the numbers of choices of option A, B, or C, respectively. For the overall likelihood, again, the likelihoods of the data for each item type are multiplied.

Hence, to apply the method in this case, one first counts the number of strategy-compatible choices n_{jk} as well as the number of choices of the dominated option n_ϕ for those item types in which strategy k does not predict a guess. The relative frequencies are estimates for $(1 - \varepsilon_k - \phi_k)$ and ϕ_k, respectively. The frequencies and estimated probabilities are plugged into equation (7) for each item type. For "guess" item types of strategy k, equation (8) is used, and all likelihoods are multiplied.

Case 3: Three-alternative choice problems without dominated option

If there is no clearly inferior option in the decision situation, any choice not matching strategy k's prediction is counted as an application error relative to this strategy. For simplicity, it is assumed that each of the other two options is chosen with equal probability $\varepsilon/2$. Then, the corresponding equation for the likelihood of the data, given item type j is:

$$p(n_{jk} | \varepsilon_k, n_j) = \left(\frac{n_j!}{n_{jk}! n_{Ak}! n_{Bk}!} \right) \times (1 - \varepsilon_k)^{n_{jk}} \times \left(\frac{\varepsilon_k}{2} \right)^{(n_j - n_{jk})} \tag{9}$$

In equation (9), n_{Ak} and n_{Bk} are the numbers of choices that do not conform to strategy k and are denoted with "A" and "B" respectively. In all item types where strategy k predicts a guess, (2/3) is inserted for ε_k which incorporates the assumption of guessing all three options with equal probability 1/3. Again, the overall likelihood of the data is computed by multiplying the likelihoods for each item type.

Discussion

Researchers investigating intuitive processes in decision making are particularly dependent on analyzing decision outcomes: First, intuitive strategies are often not accessible to consciousness and hence, verbal reports do not help much to identify the decision rule. Second, process tracing methods sometimes are unwarranted because the explicit search process induced by this method may interfere with the intuitive strategies investigated. Intuition research therefore needs inference methods that allow for valid conclusions about decision rules based on outcome data alone. Off-the-shelf analysis tools like multiple linear regression may capture important aspects of the decision process, but they have been criticized for being too unspecific for identifying specific decision rules (Bröder, 2000; Hoffman, 1960).

There are three advantages of the maximum-likelihood classification method advanced in this chapter: First, the method forces the researchers to make clear and explicit statements about the set of strategies they consider as well as the error model they assume in the response process. This may appear as a disadvantage at first glance since it looks like a severe constraint on the applicability. However, scientific inferences are *always* restricted to those strategies that are considered, and analysis techniques will always imply some error model which remains implicit. Making things explicit beforehand therefore enhances transparency. Second, the method can be applied in cases where some of the strategies predict guesses in a number of cases. These cases are hard to deal with if you use ad-hoc fit statistics like the percentage of correctly predicted choices. If one restricts oneself to those cases with clear predictions of all strategies, one (a) throws away distribution information contained in these guessing cases and hence (b) loses the ability to distinguish between strategies that can only be distinguished by these guessing cases (e.g., TTB and SC or EQW and WADD). Third, the method also provides an estimate of strategy consistency (ε) as well as confidence measures for the classification: The ratio of likelihoods provides information about how much more likely the data are if you assume strategy x rather than strategy y.

Validity of the method

Bröder and Schiffer (2003a; see also Bröder, 2003) reported high convergent validity between parameters of information search in a Mouselab setting and the outcome-based strategy classification. For example, a TTB strategy was accompanied by a less deep information search, less time spent on each item, and a more attribute-wise search than compensatory strategies like EQW and WADD. This conforms to the assumptions commonly made in process tracing research about compensatory and noncompensatory strategies. In a similar vein, Bröder and Gaissmaier (2007) found response time patterns with memory-based decisions which fitted the maximum-likelihood strategy classifications.

Also, Bröder and Schiffer (2003a) report a simulation in which data were generated by error-prone strategies, and classification accuracy was very high unless the error rates were excessively high (e.g. $\varepsilon > 30\%$). However, it must be noted that this assessment only holds for the specific item set used which matched the situation of several of their experiments. Generally, the classification will be more accurate and reliable, the more differentiating items are employed to distinguish between strategies.

Approximations of the method

Under what circumstances can simpler fit indices be used which do not require the calculation of likelihoods?

A simple situation would entail only items in which every strategy under scrutiny never predicts a "guess". In this case, simple counting of strategy-compatible choices and classifying according to the highest number of matches is always equivalent to the maximum likelihood method. However, one may wish to compute the likelihoods anyway in order to assess the confidence in the classification.

Whenever there are strategies with predicted guesses in the set, simple counting does not help. In this case, one may install a scoring rule to assess the model fit which includes the guessing cases. A *linear* scoring rule might count "0" for each match between strategy and choice and administer a penalty of "1" to each mismatch. A penalty of "0.5" is added for each item in which the strategy makes a guess. Sometimes, a *quadratic* scoring rule is suggested which might entail a penalty of "0.25" for predicted guesses and "1" for wrong predictions (e.g. Persson & Rieskamp, 2009) – that is, wrong predictions are penalized stronger than a lack of prediction. Both scoring rules include the guessing items, and one may ask how accurate these rules are as approximations.

In a computer simulation for binary choices, we generated 10,000 simulated participants for each of the strategies WADD, EQW, and TTB. The error rate ε was varied in steps of 5% from 5% to 50%, and 1,000 data vectors were generated with each error rate. Note that all strategies converge on simple guessing with the excessive error rate of 50%. Representing the experimental situation used by Bröder and Schiffer (2003b, 2006b) in a binary choice task, there were three item types to differentiate TTB, WADD, and EQW: For 25 of 52 items, TTB, WADD, and EQW all predicted the same choice. For 15 items, the prediction of TTB differed from that of WADD and EQW. In the remaining 17 items, WADD and TTB predicted the same choice, whereas EQW predicted a guess. All data patterns were classified according to the maximum likelihood (ML) method and both the linear and quadratic scoring rules.

As a result, classification accuracy was quite high up to error rates of 30%, and the linear scoring rule was somewhat better than the ML method when data were generated by WADD or TTB. However, when data were generated by EQW, about half of the patterns were misclassified as WADD. The quadratic scoring rule, on the other hand, was clearly biased in favour of EQW when data were generated by WADD and TTB. Classification rates for EQW even exceeded the correct classifications with high error rates. The ML method, however, showed neither a bias for nor against EQW. EQW is the only model in this case which predicts guesses, and the ML method appears to deal with them correctly. The quadratic scoring rule, in contrast, appears to favour models that are less precise (i.e., predict more guesses). This can be understood because the penalty for a predicted guess is less than the expected value for a wrong prediction if someone actually guessed. Hence, the quadratic rule is biased towards less precise models and should be avoided. The linear rule, on the other hand, has difficulties in distinguishing between models that only differ in items that predict guesses. If one does not aim at distinguishing them (e.g., one is only interested if someone uses a compensatory strategy in the given example, be it WADD or EQW), the linear rule approximates the ML method very well and has even higher accuracy rates when error probabilities are low. However, the only method with no apparent bias for or against models that predict guesses is the ML procedure. In the setting analyzed above, its accuracy was higher than 80% for every strategy with error probabilities up to 25%. Note that accuracy can be enhanced by using more discriminating items, and therefore unbiasedness is the most important feature.

Conclusion

For several reasons, researchers sometimes have to rely on decision outcomes to make inferences about decision rules. This is particularly the case in the investigation of unconscious and intuitive processes which might be altered by using active information search as a research tool. In the case of outcome-based analyses, model fits must be assessed. However, ad hoc fit indices are hard to arrive at in situations where some strategies predict guessing. Sometimes, this cannot be avoided since strategies can only be differentiated by items in which one strategy predicts guessing (e.g., SC and TTB). In these cases, the formulation of a simple error model and assumptions about guessing probabilities allows assessing likelihoods of choices for each of the models which in turn allows for inferences about strategies.

In all situations without predicted guesses it may still be worthwhile to compute the likelihoods since the likelihood ratios provide measures of classification reliability. It is recommended that outcome-based inferences about decision rules should *always* be conducted and cross-validated with search measures when these are available.

Outcome-based measures can also be combined with other data (e.g., decision times, see Glöckner & Hodges, 2008; Glöckner, this volume) to achieve a more fine-grained classification.

Materials and references

Materials

This chapter comes with three spreadsheet files of identical content which can be used with the programs OpenOffice Calc, Apple iWorks'08 Numbers, and

Microsoft Excel, respectively. With some practice in using spreadsheets, the reader will probably be able to implement the formulas of the three cases considered above by herself or himself, but the readymade spreadsheets cover some common applications which correspond to the three cases from the text (binary choice, three-alternative choice with an inferior option, three-alternative choice without inferior option). Individual choice frequencies can be entered in the data fields of the spreadsheets, and the program will provide estimates of error probabilities, likelihoods, and the likelihood ratio statistic. Situations with two to four strategies under scrutiny are included.[9]

Figure 4.2 shows a detail of the spreadsheet for binary items. To use the file, a specific coding convention for the options must be followed: Define one "reference strategy" first. This must be a strategy that always makes a prediction (i.e., it never predicts a guess). For example, this could be TTB because this heuristic never predicts a guess as long as cue patterns differ. In each item, the option predicted by the reference strategy (Strategy 1 in the spreadsheet) is coded "A", the other option is coded "B". In column 1 of the matrix, you find all possible item types when two or three strategies are compared (the four strategies variant is not shown here, although it is contained in the spreadsheet). Note that Strategy 1 always predicts "A", whereas Strategies 2 and 3 can predict "A", "B", or "0" (=guess), respectively. The lightly shaded second column can be used to insert the numbers of items of each item type used in your experiment. If one combination was not present in your experiment, insert "0" (like, for example, in rows 12, 13, 16, and 17). Hence, column 2 contains information about the experiment which will in most cases be identical for all participants.[10] In column 3, data are inserted for a single participant. This is just the number of "A" choices of this participant for each item type. These are essentially the only fields that should be modified in the spreadsheet, the others are cells reporting results and intermediate results.

For example, Column 5 reports the binomial coefficient (see equation 3) for each item type, i.e. the number of possibilities to arrive at the number of "A"

	Binary choice situations. Coding: Option "A" is always predicted by Strategy 1	No. of items in Experiment	No. of "A" choices for itemtype	Binomial coeffi-cient		estima-ted error proba-bility	Maximized LIKELIHOOD
1							
2							
3	**Item type**						
4	**2 strategies compared**						
5	Strategy 1=A, Strategy 2=A	20	16	4845	**Strategy 1**	0,483333	0,000012445590785
6	Strategy 1=A, Strategy 2=B	20	5	15504	**Strategy 2**	0,225	0,007239884196775
7	Strategy 1=A, Strategy 2=0	20	10	184756	**guessing**		0,000012037501448
8							
9	**3 strategies compared**						
10	Strat 1 =A, Strat 2=A, Strat 3=A	20	15	15504	**Strategy 1**	0,25	0,000390763325556
11	Strat 1 =A, Strat 2=A, Strat 3=B	10	7	120	**Strategy 2**	0,44	0,000000218766338
12	Strat 1 =A, Strat 2=A, Strat 3=0	0	0	1	**Strategy 3**	0,45	0,000000186320790
13	Strat 1 =A, Strat 2=B, Strat 3=A	0	0	1	**guessing**		0,000000152495516
14	Strat 1 =A, Strat 2=B, Strat 3=B	10	6	210			
15	Strat 1 =A, Strat 2=B, Strat 3=0	10	8	45			
16	Strat 1 =A, Strat 2=0, Strat 3=A	0	0	1			
17	Strat 1 =A, Strat 2=0, Strat 3=B	0	0	1			
18	Strat 1 =A, Strat 2=0, Strat 3=0	10	9	10			

Figure 4.2 Detail of the calculation spreadsheet (see text for explanations).

choices in column 3 in a set of items of the size given in Column 2. Column 7 provides the estimates of ε for each of the strategies, and Column 8 contains the likelihoods of the data given for each of the strategies compared, including pure guessing. The spreadsheet also computes the unconstrained model likelihood and the likelihood ratio statistic (not shown in Figure 4.2).

The data in the two-strategies example were chosen in a way to fit Strategy 2 very well: "A" is chosen in half of the cases where Strategy 2 predicts a guess, whereas it was chosen very few times, when Strategy 2 predicted option "B". Consequently, Strategy 2 produces a much higher likelihood of the data as shown in Column 8. In the three-strategies example, data were generated in a way that the majority of choices conformed to the prediction of Strategy 1 in each case, and this fact is nicely reflected in the likelihood which is about 100 times larger than that for the other strategies. It is recommended to compute the examples by hand using equations (3) to (9) in the text to cross-check them with the spreadsheet results.

Further information about how to use the spreadsheet is provided in a documentation file that comes along with it.

References to applications

The ML method to disentangle the strategies TTB, EQW, and WADD was introduced by Bröder and Schiffer (2003a) for the binary case and three-option choices with a dominated alternative. Bröder and Schiffer (2003a) also report an application and demonstrate the convergent validity of classification and process tracing measures. The binary model has been applied to memory-based choices (Bröder & Gaissmaier, 2007; Bröder & Schiffer, 2003a; 2006b; Glöckner & Hodges, 2008), and the three-option model was used by Bröder (2003) and Bröder and Schiffer (2006b). Other applications involving additional decision rules can be found in Garcia-Retamero, Hoffrage, and Dieckmann (2007), Garcia-Retamero, Hoffrage, Dieckmann, and Ramos (2007), and in Glöckner and Betsch (2008).

Summary and dos and don'ts

- For various reasons, information search data may not be available or applicable to infer decision strategies. Outcome-based methods must then be used. The method here determines the best-fitting strategy according to the maximum-likelihood principle.
  Dos
- To set up an experiment:
  - first define the strategies you want to compare;
  - create items for which strategies make different predictions (the more, the better).
- To analyze the data:

- count strategy-compatible choices and choices of option "A" in guessing cases for each strategy;
- plug the error rates into the equations, and hence;
- calculate the likelihoods of the data, given each strategy.

Don'ts
- Never interpret a likelihood before looking at the estimated error rate: The data only support a strategy if the accompanying error rate is (considerably) smaller than chance guessing.

Notes

1 In fact, decision outcomes should *always* be analyzed if available, also in addition to process tracing and process analysis data. Since information search and integration are in part logically independent, it amounts to an *empirical* question whether they are closely connected or not, and comparing search and outcome data may mutually validate both measures or point to situations where search and decision rules diverge (see Bröder, 2000, for a critique of decision research methodology).

2 Actually, this order varied between participants, but we use this specific order here for illustrative purposes.

3 It is easier to construct items with potentially different predictions of EQW and WADD if more than four cues are used. This would allow for more diffentiating patterns. However, one has to assume then that prople are able to discriminate between tiny weight differences.

4 The maximum likelihood approach is not restricted to this particular form of error distribution, but it is most simple in this case. If there are serious theoretical reasons for assuming other than equal distributions of errors across items, these must be made explicit. However, we are quite confident that the simple distribution assumed here is a useful approximation in many cases.

5 For example, these may be items for which our strategies make no predictions, but they are used to disguise the structure of critical items that enter in the analysis.

6 In principle, it is arbitrary which options are coded as "A", "B", and "C", respectively. However, it is convenient to define one "reference strategy" that always makes a clear prediction (i.e. TTB) and to define all options chosen by this strategy as "A". The non-predicted option is then coded "B", and in case of existing dominated options, we denote them with "C". Note that these are only logical codings by the experimenter and do not have to correspond to any option labels used for the participants in an experiment.

7 After several transformation steps not described here, this likelihood can be converted into the well-known likelihood ratio statistic G^2 which is a widely used indicator of model fit. Larger values denote worse model fits, and the usefulness of this statistic lies in its asymptotic chi-square distribution which makes significance tests feasible. G^2 is also computed in the computer spreadsheet supplementing this chapter.

8 Odds ratios with exactly the value 1 mean that the data are equally likely for two strategies. This does not allow for a clear classification, and it will happen predominantly in experiments with a low number of discriminating items.

9 The ML method itself is not restricted to distinguishing between only four strategies, but since there is a combinatorial explosion of theoretically possible item types with different predictions, an implementation of the *general* method is not feasible for more than four strategies, and one has to create a customized

spreadsheet including the formulas or one might rely on the parameter search based estimation procedure described in Glöckner (this volume). In an experiment, one will of course only use a very small subset of item types.
10 Exceptions are situations where items are drawn randomly, or the predictions depend on characteristics of the participants such as subjective cue hierarchies.

References

Bröder, A. (2000). A methodological comment on behavioral decision research. *Psychologische Beiträge*, *42*, 645–662.

Bröder, A. (2003). Decision making with the "adaptive toolbox": Influence of environmental structure, intelligence, and working memory load. *Journal of Experimental Psychology: Learning Memory, and Cognition*, *29*, 611–625.

Bröder, A., & Gaissmaier, W. (2007). Sequential processing of cues in memory-based multiattribute decisions. *Psychonomic Bulletin & Review*, *14*, 895–900.

Bröder, A. & Newell, B.R. (2008). Challenging some common beliefs about cognitive costs: Empirical work within the adaptive toolbox metaphor. *Judgment and Decision Making*, *3*, 195–204.

Bröder, A., & Schiffer, S. (2003a). Bayesian strategy assessment in multi-attribute decision making. *Journal of Behavioral Decision Making*, *16*, 193–213.

Bröder, A., & Schiffer, S. (2003b). Take the best versus simultaneous feature matching: Probabilistic inferences from memory and effects of representation format. *Journal of Experimental Psychology: General*, *132*, 277–293.

Bröder, A., & Schiffer, S. (2006a). Adaptive flexibility and maladaptive routines in selecting fast and frugal decision strategies. *Journal of Experimental Psychology: Learning, Memory, and Cognition*, *32*, 904–918.

Bröder, A., & Schiffer, S. (2006b). Stimulus format and working memory in fast and frugal strategy selection. *Journal of Behavioral Decision Making*, *19*(4), 361–380.

Garcia-Retamero, R., Hoffrage, U., & Dieckmann, A. (2007). When one cue is not enough: Combining fast and frugal heuristics with compound cue processing. *The Quarterly Journal of Experimental Psychology*, *60*, 1197–1215.

Garcia-Retamero, R., Hoffrage, U., Dieckmann, A., & Ramos, M. (2007). Compound cue processing within the fast and frugal heuristics approach in nonlinearly separable environments. *Learning and Motivation*, *38*, 16–34.

Gigerenzer, G. (2004). Fast and frugal heuristics: The tools of bounded rationality. In D. Koehler & N. Harvey (Eds.), *Handbook of judgement and decision making*. Oxford, UK: Blackwell.

Gigerenzer, G. (2007). *Gut feelings: The intelligence of the unconscious*. New York: Viking.

Glöckner, A. (2008). Does intuition beat fast and frugal heuristics? A systematic empirical analysis. In H. Plessner, C. Betsch & T. Betsch (Eds.), *Intuition in judgment and decision making* (pp.309–325). New York: Lawrence Erlbaum Associates.

Glöckner, A., & Betsch, T. (2008). Do people make decisions under risk based on ignorance? An empirical test of the Priority Heuristic against Cumulative Prospect Theory. *Organizational Behavior and Human Decision Processes*, *107*, 75–95.

Glöckner, A., & Hodges, S. D. (2008). Parallel constraint satisfaction in memory-based decisions. *Manuscript submitted for publication*.

Hammond, K. R., Hamm, R. M., Grassia, J., & Pearson, T. (1987). Direct comparison of the efficacy of intuitive and analytical cognition in expert judgment. *IEEE Transactions on Systems, Man, and Cybernetics*, *17*, 753–770.

Hoffman, P. J. (1960). The paramorphic representation of clinical judgment. *Psychological Bulletin*, *57*, 116–131.

Newell, B. R., & Shanks, D. R. (2003). Take the best or look at the rest? Factors influencing "one-reason" decision making. *Journal of Experimental Psychology: Learning, Memory, and Cognition*, *29*, 53–65.

Nisbett, R. E., & Wilson, T. D. (1977). Telling more than we can know: Verbal reports on mental processes. *Psychological Review*, *84*, 231–259.

Payne, J. W., Bettman, J. R., & Johnson, E. J. (1993). *The adaptive decision maker*. Cambridge: Cambridge University Press.

Persson, M. & Rieskamp, J. (2009). Inferences from memory: Strategy- and exemplar-based judgment models compared. *Acta Psychologica*, *130*, 25–37.

5 Multiple measure strategy classification

Outcomes, decision times and confidence ratings

Andreas Glöckner

Introduction

One of the core features of intuition is that at least parts of the information integration processes remain opaque to the decider. This obviously makes life for intuition researchers harder: it becomes impossible to use introspection-based methods or self-report measures to get a first idea about the processes and to derive (and later test) hypotheses (but see Witteman & van Geenen, chapter 3, this volume). Properties of the information integration process underlying intuition have to be derived from overt behaviour, physiological reactions or even by using neuronal activation measures. In this chapter we will outline a very general methodological approach and a statistical method that permits investigating intuitive as well as deliberate processes based on simple behavioural measures only. The method allows the researcher to make sound inferences about unconscious decision processes without "looking inside the brain" using expensive and effortful neuroscientific methods.

More specifically, elaborating on the approach introduced in the previous chapter (Bröder, chapter 4, this volume; for readers who are not familiar with maximum likelihood choice-based strategy classification, I suggest reading the chapter by Bröder first), I will discuss how choices, decision times and confidence judgments can be combined to make inferences about individuals' decision strategies even if there is a high overlap in predicted choices. To make the chapter more easily comprehensible, the different steps of the method will be explained using a sample research question and a sample data set, and analysis syntax and outputs will be included. First, I will introduce the sample research question and explain how to derive predictions of choice strategies from different recent decision models. Then pros and cons will be discussed of simple statistical approaches (e.g., *t*-test and correlations) that include additional measures above choice, extending choice-based strategy classification. Finally, the multiple-measure maximum likelihood (MM-ML) strategy classification method will be introduced. The MM-ML method estimates the total (maximum) likelihood for the observed choice behaviour (including choices, decision times, and confidence ratings) of a participant given the application of a certain intuitive or deliberate strategy. The resulting likelihoods for different strategies can be compared and people should be classified as users of the strategy with the highest likelihood. An estimation program will be provided that makes the method easy to apply. Finally, the broad field of applications of the method is outlined and advantages and disadvantages for decision research will be discussed.

Example research question, strategies, and predictions

Experimental task and research question

Let's consider a researcher who wants to investigate individuals' decision strategies in probabilistic inference tasks (e.g., which city has more inhabitants: Hamburg or Bonn?). In a comprehensive literature review, he or she learns about the different strategies individuals are supposed to use in such tasks. Most theories assume that individuals, when they have no specific knowledge about the criterion (e.g., city population), will not just rely on guessing. They will instead, consciously or unconsciously, utilize other pieces of information that are informative concerning the task in question, so-called probabilistic cues (Brunswik, 1955; Gigerenzer, Hoffrage, & Kleinbölting, 1991). Such cues could, for instance, be whether one of the cities has a professional soccer team or not, or whether the city is a state-capital or not. In both cases, one might assume that cities for which the cue has a positive value might be bigger than cities for which this is not the case. Each cue has a certain predictive power (i.e., cue validity) for the criterion. The objective cue validity is often defined as the probability that the city which has a positive cue value is bigger than the city which has not.[1] To put it simply, the validity of the cue "soccer team" would be .89 if 89% of the cities with a soccer team are bigger than cities without it.[2] Of course, individuals will not have direct access to these *objective* probabilities, but they will probably be able to produce some informed guesses based on prior experiences or their world knowledge. In experiments, either individuals' *subjective* cue validities might be measured using rating scales, or individuals could simply be informed about cue validities. Using existing information (e.g., participants constructing cue validities from their general world knowledge) has the disadvantage that participants might not be able or willing to reveal it completely, which might decrease internal validity of the study. On the other hand, providing information explicitly might influence decision behaviour. I would recommend starting with a decision task in which all information is explicitly provided and prior knowledge is ruled out (and to replicate the findings with prior knowledge later on).

Our specific sample research question therefore is: which strategies do individuals use in probabilistic inference tasks, in which cue validity information and cue values are explicitly provided? The orange selection task (Glöckner & Betsch, 2008c) will be used to investigate it. In this task, participants take the role of a purchaser of oranges and have to decide repeatedly from which of two orange producers to buy. To do so, they are provided with predictions of four testers which predict whether the oranges will be good (+) or bad (–) and are explicitly informed about their cue validity (see Table 5.1).

Selection of decision strategies

After the selection of a specific research question and an appropriate task the researcher has to decide which decision strategies are to be compared. A comprehensive literature review reveals a multitude of strategies that individuals might use to make choices in the considered tasks, ranging from deliberate to intuitive strategies and from complex to very simple ones. Some strategies can be excluded from consideration because despite being generally applicable they cannot be applied in the specific conditions. For instance, models which propose that options are selected on the basis of learned affective reactions (so-called affective tags, Finucane, Alhakami, Slovic, & Johnson, 2000) or comparisons to prototypes/exemplars stored in memory (e.g., Dougherty, Gettys, & Ogden, 1999; Juslin & Persson, 2002) do not apply to the specific task conditions (and the specific research question) because participants have no possibility to acquire the necessary memory contents; there is no feedback and hence no learning of affective tags in the selected task (see Glöckner & Witteman, chapter 1, this volume). The remaining strategies still differ widely in their predictions concerning cue integration and the underlying processes. A simple deliberate strategy would be the so-called "take the best"-strategy (TTB), which suggests that individuals consider the prediction of the most valid cue only (Gigerenzer & Goldstein, 1996; Payne, Bettman, & Johnson, 1988). If this cue differentiates (i.e., makes a positive prediction for one option and a negative prediction for the other), the favoured option is instantly selected. If this is not the case, the second cue is considered, and so on. Another simple strategy would be to ignore cue validities and to select the option which has the highest sum of cue values without weighting them by validity, a strategy which is called "equal weight" (EQW; Payne et al., 1988). The application of a "weighted additive strategy" (WADD), in which individuals calculate a weighted sum of cue values and

Table 5.1 Example task

	Oranges A	*Oranges B*
Tester 1 (80% validity)	+	–
Tester 2 (70% validity)	–	+
Tester 3 (60% validity)	–	+
Tester 4 (55% validity)	+	–

Note: Positive predictions for the respective option are indicated by "+" negative predictions by "–". Cue validity is provided in parentheses.

cue validities and select the option with the higher weighted sum (Payne et al., 1988), would require more effort. One possible intuitive strategy is specified by the Parallel Constraint Satisfaction (PCS) model, which predicts quick weighted compensatory information integration based on automatic processes of perception (described in detail below). Of course, further models could be considered, but for the sake of simplicity I will consider the deliberate strategies TTB, EQW, WADD and the intuitive strategy PCS as well as a random choice strategy RAND in the following analyses only.

Deriving predictions for deliberate strategies

Choice predictions for TTB, EQW, WADD. Considering the sample decision introduced in Table 5.1, TTB would predict choices for option A (because the most valid cue speaks for A), and EQW would predict a random selection between A and B because there are two positive cues for each option (unweighted sums are both equal to 0; note that in the calculation we transform cue values "+" to 1 and "−" to −1). The application of a WADD strategy can be assumed to entail a mediation step in which the explicitly provided objective validities v (e.g., .80 for tester 1) are transformed into subjective weights w. Individuals might use very different transformation functions (Glöckner & Betsch, 2008c). The simplest transformation would be to use the validities as they are ($w = v$). According to such a so-called *ignorant WADD* strategy, the weighted sum for options A and B would be 0.05 and −0.05 (this and all following calculations of strategy predictions have been done using the strategy prediction calculation sheet provided at www.intuitive-experts.de – Resources), and option A should be selected. Note, that the strategy is dubbed "ignorant" because it does not correct for the fact that in choices between two options cues with a validity of 0.50 have no predictive power at all (i.e., they predict no better than a coin-flip). Obviously, adding several non-predictive cues with $w = 0.50$ which all speak for option A would overrule all other information and lead to choices for option A only. This problem could be accounted for by correcting validity by subtracting the chance probability .50 ($w = v − .50$). In our example, the so-called *corrected WADD* strategy leads to the same weighted sums as ignorant WADD and predicts choices for A. However, please note that this is not always the case. A third possibility would be to transform cue validities using a non-linear transformation. This could be done using a log-transformed odds-ratio of the validity according to $w = \ln(v/(1 − v))$ (with $0 < v < 1$). Note that under the assumption that cues are independent and that the validities represent prior probabilities according to Bayes' theorem (which is different from the above presented definition of validities based on Gigerenzer et al., 1991), the application of these log-transformed decision weights in a WADD would lead to the mathematically optimal solution (*normative WADD*). I suggest the reader try out several sample calculations using the strategy prediction calculation sheet (mentioned above) to get a feeling about the very different choice predictions that result from the different transformations, and to compare them to the predictions of TTB and EQW.

Decision time predictions. TTB, EQW and WADD have usually been conceptualized as deliberate decision strategies which rely on explicit calculations or comparisons. For such strategies, the number of computational steps (elementary information processes, EIP; Payne et al., 1988) which are necessary to come to a decision determines decision time. It has been argued that although some computational steps might take longer than others (Lohse & Johnson, 1996), it is sufficient to use the number of EIPs to approximate decision time (Payne et al., 1988). Under this assumption, it is easy to derive decision time predictions from TTB, EQW, and WADD. In our example, TTB should take 4 EIPs (read cue1 info1, read cue1 info2, compare, select A), EQW should take 16 EIPs (read cue1 info1, read cue2 info1, add, etc., compare, select), and WADD should take 32 EIPs (read cue1 info1, read cue validity 1, multiply, read cue2 info1, etc., compare, select). Thus, WADD should show the longest decision time eight times as long as TTB and twice as long as EQW. Unfortunately, using absolute decision times for strategy classification comes with the caveat that thresholds for classification are often somewhat arbitrary (but see Glöckner, 2006). To circumvent this problem, the later reported methods are based on testing predicted time differences between different types of decision tasks within one participant instead (i.e., intra-individual comparison).

Confidence predictions. Confidence predictions could also be derived from the strategies. For TTB, it has been argued that confidence in a choice should be equal to the validity of the cue which differentiates between the options (Gigerenzer et al., 1991). For EQW and WADD confidence should be proportional to the difference between the unweighted or weighted sum of the cue values, respectively (Glöckner & Betsch, 2008c). Confidence predictions for the different strategies are also calculated in the prediction calculation sheet (see above).

Predictions of intuitive strategies

The deliberate strategies discussed so far might be contrasted with intuitive ones, which are at least partially based on automatic, unconscious processes of information integration. Two prominent intuitive models which might apply here are decision field theory (Busemeyer & Johnson, 2004; Busemeyer & Townsend, 1993) and parallel constraint satisfaction models (Glöckner & Betsch, 2008b; Holyoak & Simon, 1999). Although different in several process assumptions, both models make similar predictions concerning choices, and decision times, in the task considered here. For convenience, only the parallel constraint satisfaction model (PCS, Glöckner & Betsch, 2008b) will be considered in the further discussion (for a more comprehensive discussion of both models and tests comparing them see Glöckner, Betsch, & Schindler, in press; Glöckner & Herbold, in press). PCS models postulate that individuals form a mental representation of the decision task which can be modelled by interactive activation networks (Glöckner & Betsch, 2008b; Holyoak & Simon, 1999; McClelland & Rumelhart, 1981; Simon, Krawczyk, & Holyoak, 2004; Thagard, 1989). A specific network structure consisting of two layers of nodes (first layer: cue nodes; second layer: mutually inhibiting option nodes) has been proposed (see also Glöckner, 2006, 2008a, 2008b; Glöckner & Betsch, 2008b) and used to simulate intuition. The PCS processes operate towards maximizing consistency in the network by changing the activation of nodes. Initial advantages of the favoured option are accentuated by highlighting supportive information (i.e., cues that speak for the favoured option) and by devaluating contrary information (i.e., cues supporting the non-favoured option). PCS models basically predict weighted compensatory information integration of cue validities and cue values (Glöckner, 2006) and hence make essentially the same choice predictions as WADD. PCS models, however, make substantially different predictions for decision times and confidence. Decision time should decrease with increasing superiority of one option over the other (which makes consistency-maximizing easier) and decision times should be generally short because decisions are based on automatic processing. Furthermore, confidence should increase with increasing superiority of one option over the other. Specifically, the (absolute) difference in activation between two options after a consistent interpretation has been constructed can be understood as the confidence prediction of the PCS model.[3]

Selection of diagnostic tasks for the considered set of strategies

To determine which strategy participants are most likely to use, tasks have to be selected for which the strategies make different predictions concerning at least one of the dependent variables: choices, decision time, and/or confidence. If it is possible to derive sufficiently different choice predictions for the considered strategies, the choice-based strategy classification method discussed in the previous chapter by Bröder might suffice. When strategies with similar choice predictions are compared (e.g., WADD vs. PCS), that method is less appropriate. Furthermore, for researchers interested not merely in the outcomes but also in the processes of judgment and decision making, it seems more appropriate to use an integral measure which includes further process parameters and outcomes if these are available. Finally, even for seemingly very different strategies such as TTB, EQW, and WADD, it can be easily shown that choice predictions converge under certain parameter constellations (i.e., using certain transformation functions of cue validities for WADD).[4]

To be able to select tasks that are diagnostic for a specific set of strategies which include strategies with variable parameters often some additional assumptions concerning the parameters have to be made. Hence I pragmatically assume that users of a WADD strategy transform cues according to a WADD corrected strategy.

Diagnostic tasks can be designed in a theory-driven manner or by selecting tasks randomly from all possible tasks until sufficient differentiating tasks are included. Although the latter approach might have the advantage of representative sampling (Brunswik, 1955) the former is usually more efficient in that it allows to use fewer tasks. Hence I will rely on theory-driven design. There is no formal optimal solution to construct the most appropriate tasks, but basically types of tasks should be selected that allow pitting the specific properties of the strategies against each other (e.g., ignoring cue validities for EQW, ignoring less valid information for TTB, increasing decision time for low consistency for PCS, increasing confidence with increasing weighted difference between options for WADD).

Six types of tasks that could result from such a selection and the predictions of the considered decision strategies concerning choices, decision times, and confidence are shown in Table 5.2. In all tasks, participants are asked to choose the better of the options given the cue information. Predictions for the deliberate strategies were derived using the calculation sheet, and for PCS using the computer simulation.[5] Choice predictions of "A:B" in the table mean random choices between A and B because EQW does not differentiate between options. For decision times and confidence, results were rescaled to contrast weights.[6] Note that this procedure standardizes contrast weights and hence they can only be compared between the different tasks for one strategy (but not between strategies). The all 0 contrast weights for WADD and EQW decision times indicate that decision times should not differ.

I highly recommend deriving specific prediction tables before conducting experiments which aim at testing process models for judgment and decision making. They provide a solid basis for strategy classification and allow for deriving sets of specific hypotheses or the predictions can be used in one single statistical method like the multiple-measure maximum likelihood strategy classification.

Simple methods to investigate decision times and confidence

The predictions in Table 5.2 can, of course, be used in very different ways to test specific hypotheses concerning decision strategies. Even if one aims at strategy classification on an individual level, in many cases it can be helpful to analyze and report aggregated data first. For confidence judgments and decision times, either specific contrasts in ANOVA or correlations between observed data and contrast weights should be conducted, which take into account the whole pattern of observations. It is often useful to do a log-transformation on decision times to reduce the influence of outliers and to correct for violations of normal distribution (Glass & Hopkins, 1996). Observed choice distributions can of course also be simply analyzed using χ^2 tests (see for instance, Glöckner & Betsch, 2008c).

If one wants to differentiate between strategies which make different choice predictions (e.g., between TTB, EQW and WADD only), it is possible to use

Table 5.2 Types of decision tasks and predictions of strategies

	Types of decision tasks											
	1		2		3		4		5		6	
	A	B	A	B	A	B	A	B	A	B	A	B
Cue 1 ($v = .80$)	+	–	+	–	+	–	+	–	+	–	–	–
Cue 2 ($v = .70$)	+	–	+	–	–	+	–	–	–	+	–	–
Cue 3 ($v = .60$)	+	–	–	+	–	+	–	–	+	–	+	–
Cue 4 ($v = .55$)	–	+	–	+	–	+	–	+	–	+	–	+
	Choice predictions											
TTB	A		A		A		A		A		A	
EQW	A		A:B		B		A:B		A:B		A:B	
WADD$_{corrected}$	A		A		B		A		A		A	
PCS	A		A		B		A		A		A	
	Time predictions (contrasts)											
TTB	–0.167		–0.167		–0.167		–0.167		–0.167		0.833	
EQW	0		0		0		0		0		0	
WADD$_{corrected}$	0		0		0		0		0		0	
PCS	–0.44		–0.35		0.56		–0.16		0.07		0.33	
	Confidence predictions (contrasts)											
TTB	0.167		0.167		0.167		0.167		0.167		–0.833	
EQW	0.667		–0.33		0.667		–0.33		–0.33		–0.33	
WADD$_{corrected}$	0.63		0.23		–0.37		0.03		–0.17		–0.37	
PCS	0.62		0.28		–0.33		–0.01		–0.19		–0.38	

the maximum likelihood strategy classification method or the scoring rule both discussed in Bröder (chapter 4, this volume). Dependent on the expected error rate in strategy application, several tasks per type should be presented to the participants. As a rule-of-thumb suggestion: In simulations, I found that for 60 observations per participant (i.e., six types and ten tasks per type) the maximum-likelihood strategy classification method leads to reliable (i.e., unbiased) classifications up to an error rate of .25 between strategies which make different choice predictions (Glöckner, 2009). For strategies with equal choice predictions reliable classification is also possible as long as the effects on decision time and confidence are strong (Glöckner, 2009). In the following discussion of methods it is assumed that a researcher wants to analyze data from an experiment in which participants solved 60 decision tasks with 10 observations per type.

Strategy classification by additional t-tests for decision times. The simplest way to differentiate between two strategies which make the same choice predictions but different decision time predictions, such as WADD and PCS, is to conduct additional *t*-tests. If an individual was classified as having used one of the strategies based on choices, decision times for different types of tasks could be compared to see whether they are more in line with one or the other strategy. In this case, the types should be selected for which the strategies make the most different predictions and compared by *t*-tests. This method is easy to use and has been successfully applied in recent studies (Bergert & Nosofsky, 2007; Glöckner, 2006). In our example, the types with the most different time predictions are the types 1 and 3 (see Table 5.2). The 10 decision times each are compared.[7] Note that in the special case that one theory does not predict a difference in decision time (i.e., WADD) it has the advantage of being the null-hypothesis. We stick with this hypothesis as long as the evidence is not sufficient to reject it. This usually gives the strategy an advantage because with a low number of observations it is likely that an existing effect is not identified (i.e., a beta error occurs). To account for the problem and to do a fair test which does not prefer one strategy over the other, the alpha error could be adjusted (i.e., increased). A compromise power analysis reveals that when assuming a large effect size of $d = .80$, in our example the alpha error for testing the two models against each other should be set to *alpha* = .18 to have a beta error of the same size and hence to do an unbiased test of both models (effect size related calculations can be easily done using G-Power; Faul, Erdfelder, Lang, & Buchner, 2007). Alternatively, one might think about increasing the number of observations per type to n = 20 (overall $N = 6*20 = 120$) for which a more conventional alpha of .10 could be used according to a compromise power analysis.

Correlation with contrast weights. One of the major disadvantages of using *t*-tests is of course that only two task types can be compared at a time and hence only a subset of the available information is used. It is possible, that one comparison supports one strategy and another one a different strategy. This problem can be circumvented by calculating a correlation between decision times and decision time predictions instead. An additional advantage is that the higher number of observations considered in the analysis increases power. Hence, when testing against a correlation of $r = 0$ (which is predicted by WADD) and assuming a medium effect size of $r = .40$, the compromise alpha level could be set to the conventional alpha level of .05 in this example with $N = 60$ (Faul et al., 2007). Hence, using a correlation approach is preferable to using *t*-tests because the correlations test has a higher statistical power (in our example for correlations: power = $1 - beta = 0.95$).

Analyzing confidence judgments. The discussed *t*-test or correlation analyses can be applied in a similar manner for confidence judgments. Of course, confidence judgments do not have to be log-transformed because they are usually not skewed and contain fewer outliers. If the results concerning decision time and confidence converge, this of course increases reliability of the strategy classification. However, contrary results could cause trouble. It is simply possible that both strategies have to be rejected and the person can hence not be classified.

Widening the perspective, a similar problem applies if we use a choice-based strategy classification which indicates usage of one strategy (e.g., EQW), but we also observe a significant rejection of the hypotheses concerning decision times and/or confidence for this strategy. Of course the conflicting results should be taken into account. Perhaps times and confidence are exactly in line with a different strategy which accounted almost equally well for the choice results. All results should be taken into account simultaneously. That is exactly what the Multiple-Measure Maximum Likelihood (MM-ML) strategy classification method does, which will be introduced in the next section.

Multiple-Measure Maximum Likelihood strategy classification

Maximum likelihood (ML) estimation is a statistical method used for fitting a mathematical model to some data. ML essentially searches for a set of parameters given the model under scrutiny that most likely produced a set of data by making some assumptions on its generation process. It would be beyond the scope of this chapter to give a complete introduction to ML estimation. I will proceed as follows: First, a simple introduction is given that should provide the general idea how ML could be applied for a joint strategy classification based on choices, decision times and confidence. Second, I will intuitively describe how the method can be applied using the ML commands of the statistical package STATA. Third, in a more elaborated fashion I add the mathematical background of the method and some more details in Appendix A. A more elaborate description of the method and simulation results (e.g., model recovery simulation) can be found in Glöckner (2009). Jeckel, Nicklisch, and Glöckner (under review) have implemented MM-ML for the open-source statistical package R and describe in more detail how the program can be applied.

ML estimation for choices. As introduced in the previous chapter, ML can be used to identify the decision strategy which most likely produced the data. Under the assumption that strategies are applied with a constant error rate ε, a ML estimation can then be used to determine the likelihood of the data (given the application of the strategy and a constant error rate per person). As shown in the previous chapter (Bröder, chapter 4, this volume), the ML estimation can easily be calculated for each strategy and the resulting (maximum) likelihood values L can be used to identify which strategy most likely produced the vector of choices. In contrast, statistical packages such as STATA do estimate ε using an iterative search process which leads to the same results. For pragmatic reasons, most statistical packages report the log-transformed likelihood $LL = \ln(L)$.

ML for decision time. ML is not, however, limited to dichotomous outcomes (i.e., choices that could be in line or not in line with the prediction of a strategy). It can also be applied to continuous variables such as decision time or confidence. To apply ML estimations, one has to make assumptions about the data generation process. More specifically, the probability has to be specified that a certain value is drawn. The common assumption is that because of multiple random influences the drawn values follow a normal distribution around the population mean μ with a standard deviation σ.[8] If a strategy predicts no differences in decision times (such as WADD), all values are assumed to be drawn from this distribution. The further apart from the mean the values are the less likely is it that they are drawn. Hence, everything else being equal, the likelihood value decreases if decision times are further apart from μ. If a strategy predicts different decision times for the different types of tasks, each decision time is assumed to be drawn from a different normal distribution. The relative difference between the means of these normal distributions is predicted by the contrast weights in Table 5.2. Of course, these do not give us a good guess about the absolute difference. Hence, the contrasts have to be rescaled by a factor R which is a free parameter. It has to be estimated based on the data. For instance (and ignoring log-transformation), if a TTB users' mean decision time is 10 sec, and the mean times for the first five decision task types are 9.17 sec but for the sixth type it is 14.17 sec the rescaling factor estimation should be 5 (i.e., $10 + 5 * (-0.167) = 9.17$ and $10 + 5 * (0.833) = 14.17$; see equation 6 and Table 5.2).

Of course, we have a priori no idea how big μ_T, σ_T and R_T are (the subscript $_T$ indicates that the parameters are for decision time). Fortunately, the ML algorithm easily finds the parameters which produce the highest likelihood value. Note that WADD needs no rescaling parameter R_T, because it predicts no differences in decision times hence R_T should be zero. The same ML mechanism can, of course, also be applied to analyze confidence ratings and to estimate the parameters μ_C, σ_C and R_C which lead to the highest likelihood value for the confidence data.

Finding an overall likelihood value per strategy. Following the described procedure, it is possible to estimate for each strategy (and person) the optimal parameters and three likelihood values: one for choice, decision time and confidence, respectively. One advantage of likelihoods is that they are measures on a unitary scale and hence can be easily combined to an overall value. Under an independence assumption[9] the different likelihood values for choices, decision times and confidence can be simply multiplied to provide an overall likelihood value for the respective strategy: $L_{total} = L_{Choice} L_{Conf} L_{Time}$.

However, before it can be decided which strategy most likely produced the data, likelihood values have to be corrected for the different numbers of free parameters the strategies might have. Everything else being equal, a model with more free parameters fits data at least equally well, but usually better than a (nested) model with fewer parameters. The necessary correction is, however, easy to apply. It is done by calculating the Bayesian information criterion BIC (Schwarz, 1978) from the resulting total likelihood (see equation 9 in Appendix A). It should be noted that BIC is inversely scored and individuals should be classified as user of the decision strategy which produces the lowest BIC score. The parameters used in the MM-ML estimation are summarized in Table 5.3.

Although the underlying mathematical calculations are rather complex, the application of ML particularly in STATA or in the open-source statistical package R is very easy. With the programs provided in Appendix B, the reader will be able to estimate the parameters, the likelihood and the BIC score for each strategy. Note, that the method and the provided ML program is very general. It can be applied essentially to every cognitive task (e.g., probabilistic inferences, judgments, risky decisions, multi-attributive decisions, experience-based decisions, categorization, recognition) in which there are correct and wrong answers, and decision times and confidence can be recorded. Aside from limitations in computers' calculation capacity, the provided syntax can be used with minor modifications for any number of strategies/models that are compared, any number of task types, and any number of observations. For background information on ML, I recommend reading the book by Gould, Pitblado, and Sribney (2006). After preparing the data and loading the additional ML programs, simple estimation commands can be used, which also provide easily comprehensible output. Figure 5.1 shows the results from the sample data set.[10]

The analysis estimated the likelihood for each person and each considered strategy independently. The results of an output for comparing the data of subject 9 with the predictions of strategy 1 are presented in the upper part of Figure 5.1. The number of observations is 126 (6 frequencies for choices in task types, 60 decision times, 60 confidence rations). The resulting parameter estimates are listed as constant coefficients. In the example, the choice error rate (epsilon) was 20%, the log-transformed (and for order effects corrected) mean decision time was 8.3, the mean confidence was 99.35. The provided significance tests (which test if the estimated constant coefficient is different from zero) are usually only informative for the rescaling factors R. In this example, R_T and R_C are both not significantly different from zero.

Table 5.3 Parameters for the different strategies

	ε	μ_T	σ_T	R_T	μ_C	σ_C	R_C	N_p
TTB	x	x	x	x	x	x	x	7
EQW	x	x	x		x	x	x	6
WADD	x	x	x		x	x	x	6
PCS	x	x	x	x	x	x	x	7
RAND		x	x		x	x		4

Note: The parameter ε estimates the error rate for choices; μ_T and σ_T refer to the mean and the standard deviation for decision time, R_T is the scaling factor for the time contrast (see Table 5.2) which captured differences between decision times for different types of tasks. The parameters μ_C, σ_C, and R_C are equivalently used for confidence. N_p is the total number of estimated parameters. TTB, EQW, WADD, PCS and RAND refer to the decision strategies take-the-best, equal weight, weighted additive, parallel constraint satisfaction, and random choice strategy, respectively.

Output per person and strategy

```
                                          Number of obs   =        126
                                          Wald chi2(0)    =          .
Log likelihood = -183.40419              Prob > chi2      =          .
```

dv	Coef.	Std. Err.	z	P>|z|	[95% Conf. Interval]
epsilon						
_cons	.2000001	.0516387	3.87	0.000	.09879	.3012101
mu_Time						
_cons	8.344802	.0507628	164.39	0.000	8.245308	8.444295
sigma_Time						
_cons	.3932071	.0358947	10.95	0.000	.3228547	.4635594
R_Time						
_cons	.060684	.1135091	0.53	0.593	-.1617898	.2831577
mu_Conf						
_cons	99.35	.2675247	371.37	0.000	98.82566	99.87434
sigma_Conf						
_cons	2.072237	.1891685	10.95	0.000	1.701474	2.443001
R_Conf						
_cons	-1.56e-08	.0012632	-0.00	1.000	-.0024758	.0024757

```
Subj: 9  Strat: 1   - BIC:387.04097
```

Aggregated output BIC scores

```
result[10,5]
               TTB        EQW       WADD         PCS       RAND
Subj1    616.29834  750.64645  707.66247   708.20462  754.02627
Subj2    680.20815  683.29442  594.51436   600.86023  703.06562
Subj3    687.95338  723.55767  649.69426   648.30942  732.54342
Subj4    568.85478          0  607.4708     604.1918   636.29755
Subj5    609.33279   663.4615  597.17856    596.5238   660.28041
Subj6    745.60428  768.31551   658.2674   664.96085  777.25734
Subj7    607.99551          0  627.64811   629.75609  690.05906
Subj8    756.20214  797.55205  669.41646   640.16949  809.95366
Subj9    387.04096  387.34159  339.75653   340.35961  401.78435
Subj10   653.76097  656.44923  568.54083   573.48068  670.45377
```

Figure 5.1 Output of the Multiple-Measure Maximum Likelihood strategy classification with STATA. The top part of the figure shows the individual estimation results including the log likelihood value *LL*, the estimations of the parameters, and the BIC score. The lower part shows the overall output of BIC scores for all persons (in rows) and all strategies (in columns).

A significant rescaling factor would indicate that the specific contrast weights contribute to explain the data. The tests for *R* produce results similar (but not exactly equal) to correlations between data and contrast weights (i.e., the correlations of observed decision times with the contrast weights for the respective task types). The BIC score indicates the overall fit of data and strategy predictions for the specific participant. More precisely, it gives the corrected log-transformed likelihood for the data given the application of a certain strategy under the assumptions of a constant error rate ε, normally distributed decision times and confidence ratings, and independence between observations. Note that likelihood values (and BIC scores) result from multiplying single probabilities of each observation. Their absolute value is therefore heavily dependent on the number of observations and increases with every observation added. Likelihood scores can hence only be interpreted in relation to each other (for a discussion of the Likelihood-Ratio see Bröder, chapter 4, this volume).

The lower part of Figure 5.1 shows the output which summarizes the results of all individual comparisons. It presents the resulting BIC scores for each subject (in rows) and considered strategy (in columns; i.e. TTB, EQW, WADD, PCS, RAND). Lower values indicate a better fit. The example result of subject 9 and strategy 1 is consequently presented in row 9, column 1 of the matrix. The strategy that explains a subjects' data best can be easily determined by identifying the lowest number in the persons' row (e.g., the data of participants 9 are most likely generated by strategy 3).

Discussion

This chapter discussed how both deliberate and intuitive decision strategies can be investigated using basic behavioural measures. It was discussed how a research question is defined, strategies and differentiating types of tasks are selected and predictions for different dependent measures are derived. I recommend thoroughly going through all of these steps at the beginning of each research project and summarizing the results in a prediction table. I discussed three methods that could be used to analyze the derived predictions. Simple t-tests might be computed after applying a choice-based strategy classification (Bergert & Nosofsky, 2007; Glöckner, 2006). The method is easy to apply, but it does not take into account the whole set of predictions. Calculating correlations between observations and predictions avoids this caveat and the method has a higher statistical power. Hence it might be preferable. However, for both methods the problem arises that results from different tests on different dependent measures can contradict each other and cannot easily be integrated. The Multiple-Measure Maximum Likelihood strategy classification method circumvents this problem in that it simultaneously estimates a likelihood/BIC score taking into account all observations on the three dependent variables. It has been shown that the method produces unbiased classifications (i.e. no tendency to overestimate the usage of one or another class of strategies) and that it can differentiate between strategies even if these make the same choice predictions (Glöckner, 2009). The MM-ML method is easy to apply and it is easily extendible.[11] Besides allowing for differentiating between strategies which make similar choice predictions, the MM-ML method has three major additional advantages: a) all dependent variables are considered simultaneously and in a compensatory manner, b) strategy classification becomes more reliable because the additional variables provide convergent measures, c) inspecting the estimated parameters for choices, decision times, and confidence (Figure 5.1) provides differentiated insights into the processes and might help to improve theories or to replace parts of them that make inappropriate predictions.

Final remark

Occam's razor suggests that if two models can explain a set of data equally well, the model which is able to do so with less parameters is preferable. It has been shown that in some cases simple strategies can account equally well for data which is usually explained by more complex ones (Brandstätter, Gigerenzer, & Hertwig, 2006; Gigerenzer & Todd, 1999). However, findings have been criticized for the fact that not enough tasks were included that differentiated between the considered strategies (Glöckner & Betsch, 2008a). Deciding in favour of the more parsimonious model and arguing that this model indeed describes the underlying cognitive processes might sometimes be premature. The MM-ML method urges to think about tasks that are diagnostic on as many different dependent variables as possible and gives researchers the possibility to extend the data space before limiting thoughts to simple models only.

Dos and Don'ts

- Select a set of strategies appropriate for the research question.
- Identify types of decision tasks that differentiate between strategies.
- Derive interval-scaled predictions from all strategies concerning the dependent variables choices, decision time, and confidence. The predictions should be summarized in a prediction table.
- If a strategy does not allow deriving predictions (i.e., because it is vaguely formulated) use additional assumptions and make them explicit.
- Use a sufficient number of observations per type of decision task in the experiment.
- Determine the likelihood of individuals' data given the application of each strategy by using the MM-ML method and use the BIC score for strategy classification.
- Inspect individual level results to explore the model fit separately for the dependent variables choices, decision time and confidence.

Appendix A

Let n_j be the number of tasks of type j that are presented and let n_{jk} be the number of correct predictions of strategy k. The likelihood of observing a certain number of correct predictions n_{jk} given a constant error rate follows a binomial distribution. Hence, the likelihood of observing a set of choices given a strategy k and a constant error rate ε_k can be calculated by:

$$L_{k\,(C)} = p(n_{jk} \mid k, \varepsilon_k) = \prod_{j=1}^{J} \binom{n_j}{n_{jk}} (1 - \varepsilon_k)^{n_{jk}} \, \varepsilon_k^{(n_j - n_{jk})}. \tag{1}$$

The single free parameter ε_k can be estimated using standard statistical software packages such as STATA or, in this simple case, by:

$$\hat{\varepsilon}_k = \left[\sum_{j=1}^{J} (n_j - n_{jk}) \right] \div \left[\sum_{j=1}^{J} n_j \right] \tag{2}$$

The standard assumption is that log-transformed decision times are normally distributed (Bergert & Nosofsky, 2007, Appendix C). Under this assumption, the likelihood of observing a log-transformed decision time x given $N[\mu, \sigma]$ can be calculated by the density function of the normal distribution:

$$p(x \mid \mu, \sigma) = \frac{1}{\sqrt{2\pi\sigma^2}} e^{-\frac{(x - \mu)^2}{2\sigma^2}}, \tag{3}$$

and for a set of i independent observations $\vec{x}$ drawn from the same distribution by:

$$L_{k(T)} = p(\vec{x} \mid \mu, \sigma) = \prod_{i=1}^{I} \frac{1}{\sqrt{2\pi\sigma^2}} e^{-\frac{(x_i - \mu)^2}{2\sigma^2}}. \tag{4}$$

Under the assumption that choices and decision times are independent the likelihood of observing a set of choices and decision times given the application of a strategy k, a constant error rate for choices ε_k, and decision times that are drawn from a unique normal distribution $N[\mu, \sigma]$ is:

$$L_{k1} = L_{k(C)}L_{k(T)} = p(n_{jk}, \vec{x} \mid k, \varepsilon_k, \mu, \sigma) = \prod_{j=1}^{J} \binom{n_j}{n_{jk}} (1 - \varepsilon_k)^{n_{jk}} \, \varepsilon_k^{(n_j - n_{jk})}$$

$$\prod_{i=1}^{I} \frac{1}{\sqrt{2\pi\sigma^2}} e^{-\frac{(x_i - \mu)^2}{2\sigma^2}}. \tag{5}$$

Equation 5 should obviously only be applied for decision strategies *k1*, which predict equal decision times for all considered decisions. Let's assume that strategies $k2$ make (interval-scaled) predictions t_i which are scaled to contrast weight with $\Sigma t_i = 0$ (and equal n per category). Let's further assume that decision times for the item i are drawn from different normal distributions with means

$$\mu_i = \mu + t_i R, \tag{6}$$

in which R represents a scaling parameter. The probability for observing a set of choices and decision times drawn from different normal distributions (with equal σ)[12] can then be calculated by inserting equations 6 in equation 5:

$$L_{k2} = p(n_{jk}, \vec{x}|k, \varepsilon_k, \mu, \sigma, r) = \prod_{j=1}^{J} \binom{n_j}{n_{jk}} (1 - \varepsilon_k)^{n_{jk}} \varepsilon_k^{(n_j - n_{jk})}$$

$$\prod_{i=1}^{I} \frac{1}{\sqrt{2\pi\sigma^2}} e^{-\frac{(x_i - (\mu + t_i R))^2}{2\sigma^2}}. \tag{7}$$

Furthermore, assuming that confidence judgments are independent of choices and decision times, confidence estimation can be added to equation 7 in the same manner as decision times. From extending equation 7 and adding subscript $_T$ and $_C$ for decision time and confidence, respectively results in equation 8:

$$L_{k\,(total)} = p\,(n_{jk}, \vec{x}_T, \vec{x}_C|k, \varepsilon_k, \mu_T, \sigma_T, R_T, \mu_C, \sigma_C, R_C\,) =$$

$$\prod_{j=1}^{J} \binom{n_j}{n_{jk}} (1 - \varepsilon_k)^{n_{jk}} \varepsilon_k^{(n_j - n_{jk})} \prod_{i=1}^{I} \frac{1}{\sqrt{2\pi\sigma_T^2}} e^{-\frac{(x_{Ti} - (\mu_T + t_{Ti} R_T))^2}{2\sigma_T^2}}$$

$$\prod_{k=1}^{K} \frac{1}{\sqrt{2\pi\sigma_C^2}} e^{-\frac{(x_{Ck} - (\mu_C + t_{Ck} R_C))^2}{2\sigma_C^2}}. \tag{8}$$

The range of the scaling parameters R_T and R_C should be limited to positive numbers only to avoid advantages of a strategy due to inverse predictions.

From this likelihood value, the Bayesian Information Criterion (BIC) which takes into account the number of parameters in the model N_p and the number of observations N_{obs} that are modelled (Schwarz, 1978) is calculated by:

$$BIC_k = -2 \ln (L_{k(total)}) + \ln (N_{obs}) N_p. \tag{9}$$

The number of estimated parameters N_p is denoted in Table 5.3 (last column). The number of independent observations N_{obs} which is also used to calculate the BIC is not always equal to the number of total observations. According to STATA 10.0 Online Manual, the number of independent categories (i.e., types of tasks) should be used if it can be assumed that the instances of these categories are highly correlated. This is the case for our data. Monte Carlo simulations revealed that using the total number of observations per person (N_{obs} = 60 [tasks]* 3[choice, decision time, confidence] = 180) leads to misclassifications in favour of models with less parameters (i.e., EQW, WADD) whereas using the number of independent categories (i.e., types) (N_{obs} = 6 * 3 = 18) gives essentially unbiased results (if effect sizes are large). Because the BIC score is inversely coded, individuals should be classified as users of the strategy which has the lowest BIC value.

Appendix B

To apply the program for the MM-ML method, the data file has to be reshaped so that each observation (number of choices for a type of task not in line with the prediction of the strategy; decision time; confidence) for each participant is in a single row (see Figure 5.2). Because strategies make different predictions, for each strategy each data point is repeated as many times as strategies are compared (*strat*). The observations are coded in the variable *dv* which entails (1) the number of choices not in line with the strategy predictions for one type of items (e.g., 3, if 3 out of 10 choices are not in line with the prediction of the strategy),[13] (2) a decision time for one observation (log-transformed; if possible also corrected for order effects by using residuals after regressing on order), or (3) the confidence rating for an observation. The variable *index* codes whether it is a choice (1), decision time (2), or confidence (3) data point; the variable *total_pred* codes the total number of observations per category (for choice data points), and the contrast weight (for decision time and confidence; see Table 5.2); the variable *miss* is used for choice data points only and codes if random choices (i.e., missing) are predicted for the respective type of items (1) or not (0) (as it is often the case for an EQW strategy, see Table 5.2). The variable type codes the type of decision task (see Table 5.2).

To apply the MM-ML procedures, several estimation programs have to be defined and uploaded. The general estimation command for the full model (equation 8) with 7 parameters is:

```
program define ML_choice_time_conf
version 1.0
args lnf p mu0T sigmaT distT mu0C sigmaC distC
quietly    replace  `lnf'=ln(binomial(total_pred,    $ML_y1,   `p')-binomial(total_pred,
    $ML_y1–1,`p')) if index == 1 & miss == 0
quietly    replace  `lnf'=ln(binomial(total_pred,    $ML_y1,    0.5)-binomial(total_pred,
    $ML_y1–1, 0.5)) if index == 1 & miss == 1
```

```
quietly    replace `Inf'=ln(normalden($ML_y1, `mu0T'+abs(`distT')*    total_pred,
`sigmaT')) if index == 2
quietly    replace `Inf'=ln(normalden($ML_y1, `mu0C'+abs(`distC')*    total_pred,
`sigmaC')) if index == 3
end
```

After installing the program (e.g., by copying it into the command window), the program ML_choice_time_conf can be used as part of any ML estimation as follows:

```
ml model lf ML_choice_time_conf (epsilon: dv=) (mu_Time:) (sigma_Time:) (R_Time:)
    (mu_Conf:) (sigma_Conf:) (R_Conf:) if Participant == 1 & strat == 1
ml init 0.5 500 100 100 10 5 5, copy
ml maximize
```

"ml model" defines the model which contains the parameters listed in parentheses; *dv* is given as data variable. The "if" sub-command defines for which

	Participant	strat	index	type	total_pred	miss	dv
1	1	1	1	1	10	0	1
2	1	1	1	2	10	0	0
3	1	1	1	3	10	0	2
4	1	1	1	4	10	0	0
5	1	1	1	5	10	0	0
6	1	1	1	6	10	0	0
7	1	1	2	1	-.1666667	0	7.748332
8	1	1	2	1	-.1666667	0	7.919313
9	1	1	2	1	-.1666667	0	7.939537
10	1	1	2	1	-.1666667	0	8.149646
11	1	1	2	1	-.1666667	0	8.150661
12	1	1	2	1	-.1666667	0	8.341264
13	1	1	2	1	-.1666667	0	8.343084
14	1	1	2	1	-.1666667	0	8.350293
15	1	1	2	1	-.1666667	0	8.42072
16	1	1	2	1	-.1666667	0	8.67658
17	1	1	2	2	-.1666667	0	7.938448
18	1	1	2	2	-.1666667	0	8.227778
19	1	1	2	2	-.1666667	0	8.24798
20	1	1	2	2	-.1666667	0	8.414245
21	1	1	2	2	-.1666667	0	8.463602
22	1	1	2	2	-.1666667	0	8.478306
23	1	1	2	2	-.1666667	0	8.557699
24	1	1	2	2	-.1666667	0	8.566448
25	1	1	2	2	-.1666667	0	8.590024
26	1	1	2	2	-.1666667	0	8.62278
27	1	1	2	3	-.1666667	0	7.629199
28	1	1	2	3	-.1666667	0	7.632421
29	1	1	2	3	-.1666667	0	8.079731

Figure 5.2 Example data set coded for Multiple-Measure Maximum Likelihood strategy classification.

person and strategy the command should be executed. "ml init" defines initial values for the parameters in the order listed in the model command, and helps for quicker convergence. "ml maximize" starts the routine.

Complete syntax files (i.e., do-files) for uploading the estimation programs and carrying out a comprehensive analysis for the provided example data set can be downloaded from www.intuitive-experts.de – Resources.

Notes

1 Mathematically, this is the posterior conditional probability of the city being larger given a positive cue value $p(bigger|cue+)$. In some cases, cue validities are also provided as prior probability of a positive cue value given the city is bigger, $p(cue+|bigger)$. Note that both are usually not the same! In contrast to the former, the latter allows to calculate the normatively optimal solution for multiple cue tasks according to Bayes' theorem (under the assumption of cue independence). Hence, if a researcher is interested in comparing the quality of decisions (for instance between intuitive and deliberate strategies) I would recommend providing cue validities in the experiment as prior probabilities.

2 Note that it is always only possible to determine the cue validity with respect to a certain reference class: for instance comparing all German cities above 100,000 inhabitants. Cue validities can be very different for different reference classes. The cue state capital might for instance have a high validity for German cities, but a lower one for US cities, taking into account that some US state capitals are small administration cities.

3 A user-friendly simulation program for the example decision tasks (as well as the source code to extend it) is available at www.intuitive-experts.de – Resources.

4 This is the case, because TTB and EQW can be considered special cases of WADD with restricted weights (Bröder & Schiffer, 2003). Considering, for instance, a situation with the cue validities .86, .70, .60, and .55. In all possible cue constellations, the predictions between WADD (corrected) and TTB will be the same, because the lower cues together can never overrule the higher one. Taking a more general view, for most (if not all) sets of cue validities, there exists a validity transformation function so that WADD perfectly approximates TTB or EQW. Hence, from a very strict perspective, the choice-based classification for the simple strategies never rules out that individuals used the more complex WADD strategy.

5 The fixed parameters were: decay = .10, all positive cue-value links (+): .01, all negative cue-value links (–): –.01, link between option1 and option2: –.20, stability criterion 10 iterations without energy change of more than 10^{-6}. Cue-validity links were generated from the given cue-validities by $w = ((v - .50)*2)^2$ resulting in link weights of .36, .16, .04, .01 for the cues 1 to 4. Iterations to find a stable solution are used to predict decision time, the absolute difference between the activation of the options was used as confidence prediction. Both were rescaled to contrast weights. Due to a copy error PCS time predictions in Table 5.2 slightly differ from the ones used in the simulations reported in Glöckner (2009). The predictions reported here are the correct ones.

6 To transform a set of predictions (e.g., 1, 1, 1, 1, 1, 3) into contrast weights with a range of 1, the range of all values (e.g., range = 2) and the mean value (M = 8/6) are calculated and then the mean is subtracted from each single value and the result is divided by the range. In our example this would lead to contrast weights of: –0.167, –0.167, –0.167, –0.167, –0.167, 0.833 (which is the TTB prediction for decision times).

7 Because of the small sample (n < 30), violations of normality and variance homogeneity should be tested and corrected for, if indicated.

8 It is commonly assumed that this assumption holds for (log-transformed) decision times (Bergert & Nosofsky, 2007), and it should hold for the distribution of confidence ratings as well (which is usually less skewed).

9 A general independence assumption might of course be criticized. If one has a sound hypothesis concerning dependencies, STATA provides possibilities to correct for dependencies in observations (i.e., command "cluster") and parameters (i.e., specified in the ML model). Note, however, that inter-correlations that are caused by systematic differences between types of decision tasks (i.e., task difficulty) are already taken into account by the inclusion of the contrast weights t in the estimation.

10 The sample data set and the complete syntax are provided at www.intuitive-experts.de (Resources). General explanations and parts of the syntax can be found in Appendix B. An implementation of the MM-ML method for the open-source statistical package *R* is provided online as well.

11 Adding further dependent measures in the same estimation (e.g., information search parameters) is straightforward by including additional parameters and/or the estimation function in the estimation program. MM-ML, of course, also allows model fitting in the sense of fitting model specific parameters (e.g., Bergert & Nosofsky, 2007; Rieskamp, in press). Furthermore, correcting for clusters in the data or for dependencies between parameters (e.g., heteroscedasticity) is also easily achieved using standard options provided by the ml procedure of STATA (Gould et al., 2006).

12 Alternatively, it could be assumed that σ differs between item types and increases with increasing t_i (cf. heteroscedasticity). Although this relation can also be easily modeled in STATA ML calculations, for simplicity a constant σ should be assumed here.

13 Note that the model does not converge if a strategy is perfectly applied (e = 0). The problem can be pragmatically solved by adding one error choice to perfect strategy applicants. I prefer using "1.1" to be able to identify replaced data.

References

Bergert, F. B., & Nosofsky, R. M. (2007). A response-time approach to comparing generalized rational and take-the-best models of decision making. *Journal of Experimental Psychology: Learning, Memory, and Cognition, 33*(1), 107–129.

Brandstätter, E., Gigerenzer, G., & Hertwig, R. (2006). The priority heuristic: Making choices without trade-offs. *Psychological Review, 113*(2), 409–432.

Bröder, A., & Schiffer, S. (2003). Bayesian strategy assessment in multi-attribute decision making. *Journal of Behavioral Decision Making, 16*(3), 193–213.

Brunswik, E. (1955). Representative design and the probability theory in a functional psychology. *Psychological Review, 62*, 193–217.

Busemeyer, J. R., & Johnson, J. G. (2004). Computational models of decision making. In D. J. Koehler & N. Harvey (Eds.), *Blackwell handbook of judgment and decision making* (pp. 133–154). Malden, MA: Blackwell Publishing.

Busemeyer, J. R., & Townsend, J. T. (1993). Decision field theory: A dynamic-cognitive approach to decision making in an uncertain environment. *Psychological Review, 100*(3), 432–459.

Dougherty, M. R. P., Gettys, C. F., & Ogden, E. E. (1999). MINERVA-DM: A memory processes model for judgments of likelihood. *Psychological Review, 106*(1), 180–209.

Faul, F., Erdfelder, E., Lang, A.-G., & Buchner, A. (2007). G*Power 3: A flexible statistical power analysis program for the social, behavioral, and biomedical sciences. *Behavior Research Methods, 39*(2), 175–191.

Finucane, M. L., Alhakami, A., Slovic, P., & Johnson, S. M. (2000). The affect heuristic in judgments of risks and benefits. *Journal of Behavioral Decision Making, 13*(1), 1–17.

Gigerenzer, G., & Goldstein, D. G. (1996). Reasoning the fast and frugal way: Models of bounded rationality. *Psychological Review, 103*(4), 650–669.

Gigerenzer, G., Hoffrage, U., & Kleinbölting, H. (1991). Probabilistic mental models: A Brunswikian theory of confidence. *Psychological Review, 98*(4), 506–528.

Gigerenzer, G., & Todd, P. M. (1999). *Simple heuristics that make us smart. Evolution and cognition.* New York, NY: Oxford University Press.

Glass, G. V., & Hopkins, K. D. (1996). *Statistical methods in education and psychology* (3rd ed.). Boston, MA: Allyn & Bacon.

Glöckner, A. (2006). *Automatische Prozesse bei Entscheidungen [Automatic processes in decision making].* Hamburg, Germany: Kovac.

Glöckner, A. (2008a). Does intuition beat fast and frugal heuristics? A systematic empirical analysis. In H. Plessner, C. Betsch & T. Betsch (Eds.), *Intuition in judgment and decision making* (pp. 309–325). Mahwah, NJ: Lawrence Erlbaum.

Glöckner, A. (2008b). How evolution outwits bounded rationality: The efficient interaction of automatic and deliberate processes in decision making and implications for institutions. In C. Engel & W. Singer (Eds.), *Better than conscious? Decision making, the human mind, and implications for institutions* (pp. 259–284). Cambridge, MA: MIT Press.

Glöckner, A. (2009). Investigating intuitive and deliberate processes statistically: The Multiple-Measure Maximum Likelihood strategy classification method. *Judgment and Decision Making, 4*(3), 186–199.

Glöckner, A., & Betsch, T. (2008a). Do people make decisions under risk based on ignorance? An empirical test of the Priority Heuristic against Cumulative Prospect Theory. *Organizational Behavior and Human Decision Processes, 107*(1), 75–95.

Glöckner, A., & Betsch, T. (2008b). Modeling option and strategy choices with connectionist networks: Towards an integrative model of automatic and deliberate decision making. *Judgment and Decision Making, 3*(3), 215–228.

Glöckner, A., & Betsch, T. (2008c). Multiple-reason decision making based on automatic processing. *Journal of Experimental Psychology: Learning, Memory, and Cognition, 34*(5), 1055–1075.

Glöckner, A., Betsch, T., & Schindler, N. (in press). Coherence shifts in probabilistic inference tasks. *Journal of Behavioral Decision Making.*

Glöckner, A., & Herbold, A.-K. (in press). An eye-tracking study on information processing in risky decisions: Evidence for compensatory strategies based on automatic processes. *Journal of Behavioral Decision Making.*

Gould, W., Pitblado, J., & Sribney, W. (2006). *Maximum Likelihood Estimation with STATA* (3rd ed.). College Station, TX: Stata Press.

Holyoak, K. J., & Simon, D. (1999). Bidirectional reasoning in decision making by constraint satisfaction. *Journal of Experimental Psychology: General, 128*(1), 3–31.

Jeckel, M., Nicklisch, A., & Glöckner, A. (under review). Implementation of the Multiple-Measure Maximum Likelihood strategy classification method in R: addendum to Glöckner (2009) and practical guide for application.

Juslin, P., & Persson, M. (2002). PROBabilities from EXemplars (PROBEX): A "lazy" algorithm for probabilistic inference from generic knowledge. *Cognitive Science: A Multidisciplinary Journal, 26*(5), 563–607.

Lohse, G. L., & Johnson, E. J. (1996). A comparison of two process tracing methods for choice tasks. *Organizational Behavior and Human Decision Processes, 68*(1), 28–43.

McClelland, J. L., & Rumelhart, D. E. (1981). An interactive activation model of context effects in letter perception: I. An account of basic findings. *Psychological Review, 88*(5), 375–407.

Payne, J. W., Bettman, J. R., & Johnson, E. J. (1988). Adaptive strategy selection in decision making. *Journal of Experimental Psychology: Learning, Memory, and Cognition, 14*(3), 534–552.

Rieskamp, J. (in press). Probabilistic nature of preferential choice. *Journal of Experimental Psychology: Learning, Memory, and Cognition.*

Schwarz, G. (1978). Estimating the dimension of a model. *The Annals of Statistics, 6*(2), 461–464.

Simon, D., Krawczyk, D. C., & Holyoak, K. J. (2004). Construction of preferences by constraint satisfaction. *Psychological Science, 15*(5), 331–336.

Thagard, P. (1989). Explanatory coherence. *Behavioral and Brain Sciences, 12*(3), 435–502.

6 Studying experts' intuitive decision making online using video stimuli

Geoffrey Schweizer, Henning Plessner and Ralf Brand

Introduction

Imagine you are a soccer referee. Every weekend you are standing on the pitch and you are required to make hundreds of decisions within split seconds. Such decisions are made intuitively: instantly integrating many cues. Each of these decisions is not only observed and commented upon by tens of thousands of soccer fans, each one of your decisions may also influence the outcome of the game. Therefore, your decisions are partly responsible for the economic well-being of the competing clubs and one false decision can easily result in an undeserved loss of millions of Euros for the losing club. Additionally, fans, club officials and the media are going to criticize you rudely after most of your matches. Quite naturally, soccer referees as well as soccer clubs share an interest in training and improving referees' decision making. One newly developed decision-making training device for soccer referees is the online training program SET[1] (Brand, Schweizer, & Plessner, 2009; Plessner, Schweizer, Brand, & O'Hare, 2009). Referees are shown several short video sequences displaying critical incidents taken from real soccer matches and are asked to make a decision (e.g., foul or no foul) for each sequence. After indicating their decision, referees obtain feedback on the correctness of their decision.[2]

Recently, there has been growing interest in investigating and understanding intuitive decision making (Glöckner & Witteman, chapter 1, this volume). While numerous books have covered theoretical aspects of intuition (e.g., Hogarth, 2001; Myers, 2002; Plessner, Betsch, & Betsch, 2008; Wilson, 2002), this volume aims at presenting methods of intuition research. One of these methods is the SET program. SET constitutes an online video feedback device not only for training, but also for investigating experts' decision making. Experts and professional decision makers such as clinicians, managers or pilots seem to base a substantial part of their decisions on intuitive processing (Klein, 1999). Indeed, several definitions of intuition directly or indirectly highlight the role of prior experience in acquiring expert intuition (e.g., Betsch, 2008; see also Glöckner & Witteman, chapter 1, this volume). Intuitive processes are generally assumed to require a knowledge base in long term memory. It has been argued that this knowledge base can be represented as a connectionist network and intuitions can be thought of as the result of activation spreading between the nodes of the network (Glöckner & Betsch, 2008a). The knowledge base is acquired rather slowly, via associative learning processes or dedicated practice. It takes time for good intuitions to develop, or, in other words, appropriate mental representations that are necessary for good intuitions need to be learned (Hogarth, 2001, 2008). Experts, who by definition have had long training, are supposed to be better at solving a task intuitively than novices, who have not had the opportunity to develop the knowledge base necessary for intuitive decision making (Klein, 1999; Plessner & Czenna, 2008). Interestingly, there is also some research showing that people who know more in a particular domain actually perform worse in certain tasks than people who know less (e.g., the so called less-is-more effect; Goldstein & Gigerenzer, 2002). For example, when researchers asked a sample of American students and a sample of German students whether San Antonio or San Diego had more inhabitants, the surprising result was that more Germans than Americans guessed the correct answer (Goldstein & Gigerenzer, 2002). We think that the major difference between these two positions on the benefits of prior knowledge lies in how experts are defined. Experts in studies on the less-is-more effect have substantial knowledge regarding the content of their task, but they have hardly performed the task itself before. Americans certainly know more about both San Diego and San Antonio than Germans, but probably they have only limited experiences (if at all) in actually comparing these cities with regard to their populations. We define experts as people who are familiar with the task and have performed it many times (and years) before (cf. Ericsson, 1996). For example, soccer referees have spent considerable amounts of time judging whether an incident was foul or not, before they are asked to do so in a SET study. Although they have not used SET before, they have already performed the basic task several times.

Intuition research may particularly benefit from studies using expert participants, who decide by using their intuition. Despite this fact, so far only a minority of studies on intuition is conducted with experts (e.g., Klein, 1999; Witteman & van Geenen, chapter 3, this volume). An obvious reason for this is that research on expertise challenges scientists in several ways. First, it is usually difficult to persuade experts in a certain domain (e.g., refereeing, medicine) to come to the university's psychological lab. Sometimes they live all over the country, which would entail high travel costs. In addition, the number of experts in a certain domain can be quite limited. Thus, conducting traditional experiments with expert participants is at best difficult and takes lots of time, and at worst is simply impossible. A second challenge refers to the materials to be used in the study. To be able to optimally benefit from experts' knowledge, researchers need to use naturalistic stimulus materials (Salas & Klein, 2001). For example, when investigating soccer referees' decision making in foul situations one would prefer presenting a video of the incident to the participants over asking them to read a verbal description of the situation. This, again, challenges researchers in several ways. They need to obtain or produce a sample of fairly realistic videos, then select the most appropriate ones based on criteria established beforehand and finally have a method available to present the videos to their expert participants. Furthermore, researchers will not only want to present the videos, but to group items according to certain criteria (such as difficulty or type of foul), experimentally manipulate conditions, and record data. The SET training and research tool was developed to meet exactly these demands.

So far, SET has mainly been used for conducting research in the domain of soccer referees' decision making. We will therefore use referees' decision making as our example application. Nevertheless, we regard our approach as appropriate and exemplary for investigating experts' decision making in many fields of interest. With the use of corresponding stimulus material, SET can be easily converted for conducting research in many other areas of expert decision making.

Conceptual introduction of the method

The decision-making situation of expert soccer referees has some character-istics in common with those of experts in other domains. Referees act in environments marked by high stakes, time pressure, uncertainty and imperfect access to relevant information (Helsen & Bultynck, 2004; Mascarenhas, O'Hare, & Plessner, 2006). In addition, referees' environments often provide invalid and imperfect feedback about the quality of their decisions, which constitutes a further characteristic common to experts in other domains. Similar types of professional decision making under uncertainty and in wicked learning environments (that is: not providing proper feedback; cf. Hogarth, 2001, 2008) have been investigated for example by researchers using the naturalistic decision-making paradigm (NDM; Klein, 1999; Salas & Klein, 2001). One basic assumption of NDM states that traditional laboratory research cannot investigate experts' decision making to a fully satisfactory degree, as laboratory environments are too artificial to trigger processes that are representative of experts' decision making in real situations. Glöckner and Betsch (2008b) have followed a similar line of reasoning in discussing the commonly used Mouselab program (Payne, Bettman, & Johnson, 1988). They argued that Mouselab, although generally an extremely useful and advantageous tool, may in some situations trigger deliberate instead of intui-tive processing in participants because of the way it presents information, which might impose limitations on participants' information search behaviour (but see also Norman & Schulte-Mecklenbeck, chapter 2, this vol-ume). Although a more naturalistic presentation of stimulus material will not fully circumvent these problems, at least it may reduce some critical effects of unfamiliar tasks on participants' decision-making processes. At the same time, researchers using naturalistic stimulus materials need to be able to perform experimental manipulations in their studies to allow them to draw causal conclusions. The construction of the SET training and research tool aimed at combining these two requirements: Usage of naturalistic stimulus materials in experimental designs.

When we started creating SET, we first took a close look at referees' decision making in contact situations, i.e. situations when a referee has to judge whether a contact between two or more players was legal or foul (see also Brand, Schweizer, & Plessner, 2009; Plessner, Schweizer, Brand, & O'Hare, 2009). We conceptualize the referees' task in these situations as a perceptual categorization task (Plessner & Haar, 2006), as they have to categorize the incident that they have observed as foul or no foul. Importantly, this categorization is based mainly on the referee's perception of the incident, not on its recall from memory or on its verbal description, as in other decision-making situations (e.g., witnesses in court remembering a crime). If their decision is foul, referees additionally need to decide on an appropriate sanction (free kick, yellow card, red card). This task is extremely demanding. To make a decision in a very short time, referees need to integrate multiple cues in a complex, dynamic and probabilistic environment. In our opinion, referees' decision making can best be understood within Brunswik's Lens Model framework (Brunswik, 1952; see Figure 6.1). This framework describes how judges make decisions based on multiple cues that have a probabilistic relationship with a criterion (Doherty & Kurz, 1996; Goldstein, 2004). The main assumption is that in order to make good decisions, judges or decision makers need to have implicit or explicit knowledge about the ecological structure of the situation. That means that they need to know which cues are

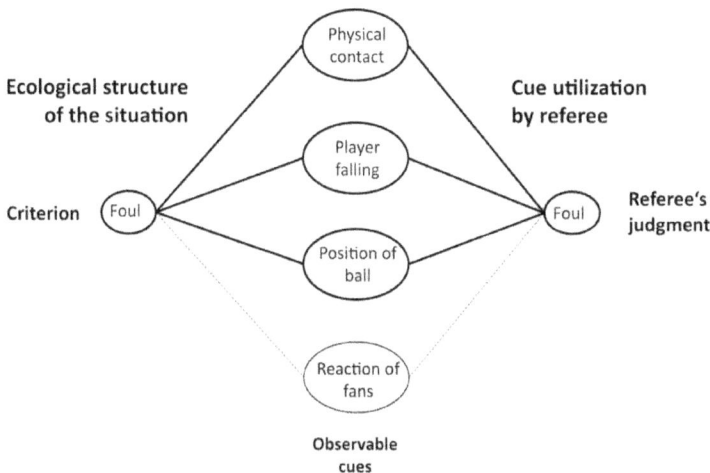

Figure 6.1 Depiction of a Brunswikian Lens for a foul situation in soccer: based on his good knowledge about which cues to use in this situation, the referee makes a correct judgment.

predictive of the criterion, and they need to make their decisions based on these cues. Imagine the following incident: A defending player collides with an attacking player and as a result the attacking player falls to the ground. Importantly, the attacking player had already passed the ball shortly before the defender tackled him. In this case, the referee has to make up his mind within a split second and call foul, a decision that can only be based on all of the above mentioned factors (if the defending player had played the ball, for example, it would not have been foul play).

One of the most characteristic features of referees' decision making is that referees have to decide extremely fast, while multiple cues need to be taken into account for a correct decision. This requires an intuitive decision: the simultaneous and very fast processing of multiple stimuli (cf. Betsch, 2008; Glöckner & Betsch, 2008b). The assumption that referees' decisions are made intuitively is further supported by the fact that expert referees frequently report that they are based on a *feeling* rather than on deliberate and analytical reasoning (e.g., Betsch, 2008; see also Dickert, chapter 10, this volume).

Robin Hogarth (2001, 2008) has extensively dealt with the question of how humans acquire intuitive abilities and what factors determine their respective quality. He emphasizes the role of feedback that is provided by certain environments. Feedback from kind environments leads to good intuitions, whereas feedback from wicked environments leads to bad intuitions. Environments are kind when they provide speedy, accurate and relevant feedback, and wicked when they provide delayed, invalid or biased feedback. Importantly, intuitions are acquired in a domain specific manner, which is why learning environments need to be representative for subsequent decision-making situations. Consequently, a training and research tool which is based on our previous considerations must allow the variation of feedback concerning decisions on incidents which are as close to real world decision situations as possible.

Application: detailed description of a video-based online research tool

In this section, we describe the structure and features of the SET tool and how these can be applied to designing and conducting online experiments with expert participants. We describe SET as exemplary tool on how video-based online research with experts can be successfully conducted and planned, so that interested scholars are provided with guidelines for how to create their own research tools. Furthermore, we give explicit advice on how to proceed when creating your own video-based online tool. Many issues addressed in the literature on online research in general apply to the SET paradigm as well, such as drop out rates, validity of results or mode effects (i.e., results obtained online differ from results obtained offline). Readers who are interested more generally in online research are referred to articles by Reips (2002), Birnbaum (2004) or Gosling, Vazire, Srivastava and John (2004).

SET is an easy to access and operate online tool, that consists of a database for storing video items, an online administration section for arranging experimental as well as training sessions and an online front end where experts participate in training as well as research. Therefore, researchers using SET do not have to visit their expert participants all across the country any more, but may instead send them an invitation to participate in an online study. Furthermore, SET is particularly designed for using naturalistic stimulus materials.

When a soccer referee takes part in the SET training program, attending a training session will usually start with the referee receiving an email by training operators which reminds him of the session. In the course of the day, the referee will log in to a website with his username and password and start his training session. A session typically starts with some pages of instructions and continues with the actual training routine. Referees indicate a decision (e.g., foul or no foul) for each of several short video sequences. Next, referees obtain feedback on the correctness of their decision. Usually, feedback is restricted to indicating right or wrong and does not elaborate on the reasons for the decision. Additionally, referees may be asked to provide further responses (e.g., decision certainty) or to answer open questions. All of the participants' responses and response times are stored in an online database for further analyses. Besides taking part in training sessions referees are asked to participate in experimental studies via the online system. For that purpose, additional participants who usually do not use the training system can be invited by simply sending them an email with username and password and a link to the online system. If further data are needed for study purposes (e.g. from a personality inventory), SET sessions can easily be complemented with a link to an established online research tool such as Globalpark or Unipark (Globalpark AG, Cologne, Germany).

SET's three basic elements (online database, online administration section and front end) are operable via a graphical user interface with text boxes, drop down lists, buttons, check boxes etc. Therefore, no programming skills are necessary for conducting research. The online database is hosted on a standard server, administration section and front end may be accessed via the internet from everywhere in the world.

Database. The database is the heart of a video-based research tool. The SET database contains some hundred video items. In order to ensure that videos are representative of referees' real-world decision making and therefore suitable for research as well as training purposes, they are carefully selected in cooperation with expert referees. Most videos are copied from television recordings. After recording, they are cut and slightly edited (e.g., score as displayed on television is masked). Of course, these videos are not perfectly naturalistic, since they show a perspective different from real-world refereeing. To achieve perfectly natural videos, one would need to record situations with head-mounted cameras worn by referees during soccer matches. However, one often has to work with the videos that are available when additional recordings are not feasible (e.g., expert referees are not allowed to wear helmet cameras in premier league matches). For our purposes it was important that videos included cues that are present in real-life decisions as well, even if it was from a perspective that does not perfectly match the perspective of a referee on the pitch.

In the database, additional information can be stored with each video item. This is very useful when you want to select video items for an experimental condition according to certain criteria. For example, in our database correct decisions for each item (e.g., foul or no foul), sanction (e.g., yellow or red card), category of foul play (e.g., kicking or pushing), origin of the video, difficulty level and other relevant information is stored. So, when you want to conduct an experiment on referees' ability to judge kicking in soccer matches from the German Bundesliga, you can select the appropriate video items via drop down lists. It is generally useful to keep all features of the database as flexible as possible, as this allows adapting to new demands and needs without consulting an IT expert every time. For example, we could change the category name "origin of video item" into "jersey colour of teams" if this seemed useful at some future point in time.

Video items are stored in the .flv format as this allows presenting them via Adobe Flash player (see below). Obviously, the quality of video items is an important issue. Unfortunately, here you have to trade-off quality against size of the file. The better the video, the larger the file. But when files become too large, playing them via the internet becomes problematic, as videos will need more time to load and will eventually stagnate from time to time. A general advice cannot be given; every researcher needs to try out how much quality she is willing to trade for speed.

Online administration section. In this section, training as well as experimental sessions are arranged. Participants' names, user names and passwords are stored here. Each participant gets a unique ID. For experimental purposes, when users do not participate in the program repeatedly, it is useful to have a number of dummy usernames that can be used repeatedly. The section also contains a grouping function, so that users can be assigned to different groups (e.g., immediate feedback group and delayed feedback group; training or experimental session). SET sessions are built up in the session section. The smallest and basic element of a session is a page. A SET session always consists of several pages. Pages serve different functions, for example text pages, video pages, decision pages, and feedback pages. These elements can be combined flexibly by researchers to serve different study goals. Researchers are provided with an overview of all existing pages. They arrange their SET session by simply selecting a page from the overview window and clicking on a symbol that moves the page to the session window. Afterwards the whole session is displayed in the session window and the sequence of pages may be altered. For example, when researchers want participants to read an instruction, then watch a video item, then make their decision and receive feedback, they simply select the appropriate pages and move them to the session window (see Figure 6.2).

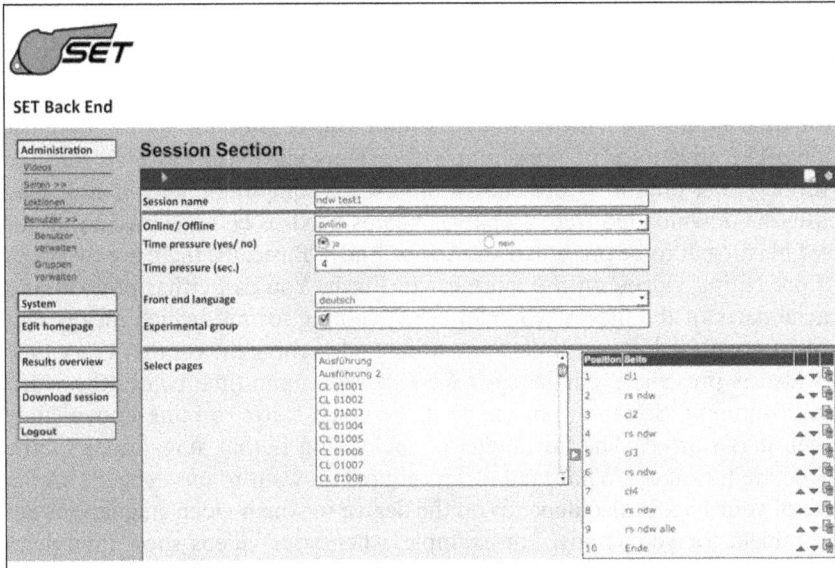

Figure 6.2 Screenshot of SET back end (session section).

Importantly, pages are not fixed, but can be created and altered by researchers. All texts for text pages can be written by experimenters and then saved for future use. Videos for video pages are taken from the database. Decision pages provide decision options for participants. After a session is completed it is saved for future use. When one wants to make minor changes to sessions (e.g., provide feedback with a different wording), one does not need to change all sessions. Instead, one simply changes the feedback page which was used in the sessions, and modifications are automatically transferred to all the sessions that use the page. The most important feature within the SET tool is the possibility of providing different kinds of feedback, as feedback plays a crucial role when training or investigating intuitive decision making. To provide feedback to referees' decisions, one needs to know which decision is correct. Again, to ensure validity for referees' real world decisions, we cooperated with experts from the German Soccer Association to obtain this information. Researchers can select delay of feedback (immediate vs. delayed), feedback content (e.g., outcome feedback vs. feedback containing additional information) or feedback presentation (e.g., single feedback for the latest decision only vs. feedback for several decisions at the same time). Of course, feedback texts can be altered. These options can for example be used to create feedback environments with varying degrees of kindness to test some of Hogarth's assumptions on the learning of intuitions (Hogarth, 2008). Participants can also be put under time pressure while making their decisions. Time pressure is indicated to participants by a shrinking timeline and may be manipulated between as well as within participants.

Front end for participation. The front end of an online research tool is the part of the device accessible to participants (see Figure 6.3). The SET front end is based on Adobe Flash, so you need an Adobe Flash plug-in to access and to use it. Flash is commonly used for presenting videos on web pages (i.e., YouTube or Google Video), and Flash can also be used for showing animations. The advantage of presenting video items via Flash Player is that the Adobe Flash plug-in is present on almost all computers, and, if not, may easily be downloaded free of charge. Videos need to be converted to .flv or .swf file format to be presented via Adobe Flash. Basically, there are two ways of presenting videos on the internet via Flash. You can either preload and cache parts of the files or you can use streaming format, which means that videos are played in real-time. Preloading and caching means that every time a video is presented, participants have to wait some time before the video starts running. Streaming means that the video starts running immediately when it is started. The advantage of preloading is that stagnations of the video are less likely. What kind of procedure you want to use depends on the size of your files. It also depends on the degree to which video stagnations are a problem for your study. For example, when your videos show interviews physicians had with patients, a short stop of video presentation is not supposed to severely affect your participants' decision-making process. On the other hand, when your participants are supposed to judge foul play in dynamic situations a stagnation of the video at the wrong time can render

Figure 6.3 Screenshot of SET front end (video item showing potential foul situation).

decision making impossible. Probably, stagnations of videos will become less and less problematic in the near future as the internet is becoming faster and technology is developing rapidly.

Storing your participants' data. Obviously, you want to store your participants' data. When implementing the storing feature into your online research tool, you first need to make up your mind on which data to store. The answer to this question depends on your research domain and methodical issues as well. When using SET, we always store participants' IDs, date of participation, the group a participant belongs to and the session the participant was engaged in. Of course, we don't have to enter any data manually; instead, they are automatically stored when a participant engages in an online session. For each video item presented, we store the item's unique ID, the correct decision(s) to be made and the decision(s) the participant actually made. Based on an online comparison between these variables, we also store whether the participant made a correct decision or not. Furthermore, we store decision times and answers to additional questions. It is useful to store the raw data (i.e., the participant's decision) as well as some data on an aggregate level (i.e., the correctness of the decision). The latter facilitate fast data analyses, while the former allow for having a more detailed look at your data. For example, after the aggregate data told us how many mistakes a referee made, we might want to know if particular decisions were especially problematic for him or if he made particular mistakes more often than others (i.e., two referees might have the same number of mistakes, but one of them frequently called no foul instead of foul while the other one called foul instead of no foul). For these reasons, one should always store the raw data, too. Data are stored in an excel file which may be downloaded and then processed with all common programs for data analysis. It is also useful to allow the possibility of having a look at your data online without having to download them first, for example, when you want to know how many people already participated in your study.

We would like to finish this section with some practical advice and some caveats. Generally, when conducting experiments online, you will have to extensively check your online tool. Participate in your experiments several times yourself. Test it with several browsers and from several computers. If you suspect that there might be a problem with a certain browser, ask your participants to download one of which you are sure that your experiment will run with. Be aware of your computer's and your browser's settings. Might different settings influence your experiment? If yes, give advice to your participants on which settings to use. When presenting video items you need to know what kind of internet connection is required for the videos to run optimally. Also, you should advise participants to shut all other applications while participating in your study, as presenting videos requires lots of working memory. Additionally, make sure that participants' computers do not start auto updates or virus scans during participation. It can also be useful to store the overall time a participant spent for your study. When it exceeds a certain time limit, you know that your participant had some break during participation, perhaps because the phone rang or it was lunch time.

It is not sufficient to make sure your online tool is working correctly at the beginning of your study. It is a compelling idea that something which has worked on the internet today will also work tomorrow. Unfortunately, this idea is wrong. So, when conducting experiments online, start your day with a brief check of your online tool. Most importantly, make sure that your participants' data are actually stored. Download and save your data every day. If you consider this advice overcautious, you will be correct for standard experiments with students or passers-by as participants. But research with experts is different. Proceeding as described above is going to take you some time, but it is also going to save you from disasters. When you lose data from a study with non-expert participants, it is annoying. When you lose your experts' data, it is a disaster. Sometimes, you cannot just conduct the study another time. Keep in mind that experts are difficult to engage as participants and that there are not many of them. Losing your sample's data can mean losing the entire population, for example when working with Premier League referees. Even if you do not lose the whole sample but if only some of your participants had problems with the internet, it can easily mean that you do not have enough participants left for statistical analyses with sufficient power. And, oftentimes, you will not be given the opportunity to re-sample some more experts.

When conducting research with expert participants it is extremely helpful to have a project partner outside the university who supplies you not only with participants, but also with the knowledge necessary for doing research with naturalistic material. In our own research project, we cooperate with the German Soccer Association's referee board. The board's members provide us with access to participants and tell us what decisions are correct in which situations, which video items can be used and many more useful things. Again, this is different from classic psychological research: When working with experts, you will have to admit that these people have superior knowledge in their respective domain – this is why you want to work with them. At the same time, experts may be quite suspicious towards your strange psychological ideas, especially when you are talking about intuition. Therefore, you should carefully prepare your first contacts with project partners and participants. It is going to depend on their first impressions of you and your work how much they are going to support you and how conscientiously they are going to participate in your studies.

Application of video-based online research to intuitive decision-making

In the section above we described in detail how to proceed when creating a video-based online research tool. In this section, we are going to describe how to apply a tool like SET to different research questions. Again, we are going to refer to the domain of refereeing, but the principles hold for other domains as well. When creating a tool like SET, it is important that one already has the research questions in mind that the tool is supposed to be applied to. As described above, SET provides several features that allow for experimental manipulations between or within groups of participants. For example, when one wants to investigate the importance of feedback for intuitive learning, one needs the feature of providing participants with feedback. This is exactly what we did in one of our first studies (Schweizer, Brand, Plessner, & Kahlert, 2009). We wanted to find out if intuitive decisions are learned better by providing immediate feedback than by delayed feedback. We hypothesized that in the case of referee decisions, immediate feedback constitutes a kinder environment than delayed feedback (Hogarth, 2008). Therefore, we invited a group of soccer experts to participate in our study. They were assigned to three different training groups within the SET tool. All groups had to watch videos and decide intuitively what calls to make (e.g., foul or not, yellow card or red card). They received different kinds of feedback on their decisions. One group received immediate feedback, the second one delayed feedback and the third one no feedback at all. We hypothesized that decisions in the first group would improve after three weeks of regular training, while decisions in the other two groups would not. This is exactly what we found when we compared the number of referees' correct decisions pre and post training. But data gathered in a study like the one described above can provide much more insight into intuitive decisions and learning processes. One could additionally investigate learning rates over the course of the training program, as some research suggests that learning multiple cues is slow and takes time. This would show how many learning trials are minimally needed to achieve learning effects. Furthermore, one could investigate if learning is fostered or hindered by different characteristics of the learning material. For example, do referees learn more from difficult or from easy incidents? The way data are stored in the SET program also allows for variations of data analysis. For example, one could examine data by using measures from Signal Detection Theory (Stanislaw & Todorov, 1999). These measures can help to distinguish if referees' improvements are due to an actually improved ability to discriminate between foul and no foul incidents or to a reduction of a bias to generally prefer one kind of decision over the other (Swets, Dawes, & Monahan, 2000). All you need for this kind of analysis is to know what kind of mistake a referee made: Did he call foul although the incident was actually legal or vice versa? So, not only do scholars need to have their research questions in mind before creating a tool like SET, they also need to consider questions of data analysis beforehand.

Further research designs could address the role of base rates for intuitive decisions (by providing different groups with different base-rates of foul or no-foul scenes), the role of instructions for decisional quality (by providing different groups with different instructions) or influences of video characteristics on decisions (by providing different groups with different kinds of videos), just to name a few. All these issues may be addressed using a video-based online tool that provides the features necessary for the above mentioned manipulations and data recordings.

Discussion

Just as all other methods reported in this book, studying experts' intuitive decision making video-based and online has its advantages and disadvantages. Advantages are obvious and have for the most part already been outlined. Research on intuition benefits from research on expertise. Successfully conducting research on expertise in turn requires two things. First, you need expert participants, and second, you need naturalistic stimulus materials. The first of these conditions can be met with an online tool and the second with the employment of video items (at least in certain domains). Therefore, video-based online studies should prove to be of great help for research on experts' intuitions.

Apart from these advantages, video-based online research also has some disadvantages. First, it takes a lot of effort to create a research tool like the one described above. SET is quite sophisticated, and without the help of experts in information technologies it is hardly possible to produce a tool like SET. Nevertheless, even when you do not have the opportunity to create your own online research tool, you do not have to refrain from online video research. If you want to conduct single studies with experts, you can make use of an already established research tool like Globalpark or Unipark. These tools can play video items online and provide many other useful features (various question types, scales and response options; filter processes and plausibility checks). Alternatively, you can contact researchers who already use an appropriate tool and ask for their cooperation. The guidelines provided in this chapter will still be useful when you do not create your own tool but instead use an already established one like Globalpark, for example when preparing your videos or deciding on which data to store. The efforts necessary to create your own video-based online research tool are particularly worthwhile when you plan a new research project which is supposed to last some time and which is going to require numerous studies over the course of the project. It does not make sense to create a tool like SET for single use. Therefore, a tool like SET should be designed for long term use, and it should be designed flexibly enough to be adapted to changing demands over your project's course. Thus, when you know that you are going to conduct numerous investigations over a longer period of time, you should strongly consider creating your own research tool as in this case your efforts and investments will definitely pay off.

The main disadvantage of investigating intuition online and video-based is the serious lack of experimental control inherent in this kind of research as compared to laboratory research (Reips, 2002). When conducting experiments online, you do not have any control over your participants' activities, nor do you know what factors are at work besides the ones implied in your experimental design. These shortcomings can hardly be resolved, so that online research will always lack internal validity compared to lab research. However, there are some things you can attempt to do to reduce the problem. Generally, it is quite easy to commit experts to your projects' goals after they have been convinced that your research is meaningful. Our referee participants, for example, hope that our research will one day lead to a better understanding of their work and furthermore to better training methods. Therefore, they can be convinced to carefully follow instructions for participation in an online session (e.g., not to interrupt the session).

A more serious threat to your experiments' results is perhaps caused by the reliance on naturalistic stimuli (i.e., video items). Although necessary when working with experts in many fields, as already mentioned above, naturalistic videos frequently cannot be created or manipulated experimentally. However, experimental manipulations of your stimulus material are generally desirable to ensure internal validity. They are in particular required for some research questions, such as studies on cue utilizations (e.g., on which cues do experts base their decisions?) or strategy capturing (e.g., what sort of decisional strategies do experts use?). One possibility to cope with this shortcoming is extensive coding and categorizing of your video items. For example, you could have experts code the cues present in the videos. Unfortunately, substantial research suggests that even experts have only limited insight into the reasons for their decisions (cf. Wilson, 2002). Therefore, coding and categorizing cannot fully substitute experimental manipulations. Nevertheless, with the SET tool we combined the benefits of naturalistic stimulus material with the merits of experimental research.

Video-based research can be combined with many other methods of intuition research as described in this volume. For example, one may use different instructions to induce intuitive or deliberate processing (Horstmann, Hausmann, & Ryf, chapter 12, this volume), one may assess participants' physiological parameters during the study (Hochman, Glöckner, & Yechiam, chapter 8, this volume) or one may ask experts to verbalize their thoughts aloud (Witteman & van Geenen, chapter 3, this volume).

Our research in the field of soccer refereeing demonstrates that a tool like SET can be applied fruitfully to conducting studies with experts (Schweizer et al., 2009). Therefore, we are currently starting to apply SET to other domains of sports decision making (e.g., refereeing in basketball, judging gymnastics). Based on our previous experience, we strongly encourage other scholars to engage in video-based online research with experts. It may at first be laborious and demanding, but it will pay off over the course of a research project. Most importantly, it will provide scientific insight into the nature of intuitive decision making that cannot be gained by using other methods. On a theoretical level, the true potentials of intuition are most completely revealed by research with experts. On an applied level, a main reason why research on intuition is currently so popular stems from the idea that professionals who have to make decisions with serious consequences frequently seem to rely on their intuitions. So, research with experts promises new discoveries that lead to a better understanding and even the improvement of real world decisions by clinicians, court judges, pilots or managers. Therefore, naturalistic research with expert participants may constitute a promising bridge between theoretical and applied research.

Summary

Important steps, dos and don'ts of video-based online research with experts
  Dos:

- Cooperate with a project partner. This partner should be an institution that experts from your domain are associated with, such as a soccer association, a training centre for pilots or the national association of fire-fighters.
- Listen to the experts you are working with – they can provide input to your research from an important perspective.
- Plan your research in detail, before you create your online research tool. Nevertheless, try to maintain some flexibility to adapt to new demands.
- Involve an expert in multimedia and IT at an early stage of your work.
- Always make sure your online tool is working correctly. You cannot be overcautious in this regard.

Don'ts:

- Don't get carried away by your fancy research tool. Be aware of the research questions it can help to answer, and be even more aware of the research questions it cannot help to answer. For these kinds of questions, carefully read the other chapters of this volume.
- Don't rely exclusively on one set of naturalistic stimuli. Try to replicate results with a set of different items, as this reduces the probability that your effect is due to some characteristic of your stimulus material. Remember, when using naturalistic stimuli you have to cope with reduced experimental control and internal validity.

Author note

Geoffrey Schweizer, Department of Sport and Exercise Psychology, University of Potsdam; Henning Plessner, Department of Social Psychology, University of Leipzig; Ralf Brand, Department of Sport and Exercise Psychology, University of Potsdam.
The SET training and research tool was developed as a part of a project supported by a joint grant (IIA1-071017/06-08) from Bundesinstitut für

Sportwissenschaft and Deutscher Fußball-Bund. SET was programmed by Benno Bartels from Insert Effect GbR in Nuremberg, Germany.

Correspondence concerning this article should be addressed to Geoffrey Schweizer, Department of Sport and Exercise Psychology, University of Potsdam, Am Neuen Palais 10, 14469 Potsdam, Germany. E-mail: geoffrey.schweizer@uni-potsdam.de

Notes

1 SET is an acronym for the German word *Schiedsrichter-Entscheidungs-Training*, which means decision making training for referees.
2 To participate in an exemplary SET session yourself, visit www.intuitive-experts.de – Resources.

References

Betsch, T. (2008). The nature of intuition and its neglect in research on judgment and decision making. In H. Plessner, C. Betsch & T. Betsch (Eds.), *Intuition in judgment and decision making* (pp. 3–22). Mahwah, NJ: Lawrence Erlbaum Associates.

Birnbaum, M. H. (2004). Human research and data collection via the internet. *Annual Review of Psychology*, *55*, 803–832.

Brand, R., Schweizer, G., & Plessner, H. (2009). Conceptual considerations about the development of a decision-making training method for expert soccer referees. In D. Araujo, H. Ripoll & M. Raab (Eds.), *Perspectives on cognition and action in sport*. Hauppauge: Nova Science.

Brunswik, E. (1952). *The conceptual framework of psychology*. Chicago: Chicago University Press.

Doherty, M. E., & Kurz, E. M. (1996). Social judgment theory. *Thinking and Reasoning*, *2*, 109–140.

Ericsson, K. A. (1996). *The road to excellence: The acquisition of expert performance in the arts and sciences, sports, and games*. Mahwah, NJ: Lawrence Erlbaum.

Glöckner, A., & Betsch, T. (2008a). Modeling option and strategy choices with connectionist networks: Towards an integrative model of automatic and deliberate decision making. *Judgment and Decision Making*, *3*, 215–228.

Glöckner, A., & Betsch, T. (2008b). Multiple-reason decision making based on automatic processing. *Journal of Experimental Psychology: Learning, Memory, and Cognition*, *34*, 1055–1075.

Goldstein, W. M. (2004). Social judgment theory: Applying and extending Brunswik's probabilistic functionalism. In D. Koehler & N. Harvey (Eds.), *Blackwell handbook of judgment and decision making* (pp. 37–61). Malden, MA: Blackwell Publishing.

Goldstein, D. G., & Gigerenzer, G. (2002). Models of ecological rationality: The recognition heuristic. *Psychological Review*, *109*, 75–90.

Gosling, S. D., Vazire, S., Srivastava, S., & John, O. P. (2004). Should we trust web-based studies? A comparative analysis of six preconceptions about internet questionnaires. *American Psychologist*, *59*, 93–104.

Helsen, W., & Bultynck, J. B. (2004). Physical and perceptual-cognitive demands of top-class refereeing in association football. *Journal of Sport Sciences*, *22*, 179–189.

Hogarth, R. (2001). *Educating intuition.* Chicago, IL: The University of Chicago Press.

Hogarth, R. (2008). On the learning of intuition. In H. Plessner, C. Betsch & T. Betsch (Eds.), *Intuition in judgment and decision making* (pp. 91–105). Mahwah, NJ: Lawrence Erlbaum Associates.

Klein, G. (1999) *Sources of power: How people make decisions.* MIT Press, Cambridge.

Mascarenhas, D. R. D., O'Hare, D., & Plessner, H. (2006). The psychological and performance demands of association football refereeing. *International Journal of Sport Psychology, 37,* 99–120.

Myers, D. G. (2002). *Intuition – its powers and perils.* New Haven, CT: Yale University Press.

Payne, J. W., Bettman, J. R., & Johnson, E. J. (1988). Adaptive strategy selection in decision making. *Journal of Experimental Psychology: Learning, Memory, & Cognition, 14,* 534–552.

Plessner, H., Betsch, C., & Betsch, T. (Eds.). (2008). *Intuition in judgment and decision making.* Mahwah, NJ: Lawrence Erlbaum Associates.

Plessner, H., & Czenna, S. (2008). The benefits of intuition. In H. Plessner, C. Betsch & T. Betsch (Eds.), *Intuition in judgment and decision making* (pp. 251–266). Mahwah, NJ: Lawrence Erlbaum.

Plessner, H., & Haar, T. (2006). Sports performance judgments from a social cognition perspective. *Psychology of Sport and Exercise, 7,* 555–575.

Plessner, H., Schweizer, G., Brand, R., & O'Hare, D. (2009). A multiple-cue learning approach as the basis for understanding and improving soccer referees' decision making. In M. Raab, J. Johnson & H. Heekeren (Eds.), *Progress in Brain Research: Mind and motion: The bidirectional link between thought and action* (pp. 151–158). Amsterdam: Elsevier Press.

Reips, U.-D. (2002). Standards for internet-based experimenting. *Experimental Psychology, 49,* 243–256.

Salas, E., & Klein, G. (Eds.) (2001). *Linking expertise and naturalistic decision making.* Mahwah, NJ: Lawrence Erlbaum Associates.

Schweizer, G., Brand, R., Plessner, H., & Kahlert, D. (2009). *Training soccer referees' decision making using the SET training tool.* Manuscript submitted for publication.

Stanislaw, H., & Todorov, N. (1999). Calculation of signal detection theory measures. *Behavior Research Methods, Instruments, & Computers, 31,* 137–149.

Swets, J. A., Dawes, R. M., & Monahan, J. (2000). Psychological science can improve diagnostic decisions. *Psychological Science in the Public Interest, 1,* 1–26.

Wilson, T. D. (2002). *Strangers to ourselves: Discovering the adaptive unconscious.* Cambridge, MA: Harvard University Press.

7 Implicit evaluation as a basis for intuition

Rob W. Holland and Marieke de Vries

Introduction

It is 16.00 hours, three hours went by since you had lunch, another three hours to go before having dinner: snack time! You walk to your local canteen and you see various kinds of chocolate bars and several kinds of fruits. What kind of process would predict the outcome of your choice in this situation? Sometimes, you might think carefully and base your decision on an analytical process, on the explicit weighing of the pros and cons of both decision alternatives. If healthiness is an important aspect of snacks to you, this might make you opt for an apple rather than a chocolate bar. On other occasions, you might act upon your first evaluative reaction towards the different options you can choose from, which might make chocolate bars the more likely chosen candidate for some of us, although others would still prefer an apple.

In the current chapter we aim to elaborate on implicit evaluative measures as a means to predict intuitive judgments and decisions. How can we measure evaluative or affective associations people have towards choice options, which could serve as a basis for intuitive judgments and decisions? We will discuss various implicit measures, including reaction time measures such as the Implicit Association Test (Greenwald, McGhee & Schwartz, 1998), and the Affective Priming paradigm (Fazio, Sanbonmatsu, Powell, & Kardes, 1986; Fazio, Jackson, Dunton, & Williams, 1995), as well as projective measures such as the Affect Misattribution Procedure (Payne, Cheng, Govorun, & Stewart, 2005). Some of these measures have been "on the market" for more than ten years and have been widely used by (social) psychologists in order to learn more about the relations between attitudes and behaviour.

The main idea of all these implicit measures of attitudes is that they tap into evaluative or affective associations with an attitude object. These associations may also serve as the basis for intuitive judgments and decisions. However, in some conditions decision makers are more likely to act upon their first affective or evaluative reactions than in other conditions. Therefore, in addition to the importance of learning more about the various implicit measures of evaluative and affective associations, it is crucial to understand the conditions in which these associations translate into judgments and decisions. To preview these conditions: People are more likely to base decisions and judgments on these associations when they are under time constraints, in a positive mood, cognitively loaded or depleted from resources (see also Horstmann et al., this volume; Glöckner & Witteman, this volume).

Conceptual introduction of the methods for measuring evaluative associations

We understand intuition as gut feelings, such as the subjective experience that something is right or wrong, or that one choice option is better than another, without being able to detail what these gut feelings are exactly based on. That is, when people rely on intuition in judgment and decision making, they rely on an evaluative association regarding a judgment or decision object, without being able to explain what this association is based on (see also Glöckner & Witteman, chapter 1, this volume). In this section, we will briefly explain some of the origins of evaluative associations and models that explain how these evaluative associations can influence intuition.

On the origins of evaluative associations

Often the basis for evaluative associations is shaped by repeated couplings between objects and affective reactions. Such a process is known as evaluative conditioning (e.g., de Houwer, Thomas, & Baeyens, 2001). Evaluative conditioning consists of repeatedly linking an object or behaviour to positive or negative affective reactions. For example, consider yourself going for dinner with someone you do not know yet. If the food served in the restaurant is delicious, the positive affective reactions towards the food become associated with the company. As a result, a positive evaluation is created towards the person. It is easy to think about the type of association that becomes linked to this person when the food is bad (so beware of what kind of restaurant you take someone to on a first date).

In research on evaluative conditioning, researchers link objects (e.g., faces or neutral objects) to affectively laden pictures (or words) by presenting these objects together with the pictures. For example, Strick and colleagues (Strick, Holland & van Knippenberg, 2008) repeatedly presented pictures of consumer products (various peppermint brands), unknown to the group of participants, together with pictures of either attractive or unattractive women on a computer screen. Subsequently, the products that had been coupled with attractive faces were evaluated more positively than the products coupled with unattractive faces (see also Strick, van Baaren, Holland & van Knippenberg, 2009).

Such evaluative associations may even be established without conscious awareness of the couplings. For example, Krosnick and colleagues (1992) repeatedly showed neutral pictures of a person, immediately followed by a subliminal flash of an affect arousing picture (either pleasant or unpleasant, dependent on the condition). Participants liked the person better when the subliminal flashes contained positive pictures (e.g., cute puppies) compared to negative pictures (e.g., snakes). Subliminal procedures for evaluative conditioning have been successful in several other studies (see e.g., Aarts, Custers & Holland, 2007; Custers & Aarts, 2005; Dijksterhuis, 2004).

Although evaluative conditioning is primarily studied as a basic process of linking affect to objects, evaluative associations can also result from cognitive processes. For example, if a good friend (e.g., John) tells you several positive stories about another person (Harry), it becomes likely that your thoughts about Harry will be positive and create positive evaluative associations. Similarly, negative thoughts will result in negative associations. The effect of cognition on shaping evaluative associations has recently been demonstrated in several studies (see e.g., Gawronski, Walther & Blank, 2005; Petty, Tormala, Briñol & Jarvis, 2006).

From evaluative associations to intuition

Clearly, objects can acquire valence outside conscious awareness and these affective or evaluative reactions can serve as the basis for intuitive judgments or decisions. The measures that we discuss in the next paragraph are referred to as "implicit" attitude measures. The term implicit suggests that people cannot consciously identify their attitudes. However, in line with recent work on the link between implicit and explicit measures of attitudes, we argue that people can become aware of their attitudes under specific conditions.

Several researchers have modelled the processes by which these associations can translate into explicit judgments and decisions. Although attitudes are often referred to as "implicit" attitudes, this terminology often seems inaccurate. According to Fazio's MODE model (e.g., Fazio & Towles-Schwen, 1999) evaluative associations translate into explicit judgments and decisions when people lack the ability or the motivation to think more systematically. If either ability or motivation is absent, a strong correlation could be obtained between implicit measures of attitudes and intuitive decisions concerning the attitude object. For example, when people have to make quick decisions or when they do not care so much about the outcome, evaluative associations will affect the outcome. Similar predictions can be derived from other dual process models such as the Reflective and Impulsive Model (Strack & Deutsch, 2004) or the APE-model (Gawronski & Bodenhausen, 2006). We will further explain and exemplify the conditions for strong or weak correlations between measures of evaluative associations and intuitive decisions in a separate section.

Implicit measures: the methods

To predict intuitive judgment and decision making with the use of implicit evaluative measures, we need to (1) be able to measure evaluative associations and (2) understand under which conditions these associations may be used in decision making. We will now detail these two steps.

Measuring evaluative associations

Although the idea of automatic evaluation processes was already part of thinking about attitudes in the mid-eighties, the use of implicit measures has become widespread since the introduction of the Implicit Association Test (Greenwald et al., 1998) and the Affective Priming Task (Fazio et al., 1995). These measures, together with a more recently introduced measure, the Affective Misattribution Procedure (Payne et al., 2005), will now be explained in more detail.

Implicit Association Test

The Implicit Association Test (IAT) is the currently most studied implicit measure for evaluative associations in social cognition research. The goal of using the IAT is to measure the relative strength of the association between decision alternatives (e.g., apple versus chocolate) and valence (positive or negative associations). Consider the opening example and imagine that we want to measure the intuitive preferences for apples versus chocolate bars. With the IAT, we aim to reveal evaluative associations individuals have with regard to apples and chocolate bars.

In the IAT, people typically use two keys on a keyboard. The task for participants is to discriminate between positive and negative adjectives as well as between words related to two object categories, for example apples and chocolate bars, as *fast* and *accurate* as possible.

Usually, the IAT consists of five blocks of responses (however, some researchers use seven blocks, see below); three practice blocks and two test blocks. An example of trials from these five blocks is depicted in Figure 7.1. In the first block, participants are shown a series of single words that appear in the middle of the screen (e.g., peace, war, paradise, fear) and they have to classify each word as "good" by pressing one button (e.g., the "A" key on the keyboard) or "bad" by pressing another button (e.g., the "6" key on the key-board). In this block people learn to assign positive valence to one specific key and negative valence to the other. In the second block, participants practise with the category words. Various words appear on the screen and have to be classified as belonging to the apple category (by pressing one key, e.g., the "A") or the chocolate bar category (by pressing another key, e.g., the "6"). The words that participants respond to are usually different examples of the category (e.g., several kinds of apples, such as Elstar, Golden Delicious, and Pink Lady, and various kinds of chocolate bars, such as Snickers, Mars, and Twix).

The third block consists of the first test block in which the tasks of the first two blocks are combined. In this block participants have to respond to positive words and words related towards apples by pressing one button (e.g., the "A"), while the other button is used for the chocolate bars and negative adjectives (e.g., the "6"). The fourth block is again a practice block. In this block, only words related to apples or chocolate bars have to be categorized, but now reversing response keys for the apples (now the "6") and the chocolate bars (now the "A"). In the fifth block, which is the second test block, the valence words and category words are again paired but now in the opposite manner: words related to chocolate bars and positive adjectives share one button while the apples and negative adjectives share the other button.

Response latencies are recorded for each response. The data of the practice blocks are not used for analysis. Subsequently, the means of the response time in the critical blocks are calculated. In the process of calculating these means, error responses are left out as well as responses that are too slow (slower than 3,000 ms) or too fast (faster than 300 ms). Still, the reaction time data are usually skewed (see e.g., Fazio, 1990). There are several manners in which researchers deal with these skewed distribution and outliers, for example by deleting outliers (reactions times deviating 3 SD from the mean), or by using a 1/rt transformation, but the most widely used method to create a normal distribution with reaction time data is a logarithmic transformation (see, for a detailed procedure for dealing with outliers, Ratcliff, 1993).

The idea underlying the IAT is that when responses to category words (i.e., the words referring to apples or chocolate bars) share a button with congruent adjectives, response latencies will be shorter compared to responses to category words sharing an incongruent button. Considering the example

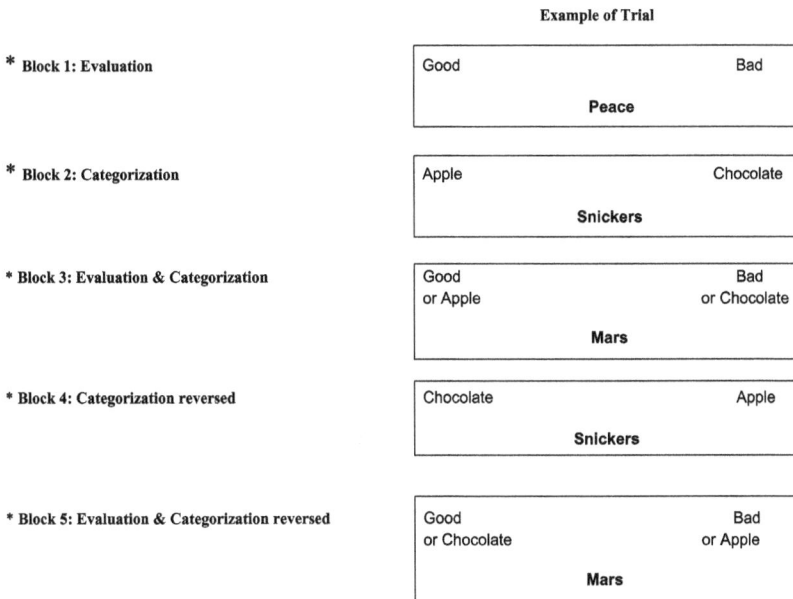

Example of Trial

* **Block 1: Evaluation**	Good · · · · · · · · · · · · · · · · Bad **Peace**
* **Block 2: Categorization**	Apple · · · · · · · · · · · · · · · Chocolate **Snickers**
* **Block 3: Evaluation & Categorization**	Good · · · · · · · · · · · · · · · · · Bad or Apple · · · · · · · · · · · or Chocolate **Mars**
* **Block 4: Categorization reversed**	Chocolate · · · · · · · · · · · · · · · Apple **Snickers**
* **Block 5: Evaluation & Categorization reversed**	Good · · · · · · · · · · · · · · · · · Bad or Chocolate · · · · · · · · · · or Apple **Mars**

Figure 7.1 The Implicit Association Task: an overview of the five blocks with examples of trials from each block.

described above, for people holding positive associations towards chocolate bars, responses are faster when the button is used for both chocolate related words and for positive adjectives (in the example above block 5) than when the same button is used for chocolate and negative adjectives (in the example above block 3). In line with this idea, somebody has more positive associations towards chocolate than to apples when the result of subtracting the response latencies in the apple/negative and chocolate/positive block (block 5) from the response latencies in the apple/positive and chocolate/negative block (block 3) is positive. This calculated mean difference of the (logtransformed) mean response times of the critical blocks is the IAT score.

Note that in the example above, we assess the evaluative associations towards chocolate bars compared to apples. In fact, this procedure is likely to measure comparative evaluations, or preferences, rather than absolute evaluative associations towards a single attitude object. Of course, decision processes often consist of comparing two decision alternatives. In such cases the original structure of the IAT may be suitable. However, sometimes we would like to test evaluations towards specific objects in which more absolute evaluations are necessary (e.g., when the decision problem concerns action versus no action, to buy or not buy a product, to go or not to go for a swim). In order to deal with this problem several researchers developed single target versions of the IAT (Wigboldus, Holland, & Van Knippenberg, 2005; Karpinski & Steinman, 2006).

The single target IAT (ST-IAT) consists of three different blocks. In contrast to the original IAT, people respond only to one category of words in addition to the valence categories. The ST-IAT starts off with a first block in which participants categorize positive and negative words. By doing this, one key becomes linked with positive responses (e.g., the "A") and one key with negative responses (e.g., the "6"), similar to the procedure of the original IAT. In the second block, however, words related to the attitude object are added to the task. For example, in order to measure attitudes towards Amsterdam participants have to respond to positive words with one key (e.g., "A") and to both negative words *and* Amsterdam related words by pressing another key (e.g., the "6"). Importantly, in order to end up with an equal number of left and right responses, the number of positive trials is doubled in this block (e.g., ten positive trials, five negative trials and five Amsterdam trials). In the third block, participants have to respond to positive words *and* to Amsterdam related words by pressing one key and to negative words by pressing the other key. In this block, the number of negative trials is doubled. The ST-IAT score is calculated by subtracting the mean logtransformed response times in block 3 from those in block 2.

Affective Priming Task

Another widely used implicit measure of attitudes is the Affective Priming Task. In this task, participants are asked to indicate as quickly and accurately as possible whether a target adjective (e.g., nice, happy, bad, stupid) is positive or negative by pressing a left "negative" or right "positive" key. Each target adjective is preceded by a brief presentation (prime) of an attitude object. This prime can either be a word or a picture. The Affective Priming Task is based on the idea that the primed attitude objects automatically activate an evaluation (Fazio et al., 1986, 1995), and in turn facilitate responses to adjectives that are evaluatively congruent, and inhibit responses to adjectives that are evaluatively incongruent. For example, consider you have positive associations with the attitude object "Hawaii", then it can be predicted that a Hawaii prime facilitates responses on positive adjectives and inhibits responses on negative adjectives.

Figure 7.2 displays an example of a typical trial in the Affective Priming Task. Each trial starts with a presentation of a fixation cross for some time (e.g., ranging from 1,000 to 2,000 ms). After the fixation cross, the prime (attitude object) is presented for 200 ms, followed by an interval (blank screen) for 100 ms. The time duration from prime presentation to target presentation is called the Stimulus Onset Asynchrony (SOA). Researchers have used various SOAs in research ranging from 100 to 450 ms. Research by Hermans and colleagues suggests that relative short SOAs (e.g., 200 ms) produce stronger affective priming effects (see e.g., Hermans, De Houwer, & Eelen, 2001). Intervals between trials are usually set to 1000 ms.

If you want to measure affective reactions towards a specific attitude object,

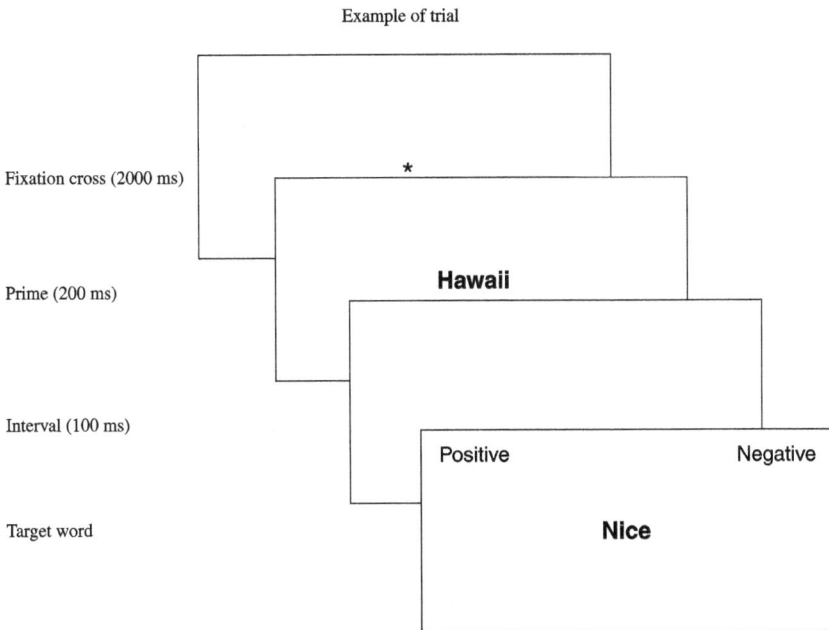

Figure 7.2 The Affective Priming Task: example of a trial.

you should include a series of trials with this object (e.g., six presentations preceding positive targets and six presentations preceding negative targets). It is wise to also include neutral primes (e.g., neutral words) or control primes (e.g., non-word letter strings) in the design, enabling you to calculate difference scores between positive and neutral trials and between negative and neutral trials (see e.g., Strick et al., 2009). The latter may be important because facilitation on positive trials is sometimes independent of inhibition on negative trials (Strick et al., 2009; cf. Cacioppo, Gardner, & Berntson, 1997).

Affective Misattribution Procedure

An implicit measure for attitudes that was developed more recently is the Affective Misattribution Procedure (AMP, Payne et al., 2005). In this measure, researchers employ the idea that people attribute affect to ambiguous objects (Murphy & Zajonc, 1993). In a way, this measure can be considered to be a modern version of the well-known Rorschach tests ("What do you see in this inkblot?"). The projection or attribution of evaluations or affective reactions makes people perceive meaningful figures in the inkblots (e.g., "I see a dragon"; Rorschach would respond: "You want to be a classic hero"). Although the AMP also makes use of misattribution processes, it is based on a more basic mechanism. Rather than misattributing implicit aspirations and motivations, it measures global affective or evaluative reactions towards objects in terms of positive or negative.

Let us assume we want to measure people's affective reactions towards names of car brands (e.g., Fiat and Hyundai) by using the AMP. We would then have the following procedure. Participants sit in front of a computer screen and are primed with a picture of a Fiat or Hyundai for 60 milliseconds, followed by a blank screen for 100 milliseconds, after which a Chinese ideograph is depicted for 100 ms, and then this ideograph is masked by a picture of black and white "noise", see Figure 7.3. Participants have to judge the pleasantness of the Chinese ideograph.

Like the IAT and the affective priming measure, the AMP does not have a cover story. Participants are straightforwardly instructed that the real-life image only serves as a warning signal for the Chinese ideograph and that they should do nothing with this image. Instead, it is the participant's task to judge the visual pleasantness of each Chinese ideograph. Participants are instructed to press a key labelled unpleasant if they judged the Chinese pictograph to be visually less pleasing than average and a key labelled pleasant if they judged it to be visually more pleasing than average. Importantly, participants are instructed to respond quickly. In order to measure affective responses to Fiat, you need a series of trials in which you prime participants with Fiat (e.g., 24 trials), but also an equal number of neutral primes (e.g., gray squares). You simply calculate the proportion of "pleasant" responses to the Chinese ideograph following the attitude object and compare this to the

Example of trial

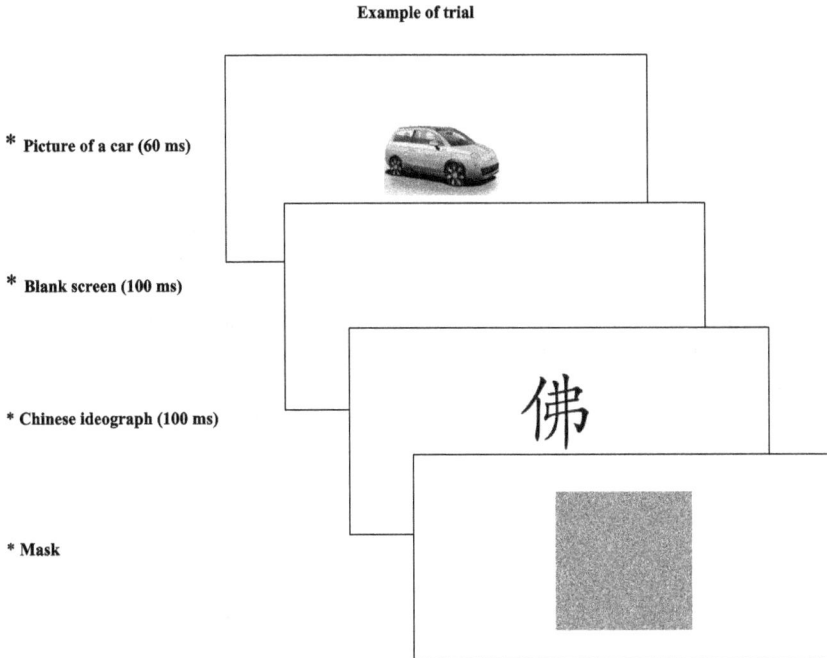

* Picture of a car (60 ms)

* Blank screen (100 ms)

* Chinese ideograph (100 ms)

* Mask

Figure 7.3 The Affective Misattribution Procedure: example of a trial.

proportion of "pleasant" responses following neutral trials. Response times are not taken into account in this measure.

Linking implicit measures of evaluative associations to explicit intuitive responses

All measures described above concern direct evaluative reactions towards objects. Such evaluative reactions could serve as the basis for intuitive responses towards these objects. In other words, we might become aware of these implicit evaluative reactions, consciously experience (part of) them, and subsequently use these evaluative or affective reactions as a guide in decision making. According to so called default-interventionist dual processing models (Evans, 2007; see also Glöckner & Witteman, this volume), intuitive processes are always activated and deliberate processes are additionally activated if possible and necessary. Several factors have been identified to influence the likelihood that deliberate processes are activated (Glöckner & Witteman, this volume; Horstmann et al., this volume). These factors should therefore also influence whether people's choices are in line with implicit evaluative associations. Without a good understanding of these factors, using implicit attitude measures to forecast intuitive reactions is useless. Most of the factors are straightforwardly derived from dual process models, such as the MODE model (Fazio & Towles-Schwen, 1999), the RIM model (Strack & Deutsch, 2004) and the APE model (Gawronski & Bodenhausen, 2006). We briefly highlight a number of these factors.

Cognitive resources

One important factor that determines whether people are likely to base their decisions on implicit associations is the amount of cognitive resources available to them. First, when people answer evaluative questions under cognitive load, for example when they have to memorize an eight-digit number (a method often used in research on cognitive load), they are more likely to decide on the basis of their first affective reaction. Indeed, several studies have shown stronger correlations between implicit and explicit measures of evaluation or decisions under cognitive load (e.g., Friese, Hofmann & Wänke, 2008; Gibson, 2008), when resources are depleted because of engagement in effortful tasks for some time (Hofmann, Rauch & Gawronski, 2007), and when people make explicit decisions under time pressure (e.g., Wilson, Lindsey & Schooler, 2000).

Motivation to think

Another implication of dual process theory is that the more motivated people are, the greater the likelihood that they engage in propositional processing and the greater the likelihood that people will move away from their first evaluative reaction. Social desirability, personal norms and values or simply vested interest may be important motivators to engage in deliberative thought. As a consequence, implicit measures will become worse predictors of decisions when social desirability concerns or vested interest increase.

Also, some people have a stronger inclination not to rely on their intuition but to think more deliberatively than others (see also Betsch & Ianello and Koele & Dietvorst, this volume). This individual difference can be gauged for example by the need for cognition scale (Cacioppo & Petty, 1982). When people start to think more deeply, first affective reactions are likely to become overshadowed by cognitive appraisals. As a consequence, implicit measures of evaluations are probably less effective predictors for decisions for people with a high need for cognition.

High thinking conditions or individual traits that facilitate deliberation may result in different decision outcomes when propositional processes and evaluative associations are incongruent, such as in the case of social desirability. Such dissociations are however not always obtained. Several studies illustrated the influence of affective reactions or evaluative associations on deliberative or systematic decisions (e.g., Pelham, Mirenberg & Jones, 2002; Todorov, Mandisodza, Goren, & Hall, 2005).

Reliance on affective reactions

A final class of factors that influence correspondence between choices and evaluative associations concerns situational influences that boost or reduce reliance on feelings. Recent studies suggest that mood states, that is, diffuse affective states, may be such a factor, with happy mood states, as opposed to sad mood states, boosting reliance on feelings and implicit evaluative associations (De Vries, Holland & Witteman, 2008a, 2008b; Holland, Hermsen, De Vries, & Van Knippenberg, 2009). In a recent study, we used an IAT to measure the implicit preference for apples versus chocolate bar. Moreover, we also measured belief-based attitudes towards apples and chocolate bars. Belief-based measures are based on explicit ratings on both the expectancy and evaluation of certain outcomes of the attitude object. Such belief-based measures have been predominantly used in the models of Reasoned Action and Planned Behaviour (see e.g., Ajzen, 1991), and are expected to correlate with deliberative decisions. Two weeks after measuring implicit and belief-based attitudes, participants in the positive mood condition were more likely to act in line with their IAT-score when they were given the choice between various apples and various chocolate bars. The choices of participants in the negative mood condition were predicted by the belief-based measure of attitudes, suggesting that negative mood induces a deliberative decision process (Holland et al., 2009). So, these studies suggest that in positive, but not in negative, mood conditions, individuals simply follow implicit evaluative associations, that is, decide intuitively.

Advantages and disadvantages of implicit measures

Implicit measures can be of great value for understanding intuitive decision making, as these measures provide an eminent tool for revealing a basis of intuition. Thus the new implicit measures are a valuable addition to the toolkit of social scientists who have been relying on questionnaires as their dominant research instrument. The use of questionnaires has serious disadvantages, such as social desirability concerns. Most importantly, compared to these questionnaires, the implicit attitude measures are closely related to core processes of intuitive reactions, as they assess the first evaluative response towards objects.

Implicit measures have been of great value for understanding attitudinal processes. Especially, it inspired researchers to differentiate in associative versus deliberative processes in evaluation (Gawronski & Bodenhausen, 2006), with implicit measures studied as a proxy for associative processes. Importantly, a great number of studies have demonstrated the predictive validity of both the IAT (e.g., Holland, Wennekers, Bijlstra, Jongenelen, & van Knippenberg, in press; see for an overview Greenwald, Poehlman, Uhlmann, & Banaji, in press) and the Affective Priming Task (e.g., Towles-Schwen & Fazio, 2006; Strick et al., 2009). Thus, a vast amount of empirical evidence already suggests that implicit measures can be good predictors of behaviour and decision making.

As with other implicit measures (e.g., with measures of implicit memory in cognitive psychology), the psychometric qualities of implicit measures are usually lower than those of explicit measures. At the same time, internal consistency scores for the IATs are usually satisfactory, with alphas ranging from .70 to .90 for IAT (Nosek, Greenwald & Banaji, 2006), and a mean alpha of .70 for the ST-IAT (Bluemke & Friese, 2008). The AMP has very good internal consistency scores, with an average alpha of .85 (Payne et al., 2005). Reliability scores for the priming measures are disappointingly low, with internal consistency scores ranging from .01 (e.g., Bosson, Swann, & Pennebaker, 2000) to .50 (Kawakami & Dovidio, 2001, see also Cunningham, Preacher & Banaji, 2001). Separate analyses for positive and negative trials may enhance internal consistency scores. For such separate valence scores, alphas of .70 have been shown (Strick et al., 2009).

Implicit measures have received a great deal of criticism (e.g., Blanton & Jaccard, 2006). One important criticism consists of the lack of strong interrelations between various implicit measures (e.g., Bosson et al., 2000). Clearly, implicit measures do not only measure evaluative associations, but they are also associated with other processes (e.g., Conrey, Sherman, Gawronski, Hugenberg & Groom, 2005). Because of measurement error and the fact that these measures do not purely tap into the evaluative processes, it is unlikely that the correlations between these measures and an outcome of interest (e.g., an intuitive decision) will be rocket high. Stated differently, correlations above the .80 are very unlikely (and you should raise your eyebrows and be very cautious if you do find such strong correlations). At the same time, this may explain why various implicit measures also lack strong interrelations (e.g., Bosson et al., 2000). Interestingly, Cunningham and colleagues (2001) were able to find stronger correlations between the IAT and Affective Priming measure when statistically controlling for measurement error.

Furthermore, it is important to carefully think about the question: "If we are measuring evaluative associations using implicit measures, what is the object of the evaluation in these tasks?". In the IAT the labels of categories are the primary objects for evaluation; exemplars only have to be categorized according to these labels and are not evaluated directly (however, when using extreme exemplars it may very well affect the IAT-effect, see below). In contrast, in the Affective Priming Task and the AMP, the specific words or pictures are the attitude object.

Preferably, you need computers in order to administer the various implicit measures. For the IAT, some researchers have developed a paper and pencil task (see e.g., Lowery, Hardin & Sinclair, 2001). However, thus far it is not completely clear how successful and valid these paper and pencil versions are. On the other hand, if you do not have a computer laboratory, it becomes more and more easy to run experiments via the internet. The software for running these programs on the internet is available (see for example the "relevant websites" listed below).

Finally, it is important to understand that implicit attitude measures are sensitive to contextual influences. For example, a Snicker may trigger more positive evaluative reactions in an Affective Priming Task when you are hungry and eager to eat something than when you just ate a 200 gram muffin (cf. Ferguson & Bargh, 2004). Also, it has been shown that IAT effects are dependent on the specific stimuli that are used for categorization in the IAT. For example, consider you want to study black-white racial attitudes with an IAT. Although generally speaking people show a negative bias towards blacks, different outcomes are found when people have to categorize exemplars like Obama, Carl Lewis, Hitler and Stalin (Mitchell, Nosek & Banaji, 2003). It is clear that these measures can tap into well-established associations that are relatively stable over time, but strong context effects are very likely as well. Needless to say, explicit measurements are also strongly context dependent.

Conclusion

Implicit measures of affective reactions or attitudes are a welcome tool in the study of intuition. By employing these measures we can predict intuitive responses when the right conditions (e.g., time-pressure, positive mood, ego-depleted) are met.

Relevant websites:

1   https://implicit.harvard.edu/implicit/ On this website you can try several different IATs, mostly even in your native language.
2   http://faculty.washington.edu/agg/iat_materials.htm. On this website you can download scoring algorithms for the IAT as well as download computer programs.
3   http://www.millisecond.com/download/samples/. This website is run by the company of Inquisit which is a good computer program to run reaction time experiments, in the laboratory or on the internet. On the website you can find examples of various implicit measures, including the IAT, the Affective Priming Task, and the AMP.

References

Aarts, H., Custers, R., & Holland, R. W. (2007). The nonconscious cessation of goal pursuit: When goals and negative affect are coactivated. *Journal of Personality and Social Psychology*, *92*, 165–178.
Ajzen, I. (1991). The theory of planned behavior. *Organizational Behavior and Human Decision Processes*, *50*, 179–211.
Blanton, H., & Jaccard, J. (2006). Arbitrary metrics in psychology. *American Psychologist*, *61*, 27–41.

Bluemke, M., & Friese, M. (2008). Reliability and validity of the Single-Target IAT (ST-IAT): Assessing automatic affect towards multiple attitude objects. *European Journal of Social Psychology*, *38*, 977–997.

Bosson, J. K., Swann, W. B, & Pennebaker, J. W. (2000). Stalking the perfect measure of implicit self-esteem: The blind men and the elephant revisited? *Journal of Personality and Social Psychology*, *79*, 631–643.

Cacioppo, J. T., Gardner, W. L., & Berntson, G. G. (1997). : Beyond bipolar conceptualizations and measures: The case of attitudes and evaluative space. *Personality and Social Psychology Review*, *1*, 3–25.

Cacioppo, J. T., & Petty, R. E. (1982). The need for cognition. *Journal of Personality and Social Psychology*, *42*, 116–131.

Conrey, F. R., Sherman, J. W., Gawronski, B., Hugenberg, K., & Groom, C. (2005). Separating multiple processes in implicit social cognition: The Quad-Model of implicit task performance. *Journal of Personality and Social Psychology*, *89*, 469–487.

Cunningham, W. A., Preacher, K. J., & Banaji, M. R. (2001). Implicit attitude measures: Consistency, stability, and convergent validity. *Psychological Science*, *12*, 163–170.

Custers, R., & Aarts, H. (2005). Positive affect as implicit motivator: On the nonconscious operation of behavioral goals. *Journal of Personality and Social Psychology*, *89*, 129–142.

De Houwer, J., Thomas, S., & Baeyens, F. (2001). Associative learning of likes and dislikes: A review of 25 years of research on human evaluative conditioning. *Psychological Bulletin*, *127*, 853–869.

De Vries, M., Holland, R. W., & Witteman, C. L. M. (2008a). Fitting decisions: Mood and intuitive versus deliberative decision-strategies. *Cognition and Emotion*, *22*, 931–943.

De Vries, M., Holland, R. W., & Witteman, C. L. M. (2008b). In the winning mood: Affect in the Iowa gambling task. *Judgment and Decision Making*, *3*, 42–50.

Dijksterhuis, A. (2004). I like myself but I don't know why: Enhancing implicit self-esteem by subliminal evaluative conditioning. *Journal of Personality and Social Psychology*, *86*, 345–355.

Evans, J. S. B. T. (2007). On the resolution of conflict in dual process theories of reasoning. *Thinking and Reasoning*, *13*, 321–339.

Fazio, R. H. (1990). A practical guide to the use of response latency in social psychological research. In C. Hendrick & M. S. Clark (Eds.), *Review of personality and social psychology: Vol. 11. Research methods in personality and social psychology* (pp. 74–97). Newbury Park, CA: Sage Publications.

Fazio, R. H., Jackson, J. R., Dunton, B. C., & Williams, C. J. (1995). Variability in automatic activation as an unobtrusive measure of racial attitudes: A bona fide pipeline? *Journal of Personality and Social Psychology*, *69*, 1013–1027.

Fazio, R. H., Sanbonmatsu, D. M., Powell, M. C., & Kardes, F. R. (1986). On the automatic activation of attitudes. *Journal of Personality and Social Psychology*, *50*, 229–238.

Fazio, R. H., & Towles-Schwen, T. (1999). The MODE model of attitude-behavior processes. In S. Chaiken & Y. Trope (Eds.), *Dual process theories in social psychology* (pp. 97–116). New York: Guilford.

Ferguson, M. J., & Bargh, J. A. (2004). Liking is for doing: Effects of goal-pursuit on automatic evaluation. *Journal of Personality and Social Psychology*, *87*, 557–572.

Friese, M., Hofmann, W., & Wänke, M. (2008). When impulses take over: Moderated predictive validity of explicit and implicit attitude measures in predicting food choice and consumption behaviour. *British Journal of Social Psychology, 47*, 397–419.

Gawronski, B., & Bodenhausen, G. V. (2006). Associative and propositional processes in evaluation: An integrative review of implicit and explicit attitude change. *Psychological Bulletin, 132*, 692–731.

Gawronski, B., Walther, E., & Blank, H. (2005). Cognitive consistency and the formation of interpersonal attitudes: Cognitive balance affects the encoding of social information. *Journal of Experimental Social Psychology, 41*, 618–626.

Gibson, B. (2008). Can evaluative conditioning change attitudes toward mature brands? New evidence from the implicit Association Test. *Journal of Consumer Research, 35*, 178–188.

Greenwald, A. G., McGhee, D. E., & Schwartz, J. K. L. (1998). Measuring individual differences in implicit cognition: The Implicit Association Test. *Journal of Personality and Social Psychology, 74*, 1464–1480.

Greenwald, A. G., Poehlman, T. A., Uhlmann, E., & Banaji, M. R. (in press). Understanding and using the Implicit Association Test: III. Meta-analysis of predictive validity. *Journal of Personality and Social Psychology.*

Hermans, D., De Houwer J., & Eelen, P. (2001). A time course analysis of the affective priming effect. *Cognition and Emotion, 15*, 143–165.

Hofmann, W., Rauch, W., & Gawronski, B. (2007). And deplete us not into temptation: Automatic attitudes, dietary restraint, and self-regulatory resources as determinants of eating behavior. *Journal of Experimental Social Psychology, 43*, 497–504.

Holland, R. W., Hermsen, B., De Vries, M., & Van Knippenberg, A. (2009). Mood and the role of intuitive versus deliberative attitude-behavior relations. Manuscript in preparation.

Holland, R. W., Wennekers, A., Bijlstra, G., Jongenelen, M. & van Knippenberg, A. (in press). Self-symbols as implicit motivators. *Social Cognition.*

Karpinski, A., & Steinman, R. B. (2006). The single category implicit association test as a measure of implicit social cognition. *Journal of Personality and Social Psychology, 91*, 16–32.

Kawakami, K., & Dovidio, J.F. (2001). Implicit stereotyping: How reliable is it? *Personality and Social Psychology Bulletin, 27*, 212–225.

Krosnick, J. A., Betz, A. L., Jussim, L. J., & Lynn, A. R. (1992). Subliminal conditioning of attitudes. *Personality and Social Psychology Bulletin, 18*, 152–162.

Lowery, B.S., Hardin, C. D., & Sinclair, S. (2001). Social influence on automatic racial prejudice. *Journal of Personality and Social Psychology, 81*, 842–855

Mitchell, J. P., Nosek, B. A., & Banaji, M. R. (2003). Contextual variations in implicit evaluation. *Journal of Experimental Psychology: General, 132*, 455–469.

Murphy, S. T., & Zajonc, R. B. (1993). Affect, cognition, and awareness: Affective priming with optimal and suboptimal stimulus exposures. *Journal of Personality and Social Psychology, 64*, 723–739.

Nosek, B. A., Greenwald, A. G., & Banaji, M. R. (2006). The Implicit Association Test at age 7: A methodological and conceptual review. In J. A. Bargh (Ed.), *Social psychology and the unconscious: The automaticity of higher mental processes* (pp. 265–292). New York: Psychology Press.

Payne, B. K., Cheng, C. M., Govorun, O., & Stewart, B. (2005). An inkblot for attitudes: Affect misattribution as implicit measurement. *Journal of Personality and Social Psychology, 89,* 277–293.

Pelham, B. W., Mirenberg, M. C., & Jones, J. K. (2002). Why Susie sells seashells by the seashore: Implicit egotism and major life decisions. *Journal of Personality and Social Psychology, 82,* 469–487.

Petty, R. E., Tormala, Z. L., Briñol, P., & Jarvis, W. B. G. (2006). Implicit ambivalence from attitude change: An exploration of the PAST model. *Journal of Personality and Social Psychology, 90,* 21–41.

Ratcliff, R. (1993). Methods for dealing with reaction time outliers. *Psychological Bulletin, 114,* 510–532.

Strack, F. & Deutsch, R. (2004). Reflective and impulsive determinants of social behavior. *Personality and Social Psychology Review, 8,* 220–247.

Strick, M., Holland, R. W. & van Knippenberg, A. (2008). Seductive eyes: Attractiveness and direct gaze increase desire for associated objects, *Cognition, 106,* 1486–1496.

Strick, M., van Baaren, R. B., Holland, R. W., & van Knippenberg, A. (2009). Humor in advertisements enhances product liking by mere association. *Journal of Experimental Psychology: Applied, 15,* 35–45.

Todorov, A., Mandisodza, A. N., Goren, A., & Hall, C. C. (2005). Inferences of competence from faces predict election outcomes. *Science, 308,* 1623–1626.

Towles-Schwen, T., & Fazio, R. H. (2006). Automatically-activated racial attitudes as predictors of the success of interracial roommate relationships. *Journal of Experimental Social Psychology, 42,* 698–705.

Wigboldus, D., Holland, R. W. & Van Knippenberg, A. (2005). *Single target implicit associations.* Unpublished manuscript.

Wilson, T. D., Lindsey, S., & Schooler, T. (2000). A model of dual attitudes. *Psychological Review, 107,* 101–126.

8 Physiological measures in identifying decision strategies

Guy Hochman, Andreas Glöckner and Eldad Yechiam

Introduction

Is a decision the product of cold cognitive processes?[1] Looking at the major theories in decision making, such as Prospect Theory (Kahneman & Tversky, 1979), subjective expected utility theory (Savage, 1954) or reinforcement learning (e.g., Sutton & Barto, 1998; Fu & Anderson, 2006), one would imagine the human mind filled with equations and flowcharts. In contrast, the intuition of most people about the human mind is that its main forces constitute emotions and affects which are more difficult to quantify (Ubel & Loewenstein, 1997), and that decisions are to a large extent the product of intuition rather than of cold calculation. Yet the fact of the matter is that science proceeds by way of quantification, and so emotional and intuitive processes, which are almost by definition not part of cold calculating cognition (cf. Böhm & Brun, 2008), are difficult to study in a scientific manner. In the present chapter we address the challenge of studying emotional and intuitive aspects of decision making using quantifiable physiological measures, which offer the possibility to add emotional and intuitive elements into mainstream formal models of decision making.

Cognitive models of decision making can be broadly classified as pertaining to two distinct, yet complementary, approaches: statistical or structural models (also known as *as-if* or *paramorphic* models) and process models. Generally speaking, structural models focus mainly on the relationship between environmental stimuli and end-results. In contrast, process models characterize the algorithms or the cognitive strategies that decision makers employ when they face situations in which judgments or decisions have to be made (Ford, Schmitt, Schechtman, Hults, & Doherty, 1989). By using process tracing techniques, such as verbal protocol analysis (see Witteman & van Geenen, chapter 3, this volume), information board, and Mouselab methodology (see Norman & Schulte-Mecklenbeck, chapter 2, this volume), these models attempt to trace the processes that take place between perception and decisions.

The merits of process tracing techniques in understanding decision strategies are unquestionable. However, since they are embedded in the historical conceptualization of human decisions as based on rational and deliberate cognitive processes (Böhm & Brun, 2008; Shafir, Simonson, & Tversky, 1993), it seems that they are not sufficiently tailored to address the specific theories they intend to investigate, especially those involving emotion and intuition (Glöckner & Betsch, 2008; Peters, Västfjäll, Gärling, & Slovic, 2006). In the last decade there has been a growing interest in emotional processes and their role in decision making (Böhm & Brun, 2008; Peters et al., 2006; see also Dickert, chapter 10, this volume). However, the bulk of these approaches mainly focus on how emotions and arousal influence choice behaviour (e.g., Ariely & Loewenstein, 2006; Lerner & Tiedens, 2006; Schwarz & Clore, 1983; see also Bless & Fiedler, 1995; Fiedler, 2001). Less attention has been devoted to the understanding of intuitive mechanisms as underlying choice behaviour in their own right, and to the direct role that automatic ("non-deliberate") mechanisms play in decision making.

Two noteworthy exceptions to this generalization can be found in the perspective of the *affect heuristic* and the *somatic marker hypothesis*. The affect heuristic (Slovic, Finucane, Peters, & MacGregor, 2002) postulates that decision makers are influenced by automatic affective responses (i.e., feelings). Specifically, affective responses provide qualitative information about environmental stimuli and choice alternatives, in the form of affective tags. Thus, these affective tags influence the way decision makers evaluate potential prospects, and affect final decision even when the stimuli that gave rise to these affects remain unconscious (Finucane, Alhakami, Slovic, & Johnson, 2000). Similarly, the somatic marker hypothesis (Damasio, 1994) suggests that decision making depends on emotions. Somatic markers are associations between environmental stimuli and affective responses. They provide information about potential advantages and disadvantages of future prospects. By focusing attention on the more advantageous prospects, while directing it away from disadvantageous prospects, somatic markers simplify the decision process, and can thus aid decision makers in reaching adaptive decisions. Similar to the affect heuristic, it has been shown that somatic markers could operate outside awareness (Bechara, Damasio, Tranel, & Damasio, 1997).

Since affective mechanisms such as the affect heuristic and somatic markers may work on an unconscious automatic level, they can be considered special kinds of "intuitive" processes in decision making. Several indirect measures, such as response time (Glöckner, 2008; see also Glöckner, chapter 5, this volume) have been proposed to investigate these intuitive processes. Research shows that measures of the autonomic nervous system's arousal can also shed light on decision makers' initial unconscious choice tendencies (Bechara et al., 1997; Fishbein et al., 2005). Thus, we argue that these measures may serve not only as indicators of covert intuitive and affective processes in decision making, but also to differentiate between the intuitive and deliberate components of decision processes.

In this chapter, we aim to show how autonomic measures of arousal, such as *Skin Conductance Response* (SCR), *Peripheral Arterial Tone* (PAT), and *Pupil Diameter* (PD), can be used to capture intuitive processes. First, decision tasks often used in this line of research are outlined. Second, the application of these autonomic measures to identify unique intuitive processes is discussed,[2] followed by a review of relevant empirical evidence. Finally, implications and future applications of the proposed methods are discussed.

Experience-based decision tasks

Researchers who aim to study emotional and intuitive aspects of decision making must equip themselves with experimental paradigms capable of differentiating cognitive deliberate processes from emotional and intuitive ones. One such class of paradigms is labelled "decision from experience" (Hertwig, Barron, Weber, & Erev, 2004). Although they may come in many shapes and flavours, these choice tasks all involve many repeated trials in which the information available to the decision maker is limited to her own experience with the outcomes of previous decisions. This basic experimental design is likely to reflect robust behavioural regularities (Erev & Haruvy, 2008), as it captures the essence of uncertainty of outcomes, as well as the structure of rewards and punishments (i.e., risk) that is specific to real-life decision situations (Bechara, Damasio, Damasio, & Anderson, 1994). But more importantly, since these experience-based tasks measure emotion-based learning (Yechiam, Veinott, Busemeyer, & Stout, 2007), and since they require many repetitions (a characteristic of high importance to physiological measures, as will be clarified in the next section), they may play an important role in the study of emotional or intuitive processes that are based on variants of conditioning (see Glöckner & Witteman, chapter 1, this volume).

One of the most frequently used experience-based tasks is the Iowa Gambling Task (Brand, Fujiwara, Borsutzky, Kalbe, Kessler, & Markowitsch, 2005). Originally, the Iowa Gambling Task was developed by Bechara and colleagues (Bechara, Damasio, Damasio, & Anderson, 1994) to evaluate neurological deficiencies resulting in decision-making impairments while leaving cognitive abilities intact (e.g., ventromedial prefrontal cortex damage), as well as to support the Somatic Marker Hypothesis.

In the original form of the Iowa Gambling Task, participants are presented with four visually identical decks of cards, labelled as A, B, C, and D (see Figure 8.1a). Participants are given an initial amount of $2,000 (in play money), and are instructed to repeatedly select one card at a time from any of the available four decks, with the goal of maximizing their total earnings. They are further told that they are free to switch from one deck to another, as often as they like; and that in order to succeed in the task they should avoid certain decks that are worse than others. No further information about the payoff structure of each deck is revealed, nor about the number of selections (which is, in reality, 100 choices).

On each trial, participants select one card and turn it over to learn the outcome of their choice. During the experiment, an accumulating payoff counter is updated after each selection. Turning any card results in an

(a) The Iowa Gambling Game

	Disadvantageous Decks		Advantageous Decks	
	A	B	C	D
	In this trial you gained $100 and lost $XX (Loss per 10 cards = $1250)	In this trial you gained $100 and lost $XX (Loss per 10 cards = $1250)	In this trial you gained $50 and lost $XX (Loss per 10 cards = $250)	In this trial you gained $50 and lost $XX (Loss per 10 cards = $250)
Net gain (per 10 cards)	-$250	-$250	+$250	+$250

(b) The clicking paradigm

A	B
	+$90

You got   +$90

TOTAL   +$90

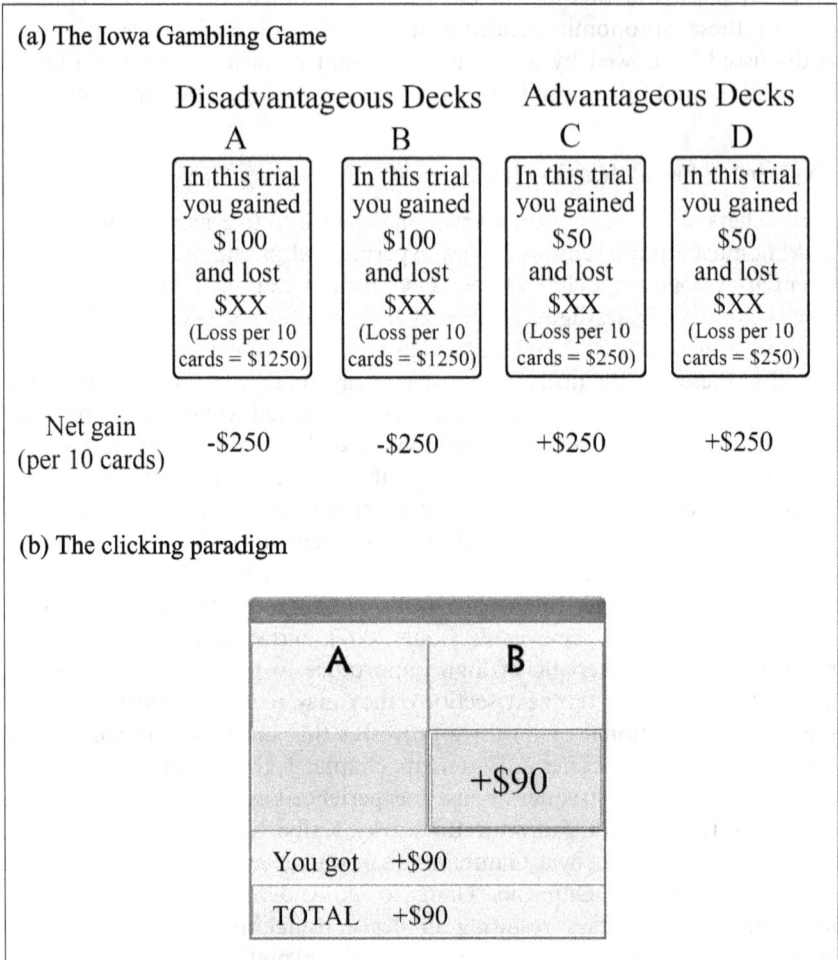

Figure 8.1 Schematic diagram of the Iowa Gambling Task (a) and a typical screenshot of the clicking paradigm (b).

immediate reward; however in some cases this gain is coupled with a simultaneous loss. Specifically, Decks A and B provide a high payoff of $100 on
each trial. However, they are occasionally (and unpredictably) coupled with
losses of high magnitude (up to $1,250). As a result, the net average loss on
each trial from these decks is $25. In contrast, Decks C and D provide small
payoffs of $50 upon each selection. Occasionally, this payoff is coupled with
losses of smaller magnitude (up to $250). Thus, the net average gain on each
trial from these decks is $25. Accordingly, Decks A and B are disadvanta-
geous, as they lead to a total net loss, while Decks C and D are advantageous,
as they lead to a total net gain. Good performance is achieved by preferring
the advantageous decks, and avoiding the disadvantageous decks.

A simplified variation of the Iowa Gambling Task (with complementary potential) is a binary experienced-based choice task, labelled "the clicking paradigm" (Erev & Haruvy, 2008). In this task, decision makers are required to repeatedly choose between two unmarked buttons, presented on the computer screen, with the goal of maximizing their total earnings (Figure 8.1b). Each selection of one of the buttons is followed by a presentation of the obtained payoff (on the selected button), and an update of the subtotal payoff counter, placed below the two buttons. Payoffs are randomly drawn from a payoff distribution associated with each selected button; however, decision makers receive no prior information about these distributions, nor regarding the number of trials to be played.

Unlike the Iowa Gambling Task, the clicking paradigm is not commonly used in studying emotional or intuitive process. However, due to its relative simplicity, it could be used to pinpoint effects of specific components of the decision scenario on choice behaviour. For example, the more complex structure of the Iowa Gambling Task makes it impossible to differentiate between risk avoidance and loss avoidance responses. In contrast, by comparing mixed payoff structures, payoffs which include both the possibility to win or lose a certain amount of money (e.g., an option producing +1 or −1 with equal likelihood) versus all-gain payoff structure of equal expected values (e.g., an option producing 0 or 2), the clicking paradigm can provide a distinction between responses to losses and risk sensitivity.

Conceptual introduction of the methods

A look into intuitive and deliberate processes governing human decision making must start from basic theories of the human mind. The dual-system approach analyzes human reasoning into two distinct yet complementary systems of processing (Epstein, 1994; Sloman, 1996): an associative system based on automatic intuitive processes, and a rational, rule-based deliberate system. Since Autonomic Nervous System activity corresponds to some of the characteristics of the intuitive system (e.g., unconsciousness, automaticity; cf. McCraty, Atkinson, & Bradley, 2004; Bierman, 2004), we postulate that it may serve as a marker of intuitive processes. In the current section, we start with a short overview of the Autonomic Nervous System. Next, we introduce three Autonomic Nervous System measures (i.e., SCR, PAT, and PD) commonly used in psychophysiological research. Finally, we discuss the application of these measures for examining intuitive as well as deliberate decision strategies.

The Autonomic Nervous System is part of the peripheral nervous system. It is predominantly an efferent system which transmits impulses from the Central Nervous System to peripheral organ systems. The main function of the Autonomic Nervous System is to maintain homeostasis in the body. To do so, it controls the heart rate, constriction and dilatation of blood vessels, contraction and relaxation of smooth muscle in various organs, visual accommodation, pupillary size, and the activity of the sweat gland. Among its many functions, the Autonomic Nervous System is responsible for the regulation and coordination of many emotional responses to environmental stimuli (Andreassi, 2000), and it usually functions in an automatic, reflexive manner.

The Autonomic Nervous System is divided into two separate branches called the Sympathetic and Parasympathetic nervous systems, based on anatomical and functional differences. The Sympathetic Nervous System enables the body to be prepared for emotionally charged stimuli, by mobilizing bodily resources to allow the organism to utilize a large amount of energy. Sympathetic responses include an increase in heart rate, blood pressure, pupil size, and sweat gland activity, and a decrease in peripheral blood vessel diameters (i.e., vasoconstriction). In contrast, the Parasympathetic nervous system is concerned with conservation and restoration of energy, by restoring bodily resources into their initial state. Parasympathetic responses include a decrease in heart rate, blood pressure, pupil size, and sweat gland activity, and increase in peripheral blood vessel diameters (i.e., vasodilatation).

Skin Conductance Response (SCR)

The term Skin Conductance Response (SCR) [also known as Electrodermal Activity (EDA), Galvanic Skin Response (GSR), or Psychogalvanic Reflex (PGR)] is used to describe a method of measuring changes in the electrical properties of the skin in response to environmental stimuli. Changes in skin conductance reflect eccrine sweat glands activity which is controlled by the Autonomic Nervous System. While the body surface is abundant with eccrine sweat glands (approximately 2 to 5 million, Fowles, 1986), they are most numerous in the palm of the hands (Andreassi, 2000). Thus, the typical (and most recommended) recording sites for SCR are the thenar and the hypothenar eminences, or the volar (palmer) surface of the distal phalanges (the fingerprint region), preferably at the participant's recessive hand.

Electrodermal activity is usually divided into skin resistance response and skin resistance level. Skin resistance level refers to the baseline level of skin resistance, while skin resistance response indicates momentary fluctuations in skin resistance. SCR and Skin Conductance Level are conductance measure units of Skin Resistance Response and Skin Resistance Level, in accordance. Conductance units are preferred instead of resistance values, since they are more appropriate for averaging and other statistical manipulations (e.g., t-tests; see Cacioppo & Tassinary, 1990 for an elaborated discussion on the advantages of conductance over resistance). In addition, conductance increases with higher levels of arousal and decreases at low levels, and does not merely fluctuate. Thus, if measuring resistance, it is recommended to convert the measuring units into microsiemens.[3]

While SCR amplitude may differ, depending on electrode size, fluctuations in response to stimulations normally range between 0.05 µS and 5 µS. In addition, the peak of skin resistance fluctuations in response to stimuli ranges from approximately 1.0 to 3.0 seconds after stimuli onset (Andreassi, 2000). A characteristic SCR waveform is depicted in Figure 8.2a. Since these are considered long lasting physiological responses, when applying SCR in experimental settings, interstimulus intervals (ISIs) should be long enough

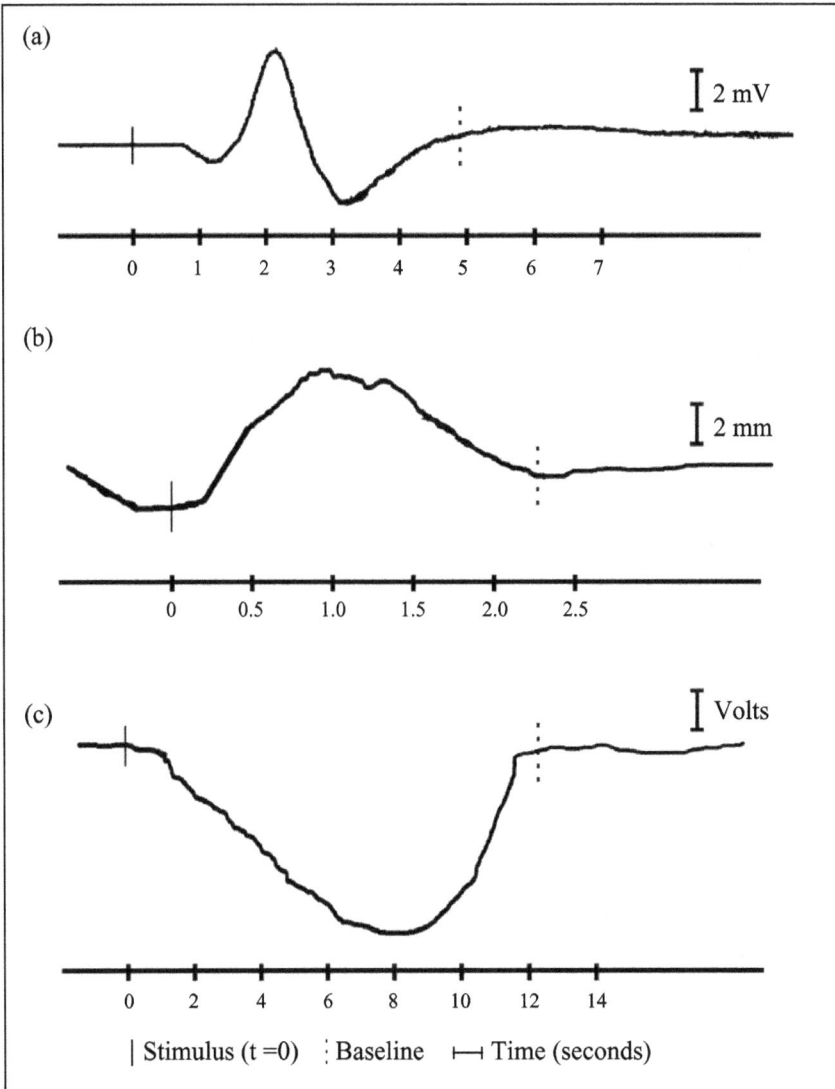

Figure 8.2 Characteristic SCR waveform (a), pupillary response to stimulation (b, indicating higher arousal), and PAT response to stimulation (c, indicating higher arousal). Note: time epochs are only approximations, and may differ depending on experimental conditions.

(i.e., at least 2 sec) not to encounter response overlapping (Tarvainen, Koistinen, Valkonen-Korhonen, Partanen, & Karjalainen, 2001).

SCR has been found to be related to numerous behavioural phenomena, such as response to novel or emotionally charged stimuli, learning, and sexual arousal (see Andreassi, 2000 and Dawson, Schell, & Filion, 1990 for a comprehensive review). However, several findings suggest a direct link between electrodermal activity and intuitive or automatic responding. For example, Tranel and Damasio (1985, 1988) found increased SCRs in response to familiar faces in a group of brain damaged patients who were unable to consciously identify them. In addition, SCR has been found to be controlled by the Anterior Cingulate Cortex (ACC) (Boucsein, 1992; Critchley, Mathias, & Dolan, 2001), a system which is directly related to emotional arousal, and in specific to response competition (Braver, Barch, Gray, Molfese, & Snyder, 2001), such as between intuitive and deliberate tendencies. Thus, it could be argued that SCR may serve as an effective measure of intuitive processes of decision making.

Pupil Diameter (PD)

The term Pupil Diameter Response (PD) is used to describe a method of measuring variations in the diameter of the papillary aperture of the eye. The pupil is the sphere that is located at the centre of the iris of the eye. One of its major functions is to control the amount of light that enters the eye. This is mainly achieved through the control of the Autonomic Nervous System over the muscles of the iris. Specifically, dilation of the pupil is caused by neurons of the Sympathetic Nervous System innervating radial fibres of the iris, whereas its constriction is by means of Parasympathetic Nervous System neurons innervating the circular fibres (Andreassi, 2000). In addition to lighting conditions, the pupil dilates in response to emotional stimuli (e.g., unexpected sound). Moreover, research show that emotionally-invoked pupillary dilations can override physiologically-invoked responses, such as intense light (Andreassi, 2000).

Typical pupillometers include an infrared light sensitive eye-camera and an infrared light source (i.e., LED). The low-intensity infrared LED is used to illuminate the eye, while the eye camera records the pupil size. Infrared illumination is required to enable recording in low-lighting environments. In addition, it facilitates accurate measures of the pupil (by contrasting the black pupil with the white corneal glint), with the measuring unit being millimetres. The pupil of the human eye ranges between 1.5 mm and about 9 mm (Guyton, 1977). In addition, pupils may dilate in response to stimuli in as little as 0.2 seconds, and peak in about 0.5 or 1.0 seconds. Thus, unlike other autonomic system measures, the pupillary response is a measure with high temporal resolution. A characteristic PD waveform is depicted in Figure 8.2b.

Similar to SCR, the pupil has been found to dilate in response to numerous psychological stimuli (e.g., Beatty, 1982; Janisse, 1974; Oka, Chapman,

& Jacobson, 2000). For example, Satterthwaite, Green, Myerson, Parker, Ramaratnam, and Buckner (2007) instructed participants to indicate which card out of two playing cards presented to them would turn up higher. Upon each selection, negative or positive feedback was given, according to their success. The results showed increased PD in response to negative as opposed to positive feedback. This is consistent with the increased emotional response often accompanying negative as compared to positive stimuli (Rook, 1984). In addition, Bierman (2004) used PD to support the somatic marker hypothesis, and found increased PD at the intuitive level when participants gazed at incorrect rather than correct stimuli. Along with the fact that PD has high temporal resolution, these findings suggest that PD too may serve as an effective measure of intuitive processes of decision-making.[4]

Peripheral Arterial Tone (PAT)

The term Peripheral Arterial Tone (PAT) is used to describe a method for measuring variations in the vascular tone (i.e., diameter of the blood vessels) at the human fingertip. Neurons of the Sympathetic Nervous System directly innervate alpha-adrenergic vascular beds, especially at distal parts of the limbs (e.g., the surfaces of the hands and fingers), and are responsible both for vasoconstriction and vasodilatation (Pillar, Bar, Schnall, Sheffy, & Lavie, 2002). Thus, PAT is considered a pure measure of Sympathetic Nervous System activity (Grote, Zou, Murphy, Peker, & Hedner, 2002; Schnall, Shlitner, Sheffy, Kedar, & Lavie, 1999).

The level of sympathetic activation is indicated by a decrease in the transparency of the blood (indexed by the amount of light received in the photoreceptor), as a function of its pulsatile volume, i.e., blood pressure. For each heartbeat, blood pressure varies between systolic and diastolic pressures. The systolic arterial pressure is defined as the peak pressure in the arteries, which occurs near the beginning of the cardiac cycle (when the heart constricts); the diastolic arterial pressure is the lowest pressure (at the resting phase of the cardiac cycle) (Klabunde, 2005). PAT is the pulse pressure – that is, the difference between the maximum and minimum pressures measured.

Essentially, PAT is a novel implementation of plethysmography to measure vascular tone in real-time. PAT measuring plethysmograph uses a pneumatic finger cup, which envelops the finger up to and beyond its tip with a uniform pressure field. Thus, it allows for exclusive measurement of arterial volume. The measuring apparatus includes a light-emitting diode and a photosensitive cell. The arterial tone affects the translucence of light through the tissue of the finger, which, in turn, affects the output measure. A computer program calculates the amount of light transmitted through the tissue of the finger in Volts. Sympathetic Nervous System activity associated with arterial constriction leads to lower values on the PAT measure (expressed by Volts). Changes in arterial constriction in response to stimuli start at approximately 1.0–2.0 seconds post-stimulus, and peak in about after 5.0 to 7.0 seconds (see, for example, Figure 8.2c). Thus, much like the SCR, when measuring PAT, Inter Stimulus Intervals should be set to at least 5.0 seconds.

Unlike other physiological measures, the PAT is not commonly used in psychophysiological research. However, similar to several PD studies (Hyönä, Tommola, & Alaja, 1995; Kahneman, 1973), increased autonomic arousal (indexed by vasoconstriction) has been found in response to increased processing demands. For example, Iani, Gopher, Grunwald, and Lavie (2007) used PAT to investigate real-time mental effort during a simulated flight task. Their result demonstrated increased arousal as the cognitive requirements of the task increased. Thus, although not directly related to emotional or intuitive processes, it seems that PAT may serve as an effective measure of intuitive processes in decision-making, especially since it is exclusively related to Sympathetic Nervous System activity.

Inferring psychological meaning from autonomic measures

Autonomic system measures may be used as markers for identifying and exploring the more covert unconscious processes of decision making (a comparison of the measures discussed in this chapter is presented in Table 8.1). However, several problems in the measurement of Autonomic Nervous System arousal may serve as an albatross around the neck of researchers aiming to relate physiological to choice behaviour. In this section we highlight these problems, and suggest several methodological concerns, that, if strictly considered, may facilitate psychological inference from physiological signals.

Noisy signals. One of the major problems in the measurement of physiological signals is the constant fluctuations in activity that are irrelevant to the psychological events being examined. For example, spontaneous electrodermal activity may occur, that is not directly related to any obvious physical or psychological stimulus. Similarly, PD fluctuations constantly occur during waking hours (Andreassi, 2000). These background variations in autonomic activity are associated with a variety of factors that cannot be easily (or accurately) interpreted. In a similar vein, although there is a relationship between sympathetic activity and emotional arousal, one cannot identify the specific emotion being elicited. Since autonomic measures serve as an index of general physiological arousal in response to physical or psychological stimulations, the specific determinants that give rise to the arousal cannot be easily inferred.

To address these problems, a one-to-one association between each unique psychological event and its corresponding physiological measure must be established (Cacioppo & Tassinary, 1990). This could be obtained by administrating stimuli in a repeated manner, and by time-locking the data relative to the events, and averaging across unique event types to parse out only the relevant information. The averaging process filters out autonomic activity that is not related to the experimental manipulation, creating an event-related measure. With this kind of averaging, changes in Autonomic Nervous System activity

Table 8.1 Comparison of physiological measures

	Temporal resolution	Measuring units	Normal range	Application simplicity	Analyzing simplicity	Required equipment
SCR	Low – between 1.0 and 3.0 seconds	Microsiemens	Approximately 1–5 μS	Medium-hard	Medium	Skin conductance coupler (galvanometer)
PD	Fast – approximately 0.5 second	Millimetre	2–9 mm	Medium	Easy	Pupillometer
PAT	Very low – up to 7 seconds	Volts	Not relevant	High	Hard	Finger-mounted plethysmograph

due to significant psychological events in the experimental trial can be specified (Beatty, 1986; Cacioppo & Tassinary, 1990).

Habituation. Another difficulty in the measurement of autonomic activity is inherent in the properties of physiological mechanisms. This is the problem of habituation, which is defined as a gradual decrease in response amplitude due to repetitive stimulation. Habituation depends on the number of stimuli presented and on the total time of the experimental procedure. Thus, this problem is particularly important in psychophysiological research, in which, as we already noted, psychological events should be administered in a repetitive manner. Although typical to several autonomic measures, habituation is most common in SCR (Aramaki, Kira, & Hirasawa, 1997). As a result, much that we know about habituation stems from research that used electrodermal activity.

For example, Aramaki et al. (1997) measured skin conductance among healthy people and found significant decrease in the amplitude (i.e., habituation) after a sequence of only three identical stimuli. In addition, a significant drop in the amplitude has been documented after approximately 15–20 minutes of examination (Elie & Guiheneuc, 1990). If stimuli are presented consecutively, and inter-stimuli intervals are short, habituation may appear even earlier (Kucera, Goldenberg, & Kurca, 2004).

Therefore, researchers who plan to use physiological measures are advised to limit each experimental session to about 20 minutes and to administer stimuli in a random order (Elie & Guiheneuc, 1990; Kucera et al., 2004). Note, however, that several experimental requirements may prohibit adherence to the above recommendations. Thus, to reduce the artefacts of habituations in these situations, researchers are further encouraged to administer equal number of trials for each stimulus type, so that when calculating the different response of the Autonomic Nervous System to these stimuli temporal effects can be cancelled out.

Baseline measurement. The momentary fluctuations in autonomic activity that occur in response to stimuli are termed phasic responses (Andreassi, 2000; Heitz, Schrock, Payne, & Engle, 2008). In contrast, the relatively stable level of autonomic arousal that is not related to stimulations (i.e., baseline level) is referred to as the tonic level. Essentially, in order to evaluate event-related changes in autonomic activity, the phasic level is calculated by subtracting the tonic level from the level of arousal measured during the experimental task. In addition, phasic levels are calculated to eliminate individual differences in amplitude (which are particularly apparent in PAT), and to thus facilitate statistical analyses on the data. Thus, reliable assessment of baseline levels of autonomic arousal is crucial to any psychophysiological research aiming to link psychological events and physiological measures.

Unfortunately, standardized conditions under which baseline measurements should be recorded do not exist. For example, the length of the baseline measurement period may vary from a couple of minutes to more than

15–20 minutes (Jennings, Kamarck, Stewart, Eddy, & Johnson, 1992). Similarly, while there is a consensus that baseline measurements should reflect autonomic activity in an inactive period, specific methods (including instructions and procedures) for this period are yet undetermined. Thus, we follow with only a brief outline of the existing options.

The most common protocol for establishing baseline measurement is to instruct participants to sit quietly and relax for several minutes, while their autonomic arousal is measured. However, some recent findings suggest that engaging participants with an undemanding cognitive task resulted in lower, more accurate baseline levels. For example, Piferi, Kline, Younger, and Lawler (2000) achieved lower baseline levels when participants were instructed to watch a relaxing video during measurement. Alternatively, another common method is to use measurement in pre-stimulus onset periods as baseline (see, for example, Tarlovsky, Yechiam, Ofek, & Grunwald, 2008).

Application

We have tried to highlight our view that it is important to incorporate autonomic arousal measures as dependent variables in decision-making research, and to make available some of the basic knowledge that is required for doing so. However, the question still remains how one might apply physiological measures to trace intuitive processes. This question is addressed in the current section.

Over the years, many applications have been proposed for autonomic system measures including, for example, in vigilance, mental workload, job-satisfaction, and personnel selection (Andreassi, 2000). One of the oldest and perhaps the most common application is for detection of deceptions. While the use of physiological measures to determine whether people are lying is interesting in its own right, in the current context we use it to demonstrate how these measures might serve as markers for underlying intuitive processes.

In a recent article, Tarlovsky et al. (2008) evaluated the PAT measure as a lie detector. In two experiments, participants had the opportunity to win monetary prizes if they were able to "beat the machine" by providing false answers to target questions presented on the computer screen without being detected. In Experiment 1, participants were initially required to provide information about their names and the names of their relatives. Upon completion, participants were presented with statement concerning the reported information (e.g., "My mother's name is Linda"), and were required to select one of two buttons, labelled "True" and "False". In reality, all statements were in fact true. However, in certain trials (marked by an on-screen green light) participants had the opportunity to provide a false answer, which, if not detected, would entail a monetary prize. Experiment 2 provided a similar task, with the exception that the personal information questions were replaced by socially undesirable previous personal behaviours (e.g., "I once hit a younger child"). During the task, PAT, heart rate, and response time were measured.

The results showed significantly increased autonomic arousal, indicated by PAT, in response to false as compared to true responses. In fact, on average, in more than 80% of the cases participants were unable to beat the PAT apparatus and to provide wrong answers without being detected. Thus, the authors concluded that PAT is a highly sensitive measure for detecting increased mental arousal which accompanies untruthful responses. However, according to Fischbein (1987), intuitive knowledge is a self-explanatory cognition that we accept with certainty as being true. Thus, the increased arousal that was found by Tarlovsky et al. (2008) could be ascribed to the dissociation between intuitive and deliberate processes of reasoning which are competing to elicit a response and create dissonance or inconsistency (Glöckner & Betsch, 2008; see also Glöckner & Witteman, chapter 1, this volume). If this is the case, it could be argued that autonomic measures serve as indicators of covert intuitive processes that compete with deliberate intentions.

It should be stressed, however, that this example highlights the difficulty of inferring psychological significance from physiological measures. Although the results of Tarlovsky et al. (2008) could be interpreted as indicating a contradiction between overt deliberate processes of lying and covert intuitive processes of knowing the truth, other plausible explanations exist. For example, these results could be interpreted as suggesting emotional arousal (e.g., excitement) which results from the prospect to gain a monetary payoff. Since conclusive research is lacking, it could be argued that in a sense, theoretical concepts support autonomic data more than autonomic measures support theoretical approaches. However, as the following examples suggest, this does not necessarily have to be the case.

Bechara et al. (1997) used SCR to trace somatic markers while normal participants and patients with VentroMedial Prefrontal Cortical (VMPC) lesions were engaged in the Iowa Gambling Task. During the task, participants were questioned about their conscious knowledge of the different decks. As predicted by the somatic marker hypothesis, normal participants exhibited increased SCR amplitude (referred to as anticipatory SCR by the authors) prior to disadvantageous choices, even before they developed explicit knowledge about the situation. Moreover, this unconscious or intuitive anticipation resulted in the overall preference of normal subjects to select the advantageous decks. By contrast, VMPC lesioned patients developed no anticipatory SCRs in response to disadvantageous decks, nor did they refrain from selecting them through the entire task. Since participants were mostly blind to the process which led to the anticipatory SCRs, it has been argued that cognitive representations of (unconscious) autonomic arousal (which may be seen as a unique form of intuitive choice strategies) guide and bias choice behaviour. Although several researchers have argued against this interpretation (e.g., Maia & McClelland, 2004), it has been supported in brain imaging studies (e.g., Critchley et al., 2001).

Similarly, in an unpublished study we (Hochman & Yechiam) used autonomic measures to examine loss aversion in monetary gambles (i.e., the tendency that loss of a certain amount of money looms larger than the gain of the same amount; Kahneman & Tversky, 1979). PAT was measured while participants were instructed to repeatedly select between two unmarked buttons (i.e., the clicking paradigm), one of which resulted in a 50/50 chance of either gaining 8.5, 6, or 3.5 or losing 1.5, 4, or 6.5 points (i.e., expected value = 1 point), and the other resulted in a constant payoff of 1 point. People showed no loss aversion and selected the alternative with negative prospects on 52% of the trials. However, although not statistically significant, median PAT amplitude in response to negative outcomes were lower compared to positive outcomes (Figure 8.3), denoting higher arousal following the outcomes from the risky option. Given the modulating role of the Autonomic Nervous System (Andreassi, 2000), we believe that the increased autonomic responses served as alerts (i.e., markers) to the decision maker to beware of potential losses. However, they did not follow this intuitive tendency because it was mitigated by other deliberate tendencies, such as the tendency to diversify between outcomes (i.e., a diversification bias; Read & Loewenstein, 1995), or to increase one's interest in the task.

The reported studies show that affective responses towards options sometimes precede choices and might influence or even determine them as postulated by the somatic marker hypothesis and the affect heuristic. One core question for the further understanding of intuition is whether these feelings determine behaviour more or less exclusively or if choices are influenced by later (presented) information. Such information might be automatically integrated or could lead to deliberate corrections of the initial feeling (cf. exclusive processing vs. interventionist models, see Glöckner & Witteman, chapter 1, this volume). The complex interplay between these kinds of processes is really not well understood and urgently demands further research (cf. Finucane et al., 2000). The application of physiological measures in simple probabilistic cue tasks (see Bröder, chapter 4, this volume; Glöckner,

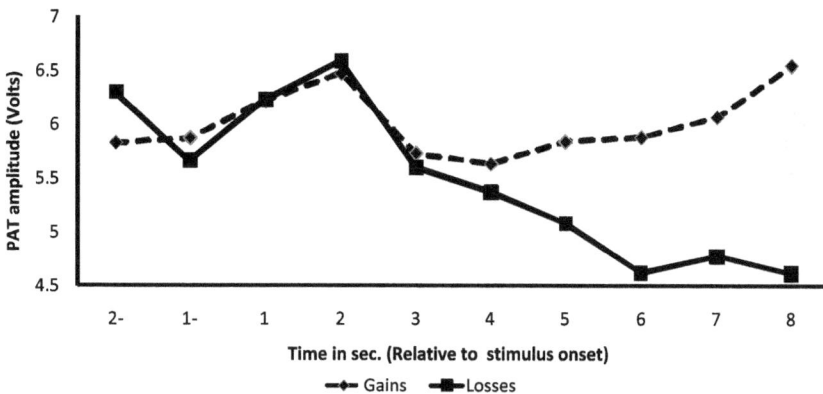

Figure 8.3 Median PAT amplitudes in response to gains and losses relative to stimulus onset.

chapter 5, this volume) might be a fruitful way to achieve this. In a recent study conducted by our group (Glöckner & Hochman, 2009, under revision), participants acquired affective responses towards two options in a simplified Iowa Gambling Task. Afterwards they were presented again with these options and shortly after (but well before individuals' choices) an additional cognitive cue (e.g., whether the option would yield a negative or a positive outcome, with certain validity) was presented. Using PAT, we observed that the additional cue not only influenced choices but also instantly modulated affective reaction. This indicates that affective responses are not only based on learned experiences but that current information is integrated into them. This can hardly be explained by simple learning models for intuition (Finucane et al., 2000), but supports more complex ones such as evidence accumulation (Busemeyer & Johnson, 2004) or parallel constraint satisfaction models (Glöckner & Betsch, 2008) (for an overview see Glöckner & Witteman, chapter 1, this volume).

Discussion

In this chapter we discussed three methods for measuring physiological reactions and how these might be fruitfully applied to investigate intuition. Physiological measures provide an interesting additional dependent variable that could provide a window into covert processes affecting behaviour. By now these measures have often been used for applied questions (e.g., lie detection, reactions in stressful situations) and for investigating behavioural phenomena (see Andreassi, 2000). We think that major progress in intuition research can be achieved by efficiently combining physiological measures to explore cognitive mechanisms underlying human behaviour. The measure might be recorded while applying the think-aloud method (see Witteman & van Geenen, chapter 3, this volume), information search tracing methods (see Norman & Schulte-Mecklenbeck, chapter 2, this volume), or video-based information presentation (Schweizer, Plessner, & Brand, chapter 6, this volume), enabling the researcher to relate the physiological reaction to subjective experiences and simple information processing strategies. Another application would be to use physiological measures in well understood somewhat more complex research tasks such as probabilistic cue tasks (Bröder, chapter 4, this volume) and to relate results concerning physiological measures to cue integration strategies determined using the choice-based strategy classification method (Bröder, this volume), or the multiple-measure maximum likelihood strategy classification method (Glöckner, chapter 5, this volume).

Using an even more comprehensive approach, physiological arousal could be included as additional dependent measure into the multiple-measure strategy classification method (Glöckner, chapter 5, this volume). Assuming that specific decision strategies (or models) allow for sufficiently clear predictions concerning the physiological arousal connected with solving subsets of tasks (e.g., more arousal for decision of type A vs. type B), the match between this prediction and the observed arousal level per person could be taken into account when trying to identify which strategy was most likely used. That is: physiological arousal could be used jointly with other measures to calculate the likelihood of the data given the application of a certain strategy.

Some theories already allow for specific predictions concerning arousal. It can be predicted that physiological arousal depends on the strength of affective reactions connected with the outcomes either by a) experience in a learning phase (Finucane et al., 2000) or b) inspection in the decision process (Busemeyer & Johnson, 2004). Parallel constraint satisfaction approaches (Glöckner & Betsch, 2008; see also Glöckner & Witteman, chapter 1, this volume) agree that experiences with options might induce affective reactions. They however claim that these affective reactions do not directly determine choices but that they are modulated by and integrated with currently available cognitive information. The model predicts that both affective reactions and cognitive information are integrated using automatic consistency maximizing processes, and that increasing inconsistency (i.e., the degree of dissonance or conflict in the mental representation of the decision task) should be related to higher physiological arousal.[5]

It might also be interesting to relate physiological measures to general tendencies towards using intuitive or deliberate strategies (see Betsch & Ianello, chapter 14, this volume; Koele & Dietvorst, chapter 13, this volume), as well as to the manipulation of decision mode (Horstmann, Hausmann, & Ryf, chapter 12, this volume). Finally, many physiological measures for autonomic activity exist. However, little is known about their concordance and divergence, especially in specific psychological situations. Thus, an investigation of the interrelation of these physiological measures as well as a cross validation with self-report scales for affect (Dickert, chapter 10, this volume) would be scientifically fruitful, both for a better understanding of the interaction between Autonomous Nervous Systems and behaviour, and to make a better match between experimental purposes and specific measures.

Applying physiological methods comes with initial costs. Apart from the costs for equipment (which has dramatically dropped in recent years), much time has to be invested to figure out the weaknesses of the specific equipment and to find efficient ways to analyze the data. For researchers who intend to work with it repeatedly it is certainly worth the effort. For single projects, we recommend to work with cooperation partners. A collection of essential resources, example data and useful links (e.g., documentations, analysis routines etc.) which comes with the book is available online (www.intuitive-experts.de – Resources).

Acknowledgment

This chapter was supported in part by the European Commission Integrated Project IP-SKILLS-35005, and also partially by the United States Air-force Grant FWR 20060084H.

Notes

1 "Cold" cognitive processes refer to reasoning under conditions of low emotion and/ or arousal. In contrast, "hot" cognitive processes refer to reasoning under conditions of high emotion and/or arousal.
2 In the process of introducing the common physiological measures, we use several technical terms that might be unfamiliar to naïve readers. Understanding these terms is not crucial to understanding this message. However, readers who wish to learn more about these terms are encouraged to find their meaning in books which specifically address psychophysiological issues (e.g., Andreassi, 2000).
3 Microsiemens (μS) is the reciprocal unit for ohm, which is the unit of resistance. To convert to μS, take the reciprocal of the ohm and multiply it by 1,000,000 [(μS = 1/ohm)*1,000,000].
4 Note that many eye-trackers (see Norman & Schulte-Mecklenbeck, chapter 2, this volume) record pupil diameter as well as fixations.
5 Technically, inconsistency is the total energy in the network after finding a stable solution (a simulation program is available at: www.intuitive-experts.de – Resources; see also Glöckner, chapter 5, this volume).

References

Andreassi, J. L. (2000). *Psychophysiology: Human behavior and physiological response*. Mahwah, N.J.: Lawrence Erlbaum Associates.

Aramaki, S., Kira, Y., & Hirasawa, Y. (1997). A study of the normal values and habituation phenomenon of sympathetic skin response. *American Journal of Physical Medicine and Rehabilitation, 76*, 2–7.

Ariely, D., & Loewenstein, G. (2006). The heat of the moment: the effect of sexual arousal on sexual decision making. *Journal of Behavioral Decision Making, 9*, 87–98.

Beatty, J. (1982). Task-evoked pupillary responses, processing load, and the structure of processing resources. *Psychological Bulletin, 91*, 276–292.

Beatty, J. (1986). The papillary system. In M. G. H. Coles, E. Donchin, & S. W. Porges (Eds.), *Psychophysiology: Systems, processes & applications* (pp. 43–50). New York: Guilford.

Bechara, A., Damasio, H., Tranel, D., & Damasio, A. R. (1997). Deciding advantageously before knowing the advantageous strategy. *Science, 275*, 1293–1294.

Bechara, A., Damasio, A. R., Damasio, H., & Anderson, S. W. (1994). Insensitivity to future consequences following damage to human prefrontal cortex. *Cognition, 50*, 7–15.

Bierman, D.J. (2004). Non conscious processes preceding intuitive decisions. *Proceedings of Bial Foundation 5th Symposium*: Behind and Beyond the Brain. pp. 100–115. Publisher and Editor: Bial Foundation, Portugal. March 31–April 3, Porto, Portugal.

Bless, H., & Fiedler, K. (1995). Affective states and the influence of activated general knowledge. *Personality and Social Psychology Bulletin, 21*, 766–778.

Böhm, G., & Brun, W. (2008). Intuition and affect in risk perception and decision-making. *Judgment and Decision-making, 3*, 1–4.

Boucsein, W. (1992). *Electrodermal activity*. New York: Plenum.

Brand, M., Fujiwara, E., Borsutzky, S., Kalbe, E., Kessler, J., & Markowitsch, H. J. (2005). Decision-making deficits of Korsakoff patients in a new gambling task with explicit rules: Associations with executive functions. *Neuropsychology, 19,* 267–277.

Braver, T. S., Barch, D. M., Gray, J. R., Molfese, D. L., & Snyder, A. (2001). Anterior Cingulate Cortex and response conflict: Effects of frequency, Inhibition, and errors. *Cerebral Cortex, 11,* 825–836.

Busemeyer, J. R., & Johnson, J. G. (2004). Computational models of decision making. In D. J. Koehler & N. Harvey (Eds.), *Blackwell handbook of judgment and decision making* (pp. 133–154). Malden, MA: Blackwell Publishing.

Cacioppo, J. T., & Tassinary, L. G. (1990). Inferring psychological significance from physiological signals. *American Psychologist, 45,* 16–28.

Critchley, H. D., Mathias, C. J., & Dolan, R. J. (2001). Neural activity in the human brain relating to uncertainty and arousal during anticipation. *Neuron, 29,* 537–545.

Damasio, A. R. (1994). *Descartes' error: Emotion, reason, and the human brain.* New York: Putnam Publishing.

Dawson, M. E., Schell, A. M., & Filion, D. L. (1990). The electrodermal system. In J. T. Cacioppo & L. G. Tassinary (Eds.), *Principles of psychophysiology* (pp. 295–324). Cambridge: Cambridge University Press.

Elie, B., & Guiheneuc, P. (1990). Sympathetic skin response: Normal results in different experimental conditions. *Electroencephalography and Clinical Neurophysiology, 76,* 258–267.

Epstein, S. (1994). Integration of the cognitive and psychodynamic unconscious. *American Psychologist, 49,* 709–724.

Erev, I., & Haruvy E. (2008). Learning and the economics of small decisions. Second draft of a chapter submitted to the second volume of *The Handbook of Experimental Economics* edited by John H. Kagel and Alvin E. Roth.

Fiedler, K. (2001). Affective influences on social information processing. In J. P. Forgas (Ed.), *Handbook of affect and social cognition* (pp. 163–185). Mahwah, NJ: Lawrence Erlbaum Associates Publishers.

Finucane, M. L., Alhakami, A., Slovic, P., & Johnson, S. M. (2000). The affect heuristic in judgment of risks and benefits. *Journal of Behavioral Decision-making, 13,* 1–17.

Fischbein, E. (1987). *Intuition in science and mathematics.* Dodrecht, Holland: Reidel.

Fishbein, D., Hyde, C., Eldreth, D., London, E. D., Matochik, J., Ernst, M., Isenberg, N., Steckley, S., Schech, B., & Kimes, A. (2005). Cognitive performance and autonomic reactivity in abstinent drug abusers and nonusers. *Experimental and Clinical Psychopharmacology, 13,* 25–40.

Ford, J. K., Schmitt, N., Schechtman, S. L., Hults, B. M. & Doherty, M. L. (1989). Process tracing methods: contributions, problems, and neglected research problems. *Organizational Behavior and Human Decision Processes, 43,* 75–117.

Fowles, D. C. (1986). The eccrine system and electrodermal activity. In M. G. H Coles, E. Donchin, & S. W. Porges (Eds.), *Psychophysiology: Systems, processes, & applications* (pp. 51–96). New York: Guilford.

Fu, W., & Anderson, J. (2006). From recurrent choice to skill learning: a reinforcement-learning model. *Journal of Experimental Psychology: General, 135,* 184–206.

Glöckner, A. (2008). Does intuition beat fast and frugal heuristics? A systematic empirical analysis. In H. Plessner, C. Betsch, and T. Betsch (Eds.), *Intuition in judgment and decision making* (pp. 309–325). Mahwah, NJ: Lawrence Erlbaum.

Glöckner, A., & Betsch, T. (2008). Modeling option and strategy choices with connectionist networks: Towards an integrative model of automatic and deliberate decision-making. *Judgment and Decision-making, 3*, 215–228.

Glöckner, A., & Hochman, G. (2009, Revised and resubmitted). The interplay of experience-based affective and probabilistic cues in decision making arousal increases when experience and additional cues are inconsistent. *Experimental Psychology.*

Grote, L., Zou, D., Murphy, P., Peker, Y., & Hedner, J. (2002). Detection of sleep disordered breathing in a general population based on the pulse amplitude. *Journal of Sleep Research, 11*, 260–287.

Guyton, A. C. (1977). *Basic human physiology: Normal function and mechanisms of disease.* Philadelphia: Saunders.

Heitz, R. P., Schrock, J. C., Payne, T. W., & Engle, R. W. (2008). Effects of incentive on working memory capacity: behavioral and pupillometric data. *Psychophysiology, 45*, 119–129.

Hertwig, R., Barron, G., Weber, E. U., & Erev, I. (2004). Decision from experience and the effect of rare events. *Psychological Science, 15*, 534–539.

Hyönä, J., Tommola, J., & Alaja, A. M. (1995). Pupil dilation as a measure of processing load in simultaneous interpretation and other language tasks. *The Quarterly Journal of Experimental Psychology* Section A, 48, 598–612.

Iani, C., Gopher, D., Grunwald, A. J., & Lavie, P. (2007). Peripheral arterial tone as an on-line measure of load in a simulated flight task. *Ergonomic, 50*, 1026–1035.

Janisse, M. P. (1974). Pupil size, affect, and exposure frequency. *Social Behavior and Personality, 2*, 125–146.

Jennings, J. R., Kamarck, R., Stewart, C., Eddy, M., & Johnson, P. (1992). Alternate cardiovascular baseline assessment techniques: vanilla or resting baseline. *Psychophysiology, 29*, 730–742.

Kahneman, D. (1973). *Attention and effort.* Englewood Cliffs, NJ: Prentice-Hall.

Kahneman, D., & Tversky, A. (1979). Prospect Theory: An analysis of decision under risk. *Econometrica, 47*, 263–292.

Klabunde, R. E. (2005). *Cardiovascular physiology concepts.* Philadelphia, PA: Lippincott Williams & Wilkins.

Kucera, Z., Goldenberg, Z., & Kurca, E. (2004). Sympathetic skin response: Review of the method and its clinical use. *Bratsil Lek Listy, 105*, 108–116.

Lerner, J. S., & Tiedens, L. Z. (2006). Portrait of the angry decision maker: how appraisal tendencies shape anger's influence on cognition. *Journal of Behavioral Decision Making, 19*, 115–137.

Maia, T. V., & McClelland, J. L. (2004). A reexamination of the evidence for the somatic marker hypothesis: What participants really know in the Iowa Gambling Task. *Proceedings of the National Academy of Science, 101*, 16075–16080.

McCraty, R., Atkinson, M., & Bradley, R. T. (2004). Electrophysiological evidence of intuition: Part 1. The surprising role of the heart. *The Journal of Alternative and Complementary Medicine, 10*, 133–143.

Oka, S., Chapman, R. C., & Jacobson, R. C. (2000). Phasic pupil dilation response to noxious stimulation: Effects of conduction, distance, sex, and age. *Journal of Psychophysiology, 14*, 97–105.

Peters, E., Västfjäll, D., Gärling, T., & Slovic P. (2006). Affect and decision-making: A "hot" topic. *Journal of Behavioral Decision-making, 19*, 79–85.

Piferi, R. L., Kline, K. A., Younger, J., & Lawler, K. A. (2000). An alternative approach for achieving cardiovascular baseline: Viewing an aquatic video. *International Journal of Psychophysiology, 37*, 207–217.

Pillar, G., Bar, A., Schnall, R., Sheffy, J., & Lavie, P. (2002). Autonomic arousal index: An automated detection based on peripheral arterial tonometry. *Sleep, 25*, 541–547.

Read, D. & Loewenstein, G. (1995). The diversification bias: Explaining the difference between prospective and real-time taste for variety. *Journal of Experimental Psychology: Applied, 1*, 34–49.

Rook, K.S. (1984). The negative side of social interaction: impact on psychological well-being. *Journal of Personality and Social Psychology, 46*, 1097–1108.

Satterthwaite, T. D., Green, L., Myerson, J., Parker, J., Ramaratnam, M., & Buckner, R. L. (2007). Dissociable but inter-related systems of cognitive control and reward during decision making: evidence from pupillometry and event-related fMRI. *Neuroimage, 37*, 1017–1031.

Savage, L. J. (1954). *The Foundations of Statistics.* John Wiley & Sons, New York: Dover Publications.

Schnall, R.P., Shlitner, A., Sheffy, J., Kedar, R., & Lavie, P. (1999). Periodic, profound peripheral vasoconstriction – A new marker of obstructive sleep apnea. *Sleep, 22*, 939–946.

Schwarz, N., & Clore, G. L. (1983). Mood, misattribution, and judgments of well-being: information and directive functions of affective states. *Journal of Personality and Social Psychology, 45*, 513–523.

Shafir, E., Simonson, I., & Tversky, A. (1993). Reason-based choice. *Cognition, 49*, 11–36.

Sloman, S. A. (1996). The empirical case for two systems of reasoning. *Psychological Bulletin, 119*, 3–22.

Slovic, P., Finucane, M. L., Peters, E., & MacGregor, D. G. (2002). The affect heuristic. In T. Gilovich, D. Griffin, & D. Kahneman (Eds.), *Heuristics and biases: The psychology of intuitive judgment* (pp. 397–420). New York, NY: Cambridge University Press.

Sutton, R. S., & Barto A. G. (1998). *Reinforcement learning: An introduction.* Cambridge, MA: MIT Press.

Tarlovsky, Y., Yechiam, E., Ofek, E., & Grunwald, A. (2008). Peripheral Arterial Tone: A missing channel in polygraph examination? *American Journal of Forensic Psychology, 11*, 313–323.

Tarvainen, M. P., Koistinen, A. S., Valkonen-Korhonen, M., Partanen, J., & Karjalainen, P. A. (2001). Analysis of Galvanic Skin Responses with principal components and clustering techniques. *IEEE Transactions on Biomedical Engineering, 48*, 1071–1079.

Tranel, D., & Damasio, A. R. (1985). Knowledge without awareness: An autonomic index of facial recognition by prosopagnosics. *Science, 228*, 1453–1454.

Tranel, D., & Damasio, A. R. (1988). Non-conscious face recognition in patients with face agnosia. *Behavioral Brain Research, 31*, 427–438.

Ubel, P. A., & Loewenstein, G. (1997). The role of decision analysis in informed consent: choosing between intuition and systematicity. *Social Science and Medicine, 44*, 647–656.

Yechiam, E., Veinott, E.S., Busemeyer, J.R., & Stout, J.C. (2007). Cognitive models for evaluating basic decision processes in clinical populations. In R. Neufeld (Ed.), *Advances in clinical cognitive science: Formal modeling and assessment of processes and symptoms* (pp. 81–111). Washington DC: APA Books.

9   Investigating causal intuitions

York Hagmayer

Introduction

In our everyday world we interact with many complex causal systems, ranging from our own body to the computer systems we use at work. In order to deal with these systems effectively we need a number of abilities. First, we have to be able to detect causal relations quickly and reliably because causal relations enable us to achieve desired outcomes by means of interventions. Research has shown that we use a variety of observable cues to differentiate causal from non-causal relations. Some of these cues even enable us to perceive causality on a single occasion. For example, we directly "see" that Fred's joke made Emma cry, although we have never heard this joke before and generally believe that jokes cause laughter rather than despair.

Second, we need an ability to make predictions about events that we have not yet observed. This is especially important for decision making, when we have to envision the causal consequences that would result from our actions. To do so, we need a representation of the causal system, which allows for such inferences. For example, when we deliberate whether to invite Fred, his buddy Tom and Emma to the same party, and we know that they individually made Emma cry, we can predict that trouble is inevitable. Research on causal learning and reasoning has shown that we use causal model representations to make predictions, which incorporate assumptions that allow inferring unobserved events and relations.

Finally, we need an ability to learn about successful courses of actions even when the causal system is beyond our grasp. For example, when dealing with our body it makes sense to learn some basics about the fundamental causal processes (e.g. nutrition and digestion). Such explicit causal knowledge allows us to evaluate novel food items, and to deliberately balance our diet. On the other hand, we have to be able to simply learn which food items suit us well, without necessarily having to understand how they affect our bodily system. In these cases, implicit causal knowledge suffices to avoid harm. Research has shown that people may use different forms of learning resulting in implicit and explicit causal knowledge.

The critical point of all three abilities described above is that the underlying cognitive processes are generally intuitive (cf. Glöckner and Witteman, chapter 1, this volume). Therefore, we will have a closer look at these processes in this chapter. In the first part, we will focus on the cues that people use to judge causality. In the second part, we will look at the assumptions people include in their causal model representations that allow them to go beyond the given information. In the third part, we will concentrate on implicit and explicit causal knowledge resulting from dealing with a causal system. In all parts a research paradigm will be introduced which allows to run studies.[1] Possible modifications and extensions will be pointed out. In addition, theoretical approaches which allow modelling the underlying cognitive processes will be briefly mentioned and pointers to the relevant literature will be given.

Cues to causality

Philosophers have analyzed the concept of causality for centuries. By doing so they did not only develop theories of causality, they also deeply analyzed our intuitions about causes and effects. Therefore philosophical writings are a good starting point to look for cues people may consider when judging causal relations (e.g. Cartwright, 1983, 1989; Eells, 1991; Glymour, 2001; Hume, 1739/1978; Woodward, 2003; Salmon, 1980; Wolff, 2007).

Box 9.1 shows a model of a causal relation. According to the model variable *C* causes variable *E*. The arrow connecting the two represents a causal mechanism by which the cause *C* generates the effect *E*. Underneath the causal model a number of theoretical assumptions about observable cues to causality are listed, which have been discussed in the philosophical literature (see Box for references). All of these cues have been shown to affect causal judgments (see Lagnado, Waldmann, Hagmayer, & Sloman, 2007, for a review).

Research paradigm

There are many ways to study which cues people use to make causal judgments. The basic idea is to experimentally manipulate the cues. If the cues are considered, they should determine whether an observed sequence of events is judged causal or non-causal. The classic paradigm to study "causal perception" has been invented by Michotte (1946) (see Figure 9.1). The paradigm builds upon our everyday knowledge about the physics of motion (e.g., the motion and collision of billiard balls). For instance, participants may observe how a dot moves towards a second, resting dot, touches the second dot and then the second dot starts to move away from the first, while the first one stops. By asking participants to describe their perceptions, Michotte was able to show that the strongest causal impression results when the cause movement precedes the effect movement, the balls touch and the second movement starts immediately (contiguity), and the two movements have the same direction and speed (similarity). Unfortunately, Michotte's paradigm has some shortcomings: (i) it confounds implicit theories of causality

---

Box 9.1

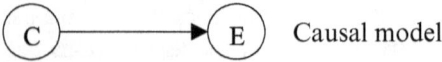

Precedence: A cause precedes its effect.

Asymmetry: The cause generates the effect, but not vice versa.

Temporal and spatial contiguity: Cause and effect are close in space and time (Hume, 1739). Cause and effect are related by a mechanism which closes the temporal and spatial gap between the cause and effect (Evans, 1993).

Resemblance: A cause and its effect share some features (Hume, 1739).

Counterfactual dependence: If the cause would not have happened the effect would not have occurred (Hume, 1739).

Covariance: Cause and effect covary (Hume, 1739); a cause increases or decreases the probability of the effect in comparison to the cause's absence (Eells, 1991)

Manipulability: By manipulating the cause the effect can be changed, but not vice versa (Woodward, 2003).

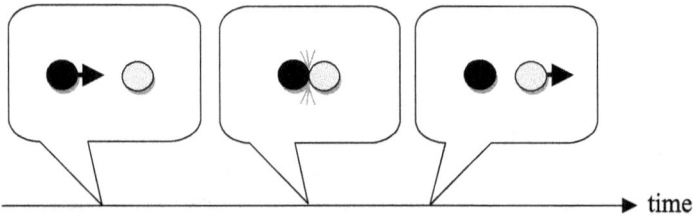

Figure 9.1 Illustration of Michotte's paradigm to investigate perceptual cues to causality. The black dot moves towards the resting grey dot, touches it, and then the grey dot starts to move.

and physics, (ii) it does not allow investigating covariation, counterfactual dependence, and manipulation which are important cues when more than one observation is made.

A more recent paradigm from developmental psychology is more suitable to investigate all cues within the same setting: The blicket detector (Gopnik, Sobel, Schulz, & Glymour, 2001). A blicket detector is a box that lights up and plays some music if a blicket (i.e., a certain type of object) is put on top (see Figure 9.2). For studies with children usually a real box is used, for adults

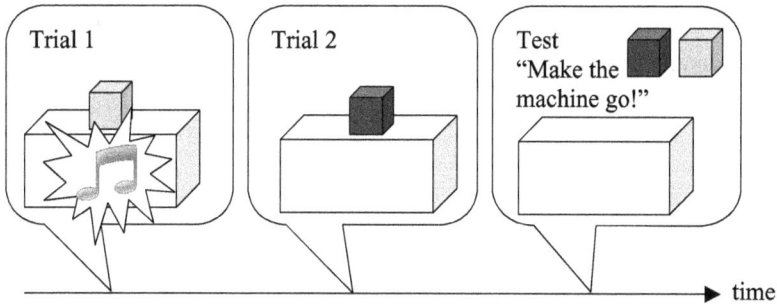

Figure 9.2 Illustration of the blicket detector paradigm to investigate cues to causality. Putting the grey block on top causes the machine to play music and light up. The black block has no effect. That means only the grey block is a blicket. See text for experimental manipulations.

a computer simulation should suffice. To investigate temporal contiguity, for example, the following procedure might be used. First the participant is shown a familiarization trial with a white block that makes the machine go off after a short interval. Next a trial with a red block is shown that leads to an immediate effect. Finally a trial with a blue block is shown that leads to the effect after some longer interval. As a test, participants are asked to choose between a red and a blue block to make the machine go. The covariation between different types of blocks and activation can be manipulated as well. The detector may only activate with a certain probability when a certain type of block is placed on top. Even counterfactual dependence can be studied. For example, the detector never activates when blue, white and red blocks are put on top individually, but it activates whenever a red or blue block is combined with the white block. In this case, the white block enables the effect, i.e. it allows the other blocks to exert their causal influence. Therefore, it is counterfactually necessary for the effect to occur. Finally, the blicket detector allows studying how people integrate different cues. For example, a block may have a strong contiguity, but no covariation (i.e., the detector lights up immediately when a block is placed on top, but it lights up with the same frequency when no block is placed on it). By factorially combining the different observable cues and running them within participants, it is even possible to determine the strategies participants use to integrate the cues (see Bröder, chapter 4, this volume; Glöckner, chapter 5, this volume).

The blicket detector paradigm also allows collecting a number of different dependent measures. Participants might be asked about causal impact directly. However, previous research on covariation estimation and the judgment of causal strength has revealed a number of biases in such assessments (see e.g. White, 2003). As an alternative, participants might be asked to determine which of the blocks are blickets (categorization task). A second alternative is to ask participants to choose a block to make the detector go (intervention task). Based on the assumption that people will prefer the block with the higher causal impact, this dependent measure allows to find out whether and how people differentiate between different causes. Note that the second and third dependent measure do not require any explicit causal judgment.

Modelling

A number of theoretical approaches can be used to model causal judgments from cues. The first possibility is a cue-based model, which assumes that people have fundamental assumptions about the cues indicating causal relatedness (Einhorn & Hogarth, 1986). Some of these cues (e.g., temporal precedence and covariation) are considered necessary, while others (e.g., contiguity and similarity) can be compensated by other cues. Observed causal relations (e.g., the collision of two billiard balls) exhibit all cues. Therefore they result in an immediate impression of causal relatedness. Observed relations that show only some cues are judged to be less causal or not causal at all. A second possibility is to use causal model theory (Waldmann, 1996; Waldmann, Cheng, Hagmayer, & Blaisdell, 2008). Causal model theory assumes that people have fundamental assumptions about causality. Based on these assumptions, people use directly observable cues and domain-specific background knowledge to infer a hypothetical causal model of the given situation (e.g., the hypothesis that the variable C is a cause of the variable E). A third approach is causal Bayes net theories. Although many take them to be merely computational models (e.g. Griffiths & Tenenbaum, 2005), others consider them to be descriptive of what people do (e.g. Gopnik et al., 2004). In short, these theories assume that people intuitively consider all possible causal hypotheses and use the available evidence and Bayesian inference to find out the most probable hypothesis (for modelling details see Griffths & Tenenbaum, 2005, or Gill, 2002).

   Summary. There is consensus that people use cues for detecting causality (cf. Lagnado et al., 2007). Some research indicates that temporal delays are the most important cue (Lagnado & Sloman, 2004). Nevertheless, there is still relatively little empirical knowledge about how people integrate different cues and whether cues can be compensated. Another interesting question is when later available evidence does change earlier causal impressions. It is obvious that we can overcome immediate impressions of causal relatedness, because we can identify mere coincidences. Yet, little is known about the conditions under which this revision occurs.

Assumptions about complex causal structures

People are usually confronted with complex causal systems involving many causes leading to a multitude of different effects which in turn have other causal consequences. Both philosophers proposing probabilistic models of causality (e.g. Eells, 1991) and computer scientists interested in causal Bayes nets (e.g. Pearl, 2000; Spirtes et al., 1993) analyzed these complex causal structures. They showed that these more complex structures have certain properties and allow predicting unobserved events and relations if certain assumptions hold. A number of cognitive scientists (e.g. Sloman, 2005; Waldmann, 1996) claimed that people acquire causal models representations that incorporate at least some of these assumptions. This enables people to make inferences about events and relations not yet experienced. Moreover, these implicit theoretical assumptions allow people to represent only the causal relations, instead of representing all possible statistical relations among the variables of a system, because the statistical relations can be inferred from the causal ones. Here is a simple illustrative example. Symptoms of the same disease tend to correlate. One possibility to represent this causal system would be to encode the statistical relations among the disease and the symptoms as well as the statistical relations among the symptoms. Alternatively only the causal relations between the disease (cause) and each symptom (effect) might be represented (common cause model, see Box 9.2). This causal model encompasses the assumption that effects of the same cause correlate. Hence, the statistical relations among the effects can be inferred and need not

---

Box 9.2

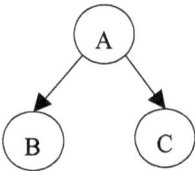

Common cause model	Causal chain model	Common effect model

Effects of a joint cause correlate

Screening off: If A is present, then the probability of C only depends on A and not on B

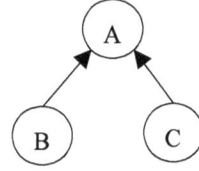

Diagnostic inferences:
(i) If both effects are present, the cause's presence is highly likely; if only one effect is absent, the cause's presence is less likely.
(ii) The probability of the cause, given an effect, depends on the presence of alternative causes of the effect and the target cause's base rate.

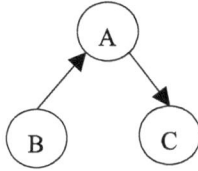

Variables within a chain correlate: If B is present, C is likely to be present

Screening off: If A is present, then the probability of C only depends on A and not on B

Causes of a joint effect are independent

Explaining away: If A is present, then B and C become more likely; if then B is revealed as present, the probability of C drops.

Prognostic inferences:
(i) If at least one cause is present, the effect's presence is highly likely.
(ii) The probability of the effect, given a cause, does not depend on the presence of alternative causes of the cause and the effect's base rate.

be represented. So the critical question is: Which are the implicit assumptions people incorporate in their causal model representations? Note that these implicit theoretical assumptions do not pertain to observable cues, but are assumptions about the implications entailed by different causal models.

The top of Box 9.2 shows three causal models with three causal variables (*A*, *B*, *C*) and two causal relations. These three models are the building blocks of all more complex models. On the left hand side a common cause model is shown, which identifies variable *A* as the cause of variables *B* and *C*; in the middle a causal chain model is shown, in which *B* causes *A* and *A* causes *C*; on the right hand side a common effect model is depicted in which *B* and *C* are the causes of their joint effect *A*. According to causal model theories these graphs not only represent causal structure, but also encompass additional theoretical assumptions. The common cause model entails a correlation among the effects. The causal chain model entails that the first cause in the chain (*B*) is correlated to the final effect (*C*). The common effect model represents the assumption that the two causes are independent and independently generate their joint effect. Hence, it entails no correlation among *B* and *C*.

A further crucial assumption made by causal Bayes net theories that might be part of people's implicit theory of causal structures is the so-called Markov assumption (cf. Pearl, 2000). Informally, it postulates that each variable in a causal system is independent of all other variables other than its causal descendants (i.e., its direct and indirect effects) once the state of its cause-variables is known. Although it sounds complicated, this assumption makes intuitively sense. The status of a variable in the world is determined by its immediate causes. If these causes are fixed, then every other event in the world can change without affecting the variable. For example, if a billiard balls hits a resting ball, the second ball will start to move. It is irrelevant whether the first ball was moved by a billiard cue, or by an earth quake. The Markov assumption has some interesting implications for the three models.[2] If the underlying causal structure is common cause, knowing about effect *B* does raise the probability of effect *C*, because the presence of effect *B* indicates the presence of cause *A*, which in turn makes the presence of effect *C* more likely. However, if the status of the common cause is known, then knowing about effect *B* tells you nothing about effect *C*, because the probability of effect *C* merely depends on the presence of *A*. This implication has been called *screening off* as the presence of the cause screens off the effects from each other. The causal chain model has similar implications. If the intermediate variable *A* is known, then the probability of *C* again only depends on its immediate cause *A* and not on *B*. By contrast, in a common effect model, the two causes are independent. Therefore knowing about one cause does not tell you anything about the second cause. However, if the status of the common effect *A* is known, then knowing about *B* does tell you something about *C*. Imagine that you observe the effect to be present. The presence of *A* increases the probability of both of its causes. Now you are informed that cause *B* is actually present. This reduces the probability of cause *C*, because *B*'s presence would suffice to explain *A*'s presence. This implication of a common effect model has been called *explaining away*.

Another set of implications of causal models concern how observations add up as evidence. Imagine that you have investigated the relations among *A* and *B* and *A* and *C* separately. You have found out that both causal relations are almost deterministic. Now for the first time you investigate all three variables in concert. You observe that *B* is present but *C* is absent. What is the likelihood of *A* being present? Assuming a common effect model, *A* should be present, because one of its causes is present. But what about a common cause model? The presence of *B* indicates that *A* is likely to be present. However, the absence of *C* strongly indicates that *A* is absent. Hence, the most parsimonious explanation is that *A* is absent and *B* was caused by some other factor. Thus while *A* is highly likely given a common effect model, it is less likely given a common cause model.

Causal models also entail a differential sensitivity to base rates. To predict the probability of an effect from its cause, the base rate of the effect is irrelevant. If we know that someone is infected with a flu virus, we know that the probability of getting fever is high, no matter how likely fever is overall. In addition, it is irrelevant whether there are many or just a few causes of the infection. By contrast, if we diagnose the presence of a cause from effects, the base rate of the cause matters. For example, if we observe someone having fever, her probability of being infected with a flu virus is still low, because (i) there are many other causes of fever, and (ii) the base rate of being infected with flu is very low. Hence, base rates and alternative causes do matter.

Research paradigm

There are many ways to study whether people's causal model representations share the implications outlined above. The basic idea of one well-suited experimental paradigm is depicted in Figure 9.3 (cf. Hagmayer & Waldmann, 2000). Participants are informed about individual causal relations that constitute a more complex causal model, e.g. the relation among *A* and *B* and the relation among *A* and *C*. Participants receive no information about the relation among the events not directly causally related, that is, the causes *B* and *C* in a common effect model, and the effects *B* and *C* in a common cause model. Moreover, they receive no information about the probability of the third variable conditional on the other two variables. For example, they do not know how likely the common effect *A* is given that cause *B* is present but cause *C* is absent. Therefore participants have to rely on their causal model representations to answer questions about these unobserved relations and probabilities. In turn, the answers tell us which assumptions are built into people's causal models.

Either the individual causal links can be instructed directly (Rehder & Burnett, 2005; Walsh & Sloman, 2007) or participants can be asked to learn

Common cause model   Common effect model

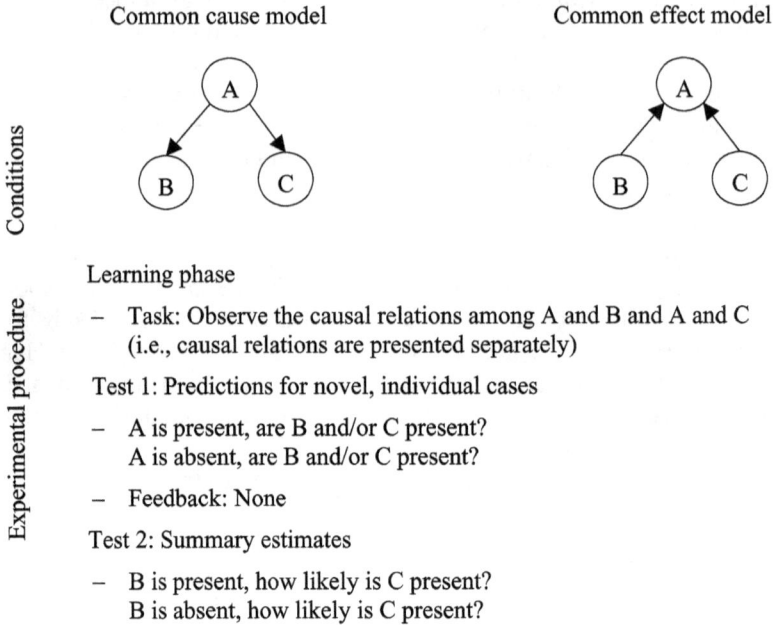

Conditions

Learning phase

– Task: Observe the causal relations among A and B and A and C
  (i.e., causal relations are presented separately)

Test 1: Predictions for novel, individual cases

– A is present, are B and/or C present?
  A is absent, are B and/or C present?

– Feedback: None

Test 2: Summary estimates

– B is present, how likely is C present?
  B is absent, how likely is C present?

Experimental procedure

Figure 9.3 Research paradigm to investigate the assumptions incorporated into
causal model representations (Hagmayer & Waldmann, 2000).

about the relations (Hagmayer & Waldmann, 2000). The advantage of a
learning paradigm is that participants receive complete information about
base rates and probabilistic causal relations in naturalistic fashion. In one of
our experiments (Hagmayer & Waldmann, 2000), participants had to learn
separately about two causal relations connecting a variable *A* to two other
variables *B* and *C*. To ensure that no covariation between *B* and *C* could
be observed, only information about one of them was presented at a time.
The data and their presentation were identical for all participants. The
learning phase consisted of 80 observations, 40 for each relation. As an
experimental factor, assumptions about the underlying causal model were
manipulated. Participants were instructed that the variables formed either a
common cause model, or a common effect model. The relation between *A*
and the other variables was quite strong, so that a high correlation among *B*
and *C* had to be expected if they were effects of a joint cause. The learning
phase was followed by a test phase in which participants' assumptions about
the covariation between *B* and *C* was assessed. First participants were shown
20 new cases in which *A* was either present or absent. Participants' task was
to predict for each case whether *B* and/or *C* would be present. No feedback
was provided. By predicting *B* and *C* several times, participants generated a
correlation between them (e.g., a high correlation was generated when participants frequently predicted B and C to be either both present or both

absent). As a second task participants were directly asked to estimate the probabilistic relation among the two. It turned out that participants gener- ated a positive correlation among *B* and *C* when they assumed a common cause model, but generated independence when assuming a common effect model. Interestingly, participants' direct estimates of *B* and *C*'s relation did not differ between the two models. So it seems that participants intuitively took the implications of the causal models into account, but were not able to explicitly state them (Hagmayer & Waldmann, 2000).

Possible extensions. The test phase can easily be changed to investigate other implications. To assess screening off, participants in a common cause condition could be presented with individual observations of (i) only the common cause, and (ii) the common cause and one effect. In both cases they would have to predict the other effect. To assess explaining away, part- icipants in a common effect condition could be presented with individual observations of (i) only the common effect, and (ii) the common effect and one cause. Now they would have to predict the other cause. In addition to these trial-by-trial predictions participants' explicit understanding of causal structures can be tested by directly asking them to estimate the respective probabilities.

Furthermore, the paradigm allows collecting data on diagnostic and prog- nostic inferences. For example, Rehder (2007) asked participants to infer the defining feature of a category from other features which were either introduced as causes or as effects of that defining feature. No specific infor- mation about the features' relations was provided. It turned out that partici- pants were sensitive to the underlying causal model. Given a common effect model, participants expected the defining feature of the category to be pres- ent when at least one cause was present; the presence of further causes increased ratings only slightly. Given a common cause model, by contrast, ratings increased gradually the more features were present.

Finally, the basic procedure can be extended to more complex models involving more causal relations. Most notably, the model could be extended to include causal feedback loops. Research with natural causal systems including feedback loops indicates that people have a hard time to under- stand the implications of these loops (Sterman, 2000). Maybe people do not have any particular implicit theory about causal loops.

Modelling

Causal model theory and causal Bayes nets can be used to model the cogni- tive processes people may employ when learning about a causal structure in a piecemeal fashion. Causal model theory assumes that people use the instruction to induce a causal model and the learning data to estimate its parameters, that is, the base rates of the causes, the strength of the causal relations, and the influence of hidden causes upon effects. Based on the model, people make predictions (cf. Waldmann et al., 2008). Causal Bayes nets would model the learning process as a Bayesian inference about the causal model and its parameters (i.e., an estimation of the respective probability distributions). Like causal model theory, it would model the tests as inferences over these causal models (cf. Griffiths & Tenenbaum, 2005).

Summary

Causal models and the assumptions built into them are currently investigated by many researchers. So far, it seems that people at least share the assumption that effects of the same cause tend to correlate, but causes of the same effect tend to be independent. This finding has been replicated in research on categorization (e.g., Rehder, 2003, Waldmann, Holyoak & Fratianne, 1995) and on causal learning (e.g. Hagmayer & Waldmann, 2000; Waldmann, 1996, 2001). Whether people's implicit theories encompass the other implications outlined above is still an open question. It seems that people's judgments and choices conform to these implications at least under some conditions. Another open question is whether people use observations that conform to these implications as cues to make inferences about causal structure. For example, people may infer a common cause model when two correlated events become independent conditional on a third event. So far, there is no evidence that people use such cues (Lagnado et al., 2007; Hagmayer, 2001).

Implicit and explicit causal knowledge

When dealing with complex causal systems people may acquire implicit and/or explicit knowledge about it. Implicit causal knowledge allows for effective action without entailing explicit knowledge about the underlying causal structure. Thus the person knows how to act without knowing how the system works.

Overview of research traditions

Before describing a research paradigm, I want to provide a brief overview of three research traditions that studied the acquisition of implicit and explicit causal knowledge through learning. Interestingly these research traditions hardly referenced each other.

The first is research on complex problem solving and systems control. Studies in this area investigated how people learn to deal with complex causal systems and whether they acquire knowledge about the causal relations within the systems (cf. Frensch & Funke, 1995). Some findings indicate that participants may acquire implicit but no explicit causal knowledge (cf. Berry & Broadbent, 1984; Dörner, 1996). Despite being able to control the system well, some participants lacked a deeper insight into the causal structure of the underlying system. However, other studies report a positive correlation between explicit causal knowledge and performance (e.g. Funke & Müller, 1988; Vollmeyer, Burns & Holyoak, 1996).

The second relevant research area is the induction of causal structure. Performance tends to be poor if people only have statistical cues available (e.g., Hagmayer, 2001). Performance increases considerably if people have several cues available (cf. Lagnado et al., 2007), or if they can intervene on the system (cf. Steyvers, Tenenbaum, Wagemakers, & Blum, 2003). As studies on causal induction generally look only for explicit causal knowledge, they almost never report findings with respect to implicit causal knowledge. One exception is Steyvers and colleagues (2003), who showed that after observing a causal system, participants tended to intervene on those variables that were most critical for determining the underlying causal structure, although they were not aware of that structure.

The third research tradition is animal cognition. Studies on instrumental learning show that rats can acquire very sophisticated causal knowledge (cf. Blaisdell, Sawa, Leising, & Waldmann, 2006). For example, Rescorla (1990) demonstrated that rats are able to learn that given Cue 1 action *Do A* yields outcome *X* and action *Do B* results in outcome *Y*, while given Cue 2 action *Do A* leads to *Y* and *Do B* to *X*. As the animals expect a certain outcome, the knowledge resulting from this learning seems rather explicit (*goal directed learning*, Dayan, 2001). However, there is a second type of instrumental learning, in which animals do not acquire any expectations about outcomes, but simply learn that given Cue 1 it is best to do *A*, while given Cue 2 *Do B* is best (*habit learning*, Dayan, 2001). Hence, in this case they only learn about the association between a cue and a reaction. Habit learning results in a form of implicit causal knowledge, the animal "knows" the best action but not its causal consequences.

Research paradigms

Given that many different research traditions ran studies, there are many extremely heterogeneous paradigms. In studies on instrumental learning, rarely more than two cues, actions and outcomes are used, all of which are generally binary and connected by simple deterministic causal links. The goal of the participants presumably is to maximize their outcomes (e.g., food and drink for the deprived animals).

In studies on causal learning and the induction of causal structure, mostly simple models with three or four binary variables are used, connected by common cause, common effect or causal chain structures. The causal systems do not contain feedback loops and the causal mechanisms are in general probabilistic but linear. And, as in animal research, learning consists of individual, independent trials. The task assigned to participants in these studies usually is to learn about the causal structure, that is, to find out how the variables are causally connected.

Research on complex problem solving in itself is very heterogeneous. Causal systems may contain between 4 and 2,000 variables, most of which are continuous. Mechanisms are linear and non-linear; in general there are feedback loops and autonomous processes. Crucially, trials tend to be dependent. That is, previous decisions affect later trials. Moreover, participants' goal usually is not to learn about causal structure but to achieve or maintain a certain goal state. Sometimes even the goal state is ill-defined (e.g., successfully manage the city of Lohausen, Dörner, 1996). Funke (2006) provides an excellent overview of different causal systems (although the chapter is in German the references are very helpful). Given that the different research paradigms are so different, it seems hardly surprising that different findings resulted.

A unifying research paradigm

Recently, we started a new line of research that aims to bridge the gaps between the different research traditions (Hagmayer & Meder, 2008). We developed a new paradigm, which allows studying the acquisition of implicit and explicit causal knowledge. The basic idea of the paradigm is to confront people with a causal system and ask them to achieve a certain goal. By repeatedly choosing among a predefined set of actions, participants learn how to deal with the system. In consequence, they may acquire different forms of knowledge: Knowledge about the best option as in habit learning (i.e. implicit causal knowledge), knowledge about expectancies and outcomes as in goal directed instrumental learning, or causal knowledge about the underlying causal system (i.e. explicit causal knowledge).

Figure 9.4 shows the two causal models we used in a first study (Hagmayer & Meder, 2008). Both models contain four variables, three binary variables that can be activated by interventions and a continuous payoff variable that is affected by these three variables. There is only one difference between the models. The first model includes a causal link connecting variables A and B, while in the second model all three variables do not causally affect each other. The three possible interventions *Do A*, *Do B*, and *Do C* are also shown. The interventions were labelled according to the variable they affected. As every intervention targeted a specific variable, it is possible for learners to infer the underlying causal model. For example, if the activation of A also results in an activation of B, then A has to cause B and therefore *Do A* indirectly affects B by way of A. The causal links connecting the interventions to the variables were deterministic; hence every intervention activated the respective variable. The variables themselves contributed a fixed amount to the final outcome. The numbers assigned to the arrows show each variable's contribution. Note that the payoffs resulting from the interventions were identical in both conditions (+80 for *Do A*, +40 for *Do B*, +60 for *Do C*).

The experiment consisted of a learning phase, in which participants repeatedly chose among the available options, and a test phase, followed by several test questions. Participants' task in the first phase was to maximize their payoffs. Each of the 30 trials referred to a separate case, in which all variables were inactive prior to any intervention. After choosing an intervention,

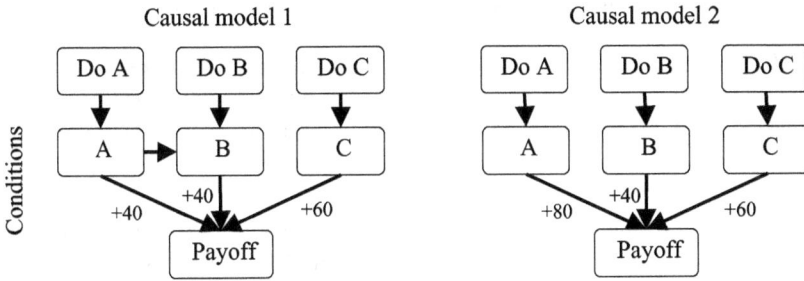

Learning phase
- Task: Maximize payoff by choosing among Do A, Do B and Do C
- Feedback: Activation of A, B and C, and Payoff

Test phase
- B is removed from the causal system
- Task: Maximize payoff by choosing among Do A, Do B and Do C
- Feedback: None

Test questions
- Estimate expected value of Do A, Do B, and Do C before B was removed
- Estimate expected value of Do A and Do C after B was removed
- Identify causal relations connecting interventions, variables and the payoff

Figure 9.4 Research paradigm to investigate implicit and explicit causal knowledge resulting from dealing with a causal system (Hagmayer & Meder, 2008).

participants received feedback which variables were activated and how much the outcome increased. After completing the first phase they proceeded to a test phase, in which they were told that variable *B* had been removed from the system. No further explanations about the consequences of this change were provided. Participants were requested to decide on interventions for ten new cases without receiving feedback. No feedback is crucial, because no new learning should result in this test phase. Again participants' target was to maximize the payoff for each case. The removal of *B* allows to test whether participants merely learned that choosing *Do A* is best or that they have encoded the causal structure. If participants simply learned which option was best, they should continue to choose *Do A* given both models as the payoffs were identical. If they learned about causal structure, they should figure out that a removal of *B* reduces the expected payoff of *Do A* to +40 given Model 1, therefore they should switch to *Do C* which has a higher payoff (+60). However, given Model 2 the removal does not affect the payoff of *Do A*; therefore intervening in *A* is still the best choice. Participants were also asked to estimate the expected payoffs of all options in both phases. This second dependent variable shows whether participants explicitly learned about the payoffs resulting from the interventions, and whether they learned about payoffs generated by each variable. Finally, participants were asked to express their assumptions about the causal system by drawing the causal relations connecting the interventions, variables and the final outcome. This third dependent variable tracks participants' explicit knowledge about the structure of the causal system.

It turned out that all participants preferred the same option after the learning phase. Roughly 50% of them also spontaneously learned about causal structure. Almost all of these participants switched from choosing *Do A* to choosing *Do C* given Model 1, and their ratings revealed that they inferred the new payoff of *Do A* resulting from the removal of *B*. Participants who showed no understanding of the underlying causal structure, neither switched their preference when variable *B* was removed given Model 1, nor did their ratings show any further inferences about the causal system. Thus a strong convergence of explicit and implicit causal knowledge resulted in this particular experiment.

Possible extensions. The basic experimental paradigm is very similar to paradigms used to study causal learning. But it can be easily extended in various ways. For example, in a set of new experiments, we used probabilistic rather than deterministic relations between interventions and effects. We also used interventions whose relation to the variables had to be learned by making choices.

One critical extension of the basic paradigm is the move from static to dynamic causal systems. By doing so, the paradigm more closely matches the paradigms used to study system control and complex problem solving. To turn the causal systems shown in Figure 9.4 into dynamic systems, causal links have to be added that connect the state of a variable at a certain point in time to a later point in time. In our own research we started with the outcome and added a decay process which decreased the outcome by 50% from trial to trial. If an intervention was chosen on a trial, its effect was added to the decayed outcome. Hence variables still had a linear effect. Otherwise the experimental procedure stayed the same. One further step would be to install dynamic relations for all the other variables within the system. For example, an activation of variable *A* at time t_0 may cause its activation at t_1 with a probability of .9. Finally, to turn the experiment into a control task, participants have to be asked to reach and maintain a certain outcome level rather than maximizing the outcome.

Modelling

Choices and answers of participants who learn about causal structure can be modelled by causal model theory (Sloman & Hagmayer, 2006). To model the choice behaviour of participants not acquiring explicit causal knowledge, it has to be assumed that these people fall back to associative learning (cf. Waldmann & Hagmayer, 2001). Causal Bayes net theories can easily model the processes underlying the choices and judgments of people who are sensitive to causal structure. To model the behaviour of other participants these theories have to assume that people have strong prior hypotheses (cf. Tenenbaum, Griffths, & Niyogi, 2007). Finally, learning and choice can be modelled by theories of associative learning (e.g., Dayan, 2001).

Summary

Many different areas of research (complex problem solving, causal learning, instrumental learning) provide theoretical approaches and experimental paradigms to study the acquisition of implicit and explicit causal knowledge. Some findings indicate that people may acquire implicit causal knowledge that allows them to act successfully without yielding explicit knowledge about the underlying causal structures. However, it is unclear which the underlying cognitive processes are. Well designed experiments will help to distinguish between different theoretical models in the future.

Final comments

Although the term causal intuition is rarely used in the literature on causal learning, reasoning and decision making, there is a surprisingly huge amount of research studying capacities that rest on intuitive processing. The paradigms presented here are a starting point for investigating these processes. To study the cues people use to derive causal judgments, it is best to manipulate these cues directly. To study the properties of participants' causal model representations it is best to ask them to make inferences about unobserved aspects of the causal system. Finally, to study implicit vs. explicit causal knowledge resulting from causal learning it is best to ask people to achieve a certain goal while dealing with a causal system, and to assess a broad range of both cognitive and behavioural measures of causal knowledge.

Challenges. Each of the paradigms proposed here has its special challenges. When running studies on people's implicit theory of causality, the most important point is to avoid confounding with intuitive theories of physics, biology or other domains. General causal cues might be contradicted or moderated by other content cues. People's general assumptions about the implications of causal structures might be overturned by domain specific knowledge.

When studying implicit and explicit causal knowledge resulting from learning, it is crucial to control (i) the background knowledge people may bring to bear, and (ii) the learning input people receive. Background knowledge may strongly bias what people learn. The same observed covariation may be judged to indicate a strong or a weak causal relation depending on previous causal assumptions (Koslowski, 1996). Controlling the learning input might be tricky if participants can decide for themselves and the causal system is dynamic. In this case, the assignment of specific goals may guide participants' actions so that equivalent learning input results. When causal relations are probabilistic, it has to be ensured that the intended probabilities are in fact observed. For example, if the probability of an event is .1, 35% of participants will not see the event within the first ten trials. To solve this problem, either the events have to be pre-fixed and only randomized in their presentation, or many trials have to be shown (often 100 or more).

Keeping these points in mind, the paradigms presented here will hopefully motivate more researchers to study causal intuitions. As pointed out above, there are still many interesting discoveries to be made.

Notes

1 The presented paradigms are a subjective selection. They were chosen because I consider them to be the paradigms which allow studying the largest number of research questions. Besides, they can easily be adapted to run both within and between-participants studies. Finally, all paradigms use causal systems that are unfamiliar. Hence, the impact of participants' background knowledge is minimized.
2 It can be proven that all of the following implications are necessary consequences of the Markov condition and the generative causal mechanisms of the model (see Pearl, 2000, for proofs).

References

Berry, D. C., & Broadbent, D. E. (1984). On the relationship between task performance and associated verbalizable knowledge. *Quarterly Journal of Experimental Psychology, 36A*, 209–231.
Blaisdell, A. P., Sawa, K., Leising, K. J., & Waldmann, M. R. (2006). Causal reasoning in rats. *Science, 311*, 1020–1022.
Cartwright, N. (1983). *How the laws of physics lie*. Oxford: Clarendon Press.
Cartwright, N. (1989). *Nature's capacities and their measurement*. Oxford: Clarendon Press.
Dayan, P. (2001). Reinforcement learning. In C. R. Gallistel (Ed.), *Steven's handbook of experimental psychology* (3rd ed., pp. 103–130). New York: Wiley.
Dörner, D. (1996). *The logic of failure*. New York: Metropolitan.
Eells, E. (1991). *Probabilistic causality*. Cambridge: Cambridge University Press.
Einhorn, H. J., & Hogarth, R. M. (1986). Judging probable cause. *Psychological Bulletin, 99*, 3–19.
Evans, A. S. (1993). *Causation and disease: A chronological journey*. New York, NY: Plenum.
Frensch, P. A., & Funke, J. (1995). *Complex problem solving: The European perspective*. Hillsdale, NJ: Lawrence Erlbaum.
Funke, J. (2006). Komplexes Problemlösen. In J. Funke (Ed.), *Enzyklopädie der Psychologie*, Band 8: Kognition. Göttingen: Hogrefe.
Funke, J., & Müller, H. (1988). Eingreifen und Prognostizieren als Determinanten von Systemidentifikation und Systemsteuerung. *Sprache & Kognition, 7*, 176–186.
Gill, J. (2002). *Bayesian methods for the social and behavioral sciences*. Boca Raton, FL: CRC Press.

Glymour, C. (2001). *The mind's arrows*. Cambridge, MA: MIT Press.

Gopnik, A., Glymour, C., Sobel, D. M., Schulz, L. E., Kushnir, T., & Danks, D. (2004). A theory of causal learning in children: Causal maps and Bayes nets. *Psychological Review*, *111*, 3–32.

Gopnik, A. Sobel., D. M., Schulz, L., & Glymour, C. (2001). Causal learning in very young children: 2-, 3-, and 4-year-olds infer causal relations from patterns of variation and co-variation. *Developmental Psychology*, *37*, 620–629.

Griffiths, T. L., & Tenenbaum, J. B. (2005). Structure and strength in causal induction. *Cognitive Psychology*, *51*, 354–384.

Hagmayer, Y. (2001). *Denken mit und über Kausalmodelle* (Thinking with and thinking about causal models). Unpublished PhD thesis.

Hagmayer, Y., & Meder, B. (2008). Causal learning through repeated decision making. In B.C. Love, K. McRae, & V.M. Sloutsky (Eds.), *Proceedings of the 30th Annual Conference of the Cognitive Science Society* (pp. 179–184). Austin, TX: Cognitive Science Society Inc..

Hagmayer, Y., & Waldmann, M. R. (2000). Simulating causal models: The way to structural sensitivity. In L. Gleitman & A. Joshi (Eds.), *Proceedings of the Twenty-second Annual Conference of the Cognitive Science Society* (pp. 214–219). Mahwah, NJ: Erlbaum.

Hume, D. (1739/1978). *A treatise of human nature*. Oxford: Clarendon Press.

Koslowski, B. (1996). *Theory and evidence: The development of scientific reasoning*. Cambridge, MA: MIT Press.

Lagnado, D. A., & Sloman, S. A. (2004). The advantage of timely intervention. *Journal of Experimental Psychology: Learning, Memory, and Cognition*, *30*, 856–876.

Lagnado, D. A., Waldmann, M. A., Hagmayer, Y., & Sloman, S. A. (2007). Beyond covariation. Cues to causal structure. In A. Gopnik & L. E. Schultz, (Eds.), *Causal learning: Psychology, philosophy, and computation* (pp. 154–172). Oxford University Press.

Michotte, A. E. (1946). *The perception of causality*. New York, NY: Basic Books.

Pearl, J. (2000). *Causality*. Cambridge: Cambridge University Press.

Rehder, B. (2003). Categorization as causal reasoning. *Cognitive Science*, *27*, 709–748.

Rehder, B. (2007). Essentialism as a generative theory of classification. In A. Gopnik & L. Schulz (Eds.), *Causal learning: Psychology, philosophy, and computation* (pp. 190–207). Oxford: Oxford University Press.

Rehder, B., & Burnett, R. (2005). Feature inference and the causal structure of categories. *Cognitive Psychology*, *50*, 264–314.

Rescorla, R. A. (1990). The role of information about the response-outcome relation in instrumental discrimination learning. *Journal of Experimental Psychology: Animal Behavior Processes*, *16*, 262–270.

Salmon, W. C. (1980). Probabilistic causality. *Pacific Philosophical Quarterly*, *61*, 50–74.

Sloman, S. A. (2005). *Causal models: How we think about the world and its alternatives*. Cambridge, MA: Oxford University Press.

Sloman, S. A., & Hagmayer, Y. (2006). The causal logic of choice. *Trends in Cognitive Science*, *10*, 407–412.

Spirtes, P., Glymour, C., & Scheines, R. (1993). *Causation, prediction, and search*. New York: Springer.

Sterman, J. D. (2000). *Business dynamics*. Boston, MA: McGraw Hill.

Steyvers, M., Tenenbaum, J. B., Wagenmakers, E-J., & Blum, B. (2003). Inferring causal networks from observations and interventions. *Cognitive Science*, *27*, 453–489.

Tenenbaum, J. B., Griffiths, T. L., Niyogi, S. (2007). Intuitive theories and rational causal inference. In A. Gopnik & L. E. Schulz (Eds.), *Causal learning: Psychology, philosophy, and computation* (pp. 310–322). Oxford University Press.

Vollmeyer, R., Burns, B. D., & Holyoak K. J. (1996). The impact of goal specificity on strategy use and the acquisition of problem structure, *Cognitive Science, 20*, 75–100.

Waldmann, M. R. (1996). Knowledge-based causal induction. In D. R. Shanks, K. J. Holyoak & D. L. Medin (Eds.), *The psychology of learning and motivation*, Vol. 34: Causal learning (pp. 47–88). San Diego: Academic Press.

Waldmann, M. R. (2001). Predictive versus diagnostic causal learning: Evidence from an overshadowing paradigm. *Psychological Bulletin & Review, 8*, 600–608.

Waldmann, M. R., Cheng, P. W., Hagmayer, Y., & Blaisdell, A. P. (2008). Causal learning in rats and humans: a minimal rational model. In N. Chater & M. Oaksford (Eds.), *The probabilistic mind. Prospects for Bayesian cognitive science* (pp. 453–484). Oxford: University Press.

Waldmann, M. R., & Hagmayer, Y. (2001). Estimating causal strength: The role of structural knowledge and processing effort. *Cognition, 82*, 27–58.

Waldmann, M. R., Holyoak, K. J., & Fratianne, A. (1995). Causal models and the acquisition of category structure. *Journal of Experimental Psychology: General, 124*, 181–206.

Walsh C. R., & Sloman, S. A. (2007). Updating causal beliefs with causal models: Violations of screening off. In M. A. Gluck, J. R. Anderson, & S. M. Kosslyn (Eds.), *A Festschrift for Gordon H. Bower* (pp. 345–357). New York: LEA.

White, P. A. (2003). Making causal judgments from the proportion of confirming instances: The pCI rule. *Journal of Experimental Psychology: Learning, Memory, and Cognition, 29*, 710–727.

Wolff, P. (2007). Representing causation. *Journal of Experimental Psychology: General, 136*, 82–111.

Woodward, J. (2003). *Making things happen. A theory of causal explanation.* Oxford: Oxford University Press.

10 Measuring affect and emotions in decision making

The affective side of intuitive information processing

Stephan Dickert

The recent interest in intuitive processes (e.g., Glöckner & Witteman, chapter 1, this volume; Kahneman & Frederick, 2002) sparks the question of how to best measure the intrinsic properties of intuition. While intuition encompasses cognitive processes (e.g., pattern recognition and memory processes), it is also widely accepted that affective reactions are a part of and contribute to intuitive processes (Böhm & Brun, 2008; Slovic, Finucane, Peters, & MacGregor, 2002). Several influential dual processing theories suggest that affect is a critical component of intuitive processes (Epstein, 1994; Kahneman, 2003; Reyna, 2004), and researchers who identify intuition as a "gut feeling" emphasize this link to affect in their conceptualization of automatic intuitive processes (de Vries, Holland, & Witteman, 2008). Price and Norman (2008) view intuition as a conscious feeling that informs decision making without conscious access to the causes of the feeling. To equate intuitive with affective processing, however, might be premature. Camerer, Loewenstein, and Prelec (2005) point out that a more useful framework recognizes that processing type (i.e., controlled vs. automatic) and processing content (cognitive vs. affective) are separate – although often overlapping – constructs. The relationship between intuition and affective experiences is undoubtedly strong yet rather complex.

Affective and intuitive processes share some of the challenges that make it difficult for researchers to measure them: a multitude of theoretical approaches, definitional inconsistencies in the literature, and limitations of standard methods to assess their intrinsic properties. Nonetheless, research on the role of affective processes in judgment and decision making has increased considerably over the last decade. The relationship between intuitive and affective processes is likewise increasingly attracting researchers' attention. Affective reactions can guide information processing in a variety of ways (including attracting attention to specific information, providing information concerning stimuli and decision outcomes, and preparing behavioural responses), all of which might fall under the label of intuitive information processing. Furthermore, affective responses to specific stimuli can be based on learned associations, which surface as intuition in expert decision making. Stable individual differences in affective reactivity may also influence how information is processed, and these trait differences could be visible in people's reliance on intuition in specific situations (see Betsch & Ianello, this volume). To better understand intuitive processes in these contexts, a closer examination of the assessment of affective processes and their relationship to intuition is necessary. The material presented in this chapter should serve as an example of how these affective processes can be measured.

Any serious attempt to address the issue of the assessment of affective experiences needs to take the rich theoretical background of the abundant research on emotions into account. I will give a short overview of the important theoretical issues, including definitional problems and structural conceptualizations, before reviewing a selection of affect measures that have been employed in recent judgment and decision-making research. The necessary brevity precludes an exhaustive treatment of the measurement of affective experiences, and instead the focus is on a selection of self-report measures that are readily usable for researchers interested in affective processes without access to more elaborate equipment (e.g., functional magnetic resonance imaging or electrocardiograms).

Theoretical issues

Definitional challenges

According to Russell (2003), researchers have not yet adequately answered William James' question what an emotion truly is. Indeed, defining the subjective experience of an emotion is a "very thorny issue" (Izard, 1993, p. 71), and considerable disagreement exists among researchers on how to best conceptualize and measure it (Izard, 2007). While most people readily concede that they know what an emotion is, few are able to generate a definition of what is both necessary and sufficient to constitute an emotional experience. If one is to measure emotional experiences, however, it is difficult to evade the definitional challenge without running the risk of negating one's own attempt to speak intelligibly on the role of affective processes in information processing.

Influenced by contemporary research on cognitive mechanisms, Schachter and Singer (1962) proposed a model of emotions that emphasizes the role of cognitive appraisal and attribution. According to this model, emotions are combinations of both physiological arousal states and cognitive processes used to interpret and make sense of the arousal. Lazarus (1991) expanded on this idea and asserted that all forms of emotions are either mediated or generated by some form of cognitive processing (e.g., cognitive appraisal, attribution, or construal processes). The role of cognition in the form of elaborate meaning analysis in the generation of emotions has also been explored by Frijda (1986). Cabanac (2002) proposes that an emotional experience is primarily a mental experience (as opposed to just a somatic reaction) characterized by its intensity and hedonic content. Recent efforts to address the definitional challenge also include the decomposition of emotions into response modes (e.g., experiential, behavioural, and physiological; Gross, 2002; Mauss & Robinson, 2009), core dimensions inherent to all feeling states (e.g., activation and valence; Russell, 2003), and causal antecedents that determine the nature of the emotional experience (e.g., cognitive appraisals; Lazarus, 1991). Some researchers have argued that emotions are biobehavioural systems with four components: subjective experience, physiological reaction, expression and behavioural response (Humrichouse, Chmielewski, McDade-Montez, & Watson, 2007). Measuring the subjective emotional experience and related behavioural response components appears to be a particularly interesting approach for research on intuitive information processing underlying judgments and decisions, as one of the basic functions of an emotion seems to be its motivational purpose to guide action (e.g., Damasio, 1994; Peters & Slovic, 2000; Zeelenberg, Nelissen, Breugelmans, & Pieters, 2008).

Another important definitional aspect central to the assessment of feeling states is the distinction between affect, emotions, and moods. The fact that different researchers use these terms in different (and sometimes contradicting) ways adds considerable complication to the endeavour to survey the literature for a commonly accepted nomenclature. The greatest disagreement seems to hover around the term "affect". While Gray and Watson (2007) define affect as an overarching broad concept that encompasses specific emotions and more general mood states, Russell (2003) uses the term *core affect* to denote the central affective experience from which more specific emotional states can be constructed. Research in judgment and decision making often uses the term "affect" to describe not an inclusive set of emotions and moods, but to refer to the relatively brief positive vs. negative experience associated with a trigger or stimulus that can guide information processing (Peters & Slovic, 2000), risk perception (Loewenstein, Weber, Hsee, & Welch, 2001; Slovic et al., 2002), and choices (Damasio, 1994). Except where otherwise noted, for the purpose of the current chapter I will refer to the term *affect* as a relatively brief positive vs. negative experience, whereas *affective experience* refers to any feeling state (including emotions and moods). Emotions are defined as specific feeling states (e.g., anger, sadness) that typically have an identifiable trigger and are object-related (i.e., we feel happy or sad *about* something), whereas moods are more enduring, low-intensity background feeling states that often do not have a conscious trigger and are characterized mainly by their valence.[1]

A distinction is also made between integral and incidental feelings, which refers to whether the affective experience is integral and inherent to an object, stimulus, or decision-making process, or whether it is incidental and unrelated to the decision task (Peters, 2006). For example, background mood states are one form of incidental affective experiences.

A further consideration for the study of affective experiences revolves around the question of whether feeling states are anticipated or anticipatory (e.g., Loewenstein et al., 2001). A feeling state that is anticipated is essentially a prediction of how one would feel if a specific event were to take place, while an anticipatory feeling state is experienced right now and influences how information is processed, but is connected to a future event. This theoretical distinction becomes important for the measurement of affective experiences in judgment and decision making because anticipated and anticipatory feeling states potentially influence the mechanisms underlying preferences and choices in different ways (see Loewenstein & Lerner, 2003; Västfjäll & Gärling, 2002).

The structure of affective experiences

Which measures are preferable to answer one's research question depends on whether one intends to measure distinct emotional experiences, background mood states, or integral affect related to an object or decision outcome, and whether these feeling states are affective forecasts or anticipatory feelings. Self-report measures typically rely on one of two basic assumptions about the structure of affective experiences: They either posit that affective experiences are best assessed as distinct emotions on concrete levels, or they decompose these experiences into a number of underlying dimensions.

Affect models of distinct emotions are particularly useful for universally recognized emotional experiences such as fear, anger, sadness, anxiety, and happiness because these feeling states have specific behavioural and cognitive consequences (Gray & Watson, 2007; Lerner, Small, & Loewenstein, 2004). Affect models that decompose affective experiences into dimensions, on the other hand, assess feeling states through a number of core dimensions (e.g., Mellers, 2000; Osgood, Suci, & Tannenbaum, 1957; Russell, 2003; Russell & Feldman Barrett, 1999; Tellegen, Watson, & Clark, 1999). The seminal work of Osgood, Suci, and Tannenbaum (1957) argues for three independent bipolar dimensions: evaluation, potency, and activation (EPA model). These components refer to the dimensions of pleasure/pain, ability/inability to influence a situation, and activity-passivity, respectively, which in combination form distinct emotions (Russell & Mehrabian, 1977). Later models reduce the number of dimensions to two (Russell, 1980; Russell & Feldman Barrett, 1999; Tellegen, Watson, & Clark, 1999), or one (Mellers, 2000; Slovic et al., 2002). While two-dimensional models usually stress the importance of valence (positive/negative) and arousal (active/passive), one-dimensional models focus on valence only.

Of particular interest for the current chapter are the two-dimensional models proposed by Russell (1980) and Watson and Tellegen (1985), which form a circumplex on which discrete emotions can be located (see Figure 10.1). The two dimensions proposed by Russell comprise valence (pleasantness/ unpleasantness) and engagement (high arousal/low arousal). These two core dimensions are thought to be inherent properties of all emotions (Russell, 2003), and each distinct emotion can be located at a specific point along the resulting two-dimensional space. A central feature of Russell's model is that

Russell

Watson & Tellegen

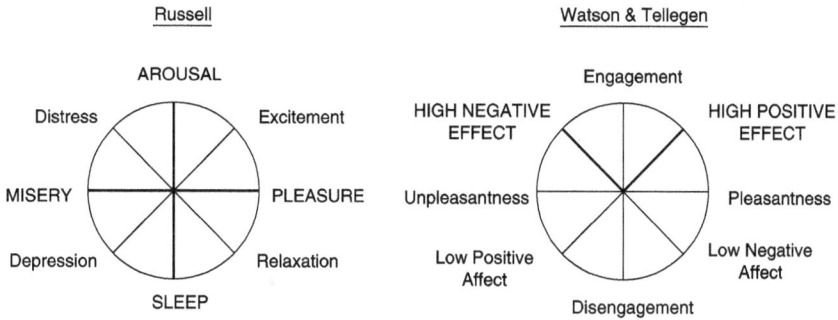

Figure 10.1 Circumplex model of affect. Taken from Russell & Feldman Barrett (1999).

valence (i.e., pleasantness/unpleasantness) is measured on a bipolar scale, which clearly classifies an emotion as either positive or negative. In this model, emotions on opposite ends tend to be highly negatively correlated (e.g., happiness and sadness), and it is suggested that affective states at opposite ends cannot be experienced simultaneously. The model described by Watson and Tellegen (1985), on the other hand, uses two scales measuring positive and negative affect,[2] which can be mapped onto the dimensional space of Russell's model at a 45-degree angle of the valence and engagement axes (Russell & Feldman Barrett, 1999). Positive and negative affect are conceptualized to be independent of each other and are therefore at a 90-degree angle. According to this model, positive and negative affect can be experienced at the same time (e.g., one might feel euphoric *yet* nervous, or sleepy *and* relaxed).

It is of note that both dimensional models encompass specific emotions at a distinct and concrete level. Furthermore, while it is possible to assess the dimensions directly by one-adjective questions (e.g., asking how positive one feels), typically several adjectives on uni- or bipolar scales are used to assess each dimension (e.g., Russell & Feldman Barrett, 1999). Tellegen, Watson, and Clark (1999) suggest that models of discrete emotions and dimensional models should not be seen as mutually exclusive, but instead as measurements of affective states at different levels in an integrated hierarchical model. Discrete emotions are at the lower (i.e. concrete) level, the underlying dimensions of positive and negative affect are at a higher (i.e., abstract) level, and at the highest level affective states are differentiated only by their hedonic content and measured on a bipolar valence dimension. This hierarchical model is quite useful for research on affect and intuition, as it allows for comparisons across specific research domains and sometimes dissonant findings. While Slovic et al. (2002) report to have used a general valence dimension (good-bad) to measure affective reactions towards environmental hazards, other researchers have focused on distinct emotions and how they influence judgments and choices (e.g., Lerner, Small, & Loewenstein, 2004; Zeelenberg et al., 2008).

Research in judgment and decision making is often concerned with the role that affective and intuitive processes occupy in choice behaviour and preference construction (Lichtenstein & Slovic, 2006). While the psychometric properties of the scales used to assess affect, emotions, and mood states are undoubtedly of paramount importance, it is often equally interesting to adapt measurements to specific decision making tasks. For example, the positive and negative affect schedule (PANAS; Watson, Clark, & Tellegen, 1988) is a measure that primarily assesses mood states, but can readily be used to measure integral affect (e.g., Peters, Slovic, & Gregory, 2003) or temperament (Watson, 2004). Similarly, personality assessment tools (e.g., the Big Five Personality Inventory; Goldberg, 1992; John & Srivastava, 1999) can be used to measure affect-related constructs and investigate their influence in choices. For example, Peters and Slovic (2000) used the neuroticism factor from the Big Five Personality Inventory Mini-Markers (Saucier, 1994) to assess negative affective reactivity and relate it to participants' choice behaviour. Before addressing specific self-report measurements of affective experiences, a quick overview of the functions of affect in intuitive information processing is presented next.

The functions of affect in intuitive information processing

Affective processes are not homogenous and can result in a variety of decision-making strategies (Pfister & Böhm, 2008). Nonetheless, some basic functions that affect has in judgment and decision making have been identified (Pfister & Böhm, 2008; Peters, 2006). Affect can serve as information and inform decision makers whether a decision option is basically good or bad (Schwarz & Clore, 2003). In this function, affect guides judgments and decisions by the affective valence that is attached to the decision options (Slovic et al., 2002). Intuitive judgments and decisions that are based on "gut feelings" are an example of how affective reactions can be a source of information. Intuitive judgments are quick, automatic, and not based on extensive conscious deliberation. The fact that gut feelings underlying intuitive judgments and choices do not necessarily have to be conscious was nicely demonstrated with the Iowa Gambling Task (Damasio, 1994; for a detailed description see Hochman et al., this volume). De Vries, Holland, & Witteman (2008) used the Iowa Gambling task to examine the effects that the affective properties of intuition have on choices. They interpret their data to suggest that mood is a moderator for the type of processing people engage in, where positive mood states can lead to greater reliance on gut feelings (i.e., intuition; Böhm & Brun, 2008). However, it needs to be pointed out that the connection between affective and intuitive processes is likely to go beyond a simple equation that only focuses on positive vs. negative mood states.[3]

Additionally, affect can serve as a spotlight, highlighting particular characteristics of decision options, leading to differential focus on specific decision attributes at the cost of neglecting others (Peters, 2006). Thirdly, affect has motivational properties that influence approach-avoidance behaviour (e.g., Gray, 1982). The motivation to approach or avoid specific stimuli, events, or decision outcomes can lead to relatively automatic and intuitive actions that do not rely on extensive deliberative information processing. Finally, Peters (2006) and Cabanac (2002) propose that affect may be used as a common currency which allows for quick (and intuitive) comparability between options on an affective level without doing extensive calculations.

Self-report scales of affect

Numerous self-report scales of affect exist and have been used in a large number of different research domains. A selection of measures used in recent judgment and decision-making research will be presented next (for other selections see Gray & Watson, 2007, and Humrichouse et al., 2007). Recall that affective experiences can be measured on several levels and that, depending on the research questions, one can focus on either distinct emotions, dimensional scales, or on a higher-order bipolar valence dimension. An overview of the measurement scales presented in this section is shown in Table 10.1.

Dimensional measures of positive affect and negative affect

Several scales exist to measure the dimensions of positive and negative affect. These vary substantially in both the number and types of items used to assess them. I will review the Positive and Negative Affect Schedule (PANAS), the Evaluative Space Grid (ESG), the Self-Assessment Manikin (SAM), and Affect Rating Dial (ARD).

Positive Affect and Negative Affect Schedule (PANAS)

In its original version, the PANAS (Watson, Clark, & Tellegen, 1988) was designed to capture positive and negative mood states along the two dimensions posited by Watson and Tellegen (1985). The original version consists of ten items for each dimension. Negative affect is measured by the unipolar adjectives *Afraid, Ashamed, Distressed, Guilty, Hostile, Irritable, Jittery, Nervous, Scared, Upset*, while positive affect is measured by *Active, Alert, Attentive, Determined, Enthusiastic, Excited, Inspired, Interested, Proud*, and *Strong*. People rate the adjectives on a five-point scale to indicate how they feel (from 0 = very slightly or not at all to 4 = extremely). This measure typically shows good reliability as well convergent and discriminant validity (reported in Gray & Watson, 2007, and Humrichouse et al., 2007; see also Watson & Clark, 1997). Watson et al. (1988) report that scale reliabilities ranged from Cronbach's alpha = .86 to .90 for positive affect and .84 to .87 for negative affect, in samples with different instructions as to the time at

Table 10.1 Overview of measurement scales

Measurement scales	Dimensions assessed	Affective experience assessable	Assessment method	Typical time	Repeated-assessment suitability
Positive and Negative Affect Schedule (PANAS; Watson, Clark, & Tellegen, 1988)	Two unipolar dimensions (Positive & Negative Affect)	Affect; Emotions (PANAS-X); Mood;	Verbal	3–5 minutes	Medium
Evaluative Space Grid (ESG; Larsen et al., 2009)	Two unipolar dimensions (Positive & Negative Affect)	Affect; Emotions; Mood	Graphical	< 1 minute	High
Self-Assessment Manikin (SAM; Lang, 1980)	Three bipolar dimensions (Valence, Activation, & Potency)	Affect; Mood	Graphical	< 1 minute	High
Affect Rating Dial (ARD; Ruef & Levenson, 2007)	One bipolar dimension (Valence)	Affect, Emotions, Moods	Graphical	< 1 minute	High
Behavioural Inhibition Scale and Behavioural Activation Scale (BIS/BAS; Carver & White, 1994)	Two unipolar dimensions (Negative and Positive Affective Reactivity)	N/A	Verbal	3–5 minutes	Low
Big-Five: Extraversion & Neuroticism (Saucier, 1994)	Two bipolar dimensions (Extroversion–Introversion & Emotional stability–Neuroticism)	N/A	Verbal	3–5 minutes	Low

Note: Repeated assessment suitability includes quick and frequent assessment for repeated-measure designs.

which to indicate their moods (e.g., some were asked to indicate how they feel at that moment, while others were asked how they felt the past few days, weeks, or year) and state vs. trait affective states. In these different samples the inter-correlation between the positive and negative affect factors varied from $r = -.12$ to $r = -.23$.

Depending on the instructions, the PANAS can be used to measure state affect or trait affect.[4] The versatility of the PANAS is also evident by its relatively simple application to objects, stimuli, and decision-relevant attributes, a property which makes it quite useful for research on integral affect in intuitive decision making. This can be done by changing the instructions so that the adjectives relate to specific decision attributes. Peters and Slovic (2007) employed an adapted version of the PANAS with both unipolar and bipolar scales to assess affective experiences and their relation to behavioural intentions. In an earlier paper, Peters et al. (2003) used similar adapted scales for measuring positive and negative affect related to a specific object (e.g., a lottery ticket). Instead of assessing general mood states, Peters and colleagues were able to demonstrate that participants' integral affective response determined both buying and selling prices of lottery tickets. Using a similar methodology, Dickert, Dieckmann, Peters, & Slovic (2004) showed that integral positive affect mediated the endowment effect (i.e., the disparity between buying and selling prices) and differences in the perceptions of the likelihood of winning money in a hypothetical lottery. The items we used to measure negative affect were *unhappy*, *upset*, *bad*, and *dislike*, and positive affect was measured by the items *happy*, *excited*, *good*, and *like*. Participants were instructed to indicate how *happy* they felt *about* the lottery ticket, which was taken as a measurement of integral affect associated with the object of evaluation. Even with this shortened and adapted version of the PANAS, internal consistency was high (Cronbach's alpha = .92 and =.90, for positive and negative affect, respectively). The resulting positive and negative affect factors were moderately negatively correlated ($r = -.30$).

Evaluative Space Grid (ESG)

Larsen, Norris, McGraw, Hawkley, and Cacioppo (2009) developed the Evaluative Space Grid (ESG) to measure positive and negative affect. This grid is a two-dimensional space with the X-axis denoting positive affect and the Y-axis denoting negative affect. Along the axes are several verbal descriptors of the intensity of the experienced affect (e.g., *not at all*, *slightly*, *moderately*, etc.), at equal distances from each other and separated by vertical (or horizontal, depending on which axis) lines. The resulting grid provides the possibility to simultaneously indicate how positive and negative one feels by selecting one of the squares in the grid. Larsen et al. asked participants to rate their affective reaction towards several 50–50 gamble outcomes that were either disappointing or outright wins (or a relief or outright losses) in a repeated-measures design. They compared the ESG to single-item scales for positive and negative affect, and found evidence for convergent validity of the grid measure. While the ESG is basically a single-item measurement of affect, it has the benefit of being quite flexible (in regard to the number and labels of intervals on each axis) and highly efficient in its use. Larsen et al. also report having successfully used the ESG for quick and continuous (every 100 ms) measurement of affect as well as for predicting facial electromyographic activity from ESG-responses.

Self-Assessment Manikin (SAM)

Based on the work of Osgood, Suci, and Tannenbaum (1957), Lang (1980) created the Self-Assessment Manikin (SAM) as a graphical, non-verbal measurement of the three dimensions underlying affective experiences identified by Osgood and colleagues (i.e., evaluation, potency, and activation). There are three rows of several manikins each, that are presented in order to assess the hedonic valence dimension (evaluation), ability to influence a situation (potency or dominance), and arousal or activity-passivity (activation). The three different rows of manikins are presented in Figure 10.2 and represent measurement on bipolar scales. For example, the first dimension measures the hedonic tone of the experienced affective state, anchored by complete happiness, pleasure, contentment, hope, and satisfaction on one side, while the other side represents an emotional state that resembles

Figure 10.2 Self-Assessment Manikin with (1) valence, (2) arousal, and (3) dominance dimensions. Taken from Lang, P. J. (1980). Reprinted with permission.

complete unhappiness, annoyance, dissatisfaction, melancholy, despair, and boredom (see Bradley & Lang, 2007 for details). Similarly, the arousal dimension is depicted by manikins that range from a completely calm and relaxed manikin to an exploding one. The anchors for the arousal dimension are extreme stimulation, excitement, frenzy, and being aroused on one side, and complete relaxation, calmness, and sleepiness on the other. Finally, the potency (or dominance) dimension is depicted by manikins of increasing size with high and low potency at the endpoints. Bradley and Lang (2007) suggest that this last dimension is of less importance in explaining evaluative judgments, and is possibly more important in situations featuring social interactions. The graphical form of the SAM makes it easy to administer in different languages and cultural backgrounds.[5] Another advantage is that it is readily usable for computer-based research and quick, frequent, and repeated assessment. Schlösser, Dunning, and Fetchenhauer (unpublished manuscript) used the SAM to show that anticipatory feelings predicted gambling decision beyond anticipated feelings and subjective assessments of probability.

Affect Rating Dial (ARD)

All self-report scales discussed thus far have either relied upon retrospective reporting of affective experiences (e.g., after a decision-making task) or upon affect ratings that could be obtained at specific intervals (e.g., between decisions). An entirely different approach is to measure affective experiences continuously, which allows for a more detailed analysis with good temporal resolution of how and when affective experiences influence information processing (Ruef & Levenson, 2007). This can be accomplished by an Affective Rating Dial (ARD) that participants use to report their subjective affective experiences throughout an experimental session. Earlier versions of this rating dial used hardware that consisted of a dial that was mounted on a faceplate and rotated 180-degrees along an affect scale anchored by *very negative* and *very positive* (e.g., Gottman & Levenson, 1985). A modern and more accessible way to use these kinds of continuous online ratings is to construct a computer-based slidebar, which can readily be moved with the mouse to indicate how participants feel at each moment of the experiment. This represents a less intrusive way to record ongoing affective experiences than interrupting the experiment at various points to ask for affect ratings. It also allows plotting an affect time course that can reveal when information processing might have been particularly influenced by people's affective experience. Fredrickson and Kahneman (1993) used an adapted and colour-coded version of the ARD that gave visual feedback for positive (green dots) and negative (red dots) affect to show that participants' retrospective evaluations of affective experience neglected the duration of the experience. Similarly, Kahneman, Fredickson, Schreiber, and Redelmeier (1993) used a "discomfort meter" rating dial to measure pain while participants endured physical pain over a short period (60 to 90 seconds).

While the continuous sampling method might be particularly suited to measure affective processes in intuitive decision making, it also has a specific drawback: it measures affective experiences along one dimension only (e.g., valence). This has two implications that need to be taken into account when considering its use: (1) it does not untangle positive and negative affect-ive states that might be felt simultaneously (as in mixed emotions); and (2) while it is possible to measure both general affective states (e.g., positive vs. negative affect) and specific emotions (e.g., anger) by using different labels for the rating dial, it cannot measure more than one dimension or specific emotion at one time.

Personality measurements

In addition to measuring affective reactions directly, it is also possible to assess people's propensity to experience affective states. As with self-report affect questionnaires, there are numerous personality instruments that are related to affective states. I will review two that capitalize on affective reactiv-ity: The Behavioural Inhibition Scale/Behavioural Activation Scale and the Big Five personality inventory.

Behavioural Inhibition Scale and Behavioural Activation
Scale (BISBAS)

The Behavioural Activation Scale and Behavioural Inhibition Scale (BISBAS) is a personality measurement for the biobehavioural systems of positive and negative affective reactivity (Carver & White, 1994). It is based on Gray's reinforcement sensitivity theory (1982) and comprises 20 individual items that are used to form one negative reactivity scale (BIS) and three positive reactivity scales (reward sensitivity, drive, and fun seeking). The three positive reactivity scales are sometimes combined to form an overall positive reactivity scale (BAS). Positive reactivity can be conceptualized as the degree to which a person is attracted to seeking out pleasure or rewards that are connected to a specific activity, object, or outcome. Similarly, negative reactiv-ity can be thought of as the motivation to stay away from punishments or aversive stimuli.

It is of note that the BISBAS is a measurement of personality dispositions and therefore not based on the affect models proposed by Russell (1980) or Watson and Tellegen (1985). However, Watson et al. (1999) and Humrichouse et al. (2007) suggest that the affective components of BIS and BAS are related to the two affect dimensions measured by the PANAS. Similar to the PANAS, the BISBAS also posits that positive and negative affective reactivity are independent constructs. Thus, individual differences in positive and negative reactivity are measured on orthogonal dimensions.

With its measurement of people's sensitivity to positive and negative outcomes, the BISBAS can be used in decision contexts that involve risky choices and decision making from experience. For example, in a variant of the Iowa Gambling Task that disentangled expected value from gain and loss cards, Peters and Slovic (2000) demonstrated that affective sensitivity predicted choices. Specifically, higher negative reactivity led to fewer choices from high loss decks, whereas higher positive reactivity[6] increased choices from high gain decks.

Big Five Inventory (BFI): Extraversion and Neuroticism

Similar to the BISBAS, the Big Five personality inventory is not a measure of affective experience per se, but is a trait measure of personality (see John & Srivastava, 1999 for an informative historical overview on the Big Five). Nonetheless, two of its five dimensions have been prominently linked to positive and negative reactivity: Extraversion and Neuroticism (emotional stability). Watson, Hubbard, and Wiese (2000) report that the average correlation between neuroticism and the negative affect scale from the extended version of the PANAS (PANAS-X) was $r = .60$. Peters and Slovic (2000) used extraversion as a measure of positive reactivity, which was predictive of choices with distinctly positive outcomes attached to them. This is in line with research by Zinbarg and Mohlman (1998), who show that individual differences in the learning of affectively-valenced associations predict choices in a card learning task. Dickert and Peters (manuscript in preparation) extend this finding and show that extraversion predicts choices from gain cards when choices are made intuitively.

The Big Five personality inventory comes in various forms with varying number of items. Some versions can be a bit cumbersome in its administration, such as Goldberg's (1992) 100 trait descriptive unipolar adjectives, especially when only two of the five personality dimensions are of interest. Saucier (1994) introduced the Big Five Mini-Markers, a shorter version with a total of 40 items, eight for each of the five scales.[7] Each item is measured on a 1–9 scale, anchored by *extremely inaccurate* to *extremely accurate*. Extraversion is measured by items such as *talkative*, *extraverted*, and *energetic*, while Neuroticism is measured by items like *envious*, *fretful*, and *temperamental*.

Specific emotions

While research in judgment and decision making has made extensive use of affect scales (such as the PANAS) and personality and affective reactivity scales, it is equally common to assess specific emotions with very short scales (e.g., three-items) or with single adjectives. Special attention has been given to regret (Connolly & Zeelenberg, 2002), but recent research has also increasingly focused on pro-social emotions like empathy in relation to charitable behaviour (e.g., Batson, 1990; Kogut & Ritov, 2005). Although there are many more specific emotions that play a role in decision making and the underlying information processing (e.g., anger, fear, sadness, etc., Lerner

& Keltner, 2000), we will examine regret and empathy constructs in more detail to show how specific emotions can be measured and ways in which they can influence information processing and decisions.

Regret

Regret, as a concept, has played a prominent role in decision-making research for more than two decades (e.g., Bell, 1982; Loomes & Sugden, 1982, Zeelenberg & Pieters, 2007). Research on regret was initially limited to the effects of anticipated vs. experienced regret on decisions. Moreover, much of the early research on regret theory confounded the effects of disappointment and regret (cf. Connolly & Reb, 2005). Disappointment is the specific feeling attached to an outcome that compares unfavourably to an alternative outcome one could have received with more luck, while regret is understood to be the result of a similar comparison but with the addition that one could have received a better outcome with a better choice.

The distinction between anticipated and experienced regret is of substantial importance to regret-based explanations of choice (e.g., subjective expected pleasure theory; Mellers, Schwartz, & Ritov, 1999). For example, Mellers and colleagues (Mellers, 2000; Mellers & McGraw, 2001) compare anticipated pleasure/regret and anticipated disappointment/elation with the emotions experienced after an outcome of a choice becomes known. These authors conceptualize feelings of regret to be on a continuum between regret and rejoicing, while the closely related feeling of disappointment is measured on a continuum between disappointment and elation. These two conceptually related dimensions can readily be assessed by single adjectives.[8] The single-adjective approach to measure regret has been used successfully in diverse research domains, including medical decision making (Connolly & Reb, 2003, 2005), decision making under risk (Connolly & Butler, 2006), financial investments (Kahneman & Tversky, 1982), and charitable behaviour (Dickert, 2008).

Empathy

Research on pro-social behaviour has focused on feelings such as empathy (Batson, 1990), sympathy, and compassion (Kogut & Ritov, 2005) to help explain decisions to help others (Slovic, 2007). While different empathy scales exist (e.g., Davis, 1994), recent research on charitable decisions has also used either single adjectives or short scales (2–5 items; e.g., Kogut & Ritov, 2005; Small, Loewenstein, & Slovic, 2007). For example, Kogut and Ritov used the compound terms *worried, upset, and sad* as indicators of empathic distress felt by participants in response to being presented with descriptions of children in need of financial help. Similarly, feelings of empathic concern were measured by the compound term *sympathy and compassion*. Using a similar methodology, Dickert (2008) showed that empathic concern predicts donations when people are in a more intuitive decision mode (i.e., when delibera-tive capacity is decreased).

Conclusion and recommendations

The goal of this chapter was to show how affective processes can be assessed with self-report measurements. As affective experiences are multidimensio-nal and multilayered phenomena with different cognitive, experiential and behavioural components, it is best to be specific about the level at which they are assessed. The dimensional measures of affective experiences are charac-terized by their assessment of affective experiences in terms of one (ARD), two (PANAS; ESG), or three dimensions (SAM). The PANAS, ESG, and ARD can easily be adapted to measure a variety of affective states, including general mood, incidental and integral affect, and specific emotions. The ESG, SAM, and ARD are especially useful for quick and repeated assessment of affective states, while the PANAS can be adapted to measure trait vs. state affect. Apart from the dimensional affect measures, two personality ques-tionnaires (BISBAS and Extraversion and Neuroticism from the Big Five) were reviewed to show that trait personality assessments related to affective reactivity can be turned into a useful individual difference measurement in experiments that involve affective and intuitive processes. Using single-adjective unipolar or bipolar scales to assess discrete emotional states is also an acceptable practice for many researchers. The advantages of dimensional measures are the good psychometric properties of some of the scales and a theoretical framework that can readily be applied to the information process-ing underlying judgments and decisions. The advantages of specific emotion measures are that they allow examining the effect of particular emotions and their behavioural and cognitive consequences.

A critical issue about research on affect and affective processes in judgment and decision making is when precisely the assessment takes place. When investigating whether affective processes are related to a decision-making phenomenon, one should think carefully about the timing of the administra-tion of the affect measure. If temporal resolution is of paramount import-ance, researchers might consider using a version of the ARD. For other measurements it is typical to have participants first go through the judgment or choice task and then later record their feelings about the available options. However, if the affective processes are hypothesized to be ongoing during the experimental task, it might be problematic to assume that an assessment after the task is indicative of feelings experienced during the task. Researchers should also consider that reporting one's feelings may inadvertently change the nature of the affective process and its relationship to behaviour, as is the case in studies on affective labelling (e.g., Lieberman et al., 2007) and the affective asynchrony effect (Peters & Slovic, 2007). During affective labelling, reporting one's feelings has been found to decrease affective responses, which was also observable on a neural level by decreased amygdala activity in

Lieberman et al. (2007). Peters and Slovic (2007) found that using measures that require more deliberative thought reduces the intuitive correspondence between feelings and behavioural intentions.

Future research on the role of intuition in judgment and decision making can benefit significantly from taking the various facets and functions of affective experiences into account. Carefully selected self-report measurements are useful in uncovering these affective processes and their relation to judgments and choices. A plethora of assessment tools and methods to measure the affective side of intuition exist. The selection presented in this chapter should be seen as a starting point and as highlighting exciting possibilities for research endeavours designed to understand the affective side of intuitive processes.

Notes

1 These feeling states often blend into each other and can trigger other feeling states. For example, when in a bad mood, one might have a higher propensity to become angry.
2 Watson and colleagues use the term *affect* as an umbrella term to include all affective experiences.
3 A more nuanced approach is provided by Camerer, Loewenstein, and Prelec (2005), who point out that processing type (automatic vs. controlled) should be conceptualized separately from processing content (affective vs. cognitive). According to this framework, intuition can have both cognitive and affective components.
4 The PANAS has also been extended (PANAS-X) to allow for the measurement of specific, lower order emotions, which include fear, sadness, guilt, hostility, joviality, self-assurance, attentiveness, shyness, fatigue, serenity, and surprise (see Gray & Watson, 2007 and Watson & Clark, 1997 for details).
5 Although it should be noted that the more widely used affective measurements (e.g., the PANAS) are available in several different languages.
6 Peters and Slovic (2000) have used both the BAS-fun scale and the Big Five personality dimension of extraversion to measure positive reactivity.
7 An even shorter version of the Big Five was recently suggested by Rammstedt and John (2007) which uses only two items per scale.
8 An alternative approach to the disentanglement of regret and disappointment by means of a seven-item scale was recently proposed by Marcatto and Ferrante (2008).

References

Batson, C. D. (1990). How social an animal? The human capacity for caring. *American Psychologist*, *45*, 336–346.

Bell, D. (1982). Regret in decision making under uncertainty. *Operations Research*, *30*, 961–981.

Böhm, G. & Brun, W. (2008). Intuition and affect in risk perception and decision making. *Judgment and Decision Making*, *3*, 1–4.

Bradley, M. M., & Lang, P. J. (2007). The international affective picture system (IAPS) in the study of emotion and attention. In J.A. Coan & J.J.B. Allen (Eds.), *The handbook of emotion elicitation and assessment* (pp. 29–48). New York: Oxford University Press.

Cabanac, M. (2002). What is emotion? *Behavioural Processes, 60*, 69–83.

Camerer, C., Loewenstein, G., & Prelec, D. (2005). Neuroeconomics: How neuroscience can inform economics. *Journal of Economic Literature, 43*, 9–64.

Carver, C. S., & White, T. L. (1994). Behavioural inhibition, behavioural activation, and affective responses to impending reward and punishment: The BIS/BAS scales. *Journal of Personality and Social Psychology, 67*, 319–333.

Connolly, T., & Butler, D. (2006). Regret in economic and psychological theories of choice. *Journal of Behavioural Decision Making, 19*, 139–154.

Connolly, T., & Reb, J. (2003). Omission bias in vaccination decisions: Where's the "omission"? Where's the "bias"? *Organizational Behaviour and Human Decision Processes, 91*, 186–202.

Connolly, T., & Reb, J. (2005). Health in cancer related decisions. *Health Psychology, 24*, 29–34.

Connolly, T., & Zeelenberg, M. (2002). Regret in decision making. *Current Directions in Psychological Science, 11*, 212–216.

Damasio, A. R. (1994). *Descartes' error: Emotion, reason, and the human brain.* New York: Avon.

Davis, M. H. (1994). *Empathy: A social psychological approach.* Boulder, CO: Westview.

de Vries, M., Holland, R. W., & Witteman, C. L. M. (2008). In the winning mood: Affect in the Iowa gambling task. *Judgment and Decision Making, 3*, 42–50.

Dickert, S. (2008). *Two routes to the perception of need: The role of affective and deliberative information processing in pro-social behaviour.* Doctoral Dissertation, University of Oregon, OR.

Dickert, S., Dieckmann, N., Peters, E., and Slovic P. (2004, November). Positive affect and the endowment effect: A mediation analysis. *Poster presented at the annual Judgment and Decision Making conference, Minneapolis.*

Dickert, S., & Peters, E. Thinking harder and choosing worse. *Unpublished manuscript.*

Epstein, S. (1994). Integration of the cognitive and the psychodynamic unconscious. *American Psychologist, 49*, 709–724.

Fredrickson, B., & Kahneman, D. (1993). Duration neglect in retrospective evaluations of affective episodes. *Journal of Personality and Social Psychology, 65*, 45–55.

Frijda, N. H. (1986). *The emotions.* Cambridge: Cambridge University Press.

Goldberg, L. R. (1992). The development of markers for the Big-Five factor structure. *Psychological Assessment, 4*, 26–42.

Gottman, J. M., & Levenson, R. W. (1985) A valid procedure for obtaining self-report of affect in marital interaction. *Journal of Consulting & Clinical Psychology, 53*, 151–160.

Gray, E. K., & Watson, D. (2007). Assessing positive and negative affect via self report. In J. A. Coan & J. J. B. Allen (Eds.), *The handbook of emotion elicitation and assessment* (pp. 171–183). New York: Oxford University Press.

Gray, J. A. (1982). *The neuropsychology of anxiety: An enquiry into the functions of the septo-hippocampal system.* Oxford: Oxford University Press.

Gross, J. (2002). Emotion regulation: Affective, cognitive, and social consequences. *Psychophysiology, 39*, 281–291.

Humrichouse, J., Chmielewski, M., McDade-Montez, E., & Watson, D. (2007). Affect assessment through self report. In J. Rothenberg & S.L. Johnson (Eds.), *Emotion and psychopathology* (pp. 13–34). Washington: American Psychological Association.

Izard, C. (1993). Four systems for emotion activation: cognitive and noncognitive processes. *Psychological Review*, *100*, 68–90.

Izard, C. (2007). Basic emotions, natural kinds, emotion schemas, and a new paradigm. *Perspectives on Psychological Science*, *2*(3), 260–280.

John, O. P., & Srivastava, S. (1999). The Big Five trait taxonomy: History, measurement, and theoretical perspectives. In L. A. Pervin & O. P. John (Eds.), *Handbook of personality: Theory and research* (2nd ed., pp. 102–139). New York: Guilford Press.

Kahneman, D. (2003). A perspective on judgment and choice: Mapping bounded rationality. *American Psychologist*, *58*, 697–720.

Kahneman, D., & Frederick, S. (2002). Representativeness revisited: Attribute substitution in intuitive judgment. In T. Gilovich, D. Griffin, & D. Kahneman (Eds.), *Heuristics and biases* (pp. 49–81). New York: Cambridge University Press.

Kahneman, D., Fredrickson, B., Schreiber, C., & Redelmeier, D. (1993). When more pain is preferred to less: Adding a better end. *Psychological Science*, *4*, 401–406.

Kahneman, D., & Tversky, A. (1982). The psychology of preferences. *Scientific American*, *246*, 160–173.

Kogut, T. & Ritov, I. (2005). The "identified victim" effect: An identified group, or just a single individual? *Journal of Behavioural Decision Making*, *18*, 157–167.

Lang, P. J. (1980). Behavioural treatment and bio-behavioural assessment: Computer applications. In J. B. Sidowski, J. H. Johnson, & T. A. Williams (Eds.), *Technology in mental health care delivery systems* (pp. 119–137). Norwood, NJ: Ablex.

Larsen, J. T., Norris, C. J., McGraw, A. P., Hawkley, L. C., and Cacioppo, J. T. (2009). The evaluative space grid: A single-item measure of positivity and negativity, *Cognition & Emotion*, *23*, 453–480.

Lazarus, R. (1991). Cognition and motivation in emotion. *American Psychologist*, *46*, 352–367.

Lerner, J. S., & Keltner, D. (2000). Beyond valence: toward a model of emotion-specific influences on judgment and choice. *Cognition and Emotion*, *14*, 473–493.

Lerner, J. S., Small, D. A., & Loewenstein, G. (2004). Heart strings and purse strings: Carryover effects of emotions on economic decisions. *Psychological Science*, *15*, 337–341.

Lichtenstein, S. & Slovic, P. (2006). *The construction of preference*. New York: Cambridge University Press.

Lieberman, M., Eisenberger, N., Crockett, M., Tom, S., Pfeifer, J., & Way, B. (2007). Putting feelings into words: Affective labelling disrupts amygdala activity in response to affective stimuli. *Psychological Science*, *18*, 421–427.

Loewenstein, G. F. & Lerner, J. S. (2003). The role of affect in decision making. In R.J. Davidson, K.R. Scherer, & H.H. Goldsmith (Eds.), *Handbook of affective sciences*, (pp. 619–642). Oxford: Oxford University Press.

Loewenstein, G. F., Weber, E. U., Hsee, C. K., & Welch, E. S. (2001). Risk as feelings. *Psychological Bulletin*, *127*, 267–286.

Loomes, G., & Sugden, R. (1982). Regret theory: An alternative theory of rational choice under uncertainty. *Economic Journal*, *92*, 805–824.

Marcatto, F., & Ferrante, D. (2008). The regret and disappointment scale: An instrument for assessing regret and disappointment in decision making. *Judgment and Decision Making*, *3*, 87–99.

Mauss, I. B., & Robinson, M. D. (2009). Measures of emotion: A review. *Cognition & Emotion*, *23*, 209–237.

Mellers, B. A. (2000). Choice and the relative pleasure of consequences. *Psychological Bulletin, 126*, 910–924.

Mellers, B. A. & McGraw, A. P. (2001). Anticipated emotions as guides to choice. *Current Directions in Psychological Science, 10*, 210–214.

Mellers, B. A., Schwartz, A., & Ritov, I. (1999). Emotion-based choice. *Journal of Experimental Psychology: General, 128*, 332–345.

Osgood, C. E., Suci, G. J., & Tannenbaum, P. H. (1957). *The measurement of meaning*. Oxford, England: University of Illinois Press.

Peters, E. (2006). The functions of affect in the construction of preferences. In S. Lichtenstein & P. Slovic (Eds.), *The construction of preference* (pp. 454–463). New York: Cambridge University Press.

Peters, E., & Slovic, P. (2000). The springs of action: Affective and analytical information processing in choice. *Personality and Social Psychology Bulletin, 26*, 1465–1475.

Peters, E., & Slovic, P. (2007). Affective asynchrony and the measurement of the affective attitude component. *Cognition and Emotion, 21*, 300–329.

Peters, E., Slovic, P., & Gregory, R. (2003). The role of affect in the WTA/WTP disparity. *Journal of Behavioural Decision Making, 16*, 309–330.

Pfister, H. & Böhm, G. (2008). The multiplicity of emotions: A framework of emotional functions in decision making. *Judgment and Decision Making, 3*, 5–17.

Price, M.C., & Norman, E. (2008). Intuitive decisions on the fringes of consciousness: Are they conscious and does it matter? *Judgment and Decision Making, 3*, 28–41.

Rammstedt, B. & John, O. (2007). Measuring personality in one minute or less: A 10-item short version of the Big Five Inventory in English and German. *Journal of Research in Personality, 41*, 203–212.

Reyna, V. F. (2004). How people make decisions that involve risk: A dual-processes approach. *Current Directions in Psychological Science, 13*(2), 60–66.

Ruef, A. M., & Levenson, R. W. (2007). Continuous measurement of emotions. In J.A. Coan & J.J.B. Allen (Eds.), *The handbook of emotion elicitation and assessmen* (pp.286–297). New York: Oxford University Press.

Russell, J. A. (1980). A circumplex model of affect. *Journal of Personality and Social Psychology, 39*, 1161–1178.

Russell, J. A. (2003). Core affect and the psychological construction of emotion. *Psychological Review, 110*, 145–172.

Russell, J. A. & Feldman Barrett, L. (1999). Core affect, prototypical emotional episodes, and other things called emotion: Dissecting the Elephant. *Journal of Personality and Social Psychology, 76*, 805–819.

Russell, J. A., & Mehrabian, A. (1977). Evidence for a three-factor theory of emotions. *Journal of Research in Personality, 11*, 273–294.

Saucier, G. (1994). Mini-Markers: A brief version of Goldberg's unipolar Big-Five markers. *Journal of Personality Assessment, 63*, 506–516.

Schachter, S. & Singer, J. (1962). Cognitive, social, and physiological determinants of emotional state. *Psychological Review, 69*, 379–399.

Schlösser, T., Dunning, D., & Fetchenhauer, D. What a feeling? The role of anticipated and anticipatory emotions in risky decisions (unpublished working paper).

Schwarz, N., & Clore, G. L. (2003). Mood as information: 20 years later. *Psychological Inquiry, 14*, 294–301.

Slovic, P. (2007). "If I look at the mass I will never act": Psychic numbing and genocide. *Judgment and Decision Making, 2*, 79–95.

Slovic, P., Finucane, M., Peters, E., & MacGregor, D.G. (2002). The affect heuristic. In T. Gilovich, D. Griffin & D. Kahneman (Eds.), *Heuristics and biases: The psychology of intuitive judgment* (pp. 397–420). New York, NY: Cambridge University Press.

Small, D. A., Loewenstein, G., & Slovic, P. (2007). Sympathy and callousness: Affect and deliberations in donation decisions. *Organizational Behaviour and Human Decision Processes, 102*, 143–153.

Tellegen, A., Watson, D., & Clark, L. A. (1999). On the dimensional and hierarchical structure of affect. *Psychological Science, 10*, 297–303.

Västfjäll, D., & Gärling, T. (2002). The dimensionality of anticipated affective reactions to risky and certain decision outcomes. *Experimental Psychology, 49*, 228–238.

Watson, D. (2004). Stability versus change, dependability versus error: issues in the assessment of personality over time. *Journal of Research in Personality, 38*, 319–350.

Watson, D., & Clark, L. A. (1997). Measurement and mismeasurement of mood: Recurrent and emergent issues. *Journal of Personality Assessment, 68*, 267–296.

Watson, D., Clark, L. A., & Tellegen A. (1988). Development and validation of brief measures of positive and negative affect: the PANAS scales. *Journal of Personality and Social Psychology, 54*, 1063–1070.

Watson, D., Hubbard, B., & Wiese, D. (2000). Self-agreement in personality and affectivity: The role of acquaintanceship, trait visibility, and assumed similarity. *Journal of Personality and Social Psychology, 78*, 546–558.

Watson, D., & Tellegen, A. (1985). Towards a consensual structure of mood. *Psychological Bulletin, 98*, 219–235.

Watson, D., Wiese, D., Vaidya, J., & Tellegen, A. (1999). The two general activation systems of affect: structural findings, evolutionary considerations, and psychobiological evidence. *Journal of Personality and Social Psychology, 76*, 820–838.

Zeelenberg, M., Nelissen, R., Breugelmans, S., & Pieters, R. (2008). On emotion specificity in decision making: Why feeling is for doing. *Judgment and Decision Making, 3*, 18–27.

Zeelenberg, M., & Pieters, R. (2007). A theory of regret regulation 1.0. *Journal of Consumer Psychology, 17*, 3–18.

Zinbarg, R. E., & Mohlman, J. (1998). Individual differences in the acquisition of affectively-valenced associations. *Journal of Personality and Social Psychology, 74*, 1024–1040.

11 Tracking memory search for cue information

Frank Renkewitz and Georg Jahn

Introduction

You cannot observe people rummaging through their memory, but we claim that to trace cognitive processes it is worthwhile to analyze non-verbal overt behaviour that indicates what information individuals search for. Imagine a salesperson watching a client picking up a brochure about a certain product, say, a washing machine. The salesperson quite reasonably assumes that the client is searching information about this product. Later at home, when trying to remember product details from the brochure, it is likely that the client turns toward the brochure again to look up information. Now, if looking up is not possible, because the client's spouse is flipping through the brochure while the two decide which machine to buy, the client trying to remember product details is still more likely to look towards the momentarily inaccessible brochure than toward other brochures within sight. In the laboratory, we can create situations in which orienting toward one or the other source of information about decision alternatives is equally easy. Then, people's orienting behaviour can indicate which information they are searching for at each moment. Orienting towards information sources occurs even if people search for the necessary information in memory and are aware that it is not accessible from the original source (Richardson & Spivey, 2000). This affords a method for tracking memory search: Gaze behaviour can indicate information sought in memory, because the eyes are likely to return to the location in the environment where the to be remembered information has been previously acquired. This has been shown for deliberate memory search. But even intuitive decision making involving automatic memory activation may be accompanied by orienting towards sources of remembered information that are present in the environment.

We demonstrate the method with a probabilistic inference task. In particular, the task is to choose between two alternatives based on probabilistic cues about their rank on a criterion dimension. Previously studied probabilistic inference tasks include identifying which of a pair of cities has more inhabitants (Gigerenzer & Goldstein, 1996), deciding which of two bugs is more likely to be toxic (Bergert & Nosofsky, 2007), and selecting the better of two products

(Glöckner, chapter 5, this volume; Glöckner & Betsch, 2008). The task studied here was to decide which of two mushrooms is more likely to be toxic. Participants learned attribute sets of six fictional mushrooms and were told how strongly the attributes suggest that a mushroom may be toxic. Thus, the attributes were probabilistic cues to the criterion dimension and varied in validity.

Studying memory-based decision making

In probabilistic inference tasks, sequential search and integration of cue information is constrained by limited cognitive resources (Newell & Bröder, 2008). An important boundary condition for cue processing is whether cue information is perceptually accessible or whether it has to be retrieved from memory. It is mainly the latter condition – inferences from memory – that induces selective and heuristic processing of cues to limit the cognitive costs of memory retrieval (Bröder & Newell, 2008; Gigerenzer & Todd, 1999).

When studying memory-based decision making, common process-tracing methods are not applicable because these require the presentation of information. What remains applicable are methods analyzing decision outcomes, response times (Glöckner, chapter 5, this volume), and think-aloud protocols (Witteman & van Geenen, chapter 3, this volume).

Outcome-based methods analyze the pattern of decisions in a series of trials. The goal is to infer which process of attribute processing may have produced the observed pattern of decisions. With specific assumptions about processing strategies, it is possible to construct trials, for which different strategies would arrive at differing outcomes. For example, a strategy that ignores less valid cues can be discerned from compensatory strategies that take those cues into account (Bröder, chapter 4, this volume).

Response times are easy to obtain and can support interpreting decision outcomes. Predictions of response time patterns across trials can be generated based on specified strategies of attribute processing. For instance, the assumption of sequential attribute processing combined with a stopping rule (LEX) yields the prediction of longer response times if the stopping rule kicks in later (Bröder & Gaissmaier, 2007).

Apart from analyses of outcomes and response times, thinking aloud can be employed to study memory-based decisions, but asking reasoners to think aloud is potentially reactive (Lohse & Johnson, 1996). Moreover, thinking aloud is impossible to reconcile with parallel and holistic cue processing, which can occur in memory-based decisions as well – the appropriate memory representation provided (Bröder & Schiffer, 2003b; Jahn, Renkewitz, & Kunze, 2007).

Process-tracing methods

Outcome-based methods and response time analyses are ideally supplemented with process-tracing methods to back up the assumptions about cue processing that are necessary to interpret decision patterns and response times (see Norman & Schulte-Mecklenbeck, chapter 2, this volume). A second reason why interest in process tracing is high is that the order of information search and attentional processes influences or even determines the outcome in choice and decision making (Bröder & Gaissmaier, 2007). The process-tracing method for memory-based decisions introduced here is similar to established process-tracing methods for decisions from presented information.

Process tracing yields a wealth of data including search patterns that can be related to strategies of cue processing. Information acquisition can be analyzed with regard to the amount of information acquired, the content of information, inspection times, and search patterns (Einhorn & Hogarth, 1981; Payne, Bettman, & Johnson, 1993). This is true for visually presented information, if Mouselab-methods or eye-tracking are used. Our goal was to explore whether similar process data can be obtained for memory-based decisions.

Conceptual introduction of the method

The core idea is to analyze patterns of eye movements on emptied information displays. When the eyes return to the location associated with the information sought even if the information is not accessible there any more, then eye movements on emptied information displays are indicative of information search in memory and eye-tracking provides similar data for memory-based decisions as for "inferences from givens".

The tendency to generate eye movements to locations where information was accessible was demonstrated by Richardson and Spivey (2000). They presented videos of four talking heads in the quadrants of the screen telling facts to remember. Immediately afterwards, participants heard a statement related to one of the facts and had to judge the statement as true or false. For this verification judgment, they had to retrieve the respective fact from memory. Eye-tracking revealed that when verifying a statement, they made more fixations in the quadrant where the sought information came from than in the other quadrants (see also Hoover & Richardson, 2008).

This and similar findings on memory for locations of objects, written words, and the spatial layout of visual scenes suggest that spatial locations are stored automatically. Attempts to remember events, objects, words, or scenes trigger eye movements to the stored locations. Whether looking at the former location just accompanies or supports memory retrieval is currently under dispute (Ferreira, Apel, & Henderson, 2008).

To use the "looking at nothing" phenomenon for process tracing in memory-based decisions, we had to establish associations between locations and cue information. Hence, our participants worked through a learning phase, in which cue values were presented in fixed locations of a spatial frame. In the decision phase, we presented two empty spatial frames next to each other and recorded participants' eye movements while they remembered cue information to decide between the two alternatives.

To test the method, we needed an independent indicator of cue processing. We designed attribute sets of alternatives such that we could use an outcome-based strategy classification. Thus, we could see whether the observed eye movement patterns showed the characteristics of cue value retrieval from memory that is associated with non-compensatory or compensatory strategies. The strategy classification discerns three prototypical strategies (one non-compensatory, two compensatory; see below) of processing binary cues varying in validity.

The three prototypical strategies are: a lexicographic strategy, an equal weight strategy and a weighted additive strategy. The lexicographic strategy (LEX, also known as "Take the Best") combines sequential cue processing with a stopping rule. Attributes are retrieved in the order of cue validity, starting with the most valid cue. As soon as the attribute values on a cue dimension differentiate between the alternatives, the one with the positive cue value is chosen. LEX is a non-compensatory strategy, because cues lower in validity are disregarded. The equal weight strategy (EQW) is a compensatory strategy that disregards information about cue validities. For each alternative, the number of positive cue values is counted and the alternative with the higher number is chosen. Weighted adding (WADD) is the second compensatory strategy and uses information about cue values and cue validities fully. Cue values are weighed by cue validity and added for each alternative. Then, the alternative with the higher result is chosen.

In chapter 1, Glöckner and Witteman characterized LEX as a *Payne-heuristic*: a shortcut strategy that relies on simple deliberate processes. In contrast, WADD can be understood as a paramorphic model. The choices expected by WADD could be brought about by a series of deliberate calculations as well as by intuitive-automatic processes. Automatic processes that approximate WADD predictions have been simulated as parallel constraint satisfaction (see Glöckner & Betsch, 2008). Similarly, EQW can be conceived as a simple deliberate or as an intuitive process. Automatic processes that match cue patterns holistically can result in choices that correspond to EQW predictions (Jahn, Renkewitz, & Kunze, 2007). In the predictions on gaze behaviour that follow we do not differentiate between deliberate or automatic variants of WADD and EQW. Instead, the predictions contrast gaze behaviour that can be expected with a non-compensatory strategy (LEX) and with compensatory strategies (WADD, EQW). The predictions tied to WADD and EQW that we test here hold independently of the implementation of these strategies as deliberate or automatic processes. In the discussion, we suggest how a more detailed analysis of gaze behaviour may discriminate between intuitive and deliberate users of WADD and EQW.

An outcome-based classification of a participant as using LEX would suggest that the participant tended to compare single cue values between alternatives. Consequently, if eye movements on emptied information frames indicate cue retrieval, then transitions between alternatives should be more frequent for LEX-users. On the other hand, EQW- and WADD-users tend to integrate cue information within alternatives before comparing them. Thus their gaze should switch less frequently between alternatives. Note that for LEX-users the frequency of transitions should depend on the position of the first differentiating cue. If the most valid cue differentiates, LEX stops early and generates fewer transitions than if more cues have to be processed until a differentiating one is found. Thus, an index of gaze transitions between alternatives that could differentiate between LEX- and EQW/WADD-users should be relative to the time required for the decision (i.e. transitions per second).

A second prediction on gaze behaviour pertains exclusively to LEX-users. For users of this strategy, memory-retrieval is more extensive the later (in descending order of validity) the first differentiating cue appears. Thus, the absolute frequency of transitions between alternatives should increase linearly with the position of the first differentiating cue. For users of EQW or WADD no such linear increase should be observed.

Taken a step further, eye movements on the empty spatial frames can also be analyzed at higher spatial resolution. Each cue value has a location within each spatial frame and fixations on these locations could indicate when the respective cue value is retrieved or processed. However, in contrast to visible displays where the reasoner has to visit a location to learn about the information there, memorized single cue values may be organized in all kinds of retrieval structures, which bear no trace of the locations within a spatial frame. Hence, fixation sequences and fixation durations within spatial frames are probably less informative than we might wish. Nonetheless, we tested a prediction relating to locations of single cue values.

It is again the LEX-strategy that should produce a characteristic pattern. LEX-users should disregard cues lower in validity as soon as a higher cue differentiates between alternatives. Hence, if fixations on the former location of a single cue value indicate its retrieval in memory, then fixations on former locations of cue values lower in validity should be less frequent in trials in which a cue higher in validity differentiates.

Application

Method

Design. The experiment consisted of a learning phase, in which the participants acquired cue knowledge about six objects, followed by two decision phases. In the first decision phase, pairs of objects were presented for binary choice. In this phase, participants were not instructed which strategy to use. Here, the aim was to identify groups of participants who spontaneously employ different strategies and to test whether these groups show different patterns of gaze behaviour as predicted in our hypotheses. We added a second decision phase to gain better control over the strategies participants used. In this phase, we presented the same binary choice items as in the first phase, but we directly instructed the participants to employ a certain strategy.

Materials. The participants learned cue descriptions of six alternatives. These alternatives were mushrooms characterized by the four cue dimensions enzyme, amino acid, mineral, and spread (see Table 11.1). Each of the cue dimensions could have three different values. In the learning phase of the experiment, participants memorized the cue patterns describing the six mushrooms. The critical cue values (see Table 11.1) that indicate a higher value on the target dimension (toxicity of the mushrooms) were not given to the participants until the learning phase was completed. In the decision phase, we presented pairs of mushrooms for binary choice.

A complete paired comparison of the six cue patterns used by us yields 15 choice items. In both decision phases of the experiment, all 15 items were presented twice to allow for a more reliable strategy classification. For the second presentation of each item, the order of the alternatives was reversed. Thus, each decision phase consisted of 30 binary choice items after two practice trials.

Figure 11.1a illustrates the way in which the alternatives and their cue descriptions were presented in the learning phase. Each mushroom was symbolized by a different geometrical figure. Verbal descriptions of the cue values appeared in four rectangular frames that were arranged along the borders of the geometrical figures. The position of the frames was constant across all alternatives. Values on the same cue dimension were always shown in the same frame (e.g., the respective value of the cue *enzyme* was presented in the lower left frame for all mushrooms). Thus, each cue dimension was tied to specific spatial coordinates.

Figure 11.1b shows a binary choice item as it was presented in the decision phases. In each trial, two of the geometrical figures representing mushrooms were presented side by side. The size of the figures was the same as in the

Table 11.1 The decision alternatives that were presented in the learning phase of the experiment.

		Cue 1: Enzyme	Cue 2: Amino Acid	Cue 3: Mineral	Cue 4: Spread	Cue pattern
	Critical cue values	tyrosinase	ergosterol	magnesium	rare	++++
Alternative	Symbol					
1	Circle	tyrosinase	canavanine	magnesium	rare	+−++
2	Square	laccase	ergosterol	magnesium	rare	−+++
3	Triangle	peroxidase	ergosterol	magnesium	frequent	−++−
4	Rhombus	tyrosinase	thiamine	zinc	medium	+−−−
5	Pentagon	tyrosinase	canavanine	potassium	rare	+−−+
6	Cross	tyrosinase	ergosterol	zinc	medium	++−−

learning phase. The rectangular frames that contained the cue values in the learning phase were now empty. So, participants had to actively search their memory for cue information to be able to decide which of the two mushrooms was likely to be the more toxic one.

Procedure. Although eye movements were tracked only in the decision phases, at the beginning of the experiment the eye tracker was calibrated which typically took about 5 min. The aim of this early calibration was to shorten the calibration procedures before the decision phases and, thus, to reduce the time gap between learning and memory retrieval in these phases.

In a first stage of the learning phase, participants learned cue descriptions of single mushrooms and were tested immediately afterwards. They were shown the spatial frame with cue values of one mushroom. Then the cue values disappeared and participants had to reproduce the different attributes cue by cue. For each cue, the three possible values were presented in random order and participants selected one of them. Acoustic feedback indicated whether the selection was correct and the correct cue value appeared in the corresponding rectangular frame. Cues were tested in order of cue validity and arranged counter-clockwise around the geometrical figure representing the mushroom. Thus, the most valid cue was tested first and its value

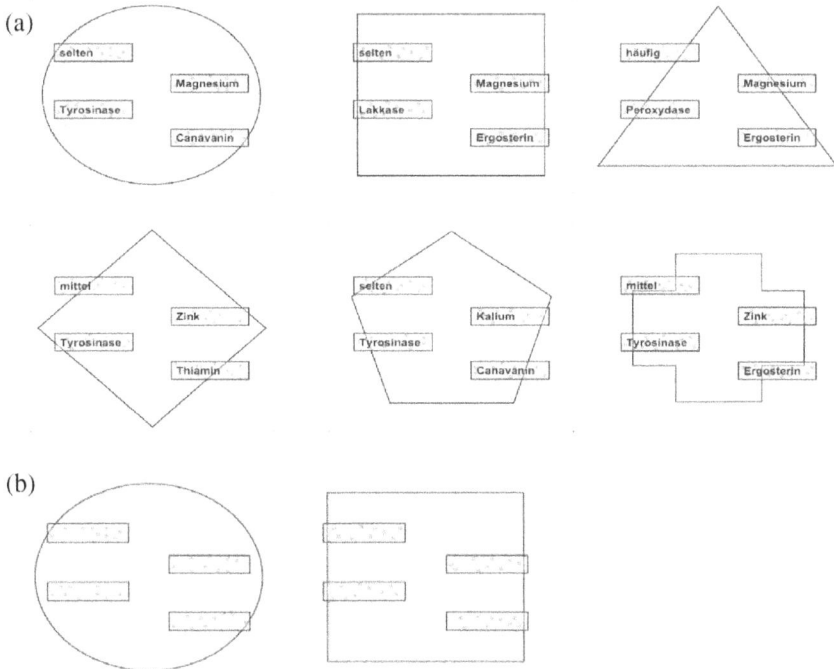

Figure 11.1 The six alternatives presented in the learning phase with the original German labels for cue values (a) and a binary choice item from the decision phases (b).

appeared in the lower left frame, the least valid cue was tested last and its value was shown in the upper left frame. Learning of single cue patterns proceeded until the first reconstruction without errors.

After three cue patterns had been learned, these three were tested and practised in the same way as in the single trials until a criterion of 11 out of 12 possible correct cue value selections was achieved. Then, the same learning and testing procedure was completed for the cue patterns of the remaining three mushrooms. Finally, all six cue patterns were tested until at least 22 of the 24 cue values were reproduced correctly. The order of cue patterns was random in learning and testing. The assignment of cue patterns to sets of three was balanced.

Before the decision phases the calibration procedure of the eye tracker was repeated. Afterwards, the participants checked their cue knowledge in a brief self-test. Again, each of the six geometrical figures was presented without the corresponding cue values. When the participants confirmed that they had tried to recall the cue values, a display of the complete cue pattern followed. Then, the experimenter told the participants that they would have to decide in a series of trials which of two mushrooms was more toxic and that they would now be informed which attributes of mushrooms indicated toxicity. Participants were told that enzymes gave the most important hint to toxicity and that only the enzyme tyrosinase would indicate toxicity. The second most important hint was the amino acid and only the amino acid ergosterol would indicate toxicity, and so on. Additionally, a list showing the attributes of the "typical toxic mushroom" was shown (tyrosinase, ergosterol, magnesium, rare). The participants were asked to repeat the attributes indicating toxicity in order of their importance while a blank screen was presented.

The 30 test trials of the first decision phase were organized in two blocks. Each block consisted of the 15 binary choice items resulting from a complete paired comparison of the six mushrooms. Within each block, choice items were presented in random order and participants responded by pressing one of two keys on a standard keyboard.

The experimenter told the participants that, in the last phase of the experiment, they would again decide several times which of two mushrooms was more toxic. However, this time they should make their decisions according to a certain rule that would be illustrated later on. This was followed by a repetition of the information about cue validities and critical cue values. After this, in each of the three strategy conditions the corresponding decision rule was explained (see above). Subsequently, an example of the application of the decision rule was given. In this example two cue patterns were used that were not part of the test set. The presentation of test trials in the second decision phase followed the same procedure that was used in the first phase.

Apparatus. The calibration dots and experimental stimuli were presented on a PC with a 19″ LCD-monitor at a resolution of 800×600 pixels. The acoustic feedback in the learning phase was presented through headphones.

Stimulus presentation during learning and testing as well as the data collection were handled by EPrime.

Eye movements were monitored by a desk-mounted SMI eye tracker. The eye camera was placed to the right of the computer monitor and approximately 80 cm from the observer's eye. The camera provided an infrared image of the right eye sampled at 50 Hz. The centre of the pupil and the corneal reflection were tracked to determine the gaze direction. On a second computer, gaze position (indicated by a crosshair) was superimposed over the stimulus display and continuously displayed to the experimenter. This allowed us to detect miscalibrations and to recalibrate the eye tracker before the second decision phase if this was necessary. The accuracy of the gaze position record was approximately 0.5 degrees of visual angle. The minimum fixation duration was 100 ms. During the decision phases, head movements were restrained with a chin rest.

Participants. Forty-three students at Chemnitz University of Technology participated in the experiment (36 women; mean age 22.8 years). They received partial course credit for their participation.

Results

The basis for the tests of our hypotheses on gaze behaviour is the outcome-based classification of participants. Hence, we begin by reporting the results of the maximum-likelihood strategy classification method (Bröder, chapter 4, this volume; Bröder & Schiffer, 2003a). We will then turn to the results on gaze behaviour and evaluate our central hypotheses.

Preparatory data analysis. The frequencies of strategy classifications in both decision phases are depicted in Table 11.2. In the first decision phase, participants were free to use any decision strategy. In this phase, three participants could not be classified based on the pattern of their choices.[1] Thirty per cent of the participants were classified as using the LEX-heuristic. Compared to similar studies on memory-based decisions in binary choice tasks, the proportion of presumed LEX users is rather low, but not exceptional

Table 11.2 Frequencies and, in parentheses, percentages of strategy classifications depending on decision phase and instructional condition.

	Strategy classification					
	LEX	*EQW*	*WADD*	*Guessing*	*unclassified*	*N*
Decision phase 1						
Free	13 (30.2)	12 (27.9)	6 (14,0)	9 (20.9)	3 (7.0)	43
Decision phase 2						
LEX	14 (73.7)	1 (5.3)	0 (0.0)	4 (21.1)	0 (0.0)	19
EQW	1 (6.3)	12 (75.0)	3 (18.8)	0 (0.0)	0 (0.0)	16
WADD	2 (25.0)	1 (12.5)	1 (12.5)	2 (25.0)	2 (25.0)	8

(see Bröder & Schiffer, 2003b; Bröder & Schiffer, 2006; Bröder & Gaissmeier, 2007; Jahn, Renkewitz & Kunze, 2007). The relatively high proportion of guessing classifications (21%) might indicate that the participants experienced the task as rather difficult.

In the second decision phase, participants who were instructed to use either the LEX- or the EQW-heuristic predominantly adopted the corresponding strategy. In both conditions, about 75% of the participants were classified as using the instructed strategy. Additionally, participants were more consistent in using a given strategy in the second decision phase than in the first phase. This is indicated by the average error rate. The error rate gives the proportion of trials in which a participant decided against the prediction of the strategy that was adopted by him or her according to the maximum-likelihood classification. The mean error rates of participants classified as using LEX, EQW and WADD in the first decision phase were 22%, 21% and 29%, respectively. In the second decision phase, the mean error rates of participants who apparently followed the strategy instructions were 17% in the LEX-condition and 15% in the EQW-condition. These figures hardly change when one includes all LEX and EQW classifications in the second decision phase. The mean error rate of the four participants classified as WADD users in this phase was 23%. Thus, there was a general tendency to stick more consistently with a given strategy in the second decision phase. For the following analyses of gaze behaviour, one might therefore expect somewhat clearer and larger effects in this phase than in the first phase.

In contrast to the LEX and EQW-conditions, in the WADD-condition the majority of the participants failed to use the instructed strategy. This suggests that the corresponding strategy instruction was not sufficiently clear or that the strategy was too difficult to apply. When we noticed that only one of eight participants in this condition was classified as using WADD, we stopped using the WADD instruction and assigned all later participants randomly to the LEX- or EQW-condition.

In the analyses of gaze behaviour we did not consider participants who remained unclassified or were classified as using a guessing strategy, because we held no hypotheses regarding the gaze behaviour of these participants. In the analyses pertaining to the second decision phase, we grouped participants according to the results of the maximum-likelihood strategy classification. If one restricts the analyses to participants who appeared to employ the instructed strategy, the descriptive pattern of eye-tracking results reported below remains the same. However, some of the results of inferential statistics change, due to the reduced power of the significance tests. For all statistical tests, we combined all EQW and WADD classifications to one category of participants who used a compensatory strategy.

In both decision phases, we excluded some participants from further analysis because of the bad quality of their eye-tracking data. We eliminated the data of a participant when gaze data were missing for more than 40% of the total time of a decision phase. This was the case for eight participants

(2 LEX, 3 EQW and 3 WADD classifications) in the first decision phase and for six participants (3 LEX, 2 EQW and 1 WADD classifications) in the second phase. Additionally, we discarded all trials (9.0% in the first phase and 8.3% in the second phase) in which the tracking data for more than 40% of the trial duration were missing.

Transitions between alternatives per second. Our first hypothesis claims that, relative to the time required for a decision, users of the LEX-heuristic should switch their gaze more often between alternatives than users of a compensatory strategy. To evaluate this hypothesis we defined two large areas of interest (AOIs), each of which covered one alternative and thus almost one half of the screen. In the centre of the screen, the two AOIs were adjacent. A *transition* was defined as two successive fixations in different AOIs. We determined the number of transitions per trial and divided this number by the trial duration (in seconds) to obtain an index of gaze transitions.

Figure 11.2 shows the means of the gaze transition index in both decision phases for groups of participants with different strategy classifications. When participants were instructed to employ a certain decision strategy, transitions between alternatives per second were indeed more frequent with LEX than with a compensatory strategy. A planned contrast between the LEX-group and the combined EQW- and WADD-groups reveals that this effect was significant, $F (1, 26) = 4.91$, $p = .036$, $\eta^2 = .16$. This indicates that different decision strategies are associated with different patterns of gaze behaviour during memory search. In the first decision phase, when the choice of a strategy was not restricted, the descriptive pattern of results was similar.

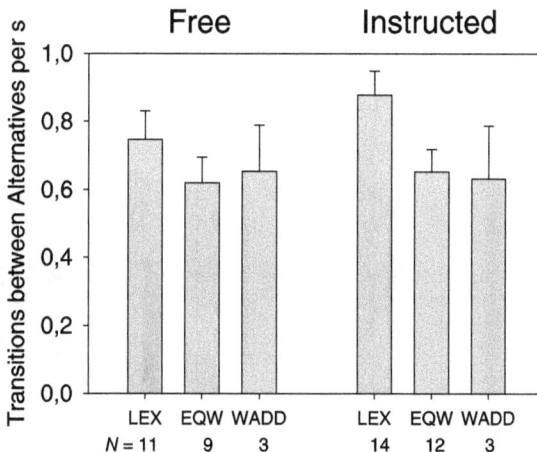

Figure 11.2 Mean number of transitions between alternatives per second in the first decision phase (free choice of strategies) and in the second decision phase (instructed strategies) for groups of participants with different strategy classifications. Error bars represent standard errors and are based on between-subjects variance in the corresponding groups.

However, the effect is less pronounced ($\eta^2 = .04$) and consequently not statistically significant, F $(1, 20) = 0.93$, p = .346.

Transitions between alternatives depending on the position of the first discriminating cue. According to the search rule implied by the LEX-heuristic, memory retrieval should occur attribute-wise and be more complete the later in the hierarchy of cue validities the first differentiating cue appears. Hence, the absolute number of transitions between alternatives should increase linearly with the position of the first differentiating cue. In contrast, for users of a compensatory strategy the position of the first discriminating cue should be irrelevant.

In Figure 11.3, the mean absolute frequencies of transitions between alternatives are plotted against the position of the first differentiating cue separately for the different groups of participants and both decision phases. With instructed strategies, users of LEX switched their gaze more often from one alternative to the other the later the first discriminating cue appeared. Neither EQW- nor WADD-users present a similar trend. For LEX-users, the linear contrast is significant (repeated measures analysis, F $(1, 13) = 12.63$, p = .004) and associated with a large effect size (partial $\eta^2 = .49$).

When participants chose freely between strategies, for LEX-users the number of gaze transitions again increased with the position of the first discriminating cue.[2] The linear effect was somewhat smaller than under instructed-strategy conditions (F $(1, 9) = 4.00$, p = .076, partial $\eta^2 = .31$). For users of compensatory strategies no systematic effect was associated with the position of the best differentiating cue.

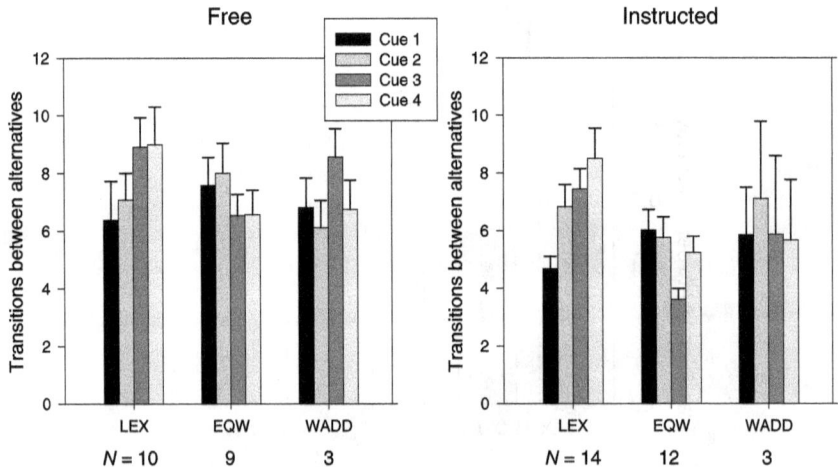

Figure 11.3 Mean absolute number of transitions between alternatives depending on the position of the first differentiating cue for groups of participants with different strategy classifications in both decision phases. Error bars represent standard errors and are based on between-subjects variance in the corresponding groups.

Fixation durations at locations of cue values. Hitherto, we analyzed the eye-tracking data at the level of decision alternatives. However, the decision strategies considered here also allow for differential predictions about the specific cue information that is retrieved from memory and the sequence in which this retrieval will occur. Although there are good reasons to doubt that memory retrieval of specific cue values will translate to clear patterns of congruent gaze behaviour (see above), we tested one of these predictions.

The LEX-strategy assumes that memory retrieval stops as soon as the first discriminating cue is found. Thus, in trials in which a cue high in validity discriminates, values of cues with a lower validity should not be searched for in memory. Inasmuch as gaze behaviour is indicative of the retrieval of specific cue values, in such trials participants should therefore not look at the former locations of cues with lower validity. In contrast, the compensatory strategies generally factor in all cue information. Consequently, the gaze behaviour of EQW- or WADD-users should not be affected by the position of the first discriminating cue and the former locations of all cue values should be fixated for about the same amount of time.

To evaluate these predictions, we defined AOIs around the empty rectangular frames that had contained the cue values in the learning phase. These AOIs were 30 pixels wider than the original frames in each direction. For each trial and each cue, we determined the summed duration of all fixations in the two AOIs pertaining to the respective cue (one AOI for each alternative). These summed durations were averaged per participant across all trials in which the first discriminating cue had appeared in the same position.

The lower part of Figure 11.4 summarizes the means of the fixation durations under instructed strategy conditions separately for compensatory strategy classifications and for LEX classifications. Contrary to the predictions, users of EQW and WADD did not look equally long at the former locations of all cues. Instead, the frames that previously contained the third and fourth cue of the validity hierarchy were generally fixated longer than the frames containing the first and second cue. As there is no reason inherent to the decision task to look predominantly at the third and fourth cue, this might be interpreted as a general gaze bias. There are at least two plausible explanations for such a gaze bias. First, the third and fourth cue (mineral and spread, respectively) always appeared in the upper part of the geometrical figures representing the decision alternatives. Thus, the gaze bias might simply reflect a preference to look at the upper part of the screen. Second, the labels describing values of the third and fourth cue (e.g., "magnesium" and "rare") were probably familiar to all of our participants. In contrast, the labels describing values of the first and second cue (e.g., the enzyme "tyrosinase" and the amino acid "canavanine") were presumably unknown to most participants prior to the experiment. Hence, the longer glance times at positions of the third and fourth cue may be caused by a preference for familiar stimuli which might also be easier to retrieve.

The second prediction about the gaze behaviour of users of compensatory strategies was corroborated under instructed strategy conditions: The position of the first discriminating cue had no systematic impact on the fixation durations at the locations of different cues. These descriptive results were confirmed in a two-way repeated measures ANOVA. There was a large and significant main effect for the factor cue, (Greenhouse-Geisser corrected) F (1.89, 26.39) = 9.84, p = .001, partial η^2 = .41. Neither the main effect of the position of the first discriminating cue (F (2.08, 29.18) = 2.59, p = .10, partial η^2 = .16) nor the interaction of both factors reached significance (F (3.33, 29.18) = 0.68, p = .59, partial η^2 = .05).

For participants classified as LEX users, a different pattern of results emerged. These participants also seem to have a preference to look at the former locations of the third and fourth cue. However, as expected, the fixation durations are now affected by the position of the first discriminating cue. But this effect does not correspond exactly to the prediction. It is not the case that cues with a low validity are only attended to if no cue higher in validity discriminates. Instead, all cues tend to receive more attention the later the first discriminating cue appears. Additionally, the results point to an interaction between the factors cue and position of the first discriminating cue. The differences in mean fixation durations between cues with high and low validity tend to increase with the position of the first discriminating cue. A two-way repeated measures ANOVA reveals that the main effect of the factor position of the first discriminating cue is significant (F (1.79, 23.28) = 9.25, p = .001, partial η^2 = .42). The interaction effect is significant at an alpha level of 0.1 (F (6.88, 89.54) = 1.84, p = .091, partial η^2 = .12), while the main effect of the factor cue does not reach significance (F (1.61, 20.89) = 1.52, p = .241, partial η^2 = .11).

As with the previous analyses, the result pattern was similar but somewhat blurred when the participants chose a decision strategy freely (see the upper part of Figure 11.4). For users of a compensatory strategy, there was again a clear preference to look at the former locations of the third and fourth cue (F (1.67, 18.34) = 4.64, p = .029, partial η^2 = .30) and no systematic impact of the position of the first discriminating cue (F (1.88, 20.72) = 0.43, p = .644, partial η^2 = .04). For LEX-users, there is a similar trend to look predominantly at the location of the third and fourth cue (F (1.72, 15.47) = 4.40, p = .035, partial η^2 = .33). The position of the first discriminating cue again seems to have an impact on the fixation durations of LEX-users, but the result pattern is less structured than under instructed strategy conditions. Thus, the effect of the position of the first discriminating cue is considerably larger than for users of a compensatory strategy, but not significant (F (2.88, 25.93) = 4.64, p = .208, partial η^2 = .15). The interaction effect was not significant either for users of compensatory strategies or for LEX-users.

Free

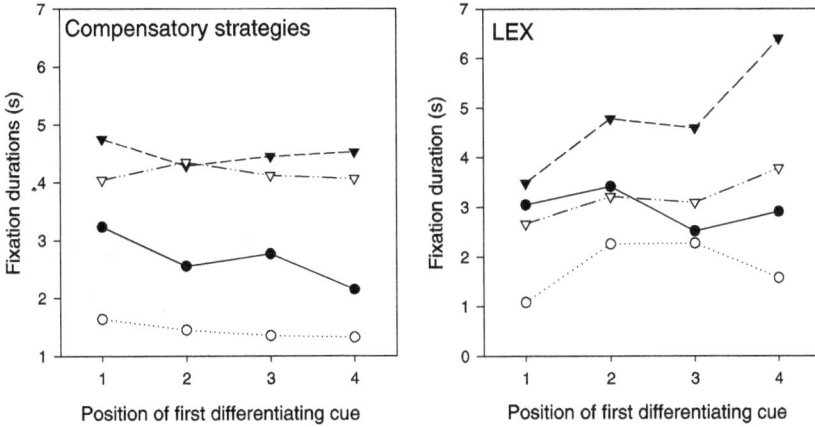

Instructed

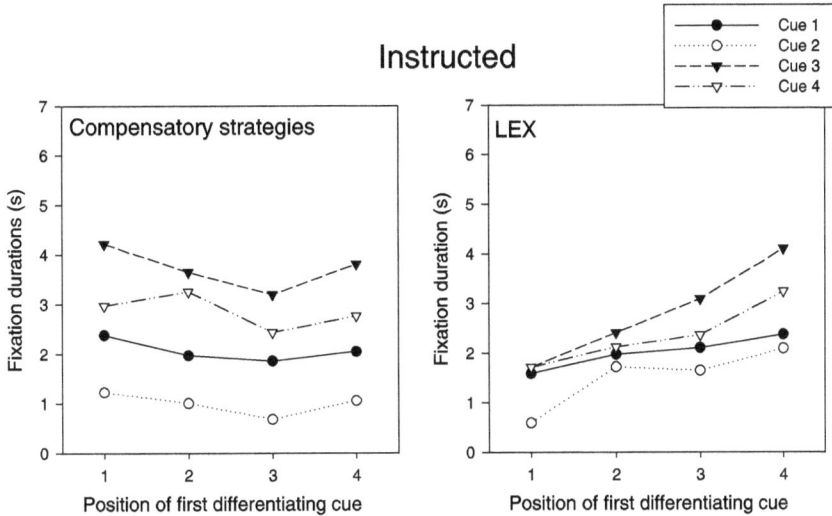

Figure 11.4 Mean fixation durations at locations of different cues depending on the position of the first differentiating cue. Data are presented separately by decision phases and by strategy classification (compensatory strategies vs. LEX).

Discussion

The main goal of the present study was to test whether different decision strategies are associated with different patterns of gaze behaviour during memory search for cue information. We tried to validate eye-tracking as a new source of process-tracing data in memory-based decision making. The results support the idea that eye-tracking has the potential to yield valuable information about the cognitive processes during memory search. Under instructed strategy conditions, we found different patterns of eye movements on emptied information displays for participants classified as using either a non-compensatory or a compensatory strategy. LEX-users switched their gaze more often between alternatives suggesting an attribute-wise memory search for information. Additionally, LEX-users switched more often between alternatives the later the first discriminating cue appeared. For users of compensatory strategies, no such increase in gaze transitions depending on the position of the best discriminating cue was observed. Thus, when we consider gazes and gaze transitions at the level of alternatives, the results for instructed participants were consistent with predictions derived from strategy-specific assumptions about memory search. This indicates that the link between memory search and eye movements demonstrated in research on the looking-at-nothing phenomenon translates into distinct and specific patterns of gaze behaviour for users of different decision strategies in the cue-learning paradigm applied here. Therefore, the tracking of eye movements seems suitable to yield data that help to uncover memory search processes in decision making.

Additionally, the results of the present study provide convergent support for the outcome-based classification method and corroborate the processing assumptions of the different decision strategies. At least at the level of alternatives, we found descriptively very similar result patterns for non-instructed participants as for instructed participants. Hence, spontaneously deciding participants with different strategy classifications apparently indeed employed different processes to arrive at their decisions. The fact that the gaze patterns conformed to the predictions also for non-instructed partici-pants furthermore suggests that memory search for cue information was often spontaneously performed according to the different decision strategies. However, throughout all analyses, we found smaller effects and less struc-tured result patterns for non-instructed than for instructed participants. One probable reason for this is that non-instructed participants applied a given strategy with more unsystematic errors than instructed participants. But the differences in error rates between instructed and non-instructed strategy conditions were not large (about 6%), so it seems questionable whether less consistent strategy use in the non-instructed strategy condition can account for the differences in effect sizes found in all analyses of eye movements. This hints to the possibility that there might be a few participants who are classi-fied as using a certain strategy but actually employ a different heuristic and therefore different memory search processes to arrive at their decisions. Obvi-ously, such participants would blur the results found under non-instructed strategy conditions.

What else could be accomplished by the application of eye-tracking in research on memory-based decision-making? A general problem of outcome-based classification methods is that different decision strategies predict similar or even identical choice patterns in many situations (see Glöckner, this volume). Therefore, there is a need for process measures. For the case of memory-based decisions, such measures are rare. Because the present study suggests that gazes and gaze transitions between alternatives differentiate between decision strategies at least at the group level, eye-tracking might yield a remedy for this problem. Hence, eye-tracking may be a useful complement to outcome-based classification methods in any study investigating manipulations supposed to affect the choice of decision strategies. In such studies, eye-tracking could provide evidence that not only decision patterns but also the underlying cognitive processes change in the expected way.

Further potential applications of eye-tracking depend largely on the degree to which fixations on former locations of cue values are indicative of attempts to retrieve these cue values. In this respect, the results of the present study were inconclusive. On the one hand, we found different patterns of fixation durations on former locations of cue values for users of different strategies. This obviously suggests that there is a link between memory search and fixations on these locations. On the other hand, the result pattern did not conform to the predictions derived from the decision strategies. There are at least three possible explanations for this finding.

First, there was a general bias to gaze predominantly at locations of cue values in the upper part of the stimulus display. This bias may simply reflect a tendency to attend to the upper part of the stimuli more than to the lower part independently of any memory search processes. The upper part of the stimuli always contained values of the third (mineral) and fourth cue (spread). The labels of these values were probably more familiar to the participants than the value labels of the first and second cue. Thus, the fact that the third and fourth cue received generally more attention than expected may have been caused by the position of the cues or by a preference for familiar value labels. Therefore, the discrepancies between predicted and observed gaze patterns may result from shortcomings in our experimental procedure. An experiment in which the position of cues is balanced across participants and in which similarly familiar value labels are used on all cues may yield the predicted result pattern.

Second, the assumptions about memory search processes of the different decision strategies could be partially wrong. For instance, it is possible that LEX-classified participants do attempt to retrieve values of cues with low validity and gaze at the corresponding positions even if a cue higher in validity discriminates, but do not consider these cue values when they integrate information to arrive at a decision.

Third, the link between memory retrieval of cue values and eye movements to the former locations of these values may simply be too weak to bring about the predicted result pattern at the level of attributes. There are several important differences between the procedures of typical studies on the looking-at-nothing phenomenon and the cue-learning paradigm applied here. Eye movements to the former location of a piece of information during memory search presuppose that the spatial location of the information is accessible in memory at the time of retrieval. Procedures of studies on the looking-at-nothing phenomenon probably foster the fulfilment of this pre-requisite. There are only few pieces of information, each piece of informa-tion has its own specific location and the retention interval is short. In contrast, in the cue learning paradigm, participants have to acquire a rela-tively large amount of cue knowledge, several cue values appear at the same location, and the interval between learning and retrieval is rather long. Therefore, to master the memory tests for cue knowledge, participants probably have to use other learning strategies than participants of a looking-at-nothing study. Thus, they are likely to organize cue values in specific knowledge structures, build associations between cue values, use mnemon-ics to store these values (for instance, acronyms of the cue values of an alternative), and so on. All of this presumably results in a memory represen-tation in which cue values are less strongly tied to their former spatial location. Consequently, the participants may more often use retrieval pro-cesses that do not direct eye movements to the former location of the sought information.

The present experiment gives no unambiguous reason to favour one of these explanations. Hence, further research will be needed to clarify if and to what degree fixations on former locations of cue values indicate attempts to retrieve these values. If such research could identify conditions under which fixations on former locations of cue values constitute a reliable indicator of memory search, the field of further useful applications of eye-tracking as a process measure in memory-based decision making seems wide and promis-ing to us. With an indicator of information search at the level of single cue values, the analysis of decision behaviour could move from the level of groups to the level of individuals or even trials. In principle, in this case all measures and analytical techniques used in Mouselab-methods could also be applicable to memory-based decisions. In conjunction with outcome-based methods, these measures and techniques allow to discriminate between a large number of strategies for decision making at the individual level (Riedl, Brandstätter & Roithmayr, 2008). Maybe most importantly, an indicator of information search at the level of cue values could aid discrimination of individuals who use deliberate and intuitive variants of WADD and EQW possible. Glöckner and Herbold (2008) present an attempt to differentiate between deliberate and automatic strategies in decision making from given information with eye-tracking data. They derive differing predictions on gaze behaviour for strategies that make identical choices but vary in their process assumptions. For instance, based on findings demonstrating that deeper levels of processing are connected to longer fixation times of the respective infor-mation, they argue that an automatic strategy relying on parallel constraint satisfaction should result in generally shorter fixations of single pieces of information than a deliberate weighted additive strategy. Additionally, they suggest that an automatic strategy based on parallel constraint satisfaction should – in contrast to a deliberate weighted additive strategy – bring about a concentration of fixations on attributes of the favoured alternative. With an indicator of memory search for cue values, hypotheses like these would also be testable in the case of memory-based decisions.

Acknowledgments

We would like to thank Anne Herbik, Diana Rösler, and Agnes Scholz for their help in conducting the experiment.

Notes

1 With the maximum-likelihood strategy classification method, a choice pattern remains unclassified if the likelihood of the pattern is the same for at least two different strategies.
2 We excluded one additional participant from this analysis. The mean reaction time of this participant was more than twice as long as the reaction time of any other participant. Consequently, also the mean absolute number of gaze transitions of this participant was an outlier and exceeded the mean number of transitions of LEX-users by the factor 3.4.

References

Bergert, F. B. & Nosofsky, R. M. (2007). A response-time approach to comparing generalized rational and take-the-best models of decision making. *Journal of Experimental Psychology: Learning, Memory, and Cognition*, *33*, 107–129.

Bröder, A. & Gaissmaier, W. (2007). Sequential processing of cues in memory-based multiattribute decisions. *Psychonomic Bulletin & Review*, *14*, 895–900.

Bröder, A., & Newell, B. R. (2008). Challenging some common beliefs: Empirical work within the adaptive toolbox metaphor. *Judgment and Decision Making*, *3*, 205–214.

Bröder, A. & Schiffer, S. (2003a). Bayesian strategy assessment in multi-attribute decision making. *Journal of Behavioural Decision Making*, *16*, 193–213.

Bröder, A. & Schiffer, S. (2003b). Take the best versus simultaneous feature matching: Probabilistic inferences from memory and effects of representation format. *Journal of Experimental Psychology: General*, *132*, 277–293.

Bröder, A. & Schiffer, S. (2006). Stimulus format and working memory in fast and frugal strategy selection. *Journal of Behavioural Decision Making*, *19*, 361–380.

Einhorn, H. J., & Hogarth, R. M. (1981). Behavioural decision theory: Processes of judgment and choice. *Annual Review of Psychology*, *32*, 52–88.

Ferreira, F., Apel, J., & Henderson, J. M. (2008). Taking a new look at looking at nothing. *Trends in Cognitive Science*, *12*, 405–410.

Gigerenzer, G. & Goldstein, D. (1996). Reasoning the fast and frugal way: Models of bounded rationality. *Psychological Review*, *103*, 650–669.

Gigerenzer, G., Todd, P. M., & the ABC Research Group. (1999). *Simple heuristics that make us smart*. New York: Oxford University Press.

Glöckner, A., & Betsch, T. (2008). Multiple-reason decision making based on automatic processing. *Journal of Experimental Psychology: Learning, Memory, and Cognition*, *34*(5), 1055–1075.

Glöckner, A. & Herbold, A.-K. (2008). Information processing in decisions under risk: Evidence for compensatory strategies based on automatic processes. *MPI Collective Goods Preprint*, No. 2008/42. Available at SSRN: http://ssrn.com/abstract=1307664

Hoover, M. A. & Richardson, D. C. (2008). When facts go down the rabbit hole: contrasting features and objecthood as indexes to memory. *Cognition, 108*, 533–542.

Jahn, G., Renkewitz, F., & Kunze, S. (2007). Heuristics in multi-attribute decision making: Effects of representation format. In D. S. McNamara & G. Trafton (Eds.), *Proceedings of the Twenty-Ninth Annual Conference of the Cognitive Science Society*. Mahwah, NJ: Erlbaum.

Lohse, G. L. & Johnson, E. J. (1996). A comparison of two process tracing methods for choice tasks. *Organizational Behaviour and Human Decision Processes, 68*, 28–43.

Newell, B. R., & Bröder, A. (2008). Cognitive processes, models and metaphors in decision research. *Judgment and Decision Making, 3*, 195–204.

Payne, J. W. Bettman, J. R., & Johnson, E. J. (1993). *The adaptive decision maker*. Cambridge: Cambridge University Press.

Richardson, D. C. & Spivey, M. J. (2000). Representation, space and hollywood squares: Looking at things that aren't there anymore. *Cognition, 76*, 269–295.

Riedl, R., Brandstätter, E., & Roithmayr, F. (2008). Identifying decision strategies: A process- and outcome-based classification method. *Behaviour Research Methods, 40*, 795–807.

12 Methods for inducing intuitive and deliberate processing modes

Nina Horstmann, Daniel Hausmann and Stefan Ryf

Introduction

Over the past years, an increasing number of studies directly comparing intuition and deliberation were published. One of the most obvious ways to learn about differences between intuitive and deliberate processes is to induce the increased application of one or the other processing mode and to measure behavioural differences. An in-depth analysis of the literature reveals that different methods to manipulate intuitive and deliberate judgment and decision making are available. For instance, participants can be instructed to decide "intuitively" or "deliberately" and their choices can be analysed.

The purpose of this chapter is to give an overview of methods for the induction of intuitive or deliberate processing modes. Several methods such as a) direct instruction, b) time constraints, c) distraction task, d) manipulation of mood, and e) enhancement of task relevance are outlined and studies are discussed to illustrate them. These methods are either well-established or seem to be promising. As Glöckner and Witteman (chapter 1, this volume) pointed out, the label intuition is used for different kinds of automatic processes. Likewise the label deliberation could encompass various processes (e.g., conscious calculation vs. in-depth analysis of reasons). Consequently, throughout this chapter it is important to keep in mind that the different methods for inducing intuition (deliberation) presented might also induce diverse types of intuitive (deliberate) processing.

This chapter is structured as follows: First, we give some theoretical background. A typical experimental design is depicted and dependent variables that could be of interest in research are outlined. Second, we describe the different manipulation methods in detail and illustrate their application by examples from the literature. Third, methods checking the success of the manipulation are presented. Finally, we discuss advantages and disadvantages of the different methods and give recommendations for experimental designs. In addition, we summarize the most important points of concern when planning a study using manipulations of processing modes.

Conceptual introduction

There is a long history of psychological models postulating two different kinds of information processing: the analytic/deliberate mode and the automatic/intuitive mode. Several theories modelling the interplay between intuitive and deliberate processes exist. Whereas one line of research conceptualizes intuition and deliberation as two completely distinct modes between which people alternate under different conditions, another line does not draw such a clear distinction and regards intuition as a default mode which can be supplemented by deliberate processes (for an overview, see Glöckner & Witteman, chapter 1, this volume). Nevertheless, there is some agreement about the properties postulated for intuition and deliberation: While intuitive processes can be described as automatic, fast, parallel, effortless, and affective, deliberate processes are thought to be accessible to conscious awareness, slow, serial, effortful, and rule-governed (see Evans, 2008).

It is assumed that people can rely on both modes for making a judgment or a decision. Which kind of processing mode is mainly involved in a specific task might depend on context factors, such as the relevance of the decision or the time available to make a decision, and personality traits. There is evidence for time-stable individual differences in decision-making styles (see C. Betsch & Iannello, chapter 14, this volume) indicating that some people tend to prefer an intuitive decision-making style, whereas others base their decision predominantly on analytical reasoning. Obviously context factors can be manipulated while personality factors cannot. Therefore, we focus on methods that are based on the manipulation of context factors.

To compare intuitive and deliberate processes directly in an experimental study, one has to make sure that the same decision task and dependent variable(s) are used for both conditions. The prototypical design for a study is illustrated in Figure 12.1. In the first step, the information upon which participants base their decision (e.g., attributes for two or more options) is presented. In the second step, the experimenter tries to achieve, by means of an appropriate experimental manipulation, that one group of participants processes this information more deliberately (deliberate condition) and the other

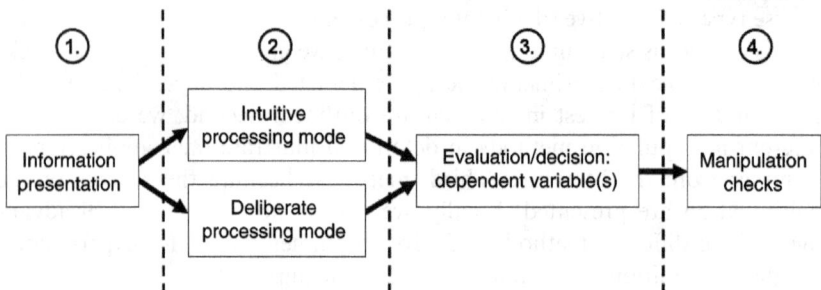

Figure 12.1 Prototypical design for a study comparing intuitive and deliberate processes.

group more intuitively (intuitive condition). In the third step, the actual judgment or decision takes place. Finally, there should be a fourth step, in which variables are measured to check the success of the experimental manipulation. Of course, the order of these four steps can be different in real experimental designs. For instance, some authors manipulate intuitive and deliberate processes first and present the information afterwards or variables for a manipulation check are measured during the experiment.

As dependent variables, outcome measures such as choices and judgments can be analysed. Recently, many studies investigated the quality (i.e., correctness) of intuitive and deliberate decisions. For instance, Wilson and Schooler (1991) examined the quality of rating strawberry jams or college courses by comparing these ratings to an expert opinion as an external criterion. Halberstadt and Levine (1999) measured the accuracy of basketball game predictions and Dijksterhuis, Bos, Nordgren, and van Baaren (2006) looked at the quality of choices between hypothetical cars. Besides decision quality, there are of course further dependent variables that are of research interest. For instance, in studies testing fit effects between intuitive and deliberate decisions and personal thinking styles (C. Betsch & Kunz, 2008) or mood states (De Vries, Holland, and Witteman, 2008a) the estimated price for the chosen object was analysed without judging its quality in comparison to normative standards. To test computational models for intuition and deliberation, choices and judgments should be compared to predictions of models for instance using the methods described by Bröder (chapter 4, this volume) and Glöckner (chapter 5, this volume). Besides outcome measures, dependent variables can of course also concern further (process) measures such as direction and amount of information search (Norman & Schulte-Mecklenbeck, chapter 2, this volume), physiological arousal (Hochman, Glöckner, & Yechiam, chapter 8, this volume), decision time and confidence (Glöckner, chapter 5, this volume), or even duration and distribution of fixations measured with eye-tracking technology. Horstmann, Ahlgrimm and Glöckner (2009), for example, induced intuitive versus deliberate processes in an eye-tracking study and investigated parameters such as number of fixations, fixation durations or direction of information search. This volume provides many examples of outcome and process measures that could be considered.

Methods

In the following we outline the conceptual framework of several methods to induce intuitive and deliberate processing modes and illustrate their application.

Direct instruction

In decision-making literature, intuitive and deliberate processes are most frequently manipulated by means of direct instructions. The basic idea underlying this method is to directly ask participants to decide intuitively or after thorough deliberation. However, the labels intuition or deliberation are not always explicitly mentioned in the instruction. Rather, the instruction focuses on one or several process characteristics and asks the participant to decide accordingly. Instructions reported in the literature differ to a great extent in the concrete wording and specific process characteristics that are accentuated. One reason for this variability may be the already mentioned heterogeneity of underlying concepts of intuition (see Glöckner & Witteman, chapter 1, this volume). Depending on the particular kind of intuition the researcher wants to investigate, participants in the intuitive condition can be instructed to a) decide fast or spontaneously, b) base the decision on (gut) feeling, or c) view the decision task holistically. In a similar manner, participants in the deliberate condition can be asked to a) analyse reasons, b) think of pros and cons, c) evaluate each piece of information, d) think carefully, or e) take one's time.

A first procedure to induce intuitive decision making is to instruct participants to decide spontaneously, fast or as fast as possible. This class of instructions refers to the speed of information processing, namely to the commonly held assumption that intuitive processes are fast (Evans, 2008). For instance, C. Betsch and Kunz (2008) asked participants to indicate which of two coffee pots they preferred by instructing the intuitive condition as follows: "Please indicate spontaneously which of the two pots you prefer" (p. 538). Schroyens, Schaeken, and Handley (2003) used a more stringent instruction to induce an intuitive processing mode: ". . . This means that we primarily want to have a look at the speed of your answers. . . . It does mean that you have to select as fast as possible the answer that you think is correct" (p. 1134). Instructions containing demands to decide fast and spontaneously can be characterized as a kind of *implicit time pressure* (Glöckner & Betsch, 2008b) which can be distinguished from explicitly given time constraints discussed in a subsequent section.

A further procedure reflecting the affective component of intuition is to instruct participants to base their decision on their feeling or gut feeling. De Vries et al. (2008a) instructed the intuitive condition in the following way: "Based on your first feelings, please indicate which of the two Thermoses you prefer to win in the lottery" (p. 5). Halberstadt and Levine (1999) used a more detailed instruction that also referred to affect:

> In particular, we are interested in the benefit of intuition in these sorts of judgments. Therefore, we would not like you to think about and analyze your reasons for liking or disliking each team. Instead, we would like you to go with your intuition or "gut feeling". Try to avoid any drawn-out analysis of your decisions, and make your predictions based on your first instinct. (pp. 522–523)

Instructions to decide intuitively can also reflect the holistic perspective of intuition, namely the integration of all or at least a high amount of information. In a recent study regarding complex problem solving, Pretz (2008) presented a very detailed instruction to participants in the intuitive condition, consisting of several processing steps and highlighting the holistic property of intuition: "(1) Imagine the situation vividly, (2) view the problem holistically, (3) trust your hunches and feelings about the problem, and (4) incubate (skip the problem and come back to it later if you get stuck)" (p. 557). Apart from the affective and the holistic property of intuition, the instruction also refers to incubation. This particular concept of intuition assumes that intuitive processes can also be time-consuming. As this assumption is similar to predictions of the Unconscious Thought Theory (Dijksterhuis & Nordgren, 2006), we refer readers to the section *Distraction Task*.

A well-established procedure to induce deliberate decision making is the instruction to analyse reasons. According to this method, participants are instructed to analyse reasons why they think or feel about each option the way they do before reaching a decision. In the majority of studies, the reasons have to be written down in a space provided. Analysis of reasons mainly reflects the rule-governed property of deliberation by providing a specific guideline how to deliberate. Additionally, the writing down of reasons forces participants to proceed serially. In a series of studies, Wilson and Schooler (e.g., 1991) asked participants to evaluate different strawberry jams or college courses on a rating scale. To induce conscious thinking about the alternatives, participants received the instruction to "analyze why you feel the way you do" about each jam or course (pp. 183/187). After tasting the different strawberry jams or reading the different course descriptions, respectively, they were instructed to write down their reasons for each alternative. They were told that the purpose of this procedure was to organize their thoughts and that their responses would be anonymous. In a study investigating the accuracy of basketball predictions, Halberstadt and Levine's (1999) instructions for the deliberate condition also contained a demand for a thorough analysis of reasons:

> In particular, we are interested in the benefit of reasoning processes in these sorts of judgments. Therefore, in order to prepare yourself for your judgments, we would like you to think about and analyze the reasons why you feel the way you do about each game, why you think each team will do well or poorly. You should list your reasons in the space provided . . . You may list any reasons that are important to your judgments, but please list at least three reasons for each game. (p. 522)

Analysis of reasons was also used by Dijksterhuis and van Olden (2006), and Levine, Halberstadt, and Goldstone (1996).

A similar procedure is to instruct participants to analyse advantages and disadvantages of the options. De Vries et al. (2008a) asked the deliberate condition to think about the pros and cons of the alternatives before reaching their decision. Likewise, C. Betsch and Kunz (2008) told participants to list them before deciding for a coffee pot: "Please have a close look at the pots and list pros and cons for each pot in the respective rows. You may take your time" (p. 538).

A further method that also reflects the rule-governed and serial property of deliberation is to instruct participants to evaluate all relevant information before reaching a decision. For instance, in their study about evaluation of college courses, Wilson and Schooler (1991) asked a group of participants to stop and think about each piece of information and rate the extent to which it made them more or less likely to take the particular course on a separate rating scale. This method was also applied by Tordesillas and Chaiken (1999) in a replication study.

The methods mentioned above to induce a deliberate processing mode are very specific in the kind of deliberation the participants are told to apply. Another procedure to induce deliberation is a simple instruction to think carefully and thoroughly about the decision task without providing further guidelines. This method takes the assumption into account that deliberation is an effortful process. In studies by Schroyens et al. (2003) and Dijksterhuis et al. (2006) participants in the deliberate condition were asked to think carefully before choosing an option.

While the methods we described so far reflect the assumption that deliberation is a rule-governed, serial and effortful process (Evans, 2008), a further class of instructions refers to the commonly-held assumption that deliberation involves rather slow information processing. That is, participants can be asked to take their time before reaching a decision. C. Betsch and Kunz (2008), and De Vries at al. (2008a) used this instruction as an additional directive besides the analysis of pros and cons.

In direct instructions, several process characteristics of intuition or deliberation can be highlighted and easily combined. Instructions can additionally be coupled with time constraints (e.g., C. Betsch & Kunz, 2008), which are outlined as a further method in the subsequent section.

Time constraints

Another commonly used method to manipulate intuition and deliberation is the implementation of time constraints. For intuition, the basic idea is to produce time pressure by limiting the decision time available. Hence, participants get a well-defined time-frame within which they have to decide. This method is based on the assumption that deliberation requires time (Evans, 2008) and therefore providing only a short time-frame is likely to reduce deliberation. Additionally, Maule and Svenson (1993) argued that time pressure reduces the cognitive resources available for analytic deliberation because the awareness of a time limit demands that resources are allocated to monitor the available time. On the other hand, thorough deliberation requires sufficient decision time. Therefore, participants in the deliberate condition are not allowed to decide before a certain time-frame has elapsed or receive weaker or no time constraint.

There are at least three methods to realize time pressure in the intuitive condition, by a) a signalforced response, b) a down counting clock, or c) an instruction to proceed quickly. First, an audible or visual warning signal can be implemented when the decision has to be made or when decision time ends. For instance, T. Betsch, Plessner, Schwieren, and Gütig (2001) defined a time limit of eight seconds within which participants should indicate their judgments. After six seconds, a visual warning signal appeared at the top of the computer screen (Study 2). Bolte and Goschke (2005) varied different time lags (Study 1: 1 and 2 seconds; Study 2: 1, 1.5 and 2 seconds) after which a response signal appeared (80-Hz tone of 100 milliseconds). Participants were instructed to decide in synchronization with the response signal by pressing a key. If no key pressure was made within 500 milliseconds after onset of the response signal, a 1,000-Hz feedback tone sounded until a key was pressed.

Second, a bar or clock counting down can be presented on the computer screen. For instance, Finucane, Alkahami, Slovic, and Johnson (2000) told participants that only a short time would be available and that a response had to be made before a clock shown at the bottom of the computer screen counted down completely from green to red. Additionally, when time had run out, a yellow sign appeared with the instruction "you must click on the scale now" (p. 6) and the participants heard a beeping sound until they made their rating. C. Betsch and Kunz (2008) used a time constraint to underline their instructions. They asked the intuitive condition to make a spontaneous decision within four seconds. The time elapsed was indicated by a ticker bar. If the participant failed to decide within this time-frame, a message box appeared demanding a choice.

Third, implicit time pressure can be implemented by way of instructions emphasizing the speed of the decision and asking to decide as fast as possible. As this procedure was outlined in the previous section, we will not go into detail at this point.

In the deliberate condition, there are at least two methods to provide sufficient time for thorough deliberation, by a) indicating a time delay, or b) implementing weak or no time constraint.

First, participants can be forced not to decide before the end of a defined time-frame. T. Betsch et al. (2001) told participants that they could not make judgments before six seconds had elapsed, and enforced this by blocking the cursor. Apart from using instructions to think deliberately, C. Betsch and Kunz (2008) further implemented time constraints to foster deliberation. The program did not activate the click buttons for the decision until after a five-second delay. Dijksterhuis et al. (2006) set a time-frame of four minutes in the deliberate condition before participants were asked to indicate their decision.

Second, weak or no time constraint can be implemented, while imposing time pressure on the intuitive condition. For instance, Finucane et al. (2000)

instructed participants in the deliberate condition to take as much time as they wanted.

The time constraints that are suitable to induce intuitive and deliberate processes depend on the experimental paradigm. To define adequate time constraints, pilot testing is advisable. For instance, in a pilot study Finucane et al. (2000) measured the time needed to solve the task in a no-time pressure condition. To obtain a value for time pressure, they subtracted one standard deviation from the mean time of the no-time pressure condition. Some studies investigate the effects of different time constraints (e.g., Bolte & Goschke, 2005). Additionally, other research findings or theories can serve as a basis to define adequate time constraints (MacGregor, 1993).

Distraction task

A further method to induce intuitive processes is the implementation of a distraction task to avoid conscious thinking about the decision task. Research on dual-task interference has shown that people have difficulties performing two tasks simultaneously, especially if the two tasks are cognitively demanding and require a lot of attentional resources (Fisk, Derrick, & Schneider, 1986). In memory research, distraction tasks are applied to prevent continuous rehearsal of the learning material or to-be-remembered information (e.g., Haist, Shimamura, & Squire, 1992).

With respect to judgment and decision-making research, the use of distraction tasks has recently won interest with a concept of intuition postulated by the Unconscious Thought Theory (Dijksterhuis & Nordgren, 2006). This theory conceptualizes intuition as a time-consuming process and therefore diverges from other models that understand intuition as a fast process: "Unconscious thought refers to object-relevant or task-relevant cognitive or affective thought processes that occur while conscious attention is directed elsewhere" (p. 96). Note that this is not necessarily a contradiction, accepting that intuition is just a label for different types of processes that partially work automatically (Glöckner & Witteman, chapter 1, this volume).

Experiments in the context of the Unconscious Thought Theory usually have three conditions: a) a conscious thinking condition (induced by instruction), b) an immediate condition (induced by time pressure), and c) a distraction condition (Dijksterhuis, 2004; Newell, Wong, Cheung, & Rakow, 2009). In the latter, a distraction task that is not relevant to the actual decision prevents conscious thinking while unconscious information integration is assumed to take place. The distraction task is added between the presentation of the relevant information and the actual decision. Typically, the time-frame used for these distraction tasks ranges from three to four minutes. The most frequently-used distraction tasks are anagram solving tasks (simple anagrams like SOUHE for HOUSE) and the so-called n-back task, in which participants are asked to monitor the identity of stimuli and to indicate when the currently presented stimulus is the same as the one shown n presentations before (often, a two-back task with digits is applied, e.g., Dijksterhuis, 2004).

In general, the decision interval for the conscious thinking condition is not self-paced and, for the sake of better comparability, has the same length as the one in the distraction condition. Comparison of outcome measures (i.e., quality of choice) in the immediate decision condition and the distraction condition indicates if an unconscious decision-relevant information integration took place during the distraction task.

Manipulation of mood

An additional approach to induce intuitive and deliberate processes is the manipulation of different mood states. Within the framework of decision making and in the context of intuition versus deliberation, unspecific mood is more frequently investigated than specific emotions. Several theoretical and empirical approaches indicate that sad mood leads people to analyse information more deliberately and thoroughly, whereas a happy mood activates more heuristic, intuitive strategies (for an overview, see Bless & Igou, 2005; Clore, Schwarz, & Conway, 1994; Forgas, 1989, 2006; Forgas & Bower, 1988). However, until now only few studies induced positive and negative mood directly with the aim of manipulating intuitive or deliberate processing modes (De Vries et al., 2008a, 2008b).

Several methods have been successfully applied to induce mood, such as for example a) presenting affective pictures or films or b) asking people to imagine a happy or sad episode from their personal past. De Vries et al. (2008a, 2008b) presented short video clips to induce either a happy mood (showing a funny film fragment from *The Muppet Show*) or a sad mood (fragment from *Schindler's List*). The presentation times of the films were 2.5 minutes. The study by Bolte, Goschke, and Kuhl (2003) induced mood states by imagination. They instructed participants to recall as clearly and vividly as possible a happy (or a sad) episode from their personal past. Participants were encouraged to form a mental image of the original episode and to evoke the emotion they had felt within five minutes. Bolte et al. (2003) gave five minutes for imagining the episode. For a general overview of further methods to induce mood and emotion, see Stemmler (2008) and Westermann, Spies, Stahl, and Hesse (1996).

Enhancement of task relevance

Another promising approach to explicitly induce a deliberate processing mode is to emphasize the relevance of the decision situation. According to the idea of an effort-accuracy trade-off (Beach & Mitchell, 1978; Payne, Bettman, & Johnson, 1988), more important decisions increase the effort to solve the task, because people want to reach a higher level of confidence before deciding. This could lead to the selection of decision strategies that are based on higher cognitive effort, potentially resulting in increased deliberation. In some of the dual-process models, the intuitive system is seen as a default mode and deliberation is only activated if necessary (so called default-interventionist models; for an overview, see Evans, 2008; Glöckner & Witteman, chapter 1, this volume). The importance of the task and consequently the desired level of confidence can be seen as a moderator variable that either induces the selection of the deliberate mode from the beginning (e.g., Chaiken, Liberman, & Eagly, 1989; Petty & Cacioppo, 1986) or the activation of deliberation after initial automatic processing (Evans, 2007; Glöckner & Betsch, 2008a; Hausmann & Läge, 2008; Kahneman & Frederick, 2002). One method to increase the relevance of the decision situation is the implementation of a performance-contingent payoff. Financial incentives are common practice in experimental economics and the effects on performance in decision making were frequently discussed (Camerer & Hogarth, 1999; Hertwig & Ortmann, 2001). Empirical findings suggest that performance-contingent payment leads to more analytical and deliberate decision making. Stone and Ziebart (1995) varied performance-contingent and random-based payment between-participants. A performance-contingent payment resulted in an extended information search and longer decision times. To experimentally induce intuition and deliberation, performance-contingent payment could be implemented in the deliberate condition while the intuitive condition is not incentivised or receives a random-based payment. However, we found no study that systematically varied incentive levels to manipulate intuitive and deliberate processes.

Another promising idea for future research is to increase the relevance of the decision task by creating a meaningful cover story, which implies personal involvement or moral dilemmas. For instance, in a study by Luce, Bettman and Payne (1997) participants were asked to imagine they were members of a charitable organization helping needy children. The decision task was to choose one child of a set of five children to support. Participants who received more detailed and vivid background information describing the children's plight spent more effort (e.g., more acquisitions in Mouselab) in the decision process. This finding provides an indication that deliberate processes are likely to be induced by a subjectively meaningful cover story of the decision task.

Manipulation check

In the experimental design of studies manipulating intuitive and deliberate processes a manipulation check should obligatorily be included. That is, one should at least implement one method to check whether the manipulation was indeed successful. Unfortunately, many studies that compare intuition and deliberation do not use a manipulation check, although suitable methods such as the analysis of decision time or strategy use inventories are available and can easily be applied.

The analysis of decision time was, for instance, used by De Vries et al. (2008a) who manipulated intuition and deliberation by means of direct instruction. They analysed the time taken to reach a decision as dependent variable and compared decision time in the intuitive and deliberate condition. The main effect of processing mode turned out to be significant, indicating a longer decision time in the deliberate condition compared to the intuitive condition. The authors concluded that the instructions successfully induced intuitive and deliberate decisions. This method can in principle be applied with every manipulation method. It was also used by Finucane et al. (2000) who implemented time constraints in their study. However, the analysis of decision time in connection with time constraints is only meaningful if participants are not forced to indicate their decision after the time-frame has elapsed in the intuitive condition or when no time constraints are implemented in the deliberate condition. In general, other techniques should be applied when using time constraints.

As a further method, inventories investigating the use of intuitive or deliberate strategies can be given subsequently to the experimental treatment. On the basis of the "Strategy Use Inventory" (SUI), Pretz (2008) classified participants as users or non-users of intuitive or deliberate strategies. The SUI consists of seven items asking for the use of intuitive (e.g., "rely on guesses or hunches") or deliberate strategies (e.g., "break the problem down into steps"). Frequency of strategy use is measured on a five-point rating scale. Pretz (2008) included only participants who reported using the instructed strategy above the mean level in further analyses. In a slightly different vein, Glöckner and Engel (2008) used a questionnaire to detect processing mode in a complex legal judgment task by asking whether participants (automatically) constructed interpretations of the evidence or analysed information in a rule-based manner. Note that such strategy use inventories are based on a particular concept of intuition and deliberation. Therefore, one has to select or develop an inventory which measures the kind of intuitive and deliberate processes the study aims to investigate.

A specific method can additionally be considered when using a distraction task. To ensure that participants actually were involved in the distraction task and did not consciously think about the decision task, performance in the distraction task can be measured. Here, it is useful to define a reasonable exclusion criterion.

To check whether the manipulation by different mood states was successful, several methods are available. For instance, De Vries et al. (2008a, 2008b) asked participants to fill out a short questionnaire consisting of five items like "To what extent do you feel happy at the moment?" (measured on a nine-point scale ranging from "not at all" to "very much"). Bolte et al. (2003) used an adjective checklist comprising separate scales for subjective happiness, sadness, and arousal and measuring on a four-point scale whether each adjective describes the current state. For a better comparison of effects within participants, Bolte et al. (2003) recorded "baseline mood" before and "induced mood" after the manipulation with the same adjective checklist and implemented a control condition without intervention.

Alternatively, inventories investigating positive and negative affect states can be implemented (e.g., PANAS; Watson, Clark, & Tellegen, 1988; for an overview see Dickert, chapter 10, this volume).

Discussion

In the research field of judgment and decision making an increasing interest in the investigation of intuitive and deliberate processes has recently developed. One possibility to investigate the properties and cognitive mechanisms underlying intuition and deliberation is to induce one of the two processing modes directly and to measure reactions on an outcome or process level. Different methods for the manipulation of intuition or deliberation such as direct instruction, implementation of time constraints or a distraction task, manipulation of mood, and enhancement of task relevance can be used (see Table 12.1). These methods might induce or prevent the usage of different kinds of intuition. While time pressure might lead people to look at fewer pieces of information, instructing them to follow their gut feeling might induce affective components of decision making. Of course, diverse types of deliberate processes are likely to be induced by the presented methods as well. For instance, the instruction to analyse reasons will probably lead to different processes than the mere instruction to think carefully.

Methodological advantages and disadvantages

In principle, the methods we described can easily be applied in an experimental design and require relatively low expenditure in material and time. So far, there is no standardized procedure to manipulate intuition and deliberation and taking into account the points concerning different types of processes discussed above one might seriously doubt whether such a method could be found at all.

Direct instruction is the most frequently used method in the literature. An important advantage of instructions is that several process characteristics can be emphasized and combined. Nevertheless, instructions involve the risk that participants misunderstand or ignore them and the real effect of the manipulation remains uncertain. It cannot be ruled out that participants make an intuitive decision and merely retain it for a certain time when they are asked to deliberate. Given that several kinds of instructions are available, it may be difficult to choose the appropriate one. It is quite likely that different instructions induce different kinds of intuition or deliberation (see also C. Betsch & Iannello, chapter 14, this volume) and researchers must know exactly what they intend to induce. When planning an experiment one has to adapt the instructions to the research paradigm or use similar studies as orientation. It is important to mention that instructions cannot always be constructed such

Table 12.1 Methods to induce intuitive and deliberate processing modes

Method	Intuitive condition	Deliberate condition
Direct instruction	*Instruct to*	*Instruct to*
	decide fast or spontaneously	analyse reasons
	base decision on (gut) feeling	think of pros and cons
	view decision task holistically	evaluate each piece of information
		think carefully or thoroughly
		take one's time
Time constraints	*Induce time pressure*	*Indicate time delay*
	by signalforced response	by blocking cursor or click buttons on the computer screen within a defined time-frame
	by a down counting clock	
	by instruction to proceed quickly	*Implement weak or no time constraint*
Distraction task	*Implement distraction*	*Implement no distraction*
	give a cognitive demanding task that has to be solved within a defined time-frame	instruct to think carefully and thoroughly within the same time-frame
Manipulation of mood	*Induce a happy mood*	*Induce a sad mood*
	by presenting positive pictures or funny film fragments	by presenting negative pictures or sad film fragments
	by asking to imagine a happy episode from personal past	by asking to imagine a sad episode from personal past
Enhancement of task relevance	*Induce low task relevance*	*Induce high task relevance*
	by implementing no or random-based payment	by implementing performance-contingent payment
	by varying parts of the cover story evoking a low desired level of confidence	by varying parts of the cover story evoking a high desired level of confidence

that properties of intuitive and deliberate processes are emphasized in a complementary way (e.g., instructions to decide fast vs. take one's time before making a decision). This is of course also partially due to the fact that some recent models assume that there is no clear distinction and complementarity between the two modes at all (see Horstmann et al., 2009; see also Glöckner & Betsch, 2008a).

Manipulation of processing modes by giving time constraints probably captures one of the basic characteristics of intuition and deliberation, namely their processing speed. Regarding intuition, time pressure can be effective to rule out deliberate processes. However, time pressure might not only prevent deliberation, it will most certainly also have further effects on information search and processing. Zakay (1993) argued that time pressure can deteriorate the decision process because participants are simultaneously confronted with two cognitive tasks: ". . . subjects keep asking themselves, 'How much time is left,' or 'How am I doing with time,' . . . The result is a typical condition of divided attention; the more resources are allocated for the time estimation process, the less resources are left for the decision process" (pp. 66–67). Additionally, it cannot be ruled out that under time pressure people also think analytically, merely trying to speed up deliberative thinking and therefore only focusing on parts of the presented information (see Edland & Svenson, 1993). Furthermore, if time pressure is too high to look up all pieces of information, the usage of non-compensatory strategies might increase (e.g., Glöckner & Betsch, 2008b; Payne et al., 1988). The combination of time pressure and a research paradigm that partially hinders information search such as in Mouse-lab seems to be particularly problematic: if intuition is understood as a holistic process of information integration, it might simply limit the information that is considered in the decision process (Glöckner & Betsch, 2008b; see Norman & Schulte-Mecklenbeck, chapter 2, this volume). Regarding deliberation, defining a time delay during which no decision is possible increases the probability that participants spend a certain time thinking analytically. However, Payne, Samper, Bettman, and Luce (2008) argued that providing a fixed time-frame for conscious thought is a poor way to induce deliberate processes. They found that a self-paced deliberation time leads to more accurate choices than fixed-time deliberation. Please note that Payne et al. (2008) used a relatively long time-frame (three or four minutes) for deliberation in order to retest the effects by Dijksterhuis et al. (2006). It is not clear if these findings hold for a shorter fixed-time deliberation as well. In any case, implementing very long time-frames for deliberation might lead to many uncontrolled effects (e.g., forgetting, distracted thoughts, inducing the feeling that the task might be hard to solve). Generally, studies implementing time constraints require some effort because pilot studies and computer-based testing are needed.

Distraction tasks that are implemented in the intuitive condition have the advantage that conscious deliberation can be almost completely prevented. As a precondition the researcher has to make sure that participants actually concentrate their attention on this task by measuring distraction task performance. One disadvantage arises with the use of a distraction task. For the sake of better comparability, the deliberate condition usually gets the same time-frame for conscious thinking as the intuitive condition receives for working on the distraction task. As mentioned above, fixed time-frames can be unsuitable to induce deliberate processes. Note that the use of a distraction task implies the investigation of a particular kind of intuition that is assumed to be rather time-consuming (cf. Dijksterhuis & Nordgren, 2006).

The induction of different mood states has the advantage that the success of the experimental manipulation is less dependent on the compliance of participants than other methods such as direct instruction, because it is assumed that mood influences on processing modes are automatic. For the induction of different mood states, many methods are available. However, until now only few studies used mood to manipulate intuitive and deliberate processes. As the induction of different mood states seems to be a promising method, future studies using this procedure are desirable.

Enhancing relevance of the decision task has the advantage that it does not intervene as much in the deliberate process as methods like instructions giving guidelines how to deliberate. Performance-contingent payment seems to be a promising method to increase task relevance. However, the financial incentives can only be applied in studies using a decision task with an external criterion of decision correctness (T. Betsch & Haberstroh, 2001). For many artificial and also real world decision tasks such a criterion cannot be defined. Although payment is common practice in economics and is also implemented in some psychological studies, we are not aware of any study that systematically manipulates intuitive and deliberate processes by different payment levels. Regarding the question how much payment is necessary to induce deliberation no standard values are available so far. Nevertheless, performance-contingent payment seems to be a promising method to enhance task relevance and thereby induce deliberation. Further, it is desirable to investigate the effectiveness of other methods such as increasing task relevance by varying parts of the cover story in future studies.

Methodological recommendations

We presented some well-established (e.g., direct instruction) as well as promising methods which so far were infrequently applied to systematically manipulate intuitive and deliberate processes (e.g., manipulation of mood or enhancement of task relevance) but are worth further research. Some studies use a combination of different methods, and, as far as we can see, there should be no disadvantages in using combined methods. Rather, it can be expected that additive effects enhance the probability of a successful manipulation. We conclude that a single application of time constraints bears essential caveats as mentioned above. Therefore, we recommend using time constraints only in combination with another method, for instance, direct instruction (see C. Betsch & Kunz, 2008).

For the experimental design of a study investigating intuitive and deliberate processes, the following points should be considered.

It is advisable to implement a between-participants manipulation as it is administered in most studies comparing intuition and deliberation. Otherwise, carry-over effects are likely to occur. To compare the effects of intuition and deliberation directly in an experimental context, one has to use the same decision task and dependent variable(s) for the intuitive and deliberate condition (see Figure 12.1).

Furthermore, qualitative data suggest that participants always exhibit a tendency to deliberate to avoid a poor performance in the experiment (T. Betsch, personal communication, October 21, 2008). Therefore, T. Betsch and his research group inform participants at the beginning of the experiment that decisions have to be made spontaneously or after thorough deliberation. After that, participants are randomly assigned to the experimental conditions. Additionally, practice tasks are implemented.

Finally, a manipulation check should be included in the experimental design. The analysis of decision time (e.g., De Vries et al., 2008a) or inventories assessing the use of intuitive and deliberate strategies (e.g., Pretz, 2008) are suitable methods that can always be applied. However, when using time constraints, other techniques than the analysis of decision time should be used. For future studies, a standardized procedure for manipulation checks would be desirable.

We hope that this chapter will be a starting point for further systematic research. The application of suitable methods will undoubtedly lead to a better understanding of intuitive and deliberate processes in judgment and decision making.

Summary

- Do not use time constraints as a single method. Research findings suggest that there are some important caveats to the exclusive application of time constraints.
- Be encouraged to use a combination of methods. We expect that additive effects enhance the probability of a successful manipulation.
- Use a between-participants manipulation.
- Use the same decision task and dependent variable(s) for the intuitive and deliberate condition.
- Include methods for checking the manipulation in your experimental design.

References

Beach, L. R., & Mitchell, T. R. (1978). A contingency model for the selection of decision strategies. *Academy of Management Review, 3*, 439–449.

Betsch, C., & Kunz, J. J. (2008). Individual strategy preferences and decisional fit. *Journal of Behavioral Decision Making, 21*, 532–555.

Betsch, T., & Haberstroh, S. (2001). Financial incentives do not pave the road to good experimentation. *Behavioral and Brain Sciences, 24*, 404.

Betsch, T., Plessner, H., Schwieren, C., & Gütig, R. (2001). I like it but I don't know why: A value-account approach to implicit attitude formation. *Personality and Social Psychology Bulletin, 27*, 242–253.

Bless, H., & Igou, E. R. (2005). Mood and the use of general knowledge structures in judgment and decision making. In T. Betsch & S. Haberstroh (Eds.), *The routines of decision making* (pp. 193–210). Mahwah, NJ: Lawrence Erlbaum Associates, Inc.

Bolte, A., & Goschke, T. (2005). On the speed of intuition: Intuitive judgments of semantic coherence under different response deadlines. *Memory & Cognition, 33*, 1248–1255.

Bolte, A., Goschke, T., & Kuhl, J. (2003). Emotion and intuition: Effects of positive and negative mood on implicit judgments of semantic coherence. *Psychological Science, 14*, 416–421.

Camerer, C. F., & Hogarth, R. M. (1999). The effects of financial incentives in experiments: A review and capital-labor-production framework. *Journal of Risk and Uncertainty, 19*, 7–42.

Chaiken, S., Liberman, A., & Eagly, A. H. (1989). Heuristic and systematic information processing within and beyond the persuasion process. In J. S. Uleman & J. A. Bargh (Eds.), *Unintended thought* (pp. 212–252). New York: Guilford Press.

Clore, G. L., Schwarz, N., & Conway, M. (1994). Affective causes and consequences of social information processing. In R. S. Wyer & T. K. Srull (Eds.), *Handbook of social cognition* (2nd ed., Vol. 1, pp. 323–418). Hillsdale, NJ: Erlbaum.

De Vries, M., Holland, R. W., & Witteman, C. L. M. (2008a). Fitting decisions: Mood and intuitive versus deliberative decision strategies. *Cognition & Emotion, 22*, 931–943.

De Vries, M., Holland, R. W., & Witteman, C. L. M. (2008b). In the winning mood: Affect in the Iowa gambling task. *Judgment and Decision Making, 3*, 42–50.

Dijksterhuis, A. (2004). Think different: The merits of unconscious thought in preference development and decision making. *Journal of Personality and Social Psychology, 87*, 586–598.

Dijksterhuis, A., Bos, M. W., Nordgren, L. F., & van Baaren, R. B. (2006). On making the right choice: The deliberation-without-attention effect. *Science, 311*, 1005–1007.

Dijksterhuis, A., & Nordgren, L. F. (2006). A theory of unconscious thought. *Perspectives on Psychological Science, 1*, 95–109.

Dijksterhuis, A., & van Olden, Z. (2006). On the benefits of thinking unconsciously: Unconscious thought can increase post-choice satisfaction. *Journal of Experimental Social Psychology, 42*, 627–631.

Edland, A., & Svenson, O. (1993). Time pressure and stress in human judgment and decision making. In O. Svenson & A. J. Maule (Eds.), *Judgment and decision making under time pressure: Studies and findings* (pp. 27–40). New York: Plenum Press.

Evans, J. S. B. T. (2007). On the resolution of conflict in dual process theories of reasoning. *Thinking & Reasoning, 13*, 321–339.

Evans, J. S. B. T. (2008). Dual-processing accounts of reasoning, judgment, and social cognition. *Annual Review of Psychology, 59*, 255–278.

Finucane, M. L., Alhakami, A., Slovic, P., & Johnson, S. M. (2000). The affect heuristic in judgments of risks and benefits. *Journal of Behavioral Decision Making, 13*, 1–17.

Fisk, A. D., Derrick, W. L., & Schneider, W. (1986). A methodological assessment and evaluation of dual-task paradigms. *Current Psychology, 5*, 315–327.

Forgas, J. P. (1989). Mood effects on decision making strategies. *Australian Journal of Psychology, 41*, 197–214.

Forgas, J. P. (2006). *Affect in social thinking and behavior*. New York: Psychology Press.

Forgas, J. P., & Bower, G. H. (1988). Affect in social judgments. *Australian Journal of Psychology*, *40*, 125–145.

Glöckner, A., & Betsch, T. (2008a). Modeling option and strategy choices with connectionist networks: Towards an integrative model of automatic and deliberate decision making. *Judgment and Decision Making*, *3*, 215–228.

Glöckner, A., & Betsch, T. (2008b). Multiple-reason decision making based on automatic processing. *Journal of Experimental Psychology: Learning, Memory, and Cognition*, *34*, 1055–1075.

Glöckner, A., & Engel, C. (2008). Can we trust intuitive jurors? An experimental analysis. *MPI Collective Goods Preprint, No. 38.* Available at SSRN: http://ssrn.com/abstract=1307580.

Haist, F., Shimamura, A. P., & Squire, L. R. (1992). On the relationship between recall and recognition memory. *Journal of Experimental Psychology: Learning, Memory, and Cognition*, *18*, 691–702.

Halberstadt, J. B., & Levine, G. M. (1999). Effects of reasons analysis on the accuracy of predicting basketball games. *Journal of Applied Social Psychology*, *29*, 517–530.

Hausmann, D., & Läge, D. (2008). Sequential evidence accumulation in decision making: The individual desired level of confidence can explain the extent of information acquisition. *Judgment and Decision Making*, *3*, 229–243.

Hertwig, R., & Ortmann, A. (2001). Experimental practices in economics: A methodological challenge for psychologists? *Behavioral and Brain Sciences*, *24*, 383–451.

Horstmann, N., Ahlgrimm, A., & Glöckner, A. (2009). How distinct are intuition and deliberation? An eye-tracking analysis of instruction-induced decision modes. *Judgment and Decision Making 4*, 335–354.

Kahneman, D., & Frederick, S. (2002). Representativeness revisited: Attribute substitution in intuitive judgment. In T. Gilovich, D. Griffin & D. Kahneman (Eds.), *Heuristics and biases: The psychology of intuitive judgment* (pp. 49–81). New York, NY: Cambridge University Press.

Levine, G. M., Halberstadt, J. B., & Goldstone, R. L. (1996). Reasoning and the weighting of attributes in attitude judgments. *Journal of Personality and Social Psychology*, *70*, 230–240.

Luce, M. F., Bettman, J. R., & Payne, J. W. (1997). Choice processing in emotionally difficult decisions. *Journal of Experimental Psychology: Learning, Memory, and Cognition*, *23*, 384–405.

MacGregor, D. (1993). Time pressure and task adaptation: Alternative perspectives on laboratory studies. In O. Svenson & A. J. Maule (Eds.), *Time pressure and stress in human judgment and decision making* (pp. 73–82). New York: Plenum Press.

Maule, A. J., & Svenson, O. (1993). Concluding remarks. In O. Svenson & A. J. Maule (Eds.), *Time pressure and stress in human judgment and decision making* (pp. 323–329). New York: Plenum Press.

Newell, B. R., Wong, K. Y., Cheung, J. C. H., & Rakow, T. (2009). Think, blink or sleep on it? The impact of modes of thought on complex decision making. *The Quarterly Journal of Experimental Psychology*, *62*, 707–732.

Payne, J. W., Bettman, J. R., & Johnson, E. J. (1988). Adaptive strategy selection in decision making. *Journal of Experimental Psychology: Learning, Memory, and Cognition*, *14*, 534–552.

Payne, J. W., Samper, A., Bettman, J. R., & Luce, M. F. (2008). Boundary conditions on unconscious thought in complex decision making. *Psychological Science*, *19*, 1118–1123.

Petty, R., & Cacioppo, J. (1986). *Communication and persuasion: Central and peripheral routes to attitude change.* New York: Springer-Verlag.

Pretz, J. E. (2008). Intuition versus analysis: Strategy and experience in complex everyday problem solving. *Memory & Cognition*, *36*, 554–566.

Schroyens, W., Schaeken, W., & Handley, S. (2003). In search of counter-examples: Deductive rationality in human reasoning. *The Quarterly Journal of Experimental Psychology: A. Human Experimental Psychology*, *7*, 1129–1145.

Stemmler, G. (2008). Induktion von Emotionen in der experimentellen Emotions-psychologie. In W. Janke, M. Schmidt-Daffy & G. Debus (Eds.), *Experimentelle Emotionspsychologie. Methodische Ansätze, Probleme, Ergebnisse* (pp. 207–224). Lengerich: Pabst.

Stone, D. N., & Ziebart, D. A. (1995). A model of financial incentive effects in decision making. *Organizational Behavior and Human Decision Processes*, *61*, 250–261.

Tordesillas, R. S., & Chaiken, S. (1999). Thinking too much or too little? The effects of introspection on the decision-making process. *Personality and Social Psychology Bulletin*, *25*, 623–629.

Watson, D., Clark, L. A., & Tellegen, A. (1988). Development and validation of brief measures of positive and negative affect: The PANAS scales. *Journal of Personality and Social Psychology*, *54*, 1063–1070.

Westermann, R., Spies, K., Stahl, G., & Hesse, F. W. (1996). Relative effectiveness and validity of mood induction procedures: A meta-analysis. *European Journal of Social Psychology*, *26*, 557–580.

Wilson, T. D., & Schooler, J. W. (1991). Thinking too much: Introspection can reduce the quality of preferences and decisions. *Journal of Personality and Social Psychology*, *60*, 181–192.

Zakay, D. (1993). The impact of time perception processes on decision making under time stress. In O. Svenson & A. J. Maule (Eds.), *Time pressure and stress in human judgment and decision making* (pp. 59–72). New York: Plenum Press.

13 The internal validity of self-report measures for intuitive and rational decision making

Pieter Koele and Guus Dietvorst

Introduction

Besides the different methods to measure the application of deliberate and intuitive processes in specific situations and under different context factors discussed in the previous chapters of this volume, the general tendency to use more intuitive or deliberate processing might be considered a trait (or state) variable which is connected with the person and to a certain extent stable over time. In this line of thought during the last three decades various measures for assessing preferences for either intuitive or rational decision-making styles have been proposed. In this chapter we will focus on the internal validity of four such instruments: Harren's (1979) Decision Making Styles questionnaire (DMS), the General Decision Making Style inventory (GDMS) of Scott and Bruce (1995), the Rational-Experiential Inventory (REI) of Epstein, Pacini, Denes-Raj and Heier (1996) and an instrument measuring the Preference for Intuition or Deliberation (PID) developed by Betsch (2004, 2008).

Harren (1979) in his DMS defines three decision-making styles: Rational, Intuitive and Dependent. The first two styles involve personal responsibility for decision-making, whereas the Dependent Style involves projection of responsibility.

Scott and Bruce (1995) add two more styles to these three: Avoidant and Spontaneous. The Avoidant style means avoiding making decisions and the Spontaneous style refers to the phenomenon that decisions just come from nowhere and are made in a split second without any reasoning.

Epstein et al. (1996) distinguish just two styles: Intuitive-experiential and Analytical-rational. The Intuitive-experiential scale was developed to measure "engagement and confidence in one's intuitive abilities"(Epstein et al. 1996, p. 392). The Analytical-rational scale is an adoption of the Need-for-Cognition scale of Cacioppo and Petty (1982) and is intended to measure "engagement in and enjoyment of intellectual activities" (Epstein et al. 1996, p. 392).

A similar distinction is made by Betsch (2004), who calls them Intuition and Deliberation. Where choices via intuition are based on implicit knowledge and use the affect towards an option as a criterion for decisions, choices through deliberation are based on explicit knowledge and are made with consideration, in a rule-governed way.

Thus it seems that the division into a rational and an intuitive style is the most fundamental and widespread among psychologists from various persuasions (Epstein et al., 1996). When focussing on this rational–intuitive division, some questions arise. How are the different styles measured? Do the instruments indeed measure what they claim to measure in a reliable way? How are these measures related to other person charateristics? In short, do these four instruments have an acceptable degree of internal validity? To answer these questions the psychometric properties of the scales will be investigated and discussed in the next section.

Decision Making Styles (DMS)

The test

The DMS questionnaire is based on the Career Making Decision model of Harren (1979, 1984). The questionnaire consists of 30 agree/disagree-items that are equally distributed among three decision-making styles: Rational, Intuitive and Dependent. The Rational style "is characterized by the ability to recognize the consequences of earlier decisions for later decisions" (Harren, 1979, p. 125), the Intuitive style by "the use of fantasy, attention to present feelings, and an emotional self-awareness as the basis for deci-sion making" (ibid.), while the Dependent Style involves "a denial of personal responsibility for decision making and a projection of that respon-sibility outside of self" (ibid.). Originally the scales referred to the deci-sion to choose a college, but the final version of the questionnaire is generic to "important decisions" (Phillips, Friedlander, Pazienza & Kost, 1985, p. 108).

Sample items of the three scales are:

Rational style

"I am very systematic when I go about making an important decision."

"I like to learn as much as possible about the consequences of a decision before I make it."

Intuitive style

"When I make a decision I just try trust my inner feelings and reactions."

"I often decide on something without checking it out and getting the facts."

Dependent style

"I really have a hard time making important decisions without help."

"I need a lot of encouragement and support from others when I make a decision."

Each scale consists of 10 items, these items are scored either 1 ("agree") or 0 ("disagree"), so scale scores range from 0 to 10, higher scores indicating a greater tendency to prefer the particular style.

Reliability

Harren (1984) found consistency coefficients of the three scales ranging from .60 to .84, and test-retest reliabilities from .76 to .85 across a two-week interval. When conducting an iterative principal component analysis on the scores of a sample of 819 undergraduates, Phillips et al. (1985) found a three-factor solution by using the Scree-test. Oblique and orthogonal rotations yielded identical results, indicating that the three factors are basically unrelated. After the orthogonal rotation the three factors accounted for 31% of the variance. Although three items loaded weakly (less than .40) and two items loaded negatively rather than positively on the expected factor, the factor-structure is in line with the hypothesized structure of the test, although the total amount of variance accounted for by the three factors is not impressive.

Construct validity

Blustein and Phillips (1990) conducted a study to establish the relation between the identity formation process of late adolescence and decision-making styles as assessed by the DMS. They distinguished four ego identity statuses: The *Moratorium* status describes persons who are exploring ideological and interpersonal issues but have not yet committed themselves to an identity, the *Identity-achievement* status refers to persons who also have been exploring and have emerged with a clear commitment to their identity, the *Foreclosure* status refers to persons who have committed themselves to the attitudes of their parents, and the *Diffusion* status is characterized by the absence of both exploration and commitment. On the basis of development theory and research Blustein and Phillips expected the following:

1   Both persons in the Moratorium status and Identity-achievement status will prefer a rational decision style without dependence on others.
2   Persons in the Foreclosure status tend to prefer a dependent, non-deliberate decision style.
3   Persons in the Diffusion status do not like rational decision making, but prefer dependent and intuitive styles.

The four ego-identity statuses were measured by an adaptation of the Extended Objective Measure of Ego Identity Status (EOM-EIS; Bennion & Adams, 1986). Subjects were 99 college students. The relations between the two sets of variables were analysed by using canonical correlation analysis.

The results show:

1   People in the Identity-achievement status tend to rely on rational decision making, but people in the Moratorium status do not; the expected negative relation with the Dependent style was not found.
2   Persons in the Foreclosure status indeed prefer a dependent decision style – other relations were not found.
3   As expected, persons in the Diffusion state seem to rely on intuitive and dependent styles but not on the rational style.

It must be noted that of the total amount of variance present in the seven variables only 20% could be accounted for by the three canonical variates.

Conclusion

The DMS appears to be a reliable measuring instrument. The theoretical three-factor structure is found, and the three subscales have acceptable reliability coefficients. The Rational and the Intuitive scale do not intercorrelate. There is some evidence for the construct validity of the test, but only in the domain of adolescent identity formation processes.

General Decision Making Style scale (GDMS)

The test

The GDMS (Scott & Bruce, 1995) consists of 25 items rated on a five-point Likert-scale. The items are equally distributed among five subscales for cognitive styles: (a) Rational, characterized by logically analyzing and evaluating alternatives; (b) Intuitive which is defined by attention to details in the flow of information; (c) Dependent, which is characterized by a need for guidance and advice by other persons in decision making; (d) Avoidant, characterized by trying to avoid decision making whenever possible, and (e) Spontaneous, defined by a need to go through the decision-making process as quickly as possible.

Sample items of the Rational and Intuitive scales are:

Rational

"I make decisions in a logical and systematic way."

"My decision making requires careful thought."

Intuitive

"When making decisions, I rely on my instincts."

"I generally make decisions that feel right to me."

Reliability

Initially Scott and Bruce (1995) intended to develop only the first four scales. They constructed 37 items that covered these four scales, and administered them to a sample of 1441 military officers. After a principal component analysis with varimax rotation a five-factor solution emerged, explaining 45% of the total variance. The first four factors corresponded neatly with the hypothesized cognitive styles. It appeared that the fifth factor had to do with spontaneity, or the time spent on decision making. Hereafter six additional items were written to cover this newly discovered dimension. The 43 items were administered to two new samples (N = 85, N = 229). In both cases the five-factor structure emerged, with 37 item-loadings over .40. After iterative item analysis 12 items were deleted, leading to the final 25-item GDMS. The total item variance explained by these 25 items was 63% in the second and 58% in the third sample. The scales seemed highly reliable in all three samples, with Cronbach's alphas ranging from .68 to .94, and a mean alpha around .80. Some of the scales correlated slightly with each other, especially the Intuitive and the Spontaneous scale (around .35), so it appears that subjects do not have a preference for just one style.

Loo (2000) also evaluated the psychometric properties of the GDMS with a sample of 223 management undergraduates and found comparable intercorrelations and Cronbach's alphas (although Dependent style had a Cronbach's alpha of only .62). When conducting an exploratory factor analysis Loo (2000) found a five-factor structure with all the items loading on their designated factor, but three items also loading higher than .30 on another factor. When conducting a confirmatory factor analysis, the five-factor model seemed to fit, which was replicated by Thunholm (2004) and Spicer and Sadler-Smith (2005). Spicer and Sadler-Smith (2005) also found substantial test-retest reliabilities for all the subscales in a sample of N = 82 with an unspecified time-interval.

Construct validity

To evaluate the construct validity Scott and Bruce (1995) correlated the five scales with a control orientation measurement. Internally controlled participants seemed more likely to use a Rational style and less likely to use an Avoidant style than externally controlled participants.

Without stating any expectations Loo (2000) correlated the five subscales to Conflict-management scales. The Avoidant style correlated with the

Avoidant Conflict-management style. The Rational style correlated negatively with the Risk and Variety components of the Conflict-management styles. The Intuitive style correlated positively with Risk and Aesthetics. Higher scores on the Dependent style were associated with higher scores on the Social value, Social interactions, and Social relations component of the Conflict-management styles. Higher Avoidant style scores were associated with higher scores on Independence, Physical activity and Autonomy. And the Spontaneous style correlated positively with the Creativity, Independence, and Variety components of the Conflict-management styles.

Thunholm (2004) explored the relationship between the GDMS and Action control, Self-esteem and Educative ability. Essentially no substantial relations were found.

Indicators for discriminant validity of the GDMS are that Scott and Bruce (1995) found differences among undergraduates, MBA-students and military officers on the Rational, Avoidant, Intuitive and Dependent style, but not on the Spontaneous style. However, it should be recognized that the reasons for the null result concerning Spontaneous style are somewhat weak because the items of the Spontaneous style were only administered to the undergraduates and the MBA-students. Although the differences among the mean scale scores in the samples are not very impressive, it seems that the military officers prefer more Rational and less Intuitive and Avoidant styles than subjects from the other samples.

Loo (2000) found that age was significantly related to two styles: older participants showed less preference for Intuitive and Avoidant style than younger participants.

Conclusion

The five scales of the GDMS seem to fit nicely into the five-factor model that was intended. The scales are fairly to highly reliable. The low intercorrelations indicate that the decision-making styles are not mutually exclusive: individuals do not use only one style. Not much can be concluded about the construct validity of the GDMS.

Rational-Experiential Inventory (REI)

The test

The REI (Epstein et al., 1996) measures two independent modes of information processing: intuitive-experiential and analytical-rational. The first version of the test consisted of two subscales: Need for Cognition, which is measured with 19 items taken from the full 45-item Need for Cognition Scale (NFC) constructed by Cacioppo and Petty (1982), and Faith in Intuition (FI), which consists of 12 items constructed by Epstein et al. themselves. The Need for Cognition-scale is associated with tendencies to carefully analyze and search for information. The Faith in Intuition-scale measures confidence in feelings and initial impressions as a basis for actions. This self-report measure of individual differences in intuitive-experimental and rational-analytic thinking is based on a theory of personality referred to as Cognitive-Experiential Self Theory (CEST; Epstein, 1990). This theory proposes that people process information by two parallel, interactive systems: a rational system and an experiential system. According to CEST, the rational system operates primarily at the conscious level and is intentional, analytic, primarily verbal, and relatively affect-free. The experiential system is assumed to be automatic, preconscious, holistic, associationistic, primarily non-verbal, and is intimately associated with affect (see Glöckner & Witteman, chapter 1, this volume).

Sample items of the Need for Cognition and Faith in Intuition scales are:

Need for Cognition

"I would prefer complex to simple problems."

"Thinking is not my idea of fun" (reverse scored).

"I find little satisfaction in deliberating hard and long for hours." (reverse scored).

Faith in Intuition

"My initial impressions of people are almost always right."

"I believe in trusting my hunches."

"I am a very intuitive person."

Respondents have to rate all items on a five-point scale ranging from completely false to completely true.

When constructing the REI, Epstein et al. (1996) used a sample of 184 undergraduates to check the factor-structure and reliability of the scales. For the NFC-scale Cronbach's alpha was found to be .87 and for the FI-scale .77. When the 31 items of the REI were entered into a principal component factor analysis with varimax-rotation, two factors emerged which accounted for 32.2% of the total variance. The first factor contained all the items of the NFC-scale and the second factor corresponded to the FI-scale and furthermore it seemed that the two factors were not related to each other. Despite these reasonable results, Epstein, Pacini and Norris (1998) created another version of the REI due to dissimilarities between the two scales in the first version. The NFC-scale was about engagement in cognitive activities whereas the FI-scale was mostly about the ability to make intuitive judgments. Also, the FI-scale contained items with a social component while the NFC-scale did not.

Furthermore the two scales were unbalanced in terms of item valence: 14 out of the 19 NFC-items were negatively stated and all 12 FI-items were positively stated. And finally: the reliabilities of the two scales differed too much.

The new version of the REI, referred to as REI-long form, consists of 40 five-point Likert scale-items divided equally over four subscales: Rational ability, Rational engagement, Experiential ability and Experiential engagement. The terms Rational and Experiential were formerly known as NFC and FI. Ability refers to a self-report of the level of ability to think logically or intuitively, whereas engagement refers to the enjoyment of using one of the two ways of reasoning.

Reliability

Pacini and Epstein (1999) administered the REI-long form to a sample of 399 undergraduates (of which 315 were female). The reliabilities of the scales were .90 for the Rationality-scale and .87 for the Experientiality-scale. When conducting a factor analysis with varimax rotation two factors emerged. The first factor (Rationality) accounted for 19.4% of the total variance and the second factor (Experientiality) accounted for 14.6%. When factor analysis was used to examine the Engagement/Ability subscales within the Rationality scale, the results showed that items could indeed be divided into Engagement and Ability items. A factor analysis on the Experientiality scale showed that positively and negatively worded items made up separate factors. Newstead, Handley, Wright and Farrelly (2004) also conducted a study with the REI-long form and found a test-retest reliability of .78 or higher on the different scales, in a sample of N = 44. Witteman, Van den Bercken, Claes and Godoy (2009) administered the REI to a sample of 774 Dutch undergraduates (almost all women). In a confirmatory factor analysis they found support for the two-factor structure of the test, and a reliability of .86 for the Rationality scale and .91 for the Experientiality scale. Both Pacini and Epstein and Witteman et al. report that the Rationality and Experientiality scales did not correlate with each other (−.04 and .04 respectively).

Construct validity

When correlating the REI-long form with personality variables, Pacini and Epstein (1999) found that the Rationality scale correlated substantially (correlations higher than .30) with the Big-5 scales Openness to Experience (.44) and Conscientiousness (.32) and negatively to Neuroticism (−.38). The Experientiality scale had no substantial correlations with any of the Big-5 factors. Witteman et al. (2009) also correlated the Rationality and Experientality scales with the Big-5 factors. In their sample of 774 Dutch students they found statistically significant but very moderate correlations between the REI-scales and the Big-5 factors – the only substantial correlations (slightly above .30) are those between the Rationality scale and Conscientiousness and

Openness to Experience. Using the first version of the REI, Shiloh, Salton and Sharabi (2002) conducted a study to test the hypothesis that intuitive responses can be predicted from variances in decision-making styles. In the study 128 students were administered the REI and the Chances Assessment Questionnaire (CAQ) which measures intuitive versus normative judgment of chances for independent events. The results showed that higher normatively correct judgments were positively correlated with the Rationality scale and negatively with the Experientiality scale.

Conclusion

The REI was designed to measure two ways of information processing, and according to its repeatedly established two-factor structure it does. The Engagement- and Ability factors within the scales do not materialize that easily, but perhaps this division is not really important. It is intriguing that the Experientiality-scale falls apart in two separate factors of positively and negatively worded items. The prominent outcome regarding the correlations of the REI with the Big-5 factors is that the Experientiality scale does not seem to be related to personality characteristics. The Rationality scale seems to have moderate positive correlations with Conscientiousness and Openness to Experience, and (only in the Pacini and Epstein 1999 study) a negative correlation with Neuroticism. Furthermore, the results show that people who score high on the Rationality scale are more likely to use normatively correct judgments than people who score high on the Experientiality scale, which is modest indication of the test's construct validity.

Preference for Intuition and Deliberation (PID)

The test

The PID (Betsch, 2004, 2008) consists of 18 items, nine of which measure a preference for Intuition and nine a preference for Deliberation. According to Betsch (2004), choices via Intuition are based on implicit knowledge and use the affect towards an option as a criterion for decisions. On the contrary, choices through deliberation are based on explicit knowledge, and are made with consideration and in a rule-governed way.

Sample items include:

Deliberation

"Before making decisions I first think them through."

"I am a perfectionist."

"I think before I act."

Intuition

"I listen carefully to my deepest feelings."

"My feelings play an important role in my decisions."

"I am a very intuitive person."

Items are scored on a five-point scale, 1 representing much disagreement and 5 much agreement.

Reliability

When constructing the German questionnaire Betsch (2004) found, using an exploratory factor analysis on 19 items (ten Intuitive and nine Deliberate), a two-factor structure which explained 31.8% of the total variance in the test scores. The two factors were identified as PID-intuition and PID-deliberation. The first scale had a Cronbach's alpha of .81 and the second .78. Hereafter a confirmatory factor analysis was conducted, using a sample of 2,132 persons, which compared a one-factor model to a two-factor model. After the elimination of one item that did not contribute anything to explained variance it appeared that the two-factor model fitted much better than the one-factor model. The internal consistency of the two scales in this sample was .77 for PID-intuition and .79 for PID-deliberation. The test-retest reliabilities with an interval of 14 days with N = 198 were respectively .76 and .59. After six months with N = 21 these were .76 and .74.

Richetin, Perugini, Adjali and Hurling (2007) investigated the psychometric qualities of the English version of the PID using a sample of 299 students. A principal component analysis revealed two factors, confirming the two-factor structure of the questionnaire. The two factors accounted for 34.7% of the variance, furthermore the factors seemed not to be correlated. The structure seemed to be quite similar to the one found by Betsch (2004), except for the fact that one item that was intended to load on the PID-intuition factor, instead loaded on the PID-deliberation factor, and two items loaded weakly on their intended factor (one belonging to the PID-intuition factor and one to the PID-deliberation factor). The internal consistencies of the two subscales were not very high: PID-intuition had a Cronbach's alpha of .62 and PID-deliberation .77. The test-retest reliabilities, conducted on a sub-sample of N = 108, were higher, respectively .83 and .76.

Witteman et al. (2009) administered a Dutch version of the PID to a sub-sample of 405 students out of the sample mentioned above. Their confirmatory factor analysis supported the two-factor structure of the test. The Deliberation scale had a Cronbach's alpha of .85, the Intuition scale of .87. The two scales were not intercorrelated (−.02).

Construct validity

Betsch (2004) validated the German version of the PID by correlating it to various individual dimensions of decision making in a sample of 293 German students. In general, correlations were low. Intuition had a correlation of .67 with the Experientiality scale of the REI and all other correlations were below .25. Deliberation correlated –.29 with Fast Decision Making, and only .20 with the Rationality scale of the REI. Betsch also examined relations with personality traits. For the PID-intuition scale no substantial correlations were found: a .24 correlation with Extraversion is almost all there is. The Deliberation scale correlated .25 with Personal Need for Structure and .35 with Perfectionism. The intercorrelation between the two PID scales was –.16.

Witteman et al. (2009) also checked the correlations between the REI and PID scales. They found a correlation of .51 between the Rationality and Deliberation scales, and of .84 between the Experientiality and Intuition scales. Within each test the scales were not correlated.

Conclusion

The PID is designed to measure Intuition and Deliberation in decision-making. This two-factor structure of the test has been confirmed repeatedly. The reliabilities of the two scales are good. The correlations of the two sub-scales with individual dimensions of decision-making and personality traits are modest.

Discussion

On of the most striking results of our investigation of four tests that intend to measure (preferences for) rational and intuitive decision-making styles is that though the scales that have been constructed have good to excellent reliabilities (both in terms of internal consistency and stability), they correlate at most moderately with variables that have been used to investigate their construct validity. But of course, a high reliability is a necessary but not a sufficient condition for a test having a high external validity.

A second point is that in general the Rational scales seem to have higher reliabilities than the Intuition scales, and they also show more substantial correlations with other variables hypothesized to be linked to a particular decision-making style. The reason for this could be, as has already been pointed out in the introductory chapter of this volume, that Intuition is a much vaguer concept (or perhaps just a label) than Rationality, and therefore less easy to measure.

A third point is the absence of any correlation between the Intuition and the Rational scales. Following Epstein (1990), Betsch (2008, p. 235) claims that Intuition is not the opposite of Deliberation, but rather, they represent two independent dimensions. This is in contrast with, for example, Hammond's

(1990) idea of a cognitive continuum, with Analytical and Intuitive reasoning as the poles of this one dimension. Notwithstanding this, the tests discussed in this chapter indeed seem to indicate that the scales they use for measuring Rationality (or Deliberation) and Intuition (or Experientiality) are independent. As Betsch (2004) remarks this implies that people can be divided into four groups: people with a preference for intuitive but not for rational decision making, people with a preference for rational but not for intuitive decision making, people with a preference for both intuitive and rational decision making, and finally a group of people without a preference for either decision-making style. What it amounts to is that we need to know which people under which circumstances prefer which decision-making style. It will not be easy to answer this question, but it is a challenge that is worth pursuing.

Finally, the existence of (at least) four tests that intend to measure (preferences for) Intuitive or Rational decision making calls for some kind of unification or standardization. The fact that the corresponding scales of the various tests do not correlate as highly as one may hope will complicate comparisons of studies using different tests for measuring Intuition and Rationality. This is not really something that will help us in understanding the important role Intuition and Rationality obviously play in judgment and decision making. Betsch and Ianello (chapter 14, this volume) explain the low correlations between the Intuition scales by the fact that very different processes are collected under the label "Intuition" and measured by the different scales. They suggest a solution to this problem by disentangling these types of processes.

References

Bennion, L. D. & Adams, G. R. (1986). A revision of the extended version of the Objective Measure of Ego Identity Status: an identity instrument for use with late adolescents. *Journal of Adolescent Research*, *1*, 183–197.

Betsch, C. (2004). Präferenz für Intuition und Deliberation. Inventar zur Erfassung von affekt und kognitionsbasiertem Entscheiden. *Zeitschrift für Differentielle und Diagnostische Psychologie*, *25*, 179–197.

Betsch, C, (2008). Chronic preferences for intuition and deliberation in decision making. In H. Plessner, C. Betsch & T. Betsch (Eds), *Intuition in judgement and decision making* (pp. 231–248). New York: Erlbaum.

Blustein, D. L., & Phillips, S. D. (1990). Relation between ego identity statuses and decision-making styles. *Journal of Counseling Psychology*, *37*, 160–168.

Cacioppo, J. T., & Petty, R. E. (1982). The need for cognition. *Journal of Personality and Social Psychology*, *42*, 116–131.

Epstein, S. (1990). Cognitive-experiential self-theory. In L. Pervin (Ed.), *Handbook of personality theory and research* (pp. 165–192). New York: Guilford Press.

Epstein, S., Pacini, R., Denes-Raj, V., & Heier, H. (1996). Individual differences in intuitive-experiential and analytical-rational thinking styles. *Journal of Personality and Social Psychology*, *71*, 390–405.

Epstein, S., Pacini, R., & Norris, P. (1998). *The Rational-Experiential Inventory, long form.* Unpublished Inventory, University of Massachusetts at Amhurst.

Hammond, K.R. (1990). Intuitive and analytical cognition: Information models. In A.P. Sage (Ed.), *Concise encyclopaedia of information processing in systems and organizations* (pp. 306–312). Oxford: Pergamom Press.

Harren, V. A. (1979). A model of career decision making for college students. *Journal of Vocational Behavior, 14*, 119–133.

Harren, V. A. (1984). *Assessment of career decision making.* Los Angeles: Western Psychological Services.

Loo, R. (2000). A psychometric evaluation of the General Decision-Making Style inventory. *Personality and Individual Differences, 29*, 895–905.

Newstead, S. E., Handley, S. J., Harley, C., Wright, H., & Farrelly, D. (2004). Individual differences in deductive reasoning. *The Quarterly Journal of Experimental Psychology, 57*, 33–60.

Pacini, R., & Epstein, S. (1999). The relation of rational and experiential information processing styles to personality, basic-beliefs and the ratio-bias phenomenon. *Journal of Personality and Social Psychology, 76*, 972–987.

Phillips, S. D., Friedlander, M. L., Pazienza, N. J., & Kost, P. (1985). A factor analytic investigation of career decision-making styles. *Journal of Vocational Behavior, 26*, 106–115.

Richetin, J., Perugini, M., Adjali, I., & Hurling, R. (2007). The moderator role of intuitive versus deliberative decision making for the predictive validity of implicit and explicit measures. *European Journal of Personality, 21*, 529–546.

Scott, S. G., & Bruce, R. A. (1995). Decision-making style: The development and assessment of a new measure. *Educational and Psychological Measurement, 55*, 818–831.

Shiloh, S., Salton, E., & Sharabi, D. (2002). Individual differences in rational and intuitive thinking styles as predictors of heuristic responses and framing effects. *Personality and Individual Differences, 32*, 415–429.

Spicer, D. P., & Sadler-Smith, E. (2005). An examination of the general decision making style questionnaire in two UK samples. *Journal of Managerial Psychology, 20*, 137–149.

Thunholm, P. (2004). Decision-making style: style, habit or both? *Personality and Individual Differences, 36*, 931–944.

Witteman, C., Van den Bercken, J., Claes, L. & Godoy, A. (2009). Assessing rational and intuitive thinking styles. *European Journal of Psychological Assessment, 25*, 39–47.

14 Measuring individual differences in intuitive and deliberate decision-making styles

A comparison of different measures

Cornelia Betsch and Paola Iannello

Introduction

Imagine the hungry friends Derek, Deborah, and Ines go to an Italian restaurant. Ines has a quick look at the menu and closes the little book with a snap (and a decision for lasagne) while Derek has not even finished reading the first page. He considers various dishes and compares prices, ingredients and calories. After a while, he finally has two options left and chooses the one with the best cost-benefit balance: the scampi-pasta is said to be excellent for a quite reasonable price. Deborah is still in the process of comparing prices and tastes, when the waiter comes and takes the orders of the group. Although she has actually not made a decision yet, she goes for a pizza, because she realizes that the other guys are hungry and are waiting for her order.

This simple scene can illustrate the consequences of different decision-making styles: some, as Derek and Deborah, might be called more deliberate thinkers, who like to think things through in a time-consuming process. They consider different aspects of the decision problem and evaluate the options on relevant attributes. Other people, like Ines, who might be called a more intuitive person, choose what immediately feels best. The results can differ in the decision outcome per se. A quick choice for the immediately appealing dish might prevent Ines from reaching the "specialties section" where the scampi-pasta is listed. A deliberate comparison of prices, calories and ingredients, on the other hand, might lead to an exclusion of lasagne or tiramisu. Ines' decision was basically influenced by sudden feelings of liking and disliking, which may mirror implicit preferences for the dishes. Derek's deliberate decision, however, is based on explicit attitudes and considerations. Deborah, who tends to deliberate very thoroughly, had to make a quick decision because she was under time pressure. She could not take into account all the information she wanted. Her dissatisfaction might not only be rooted in the pizza (instead of grilled fish), but also in the discomfort of the time pressure that prevented her from making a thoughtful decision.

In abstract terms, the inclination to decide based on intuition and/or deliberation influences the information that we use, the decisions we make and the satisfaction we experience with our decision (C. Betsch, 2008). But can we measure the individual inclination to either strategy, and if so: how? Since the topic of intuition has increasingly raised interest in the scientific community (for an overview see Plessner, C. Betsch, & T. Betsch, 2008; see also Glöckner & Witteman, this volume), a number of inventories has been published that claim to measure individual differences in intuition and/or deliberation. In these self-report measures participants have to express their agreement with statements that describe their regular handling of decision situations (e.g., *I prefer making detailed plans rather than leaving things to chance; My feelings play an important role in my decisions*). Usually the inventories consist of two scores; one expresses an inclination to intuition and one to deliberation.

This chapter gives an overview of five of the most common inventories: the Rational Experiential Inventory (REI, Pacini & Epstein, 1999), the Preference for Intuition and Deliberation scale (PID, C. Betsch, 2004, 2008), the General Decision Making Style questionnaire (GDMS, Scott & Bruce, 1995), the Cognitive Style Indicator (CoSI, Cools & Van den Broeck, 2007), and the Perceived Modes of Processing Inventory (PMPI, Burns & D'Zurilla, 1999). We compare the measures based on the assumption that intuition is a common label for different cognitive phenomena (Glöckner & Witteman, this volume). This idea is confirmed by results of a factor analysis and by the findings obtained with the scales along with their different theoretical foundations (cf. Discussion). The construct validity of the scales will also be discussed. We will finally suggest a heuristic to decide when to use which scale.

Conceptual introduction

Cognitive styles

Preferences for decision strategies can be considered as a subcategory of cognitive styles, since they involve general cognitive mechanisms such as information processing, maintaining intentions and self-regulation, but also have particular features that are specifically related to the field of decision making (Iannello, 2007; Iannello & Antonietti, 2007). The term *cognitive style* refers to consistent attitudes, preferences, or habitual strategies that affect a person's modes of perceiving, learning, judging, decision making and problem solving (Messick, 1984). Individual differences in people's cognitive functioning can be defined as cognitive style when they are pervasive and stable, that is, they appear consistently in different situations (Ausburn & Ausburn, 1978; Riding, Glass & Douglas, 1993). Cognitive styles cannot be conceived of as abilities, but rather as ways of using abilities, measured in terms of *manner* of performance (Antonietti, 2003).

Individual differences in decision-making styles have been referred to as generalized preferences or as a personality trait. The idea of decision styles as personality trait highlights the inter-temporal stability of one's decision-making behaviour across various situations. The concept of preferences mirrors the possibility that people, though within a repertoire of preferred or dominant decision styles, modulate their own behaviour according to the situation at hand. In fact, although people tend to use certain styles more frequently than others (Driver, Brousseau & Hunsaker, 1990) or have a dominant style (Rowe & Mason, 1987), they can adapt their styles to the different situations they encounter, thus showing flexibility in their application of decision styles (Hayes & Allinson, 1998; Zhang & Sternberg, 2007). As some authors suggested (Hammond, Hamm, Grassia, & Pearson, 1987), there may be joint effect of the individual style and the specific characteristic of the decision at hand. Thus, situational factors play a fundamental role in triggering the use of different decision styles, although it seems that decision style preferences are still noticeable even in decision situations that explicitly require the use of a certain style (C. Betsch, 2004). Moreover, preferred decision styles were also found to interact with experimentally manipulated styles (C. Betsch & Kunz, 2008; De Vries, Holland & Witteman, 2008). Thus, although it seems that the situation is quite influential in selecting a style the preferred style seems to play an additional role, e.g. in the subsequent subjective evaluation of the decision (C. Betsch & Kunz, 2008).

The most frequent differentiation in the field of decision-making styles is the contrast between intuitive and deliberative styles (Agor, 1989; Chaiken & Trope, 1999; Klaczynski, 2001; Stanovich & West, 2000). By and large, people with an *intuitive* style rely more on feelings to make decisions and solve problems holistically; they habitually make decisions in a fast, effortless and automatic way. People characterized by a *deliberative* style prefer to solve problems and make decisions by using analytical techniques. They tend to make slower, elaborated and planned decisions (Epstein, Pacini, Denes-Raj & Heier, 1996; C. Betsch, 2008).

Intuition and deliberation defined

The introductory chapter to this book (Glöckner & Witteman, this volume; see also Plessner et al., 2007) gives a comprehensive overview of the concepts of intuition and deliberation. In a nutshell, differences between intuitive and deliberate processes can be pinpointed to differences in the amount of processed information (high vs. low) and the kind of processing (parallel vs. serial) for intuitive vs. deliberate processes, respectively (T. Betsch, 2008). The differences between intuitive and deliberate processing are generally related to the operation of two different processing systems. When judging or deciding intuitively, the tacit or experiential system dominates, which leads to automatic processing and the use of affect and heuristics ("heuristic" is understood here as based on automatic-intuitive processes, not on cognitive shortcuts, see Glöckner & Witteman, this volume).

Deliberate processing, i.e. the operation of the deliberate or rational system, is characterized as serial, controlled, based on cognitions and using logical rules. The amount of information that can be processed consciously is substantially lower than what can be processed intuitively.

When we understand intuition and deliberation as the operation of two systems, the question occurs where the individual differences in the application of the decision styles comes from. One possibility is that there are mutually exclusive systems (Evans, 2008) – from this point of view cognitive style preferences should be responsible for the initial selection of the mode. Models that assume concurrent activation (e.g. Sloman, 2002) might explain individual differences by assuming differential allocations of resources or attention to the different processing systems. A third class of models, so-called default-interventionist models (Kahneman & Frederick, 2002; Evans, 2008) assume that deliberation is an additional process while intuition is always activated. Based on this class of models one would assume that people might have a differential threshold for the activation of deliberation.

Measurement issues

In order to measure the preferences for (habitual) intuitive or deliberate processing one has to consider how intuition and deliberation can be mapped onto measurement scales. There are several possibilities: As just outlined, intuitive and deliberate processing could be mutually exclusive, i.e. highly deliberate processing *excludes* the operation of intuitive processes (Hayes & Allinson, 1994; Myers & McCaulley, 1986; Simon, 1987). This would imply a uni-dimensional scale with intuition and deliberation as its two poles. A more generally accepted assumption, however, is that both processes can operate at the same time (Evans, 2008; Glöckner & Witteman, this volume; Hodgkinson & Sadler-Smith, 2003). This implies the necessity for two independent scales. All instruments that are reviewed in this chapter share this latter assumption and therefore measure intuition and deliberation separately on two bipolar dimensions.

Application

An individual preference for intuition and deliberation can be assessed via self-report measures that ask people to express their agreement or disagreement with several statements. Usually, the items can be divided in one set of items where high agreement expresses a preference for intuition, and high agreement on the other set expresses an inclination towards deliberate strategies. Some questionnaires reflect the conception of intuition and deliberation as personality traits (e.g. Myers-Briggs-Type Indicator, MBTI, Myers & McCaulley, 1986; Pretz & Trotz, 2007); others understand intuition and deliberation as abilities (REI, Pacini & Epstein, 1999); in most other inventories the two constructs are conceived of as styles and stable preferences or tendencies (PID, C. Betsch, 2004; GDMS, Scott & Bruce, 1995; PMPI, Burns

& D'Zurilla, 1999; CoSI, Cools & Van den Broeck, 2007). Some inventories focus on broader styles (intuitive vs. deliberate), while others are more specific about certain features of the processes (e.g. planning and knowing as features of deliberation; Cools & Van den Broeck, 2007). In this chapter we focus on the following inventories:

1   REI (Rational-Experiential Inventory, Pacini & Epstein, 1999)
    The REI scale is the first of its kind. It is based on cognitive-experiential self theory (CEST, Epstein, 2007). When it was first published (Epstein et al., 1996), the subscales need for cognition and faith in intuition assessed general processing preferences. Since then, several versions have been used by scholars. In the latest publication in which validity issues are discussed (Pacini & Epstein, 1999), the REI aims at measuring both the individual engagement in or (preference for) the rational or experiential mode of thinking and the individuals' beliefs in their own ability to successfully use that mode.

2   PID (Preference for Intuition and Deliberation Scale, C. Betsch, 2004)
    The PID is a scale that aims to directly assess strategy preferences in decision situations, instead of measuring information processing in general. The main focus of the preference for intuition scale is the reliance on affect and implicit knowledge; for the preference for deliberation scale the main focus is on the reliance on explicit cognition. Reliable translations of PID exist in six languages (German, English, Dutch, French, Spanish and Polish; Richetin, Betsch, Perugini & Giger, under review).

3   GDMS (General Decision Making Style, Scott & Bruce, 1995)
    The GDMS aims at measuring the preference for decision styles in a broader sense than just intuition and deliberation. In particular, the instrument consists of five subscales corresponding to five different styles corresponding to specific patterns of behaviour that people use in decision making: a rational style characterized by comprehensive search for information and logical evaluation of alternatives; an intuitive style characterized by a reliance on hunches and feelings; a dependent style characterized by the search for guidance from others before making decisions; an avoidant style characterized by attempts to avoid decision making whenever possible; a spontaneous style characterized by the desire to come through the decision-making process as quickly as possible.

4   CoSI (Cognitive Style Indicator, Cools & Van den Broeck, 2007)
    The CoSI assesses rather general cognitive styles; however two of them mirror aspects of deliberate processing. The three identified styles are: knowing, planning and creating. As explicated in the introductory part above, knowing, i.e. the reliance and use of explicit knowledge, is part of deliberate processing; likewise the engagement in sequential planning activities.

5   PMPI (Perceived Modes of Processing Inventory, Burns & D'Zurilla, 1999)

The PMPI assesses the awareness and perception of one's own dominant mode of coping in stressful situations. It aims at assessing coping styles rather than decision or more general information processing styles. We nevertheless decided to discuss the instrument in this chapter, as the inventory is the only one that explicitly assesses *automatic* processing (which is an important aspect of intuition). The assumed processing styles (and the respective items) refer closely to Epstein's cognitive-experiential self theory (1994) and the REI. The instrument, which consists of 32 items, distinguishes among three different perceived processing styles: rational processing, emotional processing, and automatic processing.

In our opinion, researchers should have all instruments at their disposal at no cost. We therefore prefer to employ only free instruments. Another inventory which is not free of charge is the Myers-Briggs-Type Indicator (MBTI, Myers & McCaulley, 1986). It covers the dichotomies of sensing – intuition, feeling – thinking. The MBTI was used for validating some of the discussed inventories.

In Table 14.1 we present an overview of the theoretical understanding of intuition and deliberation as proposed by the respective authors. Given our focus, we concentrate only on the scales assessing intuition and/or deliberation. A full list comprising all items of the scales can be found online at http://www.intuitive-experts.de – Resources.

Methodological considerations

For a researcher applying one or more of the scales in the experimental design, the basic motivations are usually to control for these tendencies or examine their consequences in terms of main effects (do individual differences in strategy preferences lead to different results?). The focus could also be on interactions with the actually applied decision strategy (what is the consequence of a (mis)fit between the applied and the preferred decision strategy? cf. C. Betsch & Kunz, 2008; De Vries et al., 2008). The occurrence of interactions between manipulated and preferred strategies indicate that including the assessment of individual differences might be especially useful when individuals' decision modes (Horstmann, Hausmann & Ryf, this volume) are manipulated.

Answering questions regarding intuitive and deliberate decision making could prime or activate the use of either strategy; it might also increase the awareness of strategy preferences in general. This increased awareness might lead to a heightened attention to the decision strategy and presumably activate deliberate decision strategies. Thus, the position of the inventory in the experimental procedure is important, especially if you manipulate intuition

Table 14.1 Fact sheets of five of the most common scales

	Preference for Intuition and Deliberation (PID, C. Betsch, 2004)
Subscales (number of items, reliability*)	Preference for Intuition, PID-Intuition (9 items, α = .77)
	Preference for Deliberation, PID-Deliberation (9 items, α = .79)
Definition of intuition and deliberation as given by the author/s	Intuition: a basic decision mode that uses direct affective reactions towards the decision option as the decision criterion (affect-based decision making).
	Deliberation: follows cognitions (beliefs, evaluations, reasons; cognition-based decision making). (C. Betsch, 2008)
Validity of the subscales: correlations with other scales	PID-Intuition: Faith in intuition, Fast decision making, Need for closure (-), Personal need for structure (-), PID-Deliberation (-), Extraversion, Agreeableness, Openness for new experiences, Perfectionism (-) (C. Betsch, 2004), REI Experientiality (Witteman et al., 2009)
	PID-Deliberation: Need for cognition, Personal Need for structure, Maximizing, Regret, Faith in intuition (-), Fast decision making (-), Emotional stability, Conscientiousness, Perfectionism (C. Betsch, 2004), REI Rationality (Witteman et al., 2009)
	General Decision Making Style (GDMS, Scott & Bruce, 1995)
Subscales (number of items, reliability)	Intuitive Scale (5 items, α = .79, Loo, 2000)
	Spontaneous Scale (5 items, α = .83, Loo, 2000)
	Rational Scale (5 items, α = .81, Loo, 2000)
Definition of intuition and deliberation as given by the author/s	Intuition: reliance on hunches and feelings
	Spontaneity: not explicitly specified.
	Rationality: thorough search for and logical evaluation of alternatives
Validity of the subscales: correlations with other scales	Intuitive scale: More positive decision outcomes in life, higher normative decision-making competence (Bruine de Bruin et al., 2007), Age (-), Positively valuing physical activity, aesthetics, risk (Loo, 2000)
	Spontaneous scale: Lower normative decision-making competence, More negative decision outcomes in life (Bruine de Bruin et al., 2007), Spontaneous scale: Positively valuing independence, physical activity, creativity, life style, physical prowess, risk (Loo, 2000)
	Rational scale: Higher normative decision-making competence, More positive decision outcomes in life (Bruine de Bruin et al., 2007), Negatively valuing physical activity, risk, variety (Loo, 2000)

(Continued Overleaf)

Table 14.1 Continued

	Rational Experiential Inventory (REI, Epstein et al., 1996[a]; Pacini & Epstein, 1999[b])
Subscales (number of items, reliability)	Faith in intuition[a] (12 items, α = .77) Need for cognition[a] (19 items, α = .87) Experiential Engagement[b] (10 items, α = .79) Experiential Ability[b] (10 items, α = .80) Intuitive Thinking[b] (sum of engagement and ability) (20 items, α = .87) Rational Engagement[b] (10 items, α = .84) Rational Ability[b] (10 items, α = .83) Rational thinking[b] (sum of engagement and ability) (20 items, α = .90)
Definition of experientiality and rationality as given by the author/s	Experiential system: learning system that is preconscious, rapid, automatic, holistic, primarily non-verbal, intimately associated with affect, and it has a very long evolutionary history. Rational system: inferential system that operates by a person's understanding of culturally transmitted rules of reasoning; it is conscious, relatively slow, analytical, primarily verbal, and relatively affect-free; and it has a very brief evolutionary history (Pacini & Epstein, 1999)
Validity of the subscales: correlations with other scales	Faith in intuition[a]: Positive thinking, Conscientiousness, Esoteric thinking: Belief in the unusual, Formal superstition, Naïve optimism: stereotypical thinking, Pollyanna-ish thinking, Dominance, Depression (-), Anxiety (-), Self-esteem, Heuristic processing, Femininity (Epstein et al., 1996), Preference for intuition (C. Betsch, 2004) Experiential Engagement[b]: Experiential Ability (Pacini & Epstein, 1999), MBTI Intuitive, MBTI Thinking (-) (Pretz & Trotz, 2007) Experiential Ability[b]: Experiential Engagement (Pacini & Epstein, 1999), MBTI Intuitive, MBTI Thinking (-) (Pretz & Trotz, 2007) Intuitive Thinking[b] (sum of engagement and ability): Paranormal beliefs, Belief in astrology, feng shui, religion, Seeing purposes in random/artificial/natural events (Lindeman & Aarnio, 2007), Inspiration (Thrash & Elliot, 2003) Need for cognition[a]: Global constructive thinking, Absence of negative overgeneralization, Behavioural coping: action orientation, conscientiousness, naïve optimism (-), Dominance, Racism (-), Depression (-), Anxiety (-), Self-esteem, Stress (-), Drinking (-), General health, SAT (math & verbal), GPA, Heuristic processing (-), Masculinity (Epstein et al., 1996), Preference for deliberation (C. Betsch, 2004)

	REI continued

Rational Engagement[b]: Rational ability (Pacini & Epstein, 1999), MBTI Intuitive, MBTI Thinking (Pretz & Trotz, 2007)

Rational Ability[b]: Rational Engagement (Pacini & Epstein, 1999), MBTI Thinking (Pretz & Trotz, 2007)

Rational thinking[b] (sum of engagement and ability): Paranormal beliefs (-), Belief in astrology, feng shui, religion (-), Seeing purposes in random/artificial/natural events (-) (Lindeman & Aarnio, 2007), Knowing style, Planning style (Cools & Van den Broeck, 2007), Inspiration (Thrash & Elliot, 2003)

Cognitive Style Indicator (CoSI, Cools & Van den Broeck, 2007)

Subscales (number of items, reliability)	Knowing style (4 items, α = .73) Planning style (7 items, α = .81)
Definition of knowing and planning as given by the author/s	Knowing characteristics: Facts, details, logical reflective, objective, impersonal, rational, precision, methodical Planning characteristics: Sequential, structured, conventional, conformity, planned, organized, systematic, routine
Validity of the subscales: correlations with other scales	Knowing: Rationality REI, MBTI Sensing, MBTI Judging, MBTI Perceiving (-), MBTI Thinking, MBTI Extraversion (-), MBTI Introversion, Agreeableness (-) Planning: Rationality REI, MBTI Sensing, MBTI Intuiting (-), MBTI Judging, MBTI Perceiving (-), Conscientiousness, Openness (-) (Cools & Van den Broeck, 2007)

Perceived Modes of Processing (PMPI, Burns & D'Zurilla, 1999)

Subscales (number of items, reliability)	Automatic Processing, AP (10 items, α = .82)
Definition of intuition and deliberation as given by the author/s	Automatic Processing: focus on the speed and efficiency of processing (minimal time and effort) and the immediate knowing of how to cope based on past coping experiences
Validity of the subscales: correlations with other scales	Automatic Processing: Faith in Intuition, Positive Problem Orientation, Rational Problem Solving, Impulsivity/Carelessness Style, Avoidance Style, Suppress Competing Activities, Restraint Coping, Conscientious, Problem Solving, Cognitive restructuring, Express Emotions, Social Withdrawal, Anxiety (-) (Burns & D'Zurilla, 1999)

* minimum alpha reported in the original article
a: Epstein et al., 1996
b: Pacini & Epstein, 1999

and deliberation as decision strategies. It can therefore be useful to apply the inventory in a separate session scheduled before the actual experiment is run. If this is not possible you can also add the inventory to the set of demographic variables at the end of the study.

To use the scales in statistical analyses, the means of all items of each subscale are calculated. Some items need to be reverse coded (e.g. "I don't like situations that require me to rely on my intuition" is an item that contributes to the PID-Intuition scale). The scale means can be correlated with other variables or used as covariates. The most preferable way of analysing effects of decision styles is to enter the variables and their interactions (or interactions with other relevant variables) in a regression analysis. Before calculating the appropriate interaction terms the variables need to be centred to reduce multicollinearity (subtract the variable's mean from each value; Aiken & West, 1991). This kind of analysis allows for using the variables as sole predictors and as moderators (e.g. Richetin, Perugini, Adjali & Hurling, 2007: the implicit attitude predicted sensory evaluation of soft drinks only for highly intuitive people). Moderator analyses determine if a treatment has differential effects for participants with different decision style preferences.

For illustrative reasons it might nevertheless be useful to compare intuitive and deliberate decision-types in ANOVAs: Perform two median-splits, one on each variable, and classify the people above the median of the intuition scale and below the median of deliberation scale as intuitive, and vice versa as deliberate. Note that with this kind of analysis a lot of information is left out, as there is a substantial number of subjects who do not fall in either of these two categories. Moreover, it is theoretically difficult to use only these two mutually exclusive categories as most theories assume the independent operation of the two systems. However, this artificial dichotomization allows for an approximate estimation of the "pure" effect of the operation of either intuition *or* deliberation.

Discussion

Relations between the scales

With five different inventories to assess individual differences in decision-making styles the question of course arises if there is an overlap of the scales that claim to measure the same construct and where the scales make unique contributions. Following the idea that intuition is a common label for different cognitive processes it is further relevant to determine if different aspects of intuition and deliberation can be assessed by the existing scales. To gain insight into the relation between the scales we presented German translations of the scales to 74 subjects (first year psychology students of the University of Erfurt, 76% were female with a mean age of 21.5 years, $SD = 3.4$). The PMPI automatic items were adapted to the decision-making context, i.e.

"I am often aware of how to cope with a stressful situation even before I review all its aspects" was reformulated to "I am often aware of how to decide even before I review all its aspects". The participants filled in the scales in a classroom setting.

We performed an exploratory factor analysis (main components, varimax rotation) with the means of the sub-scales as variables. This method allows evaluating the overlapping variance of the separate scales. Scales that assess similar features should load on the same factor. We expected at least two factors, preference for intuition and preference for deliberation. The existence of more than two factors can be interpreted as an indicator of separate features of intuition and deliberation that can be measured with the existing scales.

A scree-test suggested a four factor solution (factor loadings: Table 14.2; 83% explained variance). The scales GDMS_intuition, PID_intuition, REI_experiential_ability and REI_ experiential _engagement load high on the first factor (26%) and below 0.30 on the other factors. Referring to the content of the items we label this factor *affect-based decision making* (i.e., by heart, hunches, and feelings). This was substantiated by post-hoc item analyses: the correlation with the scale mean was highest for items that verbalize the use of affect (e.g. "I tend to use my heart as a guide for my actions" (REI), "My feelings play an important role in my decisions" (PID)).

The factor analysis revealed another aspect of intuition: *Automatic and spontaneous decision making* (i.e., based on experience, immediacy). The scales GDMS_spontaneous and PMPI_automatic constitute this factor, along with GDMS_deliberation that loads negatively on this factor (total variance: 15%). Characteristic items are "I make quick decisions" (GDMS),

Table 14.2 Results of the factor analysis (main components, Varimax rotation), N = 74

	Factors			
	Affect-based decision making	Cognition-based decision making	Planned, structured decision making	Automatic and spontaneous decision making
PID_intuition	**.938**	−.148	−.023	−.076
GDMS_intuition	**.798**	−.204	−.085	.276
REI_experiential_engagement	**.904**	−.059	−.176	−.039
REI_experiential_ability	**.862**	.113	.119	.134
GDMS_deliberation	−.095	**.558**	**.611**	**−.404**
PID_deliberation	−.001	.392	**.809**	−.230
REI_rational_engagem	−.042	**.901**	−.023	−.080
REI_rational_ability	−.165	**.892**	.135	.075
CoSI_knowing	−.018	**.821**	.335	−.066
CoSI_planning	−.077	−.004	**.915**	.184
GDMS_spontaneous	.098	−.196	−.263	**.825**
PMPI_autom	.074	.101	.179	**.897**

Note: Correlations between the single scales can be found in Table 14.3 in the Appendix.

"I typically figure out the way to decide swiftly" (PMPI). Pretz and Trotz (2007), who used the REI and another scale (MBTI) in a common factor analysis, divide automatic decision making into holistic and heuristic. Future analyses with more subjects should examine whether the automatic factor includes these aspects as well.

Regarding preference for deliberation, the factor analysis revealed two factors. One factor constitutes *cognition-based decision making* (i.e., decisions following analysis, logic, and careful thinking processes). The scales CoSI_knowing, REI_rational_engagement, and REI_rational_ability load high on this factor; the factor loadings for PID_deliberation and GDMS_deliberation are somewhat lower (but still over 0.30; total variance: 24%). Characteristic items are "I make detailed analysis" (CoSI), "I study each problem until I understand the underlying logic" (CoSI), "I enjoy solving problems that require hard thinking" (REI).

The final factor is the inclination toward *planned, structured decision making* (i.e., following plans and agendas, pursuing definite goals; total variance: 18%). CoSI_planning, GDMS_deliberation and PID_deliberation load high, and CoSI_knowing loads moderately on this factor. Items that characterize the factor are "I double-check my information sources to be sure I have the right facts before making decisions" (GDMS), "I prefer making detailed plans rather than leaving things to chance" (PID).

The factor analysis was conducted with only 74 subjects; further, we applied German translations instead of original versions and an adapted version of the PMPI scale. With this in mind, one needs to interpret the results with caution if we refer to the original scales. However, it was important to us to test if all existing scales relate to the same idea of intuition or if they, as implied in their respective definitions of intuition, relate to rather different aspects of intuition.

In sum, our factor analysis along with other work (e.g. Pretz & Trotz, 2007) identifies different aspects of intuition and deliberation based on the analysis of existing scales and items. Intuition can therefore be seen as a broad concept hosting aspects of affect-based, automatic, spontaneous, and heuristic decision making. Aspects of deliberation seem to be a more "crystallized" knowledge part and a rather procedural planning aspect. It seems valuable to assess the relations between deliberation and different aspects of intelligence. Substantially more work is needed to theoretically shape and sharpen the identified aspects and assess which processes underlie each aspect. A theoretical overview that could serve as a starting point is given by Glöckner and Witteman (this volume).

Construct validity

In this section we evaluate the construct validity of the scales, referring to the definitions used by the authors of the scales and the correlations we found in our analysis. We will report the findings sorted by scales and accentuate which aspects of intuition are covered by the findings obtained with the scales. In the Conclusion section we will provide a heuristic for selecting a scale depending on the aspect of intuition of interest.

The REI strives to assess experiential ability and engagement and rational ability and engagement as proposed by CEST (Pacini & Epstein, 1999). Findings with the REI show that experiential thinking is associated with increased use of heuristics (Epstein et al. 1996), such as ease of retrieval (Danziger, Moran & Rafaely, 2006); gambler's fallacy (Shiloh, Salton, & Sharabi, 2002). Other studies show that rational thinking is inversely related to non-optimal (heuristic) responses and positively related to the occurrence of optimal, normative solutions, while experiential thinking was unrelated or positively related (ratio bias, Pacini & Epstein, 1999; Alonso & Fernandez-Berrocal, 2003; proportion dominance, Bartels, 2004). Rational thinking increases the ability to adequately handle statistical information (Berger, 2007). The REI has thus been successfully applied in the prediction of heuristic and normative decision making. The correlations with other constructs (cf. Table 14.1 for references) further suggest a relation between experientiality and affective decision making (e.g., with PID-I, MBTI-Intuitive). Rationality on the other side was found to correlate positively with variables that express cognitive abilities (such as verbal & math scholastic aptitude test). In sum, the REI can be valued as a measure which assesses the inclination to experiential vs. rational decision making with emphasis on heuristic vs. normative processing.

The PID assumes individual inclinations towards intuitive decision making (based on affective reactions towards the decision option) and deliberate decision making (based on beliefs, evaluations, reasons). This is supported by findings showing that intuitive participants included affective reactions in their choices, while deliberate participants refrained from doing so (Schunk & C. Betsch, 2006; C. Betsch & Kunz, 2008). Correlations (cf. Table 14.1) further support the relation of PID-intuition to increased use of affect. Moreover, intuitive subjects are faster in decisions (Schunk & C. Betsch, 2006; C. Betsch, 2004) which may also point to the use of affect. Different manipulations of intuitive decision style (with instructions to decide quickly/by heart/ intuitively; see also Horstmann, Hausmann, & Ryf, this volume) interacted with the preference for intuition. This suggests functional equivalence of the personal inclination and the instructed ways of deciding (C. Betsch & Kunz, 2008). The same is true for preference for deliberation which interacted with the manipulated strategy (manipulated with the instruction to "think about the decision"). The reliance on implicit vs. explicit knowledge covers another difference between intuition and deliberation (Richetin et al., 2007). Regarding this aspect, the decisions of intuitive (deliberate) participants were better predicted by implicit (explicit) attitudes. In sum, the PID can be valued as a measure which assesses the inclination to intuitive vs. deliberate decision making with an emphasis on the affect-cognition and on the implicit-explicit distinction.

The GDMS differentiates intuitive from spontaneous decision making. In our factor analysis reported above, the two scales load on the affect-based and automatic factors, respectively. The findings with the GDMS show that there are indeed differences in the predictive validity of the two intuition scales: while intuition (as well as deliberation) were related to positive decision outcomes and better normative decision making, the opposite was true for spontaneous decision making (Bruine de Bruin, Parker & Fischhoff, 2007). Studies that allow conclusive thoughts regarding the processes underlying intuition and deliberation are lacking. Further, the existing correlational data with other constructs (Table 14.1) do not contribute to the question of content validity either, as the scales are related to conflict management styles or life values in general (Loo, 2000). In sum, the value of the GDMS may especially lie in contributing "spontaneity" to the assessment of intuition. In our view, the intuition and deliberation scales should be more thoroughly validated. Moreover, additional credits may also come from the (omitted) avoidant and dependent decision style scales that provide, to our knowledge, the unique possibility of assessing these styles.

The CoSI is quite a young instrument, which may explain why there are to date no published experimental findings. From correlation results the authors of CoSI conclude that knowing indicates "a preference for logical, analytical, and impersonal information processing. Theoretically, this style is similar to existing conceptualizations of the analytic pole" (Cools & Van den Broeck, 2007, p. 380). Planning on the other hand was characterized (among others, Table 14.1) by relations to rational ability and adaptation (which implies efficient and rule-based problem solving). The value of this inventory is that it differentiates between the inclination to do things based on explicit knowledge (cognitive decision making) and the inclination to engage in goal directed planning. Both scales contribute to different aspects of deliberation, as became evident in our factor analysis reported above. Future studies should aim at evaluating both scales' predictive validity.

The PMPI finally relates to the specific task of coping and the preferred way of doing so. However, it aims on tapping the reliance on automatic reactions, which is an aspect of intuition that is discussed very often. We therefore included this scale (in a reformulated decision-version) in the factor analysis and this chapter on decision styles. Automatic processing is speedy and efficient processing (minimal time and effort) and the immediate knowing of how to decide based on past experiences. Correlational results are reported in Table 14.1. The pattern reveals a relation to intuition as well as to rational problem solving (Burns & D'Zurilla, 1999). In sum, the PMPI automatic scale might be useful to access automatic, experience based decision making.

Further issues

The spontaneous aspect of the GDMS_spontaneous scale is related to quick and imprecise actions; this rather negative aspect is definitely not mirrored in the PMPI_automatic scale, which taps precision based on expertise and experience. Future analyses should distinguish these two aspects: being fast due to volatile, unsystematic and possibly erratic spontaneity or due to reliance on automatic processing, which profits from experience and parallel processing capacity.

The REI, the PID and the GDMS all include items that literally use the term "intuition". This could activate different lay-epistemological ideas of what intuition is (e.g. using affective and emotional hunches as well as cognitive heuristics). This common item-wording can artificially increase the correlation between the scales. In further studies only the items that do not mention the term intuition could be subjected to a factor analysis. Future attempts to improve the measures should avoid formulating items in this problematic way. Deciding based on feelings, on heuristics or on spontaneous and automatic reactions can be separately formulated as single items and should not be intermixed with asking if one uses one's intuition. We conclude that it seems desirable to have a new measure available that assesses the four different aspects of intuition (automatic, affective, spontaneous, heuristic) and the two aspects of deliberation (knowing, planning).

One prominent example in which using the term *intuition* as a joint label for different aspects has led to inconsistent results is the occasional appearance of gender effects. Some results supported the common idea that women are more intuitive than men (Pacini & Epstein, 1999; Parikh, 1994), other studies did not find any differences between women and men (Taggart, Valenzi, Zalka & Loewe, 1997), and yet others even found that women are more deliberative than men (Allinson & Hayes, 1996). These inconsistencies may be a consequence of confusing different aspects under one broad construct, thus leading to the speculation that probably intuition and deliberation are not affected by gender per se (Graham & Ickes, 1997). For example, some studies focused on the emotional and affective components of intuition (Graham & Ickes, 1997; Simonton, 1980), where women generally tend to score higher than men. Taking the different aspects into account might lead to different predictions regarding gender differences which should be considered in future studies on "intuition".

On close examination, it is not evident whether the different scales focus on preferences, abilities, beliefs or actual use of the strategies. As Leonard, Scholl and Kowalski (1999) point out, self-report stylistic measures make references to different levels of analysis which mirror distinct operationalizations of the constructs. For example, whereas in GDMS items are mainly phrased as expression of habits, in PID they are conceived also as personal beliefs, preferences, and habits. These levels of analysis may or may not coincide. In fact, while people may have an ideal or preferred decision-making style (e.g. for socially desired deliberation), it could be the case that their actual decision behaviours are totally different from this ideal one (e.g. by acting spontaneously). Future developments may want to consider these different levels and specify if one expects different predictions. Besides, it seems difficult to differentiate abilities and actual use in a self-report measure. Even though self-report questionnaires are the most commonly used method in studying individual differences in preferences for intuition and deliberation, they appear to capture only partial aspects of these constructs, thus providing a measurement that does not allow a comprehensive evaluation of these concepts. Parallel or automatic processing, for example, might only be partially assessable by self reports.

Conclusion

Based on the empirical findings reported above we suggest that researchers should first think about the aspect of intuition they are interested in (heuristic, affective, spontaneous, automatic intuition). If one is interested in heuristics vs. normative decision making the REI seems especially suitable. If the dichotomy of affect-cognition is the focus the PID seems appropriate; moreover, it has been successfully applied in the improvement of the predictive validity of implicit and explicit attitudes. When spontaneous decision making is assessed the GDMS is especially interesting. For automatic decision making an adapted version of the PMPI seems to be promising. It is necessary, as discussed above, to keep in mind the possibly different predictions of spontaneous (possibly erratic) and automatic (experience based) decision making. When different aspects of deliberation are of interest, the CoSI seems to be promising with its differentiation between knowing and planning.

Overall, the existing scales already provide an easy way to control for stable tendencies to decide intuitively and deliberately and to examine the consequences of these tendencies in terms of main effects and in terms of interactions with actually applied decision modes. Including the assessment of individual differences can be generally useful whenever decisions are involved, and specifically when there is a focus on the influence of intuitive and deliberate processes. Our analysis has shown that people do not mean the same when they talk about intuition. Before selecting an inventory, you definitely need to carefully consider what the theoretically relevant aspects of intuition in your study are. Moreover, researchers are challenged to theoretically shape and sharpen the identified aspects and to assess which processes underlie each aspect.

Materials and references

The items of the respective scales can be downloaded as an online-resource at http://www.intuitive-experts.de – Resources. If you use the scales, please mind referring to the original articles.

Dos and don'ts

Dos

- Think about the kind of intuition you want to measure: What kind of process are you interested in?
- Carefully choose the position of the questionnaire in the experimental procedure.
- Use the scores and theoretically interesting interactions as predictors in regression analyses.

Don'ts

- Try to avoid changing the wording, the number of items etc. and try to retain the original version of the scale to facilitate a comparison between the scales.

Appendix

Table 14.3 Correlations among scales: bold correlations (r > .23) are significant on a .05 level or higher; N = 74

	2 CoSI planning	3 GDMS int	4 GDMS delib	5 GDMS spont	6 GDMS avoid	7 GDMS depend	8 PID int	9 PID delib	10 PMPI autom	11 REI exp_e	12 REI exp_a	13 REI rat_e	14 REI rat_a
1 CoSI knowing	**0.28**	−0.17	**0.67**	**−0.26**	−0.12	−0.20	−0.12	**0.60**	0.04	−0.14	0.04	**0.68**	**0.70**
2 CoSI planning		−0.09	**0.43**	−0.11	**−0.33**	−0.01	−0.10	**0.62**	**0.27**	−0.21	0.05	0.04	0.16
3 GDMS intuition			**−0.32**	**0.36**	0.13	0.03	**0.72**	**−0.23**	**0.23**	**0.66**	**0.60**	**−0.23**	**−0.32**
4 GDMS delib				**−0.56**	−0.15	0.04	−0.15	**0.77**	−0.21	**−0.26**	0.02	**0.46**	**0.59**
5 GDMS spont					−0.05	−0.07	0.11	**−0.43**	**0.54**	0.08	0.12	**−0.27**	−0.17
6 GDMS avoid						0.21	−0.08	**−0.23**	**−0.23**	−0.06	−0.21	−0.19	**−0.24**
7 GDMS depend							0.06	0.08	**−0.32**	−0.13	−0.15	**−0.28**	**−0.41**
8 PID intuition								−0.05	−0.03	−0.13	−0.15	−0.15	**−0.30**
9 PID delib									−0.01	**0.85**	**0.73**	**0.36**	**0.41**
10 PMPI autom										0.04	0.22	0.02	0.15
11 REI exp_e											**0.68**	−0.08	−0.21
12 REI exp_a												0.02	0.02
13 REI rat_e													**0.71**

References

Agor, W. H. (1989). *Intuition in organizations.* Newbury Park CA: Sage.

Aiken, L. S. & West, S. G. (1991). *Multiple regression: Testing and interpreting interactions.* Newbury Park, London: Sage.

Allinson, C. W. & Hayes, J. (1996). The Cognitive Style Index: a measure of intuition analysis for organizational research. *Journal of Management Studies, 33,* 119–135.

Alonso, A. & Fernandez-Berrocal, P. (2003). Irrational decisions: attending to numbers rather than ratios. *Personality and Individual Differences, 35,* 1537–1547.

Antonietti, A. (2003). Cognitive styles assessment. In *Encyclopaedia of psychological assessment* (Volume I, pp 248–253). London: Sage.

Ausburn, L. J. & Ausburn, F. B. (1978). Cognitive styles: some information and implication for instructional design. *Educational Communication and Technology, 26,* 337–354.

Bartels, D. M. (2004). *Proportion dominance: Individual differences and domain generality of sensitivity to relative savings.* Poster presented at the meeting of the Society for Judgment and Decision Making, Minneapolis, Minnesota.

Berger, C. R. (2007). A tale of two communication modes: when rational and experiential processing systems encounter statistical and anecdotal depictions of threat. *Journal of Language and Social Psychology, 26*(3), 215–233.

Betsch, C. (2004). Präferenz für Intuition und Deliberation. Inventar zur Erfassung von affekt- und kognitionsbasiertem Entscheiden [Preference for Intuition and Deliberation (PID): An Inventory for Assessing Affect- and Cognition-Based Decision-Making]. *Zeitschrift für Differentielle und Diagnostische Psychologie, 25,* 179–197.

Betsch, C. (2008). Chronic preferences for intuition and deliberation in decision making: Lessons learned about intuition from an individual differences approach. In: H. Plessner, C. Betsch, & T. Betsch (2008) (Eds.). *Intuition in judgment and decision making* (pp. 231–248). Mahwah, N.J.: Lawrence Erlbaum.

Betsch, C. & Kunz, J. J. (2008). Strategy preferences and decisional fit. *Journal of Behavioral Decision Making, 21,* 532–555.

Betsch, T. (2008). The nature of intuition and its neglect in research on judgment and decision making. In H. Plessner, C. Betsch & T. Betsch (Eds.), *Intuition in judgment and decision making* (pp. 3–22). Mahwah, NJ: Lawrence Erlbaum Associates Publishers.

Bruine de Bruin, W., Parker, A. M., & Fischhoff, B. (2007). Individual differences in adult decision-making competence. *Journal of Personality and Social Psychology, 92,* 938–956.

Burns, L.R. & D'Zurilla, T.J. (1999). Individual differences in perceived information-processing styles in stress and coping situations: Development and validation of the Perceived Modes of Processing Inventory. *Cognitive Therapy and Research, 23,* 345–371.

Chaiken, S., & Trope, Y. (1999). (Eds.) *Dual-process theories in social psychology.* New York: Guilford Press.

Cools, E. & Van den Broeck, H. (2007). Development and validation of the Cognitive Style Indicator. *The Journal of Psychology, 14,* 359–387.

Danziger, S., Moran, S., & Rafaely, V. (2006). The influence of ease of retrieval on judgment as a function of attention to subjective experience, *Journal of Consumer Psychology, 16,* 191–195.

De Vries, M., Holland, R., & Witteman, C.L.M. (2008). Fitting decisions: Diffuse affect and intuitive versus deliberative decision strategies. *Cognition and Emotion*, *22*, 931–943.

Driver, M. J., Brousseau, K. R., Hunsaker, P. L. (1990) *The dynamic decision maker*. New York: Harper and Row Publishers.

Epstein, S. (1994). Integration of the cognitive and the psychodynamic unconscious. *American Psychologist*, *49*, 709–724.

Epstein, S. (2007). Intuition from the perspective of Cognitive-Experiential Self-Theory. In: H. Plessner, C. Betsch, & T. Betsch (2007) (Eds.). *Intuition in judgment and decision making* (pp. 23–37). Mahwah, N.J.: Lawrence Erlbaum.

Epstein, S., Pacini, R., Denes-Raj, V. & Heier, H. (1996). Individual differences in intuitive-experiential and analytical-rational thinking styles. *Journal of Personality and Social Psychology*, *71*, 390–405.

Evans, J. S. B. T. (2008). Dual-processing accounts of reasoning, judgment, and social cognition. *Annual Review of Psychology*, *59*, 255–278.

Graham, T., & Ickes, W. (1997). When women's intuition isn't greater than men's. In W. Ickes (Ed.), *Empathic accuracy*. New York: Guilford

Hammond, K. R., Hamm, R. M., Grassia, J., & Pearson, T. (1987). Direct comparison of the efficacy of intuitive and analytical cognition in expert judgment. *IEEE Transactions on Systems, Man, & Cybernetics*, *17*, 753–770.

Hayes, J., & Allinson, C. W. (1994). Cognitive style and its relevance for management practice. *British Journal of Management*, *5*, 53–71.

Hayes, J., & Allinson, C. W. (1998). Cognitive style and the theory and practice of individual and collective learning in organizations. *Human Relations*, *51*, 847–871.

Hodgkinson, G. P., & Sadler-Smith, E. (2003). Complex or unitary? A critique and empirical reassessment of the Allinson-Hayes Cognitive Style Index. *Journal of Occupational and Organizational Psychology*, *76*, 243–268.

Iannello, P. (2007). Stili cognitivi e decisionali: il ruolo dell'attività lavorativa. *Imparare*, *4*, 39–62.

Iannello, P., & Antonietti, A. (2007). Relationships between decision styles and thinking styles. In *Abstracts of the Workshop on Cognition and Emotion in Economic Decision Making* (pp.49–50). European Association of Decision Making.

Kahneman, D., & Frederick, S. (2002). Representativeness revisited: Attribute substitution in intuitive judgment. In T. Gilovich, D. Griffin & D. Kahneman (Eds.), *Heuristics and biases: The psychology of intuitive judgment* (pp. 49–81). New York, NY: Cambridge University Press.

Klaczynski, P. A. (2001). Analytic and heuristic processing influences on adolescent reasoning and decision-making. *Child Development*, *72*, 844–861.

Leonard, N. H., Scholl, R. W. & Kowalski, K. B. (1999). Information processing style and decision making. *Journal of Organizational Behavior*, *20*, 407–420.

Lindeman, K. & Aarnio, M. (2007). Superstitious, magical, and paranormal beliefs: An integrative model. *Journal of Research in Personality*, *41*, 731–744.

Loo, R. (2000). A psychometric evaluation of the General Decision-Making Style Inventory. *Personality and Individual Differences*, *29*, 895–905.

Messick, S. (1984). The nature of cognitive styles: problems and promises in educational practice. *Educational Psychology*, *19*, 59–74.

Myers, I.B. & McCaulley, M.H. (1986). *Manual: A guide to the development and use of the MBTI*. Palo Alto, CA: Consulting Psychologists Press.

Pacini, R., & Epstein, S. (1999). The relation of rational and experiential information processing styles to personality basic beliefs, and the ratio-bias phenomenon. *Journal of Personality and Social Psychology*, *76*, 972–987.

Parikh, J. (1994). *Intuition: the new frontier of management*. Oxford: Blackwell Business.

Plessner, H., Betsch, C., & Betsch, T. (2007) (Eds.). *Intuition in judgment and decision making*. Mahwah, NJ: Lawrence Erlbaum.

Pretz, J.E. & Trotz, K.S. (2007). Measuring individual differences in affective, heuristic, and holistic intuition. *Personality and Individual Differences*, *43*, 1247–1257.

Richetin, J., Betsch, C., Perugini, M. & Giger, J.-C. (under review). *Cross-cultural comparison of the Preference for Intuition and Deliberation scale*.

Richetin, J., Perugini, M., Adjali, I., & Hurling, R. (2007). The moderator role of intuitive versus deliberative decision making for the predictive validity of implicit and explicit measures. *European Journal of Personality*, *21*, 529–546.

Riding, R. J., Glass, A., & Douglas, G. (1993). Individual differences in thinking: cognitive and neurophysiological perspectives. *Special issues: Thinking. Educational Psychology*, *13*, 267–279.

Rowe, A. J., & Mason, R. O. (1987). *Managing with style: a guide to understanding assessing, and improving decision making*. San Francisco: Jossey-Bass Publishers.

Schunk, D. & Betsch, C. (2006). Explaining heterogeneity in utility functions by individual preferences for intuition and deliberation. *Journal of Economic Psychology*, *27*, 386–401.

Scott, S.G., & Bruce, R.A. (1995). Decision-making style: the development and assessment of a new measure. *Educational and Psychological Measurement*, *55*, 818–831.

Shiloh, S., Salton, E., & Sharabi, D. (2002). Individual differences in rational and intuitive thinking styles as predictors of heuristic responses and framing effects. *Personality and Individual Differences*, *32*, 415–429.

Simon, H. A. (1987). Making management decisions: the role of intuition and emotion. *Academy of Management Executive*, *1*, 57–64.

Simonton, D. K. (1980). Intuition and analysis: a predictive explanatory model. *Genetic Psychology Monograph*, *102*, 3–60.

Sloman, S. A. (2002). Two systems of reasoning. In T. Gilovich, D. Griffin & D. Kahneman (Eds.), *Heuristics and biases: The psychology of intuitive judgment* (pp. 379–396). New York, NY: Cambridge University Press.

Stanovich, K.E., & West, R.F. (2000). Individual differences in reasoning: Implications for the rationality debate. *Behavioral and Brain Sciences*, *23*, 645–726.

Taggart, W. M., Valenzi, E., Zalka, L., & Lowe, K. B. (1997). Rational and intuitive styles: commensurability across respondents' characteristics. *Psychological Reports*, *80*, 23–33.

Thrash, T. M., & Elliot, A. J. (2003). Inspiration as a psychological construct. *Journal of Personality and Social Psychology*, *84*, 871–889.

Witteman, C., van den Bercken, J., Claes, L. & Godoy, A. (2009). Assessing rational and intuitive thinking styles. *European Journal of Psychological Assessment*, *25*, 39–47.

Zhang, L. F., & Sternberg, R. J. (2007). *The nature of intellectual styles*. Mahwah, NJ: Lawrence Erlbaum Associates.

15 Tracing intuition
Summing up and exemplified method applications

Cilia Witteman and Andreas Glöckner

In this volume we have presented many different methods that might be applied to study intuitive and deliberate processes in decision making. In this final chapter we will illustrate how each of these methods elicits different aspects of intuition. This may help researchers choose the method that suits their research question best. Before coming to this exemplification, we would like to repeat some core issues from the book.

First, intuition should not be seen as a homogenous concept. Different kinds of intuition should be differentiated based on the underlying processes. Without claiming to be exhaustive we suggested distinguishing between associative, matching, accumulative, and constructive intuition (Glöckner & Witteman, chapter 1, this volume). In line with this argument, the analysis by Betsch and Ianello (chapter 14, this volume) indicates that when looking at stable preferences for decision-making styles (as a kind of traits), a sufficient differentiation is crucial to obtain useful results. Furthermore, as discussed by Horstmann, Hausmann, & Ryf (chapter 12, this volume), different methods often used to manipulate decision modes are likely to induce different kinds of intuitive (and deliberate) processes. Before designing studies we recommend that researchers decide which specific kind of processes they aim to investigate. This specification of intuition should also be done when reporting results. Overly wide interpretations concerning "intuition in general" should be avoided. In short, we recommend avoiding the term intuition without further qualification.

Second, many current models of intuition assume that there is an interaction between different kinds of intuitive and deliberate processes (Glöckner & Witteman, chapter 1, this volume). Hence, it cannot be expected that people use either one or the other exclusively. According to default-interventionist models, some kinds of intuitive processes (e.g., feelings as a result of associative intuition or interpretations as a result of constructivist intuition) are always activated first, and it depends on the situation if further deliberate processes are activated or not.

Third, we recommend that, in order to shed light on the processes, researchers should try to collect as many dependent measures as possible to be able to compare observations with the predictions of different models, and to use as many different methods as possible simultaneously or consecutively with the same task. If models are not sufficiently well specified to derive predictions, we recommend that researchers either ask (the authors of the models) for specifications or, if this is not feasible, specify the model themselves and make the underlying assumptions explicit.

In the next section, we will illustrate how the methods described in the book might be applied to research questions in the domain of legal decision making, but readers may replace legal with any other professional domain (for example medicine, economics).

Applying the methods

Think-aloud and cognitive process analysis: increasing understanding, generating hypotheses and materials

Suppose, then, that the aim is to study different kinds of intuitive processes in legal decision making. To improve the general understanding of the underlying processes, of the interplay between intuitive and deliberate processes and of the information structures used, it seems most useful that researchers start with a think-aloud study and a cognitive process analysis (Witteman & van Geenen, chapter 3, this volume). Judges are presented with a representative case, and are asked to verbalize everything they are thinking while solving the case. The format and contents of their reasoning are derived from an analysis of the think-aloud protocols. Hence, the researcher gets a first idea about relevant information, but also about people's information integration processes and information structuring. Based on these data, first hypotheses can be derived (and later tested) about which kind of intuitive processes plays a major role in this domain: Do judges just react in a stimulus-response manner (associative intuition); do they accumulate evidence and automatically add it up (accumulative intuition); do they mainly match the evidence to previous cases (matching intuition); or do they construct consistent interpretations of the case (constructive intuition)? Furthermore, it may be investigated whether there are differences in information processing and structures between lay people and experts by assessing differences in mental representations.

Mouselab: get a first grasp on information search

The elicited contents of the decision processes can subsequently be used in a Mouselab matrix presentation (Norman & Schulte-Mecklenbeck, chapter 2, this volume). If for example judges use facts about the situation such as precipitating events (an extremely dominant father, being made redundant), individual characteristics of the defendant (aggressive) and consequences (a supposed crime) in their reasoning, these facts can be presented in a standard Mouselab matrix and people's information search can be recorded and analysed. Although Mouselab is likely to influence intuitive processes, for pragmatic reasons it could nevertheless be used to get a first idea about information use and the order of information search.

Eye-tracking: in-depth information search analysis and process analysis based on fixation parameters

Eye-tracking studies, which are generally preferable for the study of intuitive processes but technically more demanding than Mouselab, may be used in a subsequent step to check whether the same results are found if information is presented all at once, and is not, as in Mouselab, initially hidden. Additional measures such as shifts in attention, single fixation durations and the number of repeated information inspections can be used to test very specific hypotheses about processes (Norman & Schulte-Mecklenbeck, chapter 2, this volume; for recent extensions see also Glöckner & Herbold, in press; Horstmann, Ahlgrimm, & Glöckner, 2009). If, for instance, people only look at the core facts of a case and instantly feel that the defendant is (not) guilty, they may rely on associative intuition, which may be corroborated using physiological measures (see below). If people perform a very quick scan of the whole information with short fixations on all pieces of information, they may rely on accumulative or constructive intuition. Long fixations and repeated information inspections may, in contrast, indicate the (additional) use of deliberate strategies.

An interesting potential extension is to use eye-tracking to trace information search in memory (Renkewitz & Jahn, chapter 11, this volume). If previously presented information is no longer visible, people are expected to look at the position where it was before, and the eye-tracker follows such memory-based information search. The applicability of this method to complex decision problems such as legal judgments, however, still has to be tested.

Both cognitive process analysis and eye-tracking (and to a limited degree also Mouselab) give hints of how much of the reasoning consists of deliberate linking of facts, and where which kind of intuitive processes are probably used. For decision making in legal cases, judges, but also lay persons (jurors), often report that they do not combine facts according to specific mathematical rules, but that they construct interpretations and stories and test them using deliberate reasoning (Glöckner & Engel, 2008; Pennington & Hastie, 1992; Simon, 2004). Hence, constructivist intuition seems to play a core role in interpreting the evidence of a case.

Strategy classification methods: statistical analysis of processes based on multiple dependent measures

The underlying information integration processes may further and more explicitly be investigated using the maximum-likelihood method (Bröder, chapter 4, this volume) or the multiple-measure maximum likelihood strategy classification method (MM-ML; Glöckner, chapter 5, this volume). For instance, mathematically well-defined models for accumulative intuition (Busemeyer & Johnson, 2004) and constructivist intuition (Glöckner & Betsch, 2008) might be used to derive predictions about choices, decision time and confidence in different cases and judges' or jurors' behaviour can be statistically compared with these predictions. More precisely, with both these methods, the researcher can test which information integration process has most likely produced the overall behaviour in the decision task (choice, decision time, confidence rating). Both methods can be applied to test models including any kind of intuitive and deliberate processes. The methods require specific predictions about which decision will be made (and for MM-ML also predictions concerning decision time and confidence) from each model considered. Because choice predictions of different models quite often overlap, the MM-ML, which includes predictions of time and confidence, is the preferable method to investigate models that include intuitive processes. As mentioned above, we suggest that researchers focus on models that are well specified or that they explicitly make additional assumptions if necessary to derive clear predictions.

All of these methods lead to insight into the processes and strategies in decision making. The researcher may find that judges, although using a lot of deliberate reasoning for double-checking, rely heavily on constructivist intuition and base the decision (guilty or not guilty) more on a constructed overall interpretation of the evidence than on deliberate weightings of a number of pros and cons (Glöckner, 2008). In a different stage of the process (i.e., legal assessment) or in a different legal system (cf. common law vs. private law), they might rely more on matching intuition by comparing the current case to earlier cases.

Online video studies: externally valid materials

If the researcher is particularly interested in decisions of expert judges, using online videos is a good option (Schweizer, Plessner, & Brand, chapter 6, this volume). The researcher presents a court case to be solved not on paper, but on video. This provides a richer and more naturalistic information format which reduces problems of external validity. Many questions about the underlying processes of the legal professionals' decisions could be answered by manipulating aspects in the video (the order in which the witnesses appear, the ethnicity and gender of the defendant) or by analyzing decisions (verdicts), and eye-fixations or verbal protocols to identify the information that was used.

Physiological measures: towards a differentiated view of the relation between intuitive processes and affect

Some kinds of intuitive processes (e.g., associative intuition, according to the somatic marker hypothesis or the affect heuristic) are accompanied by physiological arousal, such as higher heart rate or sweating. This is taken to reflect an affective reaction. It is often assumed that deliberation is accompanied by low or no arousal (i.e., no affective reaction). Nevertheless, from our point of view it is oversimplified to assume that increased levels of arousal can per se be used to differentiate between deliberation and intuition. According to the prevailing default-interventionist models (Glöckner & Witteman, chapter 1, this volume), such a clear distinction cannot be made, because intuitive processes always come first and it is unclear whether the later activation of deliberation has an influence on this arousal. Nevertheless physiological reactions might be a useful additional dependent measure for identifying which processes are used (Hochman, Glöckner, & Yechiam, chapter 8, this volume). If specific hypotheses become available, physiological arousal can be used to differentiate between different kinds of intuitive processes by manipulating the assumed sources for arousal. As discussed in chapter 8 (for details see also Glöckner & Hochman, under review), associative intuition (according to the somatic marker hypothesis) assumes that arousal is dependent on previous learning, accumulative intuition (according to evidence accumulation models) might predict that the overall affective evaluation of an option is dependent on the aggregate of the facts speaking for and against it, and constructivist intuition (according to parallel constraint satisfaction models) postulates that arousal is induced by inconsistency of information and increases with increasing conflict between pieces of information (everything else being equal). These potential sources for arousal can be independently manipulated to disentangle the different processes.

In a somewhat simpler application example, one might investigate whether judges or jury members have a higher physiological arousal and thus show a more affective reaction in cases in which they decide guilty as compared to not guilty and how this arousal relates to their level of confidence and the time for deliberation.

Self-report measures of affect and arousal: the pragmatic alternative

For pragmatic reasons, the influence of affect and arousal on decisions may also be assessed by asking participants to fill in self-report questionnaires (Dickert, chapter 10, this volume). Since both physiological and self-report measures of affect have their drawbacks (feasibility, reliability) the best option is to use both. It may, however, not be easy to hook up legal experts or judges to physiological instruments, and asking them to report their moods may be the most a researcher can do.

Measuring causal intuitions: intention matters in law

In legal decisions, judgments of causality and intention play a crucial role for the legal assessment of a case. If the judge thinks, for example, that the defendant has caused the situation by their own actions (intentionally assaulting a person), they will hold the defendant more responsible for the situation than if they think external factors (being provoked) were the cause, and consequently judge more harshly. Less explicit beliefs about causality will often sway judgments. It would thus be very valuable to be able to assess judges' implicit causal beliefs. By showing people causal representations, such intuitions might be revealed (Hagmayer, chapter 9, this volume).

Implicit measures: getting a hold of socially undesirable influences

The implicit associations that influence decision making may further be assessed by different implicit measures (Holland & de Vries, chapter 7, this volume). Such a measure may, for example, show that some jurors tend to have racial or gender stereotypes, which will influence their decisions unless they are made aware of them and overrule them by deliberate thoughts. Socially undesirable influences or associations are hard to measure with questionnaires and implicit measures might be preferred.

Manipulation of decision modes: influencing modes and measuring effects

All of the above methods may be applied to decision strategies as they occur spontaneously, or to strategies that are manipulated in an experiment. Decision processes may for example be influenced by instruction. Researchers may design an experiment in which they directly instruct participants to decide either intuitively or deliberatively, or they may constrain the available decision time or induce a positive mood, both of which are known to induce specific kinds of intuitive decision making (Horstmann, Hausmann, & Ryf, chapter 12, this volume). As mentioned above, a researcher should be aware that different instructions induce different kinds of intuitive and deliberate processes.

Measuring individual decision styles: preferences for specific sub-processes

Finally, if the researcher is interested in the mediating role of individual differences in the preference for either intuitive or deliberative decision making on the decision strategy applied, all of the above methods can be combined with one of a number of available self-report questionnaires (Betsch & Ianello, chapter 14, this volume), most of which have established internal validity (Koele & Dietvorst, chapter 13, this volume). Here again, intuition should not be used as a homogenous concept. The different aspects should be specifically measured and interpretations should focus on that specific aspect of the general preferences in decision strategies.

Final remarks

Research on intuitive processes is as complex as it is fascinating. In this volume, we have given theoretical and methodological foundations for research on intuitive and deliberate processes and their interplay. The book gives an overview of methods that can be used in this research. We hope that it inspires lots of further research which will then, of course, lead to further improvement of the discussed methods. We look forward to the next edition of our book.

References

Busemeyer, J. R., & Johnson, J. G. (2004). Computational models of decision making. In D. J. Koehler & N. Harvey (Eds.), *Blackwell handbook of judgment and decision making* (pp. 133–154). Malden, MA: Blackwell Publishing.

Glöckner, A. (2008). How evolution outwits bounded rationality: The efficient interaction of automatic and deliberate processes in decision making and implications for institutions. In C. Engel & W. Singer (Eds.), *Better than conscious? Decision making, the human mind, and implications for institutions* (pp. 259–284). Cambridge, MA: MIT Press.

Glöckner, A., & Betsch, T. (2008). Modeling option and strategy choices with connectionist networks: Towards an integrative model of automatic and deliberate decision making. *Judgment and Decision Making, 3*(3), 215–228.

Glöckner, A., & Engel, C. (2008). Can we trust intuitive jurors? An experimental analysis. *MPI Collective Goods Preprint, No. 38. Available at SSRN:* http://ssrn.com/abstract=1307580

Glöckner, A., & Herbold, A.-K. (in press). An eye-tracking study on information processing in risky decisions: Evidence for compensatory strategies based on automatic processes. *Journal of Behavioral Decision Making.*

Glöckner, A., & Hochman, G. (under review). The interplay of experience-based affective and probabilistic cues in decision making: Arousal increases when experience and additional cues are inconsistent.

Horstmann, N., Ahlgrimm, A., & Glöckner, A. (2009). How distinct are intuition and deliberation? An eye-tracking analysis of instruction-induced decision modes. *Judgment and Decision Making, 4*(5), 335–354.

Pennington, N., & Hastie, R. (1992). Explaining the evidence: Tests of the Story Model for juror decision making. *Journal of Personality and Social Psychology, 62*(2), 189–206.

Simon, D. (2004). A third view of the black box: cognitive coherence in legal decision making. *University of Chicago Law Review, 71,* 511–586.

Author index

Subject index

For Product Safety Concerns and Information please contact our EU
representative GPSR@taylorandfrancis.com
Taylor & Francis Verlag GmbH, Kaufingerstraße 24, 80331 München, Germany